Philosophers Ancient and Modern

EDITED BY

Godfrey Vesey

CAMBRIDGE UNIVERSITY PRESS

CAMBRIDGE
LONDON NEW YORK NEW ROCHELLE
MELBOURNE SYDNEY

Published by the Press Syndicate of the University of Cambridge
The Pitt Building, Trumpington Street, Cambridge, CB2 1RP
32 East 57th Street, New York, NY 10022, USA
10 Stamford Street, Oakleigh, Melbourne 3166, Australia

Library of Congress catalogue card number: 86-17597

British Library Cataloguing in Publication Data

Philosophers ancient and modern.—(Royal Institute of Philosophy lecture series; 20)
1. Philosophy, European
I. Vesey, Godfrey II. Philosophy III. Series
190′.9 B72

ISBN 0-521-33799-2

Library of Congress Cataloguing in Publication Data

Philosophers, ancient and modern.
(Royal Institute of Philosophy lecture series; 20)
"Supplement to Philosophy 1986."
Includes indexes.
1. Philosophy. I. Vesey, Godfrey Norman Agmondisham. II. Annas, Julia. III. Philosophy. 1986 (Supplement) IV. Series.
B74.P48 1986 100 86-17597

ISBN 0-521-33799-2 (pbk.)

Printed in Great Britain by Adlard & Son Ltd, Bartholomew Press, Dorking

Contents

Contents

Preface

In 1985, for the first time, it was possible to sit an examination in philosophy for the General Certificate of Education. The examination was at Advanced level, and was set by the Associated Examining Board. In 1986, the AEB was joined by the Joint Matriculation Board in providing 'A' level examinations in philosophy. There have been talks about other GCE Boards following suit.

Anyone who studies the AEB and JMB 'A' level philosophy syllabuses will be struck by the extent to which the two Boards, despite the difference in the design of the syllabuses, agree in their choice of classical philosophical texts to prescribe: Plato's *Republic*, Aristotle's *Nicomachean Ethics*, Descartes' *Meditations*, and so on. They may also be struck by the omission, from the lists of reading suggested by the Boards, of commentaries on the prescribed texts.

The 1985/86 programme of Royal Institute of Philosophy lectures was intended to repair this omission. All the lectures in this volume are specifically on the texts prescribed by one or other, or both, of the two GCE Boards.

I invited the lecturers to provide 'critical expositions of the prescribed texts, exemplifying the highest standards of analysis and evaluation, but expressed in such a manner as to make them accessible to sixth-formers without previous acquaintance with philosophy'. How far they succeeded is for the reader to judge. It is easier to preach accessibility than to practise it. I found this out for myself when I tackled the section of Hume's first *Enquiry* in which he gives his answer to 'the most contentious question of metaphysics, the most contentious science', the question of liberty and necessity. Philosophy simply is not simple.

The lectures were given, as usual, at the Institute's London headquarters, 14 Gordon Square. They were remarkably well attended. I suppose this was because most of the texts prescribed for the 'A' levels are also required reading for philosophy students at universities and polytechnics. Aiming at one, fairly well-defined, audience, the lectures in fact attracted a considerably wider one. I hope this volume does the same.

The format of the volume differs slightly from that of earlier ones in the series: before the lecture(s) on a philosopher's text(s) there is a short biographical and bibliographical note. In some cases I have based the bibliographical part of the note on suggestions made by the lecturer.

Godfrey Vesey

The Open University

Plato

Plato (*c*. 427-347 BC) was born into a wealthy and aristocratic Athenian family. He cherished the ambition of entering politics when he came of age, but was disillusioned first by the injustices of the oligarchic government in which his relatives Charmides and Critias were involved, and later by the action of the democracy which succeeded it, particularly the trial and execution of Socrates in 399 BC. In his best-known dialogue, *The Republic*, he sought to provide a theoretical foundation for a government which would embody the justice he had found to be lacking in the actual governments of his day. His only active intervention in politics, in the intended role of adviser, was an unsuccessful one in Syracuse, Sicily. Details of it are given in his *Seventh Letter*. Some time before his second visit to Sicily, in 367 BC, he founded the school known as 'the Academy'. His career as a writer of dialogues may have begun before this. In his early dialogues, he memorialized Socrates and his method of philosophizing by making him chief participant and questioner. His teaching in the Academy was interrupted for a third visit to Sicily in 361-360 BC, when he was nearly seventy. He survived an illness caused by the hardships of the journey, and died aged about eighty-one.

How far the views of the Platonic Socrates correspond to those of the historic Socrates is a matter for dispute. Plato's most famous pupil, Aristotle, treated Plato's theory of Forms as a theory of universals (on which, see J. O. Urmson's lecture in this volume), and held that Plato, unlike Socrates, regarded universals as existing apart from particulars. But Aristotle's interpretation of Plato's theory as being primarily a theory of universals is questionable, since he largely ignored the significance Plato attached to opposites, or contraries, such as large and small, being present together in visible things (*Republic* VII, 524c).

The most convenient one-volume collection of Plato's dialogues is *The Collected Dialogues of Plato, including the Letters*, edited by Edith Hamilton and Huntington Cairns (New York: Pantheon Books, a division of Random House, 1961). The edition of *The Republic* prescribed by the AEB and JMB is Plato, *The Republic*, translated with an introduction by Desmond Lee, second edition, revised (Harmondsworth: Penguin Books, 1974).

For those who want to take their study of Plato's *Republic* further, the following reading is suggested:

J. Annas, *An Introduction to Plato's Republic* (Oxford University Press, 1981)

N. White, *A Companion to Plato's Republic* (Oxford : Blackwell, 1979)

I. M. Crombie, *An Examination of Plato's Doctrines*, 2 vols. (London: Routledge and Kegan Paul, 1962)
R. Robinson, *Plato's Earlier Dialectic*, 2nd edn (Oxford: Clarendon Press, 1953)
G. Vlastos (ed.), *Plato* I (London: Macmillan, 1971)
T. Irwin, *Plato's Moral Theory: the Early and Middle Dialogues* (Oxford University Press, 1977)
R. Axelrod, *The Evolution of Cooperation* (New York: Basic Books, 1984) (a development of the theory of justice outlined in *Republic* 358–359)

Plato, *Republic* V–VII

JULIA ANNAS

The long section on knowledge and the philosopher in books V–VII of the *Republic* is undoubtedly the most famous passage in Plato's work. So it is perhaps a good idea to begin by stressing how very peculiar, and in many ways elusive, it is. It is exciting, and stimulating, but extremely hard to understand.

The passage fits into the context of the whole *Republic* in the following way. Socrates, the main character in the dialogue, has been discussing with two friends, Glaucon and Adeimantus, what justice is, in both individual and state. Socrates argues that a state would be governed in a just way if it were ruled by a special type of person whom he calls 'Guardians'—people who are intelligent, and who also have good qualities of character. He bases his claim that a state would be just if Guardians ruled it on the claim that only they have the ability to reason for the good of the whole state, rather than for their own selfish concerns or the interests of a class. Now since Plato's time many political thinkers have had similar thoughts; but hardly anybody has gone on to take the surprising step which Plato does in book V—that is, to claim that the ideal rulers would not just be intelligent and disinterested, but would be *philosophers*. Plato is quite aware that this is, to most people, a highly peculiar claim to make, and this is doubtless why when he defends it in books V–VII he writes in the way that he does—in a very urgent and vivid style, quite unlike that of any modern philosophy textbook or article.

The account has three parts. Firstly (474c–484a), Plato claims that it is philosophers, and not the rest of us, who have knowledge. Then (484a–502c) he shows why philosophers are not valued in society as it is. Lastly (502c–521b) he gives us three pictures, generally known as Sun, Line and Cave, which give us some idea of what the knowledge is like which the philosopher has.

In these passages Plato has much to say about knowledge and the objects of knowledge, quite independently of the ideal state. I shall begin by discussing the first and the third sections, in which he does this. I shall conclude by returning briefly to the second section and to the question of how Plato's theories of knowledge and reality affect his original claim that it is the people with knowledge, the philosophers, who should be our rulers.

At the beginning of the first section, Socrates defends his outrageous claim by explaining what he means by 'philosopher'. He means, he explains, someone who loves wisdom (or knowledge; Plato seems to use the words interchangeably here) and so loves to know the truth—all of it. Glaucon misinterprets this. He thinks that Socrates means someone who loves to study a lot of subjects and to know a large number of facts. Plato puts this in because it is a natural first reaction to think that someone who has knowledge is someone who, as we put it, knows a lot. If so, then to love knowledge would be to study and enquire a great deal, to be curious about a lot of things. Many of us share Glaucon's reaction; we tend to admire scientists and other people who want to find out about many things, and many kinds of thing.

Plato's attitude to this may surprise us, for he obviously despises it. He compares people who are curious to find out different kinds of information to 'sight-lovers', people who rush round seeing as many plays as they can. Nowadays he would probably compare them to tourists who rush round 'seeing a lot of sights'. Plato thinks that knowledge is something more serious and worthwhile than the urge to inquire into things and discover new facts; far from respecting the desire to collect and discover new information, he represents it as a kind of trivial sightseeing.

But what then is knowledge, if it is something deeper than discovering facts? Plato tries to tell us in two ways. Firstly, he tries to give us some idea of what it is directly (475e–476e), though he recognizes that this will not be very convincing to people who do not share many of his assumptions. The sight-lovers, he says, are like people who are merely dreaming. They are absorbed in what they see and experience, and are content with that. Their mistake is that they do not use their minds. If they did, it would be like waking up; they would realize that the world of sights and facts they found so interesting was like a dream compared with the real world. Plato does not say much here about what he thinks reality is, except that it is not the way we would think it to be if we relied on sense-experience. We assume from experience that there are many things and kinds of thing that are good and bad, just and unjust; but when we start to think about it, he says, we find that strictly what is just or good is one single thing—something we can grasp only in thought. What Plato means is what we might call the nature of justice and goodness. We can recognize just actions merely from being taught how to pick them out; but to grasp the nature of justice requires that we think about it and find out what it is which makes all such actions just. Elsewhere Plato calls such natures Forms. Knowledge, then, is a matter not of acquiring more facts and sights, but of thinking about the ones we have, and of grasping the underlying natures, the Forms. We may be able to recognize good and bad actions, but until we have a grasp of the nature of goodness we do not really understand these good and bad actions.

So far, then, Plato has claimed that knowledge is not a matter of getting more information, but rather of reflecting on what we have, and of making sense of that by thinking about it—by trying to *understand* it, as we would put it. The true lover of wisdom is not the person who wants to discover more facts, as Glaucon thought, but the person who wants to understand the facts we have. In the twentieth century we are brought up to agree with Glaucon rather than Socrates here, to admire explorers and discoverers just for their curiosity about things. Hence Plato's notion of knowledge may at first seem strange. Plato himself realizes this (after all, Glaucon's reaction would presumably seem natural to many) and so he goes on (476d–e) to produce an argument to convince the person who does not already share his assumptions.

The argument is simple in structure but difficult in detail, and there has been and still is a great deal of controversy about it. Two points in particular are important.

Firstly, Plato is not here trying to define what knowledge is. This is something which is often done in modern discussions. Philosophers often start from a notion like belief, which seems simpler than that of knowledge, and go on to define knowledge in terms of conditions on belief. (For example, knowledge may be defined as true belief which is justified in certain kinds of way.) In this argument Plato works the other way—he defines *belief* in terms of what knowledge is. (Lee translates the Greek word *doxa* by 'opinion'; but 'belief' is a much more natural word to use.) To do this, Plato assumes that we have an implicit grasp of what knowledge is. This does not mean, of course, that we are clear about it—as we have seen, we may well fall into Glaucon's mistake of associating knowledge with fact-grubbing rather than with reflection and understanding. But Plato thinks that if we turn our attention to knowledge and make ourselves get clear about what it involves, we will be forced to accept his conclusion—that it is not the sight-lovers or people like them who are entitled to say that they have knowledge, but people who by using their minds have come to understand the reality which underlies the sights we see.

The argument, then, examines the notion of knowledge that we have, and concludes that this leads us to see that it is reflection, not using our senses, which gives us knowledge. One important consequence of this is that it turns out that we know much less than we thought we did. For in everyday life we have no hesitation in saying that we know lots of facts, whether we can understand them or not, and whether we have reflected about them or not. Plato is by no means the first or last philosopher to think that if we look hard at what knowledge involves, we will find that we actually know much less than we thought we did. One of the most puzzling features of knowledge is just this: we use the word, perfectly correctly, all the time, and yet it does not take much reflection to get us to admit that there is a problem as to whether we do know much of what we think we know.

We may well, however, want to criticize Plato for taking the notion of knowledge itself so much for granted here. In a later dialogue, the *Theaetetus*, he tries to define knowledge *before* asking how much we really know, and finds that it is harder than he thought: he cannot come up with a satisfactory definition.

The other main point to bear in mind about this argument is that it may sound more peculiar to us than it should, because of a fact about ancient Greek. Throughout this passage Plato talks of *what is* and *what is not* in a way which sounds odd in English. The problem is that the Greek verb *to be*, *einai*, is used in a very broad way, which covers ground for which in English we use three verbs, *to exist*, *to be true* and *to be something* (the last being the 'predicative' use). When Plato says that knowledge is related to *what is*, this could mean that knowledge is of what exists, or that knowledge is of what is true, or that knowledge is of what is something—is just, is large, and so on. We can't tell which he means just from the verb he uses. We have to find out what he means by looking at the whole argument, as well as related passages and the way other writers use the word. In the past many scholars have assumed that *is* here meant *exists*, and sometimes have even translated it that way. (The first edition of Lee's Penguin translation did this, which is one reason why it is important to use the second edition, where the translation is much less free). It is better to translate the Greek just by *is* and *is not*, since the fact that this is odd English reminds us that we have to interpret here to see what Plato is getting at.

What does Plato mean by *is* and *is not* here, then? We make best sense of the argument overall if we take him to be talking about *what is something*. When Plato says that knowledge is of what is, he is saying that what you know is the way you think it is. You can know that Paris is in France, for example, because Paris is, in fact, in France. This may sound disappointingly banal, and much less exciting than a claim about existence. But we shall see that Plato's conclusion is far from banal.

In the first stage of the argument, Socrates gets Glaucon's agreement to points about knowledge which are taken to be obviously true (476e–477b). Two main claims emerge.

The first is that not only is knowledge of what is what you think it is (which we have seen to be fairly trivial) but there is a state opposed to it, ignorance, which is 'related' to what is not what you think it is. If knowledge is getting it right, ignorance is getting it wrong, having a belief which is confused or misconceived or in some way off the mark. Belief, Plato says rather surprisingly, must lie between these states.

Why? Here his reason is that the objects of belief come between those of knowledge and those of ignorance, but this is not very helpful. Later on in the argument (478c) Plato says more helpfully that it must be 'between' the other states because it is 'clearer' than ignorance and 'darker' than knowledge. We have, that is, a picture in which ignorance is the state in which one is completely in the dark and confused about something. Having a belief is clearer than *that*, but still darker and more confused than knowledge, which is the state of being completely clear about whatever it is. This is a fairly natural picture; we do talk of the person who understands something as being clear in their mind about it. We shall find Plato making extensive use of the metaphor of knowledge as light and clarity and ignorance as darkness.

The second claim is that knowledge, and its object, *what is*, come in degrees. 'What fully *is* is fully knowable, what in no way *is* is entirely unknowable.' And Plato talks of 'what absolutely *is* and what altogether is not'. I have said that by 'what is' Plato here means 'what is something—is just, is large, etc.'—but how can something *absolutely* be just, or large?

Perhaps we can get some help from something which is said about knowledge slightly later. Knowledge is *infallible*, while belief is fallible (477e). That is, if you know something, then not only are you in fact right, you *couldn't be wrong*. To know something fully, then, is to have complete understanding of it of a kind which excludes the possibility of being wrong. I don't have understanding of a subject, insight into it, if I make a claim, and it turns out to be true, but it could just as well have been false.

Now if knowledge is, as Plato is suggesting, a state of being completely clear about something, of total understanding with no muddle or misconception, then it is tempting to think that this clear state of the knower reflects a clarity in the object. *What you know* must not only be the way you think it is, but must be that in a totally clear and transparent way; for it must be something you can't be wrong about. We might well want to query this move from the nature of knowledge to the nature of its object; but it is at least a very natural thought, and in this argument Plato is working from what we find natural to think about knowledge.

The second stage of the argument (477c–478b) is longer, but much simpler. Knowledge and belief are two different faculties. Like sight and hearing, they relate us to the world in different ways; and so strictly speaking their objects are different, just as strictly speaking what we hear is not the same as what we see. Plato is arguing here by analogy, in a reasonably convincing way.

The third stage (478b–478e) draws conclusions from the earlier stages. If knowledge and belief have different objects, and knowledge is of what is, i.e. of what is what you think it is, belief must have a different object. But belief cannot be of what is *not*, i.e. what is not what you think it is. (Plato's argument seems shaky here. Why can't there be a belief about what is not what you think it is, namely a false belief? This is another of the questions which Plato will reconsider in dialogues later than the *Republic*.) And we have seen that the objects of belief must be 'between' those of knowledge and ignorance. So belief has as object what both is and is not—that is, is and is not just, is and is not large, and so on.

This is a perfectly sound conclusion from what has gone before. We might just want to rebel at this point, and say that all that shows is that there is something wrong with the notion of knowledge from which we got to this point. For how can anything both be and not be just, large, or whatever?

This is what Plato shows us in the final section (479a–480a). He returns to the sight-lovers who are absorbed in what they can see and think that that is all there is. But any just action, he says, will seem unjust from some point of view; anything large will seem small from some distance; anything beautiful will seem ugly from some perspective. We can always say of any such thing not only that it is just, beautiful or large, but also that it is not. So there are things that are and are not, namely the things that concern the sight-lover. And these can be objects of belief only, not of knowledge. It is the philosophers after all, and not the sight-lovers, who have knowledge.

Everything here hangs on the claim that if anything is large, beautiful, just, or the like, it will also turn out to be the opposite, from some point of view. Plato does not, it must be said, do much here to make this claim plausible. And there are two main unanswered problems here.

Firstly, does Plato think that *everything* that we see and otherwise experience will let us down in this way, so that we can't have knowledge of it? The argument was directed at the sight-lovers, who stop at the level of sense-experience, which suggests that Plato does mean to downgrade all sense-experience to the level of belief. But the argument itself can hardly do that; it is limited to terms like *just, ugly* and *large*, which have opposites. Not everything we experience by the senses is like this—for obviously we are not always having experience of opposed qualities. Plato is getting us to admit that we cannot *know* that the things we see are long, or just, on the grounds that they might also turn out to be short or unjust. But what about the things we see that are red, or round, or men or horses?

If we think that the argument relies on the notion of opposites, then it seems that Plato has not shown us that we can't know that things are red and round. For how could we be convinced that something that is red or round is also not red or not round? And even if we believe that we could think up circumstances where something was, say round and not round, we can hardly extend this to terms like *man* or *horse*. How could anything be a man and not a man, or a horse and not a horse? And if so, then the argument will not show that we can't know anything that we find out with the senses, only that we can't know anything that we experience that can be one of a pair of opposite terms.

But if, as I suggested, we take seriously the way the argument is directed against the sight-lovers, we will take it that Plato *does* mean us to extend the argument to everything that we can sense. And in what follows this does seem to be what he thinks the argument shows. In which case there is the difficulty that in making the argument rely on *opposites* he seems to have proved much less than he needs to prove.

The actual argument, then, in its reliance on opposites, seems to prove less than the conclusion which most people unhesitatingly draw from it—namely, that we cannot have knowledge or understanding of anything which we experience by the senses. This apparent mismatch of argument and conclusion is one of the most striking and controversial aspects of this whole passage. Scholars have discussed this argument at length, but it is fair to say that there is still no generally agreed consensus as to whether Plato's argument is in fact inadequate, and, if so, how it is.

Secondly, we have been given an argument to show us that most of what we would claim to know turns out to be mere belief, but we have not been given much idea of the alternative. What is it to have understanding, and what are its objects like? For help on both these points we have to turn to the three pictures or allegories of Sun, Line and Cave.

Plato gives us three pictures which are linked together, and he later tells us to take them together. Many people are tempted to do what Lee does in his book (pp. 458–459), which is to make a composite account or diagram in which all three contribute to a single picture. The trouble with this is that Plato has deliberately made it difficult for us to do this; the pictures just do not fit together at crucial points. Plato is deliberately giving us three *different* pictures to make *different* points. They do not add up to a single definitive picture, because he is not in a position to give us any such thing. He emphasizes (506b–d) that he has only belief, not knowledge, about the Good, the object of knowledge. That is why he gives us allegories and pictures, which he considers a second-rate form of teaching. He is appealing to our imagination because he cannot himself give us the kind of understanding which he is talking about and which he wants to urge us towards. It is a fundamental mistake to look in these passages for a fixed picture of 'Platonism' as a set of doctrines. Plato is telling us that we shall gain understanding by learning to think for ourselves, and so telling us a fixed set of things to believe is the last thing he wants to do.

The Sun passage draws a contrast between the two worlds that we have seen contrasted before—the world of the sight-lovers and that of the philosophers. We are familiar with the visible world and can appreciate how everything in it is visible because of the sun. Plato stresses that the sun is also the cause of the existence of everything visible, not just its visibility. We were told before that unlike people who are absorbed in things that they can see and experience, philosophers use their minds to think about a reality different from and underlying the things we can see. Now we are told that this reality is, in its structure, *like* the things that we can see. The philosopher is concerned with things that can be thought of, rather than things that can be seen, since his concern is to reason rather than to collect facts. Now Plato tells us that these stand to the Good the way that the things that we can see stand to the sun. It is because of the Good that they can be thought of (that is, it makes them 'intelligible'). And, just as the sun makes things grow as well as be seen, so this reality that can only be thought of depends on the Good not only for its 'intelligibility' but for its existence.

It is not surprising that from the time that the *Republic* appeared, 'Plato's Good' became a way of referring to something particularly obscure. In this passage Socrates frequently apologizes for the strange and outrageous nature of what he is saying. Plato is trying to give us a general grasp of what he means, rather than claiming to be able to spell it out in detail. And what he does say is very striking. Many philosophers have agreed in principle with Plato that we will only achieve understanding of the true nature of the world by thinking about its underlying structure, not by paying attention to the kind of thing we can see and experience through the senses. For example, many have thought that it is the mathematical structure of matter, and not those of its properties that we can sense, that is both fully comprehensible and what is ultimately real in the world. Plato makes it clear in the later books of the *Republic* that he has a similar respect for mathematics, and indeed he thinks that years of training in the mathematical sciences is a necessary preliminary to progress in philosophy. But he also insists that the knowledge we have of what is basic in the world is not 'value-free' or 'scientific' in the narrow sense. Rather, goodness is in some way fundamental to all our basic understanding of the world, because goodness is fundamental in the world.

Nowadays, this claim that all knowledge must start from grasp of what is good, may seem quaint and unscientific. Even if we feel some sympathy with it, we are likely to wish that Plato had been more specific in this passage and said something more precise and helpful about the way in which goodness is basic in the world and our understanding of it. But we should not confuse what he says here with a shallow optimism about the world. Plato does not think that if we look at the world around us we will find that goodness is fundamental in it. For if we merely look around us and do not try to get behind the everyday facts we experience, the facts that the sight-lovers are so curious about, we will certainly not find much goodness, and the idea that we cannot understand anything unless we appreciate its dependence on the Good sounds naive and silly. What Plato means is that if we stop being absorbed by everyday facts and penetrate behind the world we can see—if we 'wake up' as he put it earlier, and start using our minds to discover the natures of things—then we will find that the true reality which we can only grasp by an effort of thinking is dependent on the Good.

Plato makes it clear to us, both by the figurative way of writing and by the way Glaucon responds, that he is not in a position to say much either about what the Good is or about the way in which things are ultimately dependent on it. None the less, Plato is convinced that there is a right and a wrong way to approach our knowledge of the world. We get knowledge of ourselves and the world we live in through the various sciences and the ways we try to unify and co-ordinate their results. Plato is in the *Republic* concerned both with our mathematical and scientific view of the world and with our knowledge of society. In both cases we will be on the wrong track if we assume that the goals and methods of our results are value-free. Our most abstract knowledge and its objects depends on the Good; all enquiry is at bottom an enquiry into what is valuable.

The Line makes an entirely different kind of point. It is a picture designed to bring out what kind of thinking it is which Plato values so highly. It introduces two important new features. The world of our sense-experience, already compared with a dream, is here repeatedly likened to an image or reflection of an original. The image/original relation illuminates several aspects of the relation between the world we experience and the world we can only grasp by thinking. And the kind of thinking which enables us to escape from the world of images turns out to be mathematical thinking.

The first feature is one that we cannot miss about the Line. The image/original relationship dominates the whole figure. We are told that to picture the relationship of the world of experience to the world of thought we should imagine a line divided into unequal parts by a ratio, with each part again divided in the same ratio. (Note that Lee (p. 310) assumes, as do most scholars, that the part representing the world of thought is the larger of the two unequal parts. Plato doesn't say this, however; we are equally free to imagine it the other way round, with the larger part representing the world we experience by the senses.)

In the part representing the world we experience (here called the world of belief or opinion, not just the world we see) the relation of the parts is that of image to original. There are two ways of experiencing or acquiring beliefs about things—indirectly, through their images, shadows or reflections, or directly, by considering the things themselves. The former state is called *eikasia*, which Lee translates by 'illusion'. This is perhaps not an ideal translation, for 'illusion' suggests that we are wrong, whereas Plato means only that our grasp is indirect. The latter state is straightforward belief.

In the world of thought there is something analogous. There are two ways of thinking about objects of thought like mathematical objects. One way is indirect—mathematical reasoning or *dianoia*. It does study objects like squares and triangles, but does so indirectly, by relying on things that we can see, like diagrams; hence it is compared with the state of indirectly seeing things via their shadows. The other stage is like straightforward belief—it is a state of thinking directly about the objects of thought, not in a way mediated by anything which in any way relies on experience.

Plato's discussion of these two kinds of thinking is very compressed. It becomes a little clearer in the light of discussions in later books where he is talking about the kind of mathematical studies that the Guardians will have to go through before they can become philosophers. It is clear that Plato thinks that mathematicians are at fault in that they rely on empirical facts and methods for their results—on calculations and diagrams. This is what he refers to in this passage as being forced to use assumptions. It is only the philosophers who have a direct grasp of objects of thought, including the objects of mathematics. They do this because they think in a specially trained way which Plato here calls dialectic. Again, Plato says more about dialectic later in the *Republic*, but on a very high level of generality; we never get a very precise picture of just what form it will take. But we are told enough to know that it will involve the most ruthless possible questioning of all assumptions and of every point at which one's procedures might be relying on what we know to be true merely from experience. Dialectic is not satisfied until abstract reasoning has been tried and tested in all possible ways; and as a result it is dialectic which gives us, as the Line makes clear, a direct grasp of the objects of thought, one which does not rely at any point on thinking of them indirectly, through their 'images'.

So, both in the world of experience and in the world of thought, we can have one of two attitudes. We can be absorbed by a thing's reflections or shadows or images or reproductions of it. Or we can be interested in the original. Obviously in everyday life we are not often, if ever, very interested in shadows and reflections, to the extent of neglecting the originals, things like animals and trees, and of grasping the latter by means of the former. Plato's main interest in this state is that it provides the analogy for what happens in the world of thinking, something which is otherwise difficult to describe: even when we start to use our minds instead of being content with experience we can be doing this in two ways. We can treat the objects of our thought in a way which continues to rely on experience—or we can grasp them directly, by *pure* thought, which involves rigorous procedures of thinking which Plato calls dialectic.

One question most people would like to press is: How does the Good come into this direct grasp by means of pure thought? Plato has been so emphatic about the Good in the Sun passage that it is rather surprising that it does not seem to come into the highest kind of thinking here. Plato cannot make any connection because of the way he is writing. There is no room in the Line for the Sun, so to speak; they are different pictures and they do not fit together. Each gives us a partial picture, but we cannot add them together; we just have to remember that each gives us only part of the whole truth.

So far the Line has filled out the idea that the world of thought is distinct from, though analogous to, the world we experience. But it adds a crucial point, which in a short passage is repeated three times. The image/original relation, so prominent *within* each part of the Line, also relates its two parts; the originals in the world of experience, solid objects like trees and animals, are in turn the images or shadows of the objects grasped by thought. The Line is continuous; the two middle sections are the same size; and the same relation holds between each section and the one above it. Plato is emphasizing, in several ways, that we move on from the world of experience to the world of thought by doing the very same thing we can do *within* the world of experience—that is, moving on to the original from the image.

Suppose I look at a reflection of a tree and think, 'That's a tree'. This isn't false, and yet what I am looking at is not a *real* tree. I can, however, turn and look at the real tree. Suppose that I then think of the tree, not as a tree which I can see and touch, but as an example of a geometrical shape. This is, according to the Line, the same kind of thing as turning from the reflection to the real tree. This process of starting to think about what we experience has already been called waking up from a dream, and in the Cave it will be described as being forcibly released from bonds and dragged round. Sometimes Plato stresses that it involves a rejection, even a violent rejection, of the world of experience and the habits we have built up round that. But in the Line he stresses that these 'two worlds' are in a way also continuous. We go from the lowest state, that of absorption in the reflections of visible objects, to the highest, the direct grasp by pure thinking of objects of thought. All the time we are doing the same thing at different levels—namely, move from the image to the original, from indirect and second-hand grasp to direct apprehension of the thing just as it is.

The basic idea is the same as that in the Sun. It is by thinking that we grasp the true realities, the natures of things; everyday experience reveals to us only inferior things, shadows and images compared with the world of reality. But what the Line makes clear is that Plato's 'two worlds' leave open a number of possibilities. We can be in a state which is, for example, comparatively clear about the world of experience but still comparatively in the dark about objects of thought. We can see how the Line fills out the earlier abstract picture of ignorance as a state of total dimness, and understanding as a state of complete clarity, with various states of enlightenment in between.

The other striking feature of the Line is the way in which it is *mathematical* thinking which opens up the world of thought for us. Plato considers only mathematical thinking as leading us to see the originals of this world as images in the world of thought, and considers only mathematical thinking as a kind of prelude to dialectic or rigorous philosophical thinking. We may wonder why there are no other alternatives. This, again, is something which becomes a littler clearer later on in the *Republic*. Plato insists that philosophers should first spend years doing mathematical studies, because this is the best kind of thinking to get one to rely on reasoning rather than experience. It is mathematics which gets one to reason in what we would call a formal way, and thus to obtain truths without relying on our experience. But the Line does not say that only mathematics can do this; and there is nothing corresponding in the Sun or the Cave.

The Cave is Plato's most famous representation of the idea that we do not have the understanding of ourselves or the world that we think we do. We normally think that we have quite a lot of knowledge; we certainly do not think of ourselves as totally benighted. But in fact we are really like prisoners chained in an underground cave, seeing only shadows cast by a fire on the wall. As Plato makes clear, there are a lot of stages that we have to go through even to become clear about the world of our experience, and many more, some of them very hard, before we achieve any understanding of the world outside the cave, that is, the real world which we can grasp only by thought and reasoning. Plato describes how the prisoner can be set free, turn round, come to understand that the things he thought were real are only shadows; and then gradually get outside the cave and discover the nature of the real world. Clearly we cannot put all these details together with the stages of the Line. (If you look at Lee's diagram (pp. 458–459) you will see how hard it is to do this.) Plato is quite aware that we get into problems if we demand something to correspond to every detail of the analogy in a literal-minded way. However, the details of the prisoner's release and ascent are not there just for decoration. They bring out two points which Sun and Line could not do.

The first is that enlightenment is a long and complex process, and complete understanding far away, and not nearly as easy to achieve as the previous figures may have suggested. The prisoner has a long way to go, and we can easily see why most of us might not make it all the way, or even very far. The second is that one reason why this is so is that we do not live in societies that encourage it. The prisoners are chained; they have to be released by someone else; someone who descended into the cave from the world above would be sneered at and rejected. Society as it is does not value understanding. It encourages people to remain absorbed at the level of images and appearances. It helps us to build up habits of lazy acquiescence in the world of our experience which are hard and unpleasant to break. The Cave is Plato's picture of the human condition—we all begin by assuming that experience reveals to us the way that things really are, and it takes effort for everyone to come to stop relying on experience and see that reality is revealed by thinking, not just by the senses. But it is not just a picture of the human condition. It is a picture of people in a bad society, one which encourages people to live by appearances and discourages them from thinking about the way things really are.

We can see that for Plato relying on experience covers more than just assuming in an unthinking way that the things we see, like trees, are what is real. It also covers taking over beliefs, some of them important like our beliefs about justice, which are second-hand, picked up from society in the way the prisoners see the shadow-pictures on the wall of the Cave. In this way the Cave brings out in more detail some of the implications of the Sun passage; understanding is not just a matter of doing mathematics or pure abstract thinking, it is also grasping the Good and the dependence of everything on the Good. To accept the world of experience as real is also to have second-hand values and to be an unreflective person. The person who comes to have the kind of understanding that mathematics and philosophy can give is also someone who has a true grasp of what is valuable and worthwhile.

Many philosophers have thought that we know much less than we think we do. But few have gone as far as Plato does in two ways. He thinks that the state of most people is radically unlike the way they think it is. As far as having any knowledge goes, we are like the prisoners in the Cave—as far from true understanding as it is possible to be. And few philosophers have had as much confidence as Plato does in the powers of thinking. All through the central books of the *Republic* Plato does all he can to contrast two attitudes. On the one hand there is reliance on experience—confidence that the world is the way our senses report it, reliance on the values that society teaches us. For Plato this will never achieve any truth. It is passive and uncritical, and is repeatedly compared with being asleep and dreaming, or with being absorbed in images or reflections, grasping the originals only dimly through these or not at all. By contrast, starting to think about one's experience is compared with waking up, becoming active, breaking the bonds of inert habit. It puts us in touch with the way things really are—indirectly at first, but then by a direct and unmediated grasp. The kind of thinking which Plato stresses is the most abstract kind, mathematics and philosophy, which relies least on and takes least interest in the particular details of the world we experience. Only this, he thinks, has any hope of leading us to understand the world and ourselves, and to come to have a true insight into what is valuable.

We may criticize Plato for setting us too simple an opposition here. We may feel that in these passages too much has got lumped together on the side of experience. Relying on the senses is taken to involve a passive and uncritical attitude, and accepting the reality of what the senses report is run together with accepting second-hand opinions about values. Plato is so eager to downgrade the senses because he has not bothered to analyse very carefully what 'the senses' covers. Analogously, he is so lyrical in his praise of thinking and its objects because he has not seen that there are many distinctions that could be made. One is that of critical thinking as opposed to taking things for granted. Another is that of pure thinking as opposed to relying on experience. Still another is that of exact thinking as opposed to vague, imprecise reliance on the way things usually are. In this passage Plato runs these contrasts together and produces grand conclusions which arguably rely on conflating different kinds of thing. In his later works Plato comes to pay more attention to this kind of distinction, just as he also begins to ask what knowledge is before asking whether we have any. The result is that we no longer get the kind of grand scheme and large claim which we find in the *Republic*'s central books.

We have seen that Plato thinks of understanding as involving the rigour and precision of mathematics, but also as being a grasp of what is truly good. This is one of the aspects of his thought which is least familiar in the twentieth century, for usually mathematical rigour is *opposed* to study of value; the latter is often thought of as imprecise and unscientific. As we have seen, Plato thinks that knowledge of value is actually fundamental to any true understanding. If we bear this in mind we may see why he thinks that philosophers should be rulers. His Guardians will have both the qualities that we think a great mathematician or scientist has, and the qualities that we think a great politician has. He does not think, as we tend to do, that these kinds of quality are basically different, and that one person is unlikely to have both of them. (He would certainly agree that in present day society one person is very unlikely to be able to develop both kinds of ability and talent.) We might agree with Plato that *if* there could be people such as he describes—with a grasp of reality and true value—then it might be best if they were in charge of society; but we might want to question whether these different types of talent could in fact be combined.

We can see some of these difficulties surfacing in the second section of these books—the discursive account of the excellent qualities of the philosopher ruler, and the reasons why these are not valued in society as it is. It is quite clear why Plato thinks that people with philosophically grounded knowledge of the kind he indicates would know better what to do than people who lack it, people who just muddle through and see no need to learn. Plato makes the point by his analogy of the ship whose crew insist that sailing needs no expertise beyond what anyone can have without trying. What he describes is obviously crazy, and he is clearly right, up to a point. If you have a task that needs an expert, and you have an expert, then it is clearly irrational to refuse to let the expert do it. It is quite another matter, of course, whether Plato is right that governing is such a task, or that it is obvious that only a few people can become such experts, so that most people's intelligence is despicable. (The passage does contain some unpleasant and unnecessary snobbery about the capacities of ordinary people.)

Suppose we agree that ruling is a task which needs expertise. How does the kind of philosophically grounded understanding which Plato has been sketching produce such expertise? Plato does his utmost in this passage to stress that the person with understanding is like a person with a practical ability. He is like the ship's captain, or a doctor—he can get the right results, because he has the ability to see what needs to be done in each circumstance. The doctor's knowledge enables him to see what each patient requires; the sea-captain has to be sensitive to changes in the weather and the ship and meet each changed circumstance with the appropriate response. Rulers need philosophically grounded understanding because only this enables them to weigh up each situation properly.

And yet Plato has done everything he can in these books to stress that understanding comes from breaking away from, waking up from, absorption in the world of our experience. He has emphasized mathematical and other abstract thinking, and the distance between grasp of reality and the way that most of us live. And so we find passages like this one (500b–c): 'The true philosopher ... whose mind is on higher realities, has no time to look at the affairs of men, or to take part in their quarrels with all the jealousy and bitterness they involve. His eyes are turned to contemplate fixed and immutable realities, a realm where there is no injustice done or suffered, but all is reason and order, and which is the model which he imitates and to which he assimilates himself as far as he can.' Plato goes on to say that it is just because he has no interest in 'the affairs of men' that the philosopher will make the best ruler; it is because he knows what he is talking about and does not muddle through that he will best be able to organize society. But we must surely feel a tension here. Surely the more theoretical our studies get, the less practically able they will make us? The more one ceases to care about society the less one will have the engagement with it that is necessary if one is to be an effective ruler.

In passages like the one just quoted, Plato simply asserts that knowledge based on abstract thinking, which takes one away from interest in the world of experience, is not just compatible with effective dealing in that world, but actually enables one to do it best. But he admits that the people who become philosophers will not want to 'go down into the Cave' and rule. Once you have achieved understanding such as Plato describes, you lose interest in anything else. And despite what he says it is hard to believe that rulers who hate every moment of ruling will be good rulers, never mind the best possible. In the later dialogue *Theaetetus* Plato admits that the philosopher will be, not a useful organizer, but an unworldly person, someone who does not know his way around town, someone to whom politics is of no interest, so that if he is compelled to participate by personal need he is all at sea. We will probably find this a more realistic appraisal of the effect on someone of spending many years on unremittingly abstract studies. Plato's faith in the *Republic* that theoretical understanding leads to practical ability is, like much else in these books, inspiring but unrealistic about human nature.

We may sympathize with some of what Plato says in these books about knowledge and understanding—that we will achieve it only by thinking for ourselves, not by taking the world we experience for granted. But we are not likely to sympathize very much with his conclusions, and if we don't it is likely to be on two main grounds. Firstly, we may think that Plato greatly exaggerates the power of pure thinking, and that he does so partly because he tends to identify any independent and critical thinking about ourselves and the world around us with pure abstract thinking like mathematical thinking. At the very least Plato needs to make a great many more distinctions than he does to clarify his contrast between the world of thought and the world of experience. And secondly we are less likely to think that years of highly theoretical study will make us the best people to run society. Plato's philosopher-rulers are an impossible ideal, even though in the process he has said much that is true and valuable about the love of understanding and our continuing search for it.

Ethics in Plato's *Republic*

NICHOLAS DENYER

Why should I be just? What have I to gain if I am decent, honest, moral, upright, fair and truthful? Other people benefit if I am just, but do I? And doesn't it seem clear that sometimes the benefit that other people receive from my being just is a benefit received at my expense? Perhaps then I have no adequate reason to be just. Perhaps if I have any sense I will not bother.

An important strand of modern moral philosophy regards such questions as misconceived. It holds that being just, or taking the moral point of view, is quite different from being concerned for one's own self-interest, and thus that what one *morally* ought to do is quite different from what one ought to do on grounds of self-interested *prudence*. Furthermore, even if doing what I morally ought could be proved to advance my own self-interest, and even if a proof of that did persuade me to do what I morally ought, nevertheless, what the proof would persuade me to practise would not in any strict sense deserve the name of morality. On the surface no doubt my behaviour would be just like that of people who are genuinely moral. They, for instance, would not give short change, and neither would I. But their reason for not cheating would be that cheating is wrong. My reason would be that cheating does not pay. And this, according to the modern view I have mentioned, makes a big difference. They would be moral, I would only seem so.

Such thoughts come naturally to many people in modern times. They did not come naturally to the Greeks. From Plato's report, and we have no reason to doubt its truth, we gather that Greek popular opinion felt no qualms about commending justice on the grounds that it pays, in either this life or the next, for it wins one a good reputation among gods and among one's fellow human beings (*Rep.* 363). On reflection this way of commending justice sounds slightly paradoxical. The benefits that it claims for justice are not immediate or intrinsic. Only in the longer term do you gain by being just, and your gains depend upon the continued existence of a custom whereby those who are just receive the admiration and approval of others. By failing to mention benefits more intrinsic or immediate than these, this popular view raises the suspicion that justice has no such benefits, indeed that justice in itself has definite drawbacks by comparison with injustice. Why then should we have a convention encouraging justice if it is only the existence of such a convention that makes justice preferable to its opposite?

This paradox in popular opinion was ingeniously handled in a theory developed by the philosophers (*Rep.* 358–359). We can understand the theory easiest if we consider how it applies to a simplified case. There are two super-powers, each with a choice between arming and disarming. There are then four possible outcomes of their choices. Suppose that what each super-power would like most is the outcome in which it alone is armed and thus able to dominate the other; that what each would like least is the outcome in which it alone is disarmed and thus dominated by the other; and that since arming costs money and brings no further safety if the other is arming too, each super-power would prefer the outcome in which neither arms to the outcome in which both do. But what outcome will result? Each super-power can reflect that whatever the other does it is better off arming; and so even though both would prefer that both were disarmed, the natural thing is that both will arm. Both super-powers have strong reason to escape the natural outcome by creating a convention against armaments, in spite of the fact that arming, considered in itself, is preferred to being disarmed. According to the theorists whom Plato mentions, two people each with a choice between aggressing against the other and treating the other peaceably are in the position of our super-powers. This is why they will create conventions in favour of justice even though the immediate and intrinsic benefits of being just are much less than those of being unjust.

There are two complications here. The first is that Plato slightly misreports the theorists he describes. He says that the conventions in favour of justice are made to avoid the two extreme outcomes in which there is unreciprocated aggression. This is mistaken. There is no need of conventions or anything else to avoid the two extreme outcomes. For those two outcomes are highly unstable. The underdogs can immediately improve their position by ceasing to co-operate. The outcome that it takes conventions of justice to avoid is that in which each party fights against the other. And this outcome is as much intermediate between the two extremes as is the outcome in which both parties are peaceful. The second complication is that we should ideally extend our analysis from the simplest possible case of just two people to the real world in which there are many more than two people capable of benefiting at one another's expense by that behaviour which convention will agree to forbid as unjust. This extension to the real world raises several points of difficulty and interest. But perhaps we need not consider them here. For even the simplest case shows how the philosophical theory resolves the paradox presented by Greek popular opinion.

Now Plato of course agrees neither with popular opinion nor with the philosopher's refinement of it: that, he is sure, is not the way to talk about justice. In this respect he would agree with the important strand of modern moral philosophy that I spoke of earlier. But he would agree with it in this respect alone. The modern view thinks it wrong to commend justice by connecting it to self-interest, however weak the connection may be. Plato thinks that justice can and should be commended by connecting it to self-interest. His quarrel with his contemporaries is that they do not make the connection nearly strong enough.[1]

Imagine someone commending health and sanity in the way that Plato's contemporaries commended justice: 'Of course, if you consider things in isolation, you will see that it is not at all good for you to be healthy and much better to be sick; but if you look at things in the broader perspective you will see that all things considered you are in fact better off being healthy. For that saves you from being locked up in quarantine or stabbed with syringes and from other unpleasant fates that social convention has established for the sick.' This recommendation of health hardly sounds strong enough. There must be more to be said for health than this. For health is worth having for its own sake, and not merely for the sake of what comes from it. Moreover, while health is also worth having for the sake of what comes from it, these further benefits of health are not limited to those conferred by a social convention. For while you can avoid unpleasant surgery by the mere appearance of health, there are other benefits of health that only actual health can produce. If for example your good health is merely apparent it is not likely to lead to a long life.

Plato wants to commend justice to self-interest in terms as strong as those in which we have commended health. Justice is the health of the soul (*Rep.* 444–445). Its benefits are huge and immediate and far from wholly dependent upon social convention. And the project of the *Republic* is to prove this point.

Plato's strategy falls into two main stages. The first is to define what exactly it is for someone to be just. Only then does he proceed to the second stage of arguing that justice so defined is indeed as good as he claims it is. He maintains elsewhere, in such dialogues as the *Meno*, that this is the best way to proceed in answering any question, and that we had better establish what something *is* before we can have any clear understanding of what it is *like*. Let us then take these two main stages in turn.

Central to Plato's attempts to define justice is the analogy between the individual and the city. Any proposed definition of what makes an

[1] Hence I am in thorough disagreement with H. D. P. Lee, *Plato: the Republic* (Harmondsworth: Penguin, 1955), 28–29.

individual just can be tested by applying it to cities and vice versa. For justice will be the same thing on both the small scale and the large (*Rep.* 368–369, 434). What exactly is Plato's assumption here? And is it sound? It is fairly natural to assume that if a single word applies to two different things, then this must be because of a single feature that the two different things have in common. But this natural assumption is in fact false. What is more, Plato knows that it is false and in the *Republic* tells us why. We apply the term 'just', he points out, not only to people but also to actions. And this is not simply a pun, like applying the word 'fair' to both hair and trials; for there is something that makes it appropriate to apply the one word 'just' to actions as well as to people. But what makes it appropriate is not a single feature common both to just people and to just actions. People are just, says Plato, if the three parts of their soul are organized in the right way. But there are no such three parts to a just action. On the contrary, says Plato, what makes it correct to call an action just is that it conserves such an organization among the three parts of the soul (*Rep.* 444).

Plato's analogy between the just city and the just person relies therefore on something other than this natural but erroneous assumption. His remarks about how justice must be one and the same feature both for a smaller thing—an individual—and for a larger—a city—perhaps mean rather that if a single term applies both to wholes and to parts of those wholes then there must be a single feature common to both whole and part. But not even this principle seems entirely sound. An Irish joke is a whole, one of whose parts may be an Irish word. But the word and the joke will not share a common feature that makes them both Irish. The joke will be Irish because it describes Irish people acting in a way supposedly characteristic of them; the word will be Irish because it is used mainly by Irish people. The part/whole principle seems sound only if we incorporate an important qualification: only if the term that applies to both whole and part tells the stuff out of which a thing is made will it be certain to apply to both part and whole in virtue of exactly the same feature. For example, if a chain is golden, and a link of it is golden, then both are golden in virtue of exactly the same feature present in them both; for there is present in each the single stuff gold. The trouble is however that with this qualification the part/whole principle will not serve Plato's purpose. For just cities and just people are not made just by the presence of a stuff justice, as gold links and gold chains are made gold by the presence of the stuff gold. For if Plato is right, the justice of a city or an individual is not a stuff it contains, but a structure in which its parts are organized. Thus Plato's assumption that justice must be the same thing for both city and individual seems to be without adequate justification.

Let us however put this difficulty to one side and examine how Plato pursues his analogy between the city and the individual. The city that he describes is clearly in some sense an ideal city. But in calling it ideal we should be careful to distinguish it from the Utopian fantasies of some later thinkers. Plato does not for example imagine that the forces of history are working on behalf of his city and are sure eventually to produce it. On the contrary, he concedes that his city is unlikely ever to come about, and gives some acute analysis of the social mechanisms which so corrupt the only people capable of instituting that city as to make them the greatest obstacle to its institution (*Rep.* 491–495). Again, Plato does not imagine that once instituted his city would be perfectly stable and live happily ever after. On the contrary, he tells us something of how it will eventually decline (*Rep.* 546–547). And, finally, Plato does not imagine that his city enjoys an existence free from war or from all problems of producing and distributing material goods. On the contrary, his city contains one class to fight and another to produce. In all these respects Plato's city contrasts strongly with, for example, the scientific communism of which Marxists speak.

A similar point should be made about the just individuals whom Plato describes. Their life is no doubt in some sense ideal. It should nevertheless be distinguished from, for example, the ideal life of which Plato had dreamt in his earlier dialogue, the *Phaedo*. There Plato had imagined an ideal existence in which the intellect was altogether severed from everything bodily, and that meant from everything to do with sensation, perception, appetite and emotion. In the *Republic* by contrast Plato imagines no such thing. Here just individuals are not simply intellects, for their souls contain two other parts. Yet this is not because Plato has, by the time he writes the *Republic*, revised his low estimation of our unintellectual parts. Think for instance of the simile at 588 which compares our unintellectual parts to beasts, the intellect to a human being; or think of the remarks on self-control in 431. The *Republic's* ideal individuals then, like its ideal city, are described not in terms of thoroughgoing Utopian fantasy, but in terms that make many concessions to the uncomfortable reality in which we continue to live: the uncomfortable reality of embodiment.

The three parts of the ideal city are fairly straightforward, as is the argument that Plato gives for them. The argument is that there are three jobs that need to be done, and that since a job is done best if done by a specialist these three jobs need to be done by three distinct classes. Less straightforward perhaps are the three parts of the soul. What in particular are we to make of the second part, the part that corresponds to the Auxiliaries, and which Plato calls by the words *thumos* and *thumoeides*?[2] And if this second part is so hard to understand, can we be

[2] On the difficulties in translating these words see Lee, op. cit. in note 1 above, 184–185.

sure that we have really understood what Plato means by the other two parts when we learn to call them reason and appetite?

There is a danger here. 'Reason' and 'appetite' are words readily associated with a theory of the human soul and of human action and motivation quite different from that presented in the *Republic*. This is the theory of a bipartite soul. Let me present it in caricature. The soul contains just two parts, reason and appetite. Your appetite consists of all your desires, and it is your appetite and your appetite alone which sets you the end for which you act. But appetite by itself cannot get you to act. For to act you need not only an end but also some beliefs about what you can do to attain that end. And appetite consists only of desire, not of any beliefs at all. It is reason and reason alone which provides you with beliefs about how to attain the ends set by appetite. But this is all that reason does. It cannot itself supply ends or criticize the ends supplied by appetite. Therefore reason by itself can no more get you to act than can appetite by itself. The co-operation of both parts is necessary to produce an action. And indeed sufficient. For you will do something when and only when you believe that it will produce an effect that of all attainable effects is that for which you have the strongest desire.

That is one theory about reason and appetite. If it is correct, there is no room for any extra factor leading to action. If we adopt it, we will find it hard to see what Plato could possibly have meant by the thumoeidic part of the soul. We will perhaps start to suspect that maybe the thumoeidic part is a fiction, imagined to support an untenable analogy between the city with its three parts and the individual who without that imaginary extra part has only two.

What the *Republic* means by reason and appetite is not however what the bipartite theory means by them. For one thing, Republican reason and Republican appetite are each capable of setting goals to be attained by action. Each of them in other words does some of what is done by bipartite appetite. But each does it in a rather different way. For not just anything that sets you your goals would be a Republican appetite. To be a Republican appetite it has to be something that sets you a goal in the way that for example hunger sets you the goal of food or thirst that of drink. It has to be that special sort of goal-setter that is felt as painful while it persists and that brings pleasure when removed by attainment of the goal that it sets. Likewise Republican reason is not just any setter of goals. Republican reason sets you a goal by its calm and deliberated apprehension that such a goal is good. Both Republican reason and Republican appetite are goal-setters. But they set goals in quite different ways. It is one thing to feel hungry, that is, for appetite to set you the goal of food. It is another thing for reason to set you the goal of food, as it does when you realize that it would be best for you to eat now since you will not have another chance for some time to eat the food that you need.

Some marks of the difference between reason and appetite are already implicit in this example of food. The first is that appetite can be out of line with reason. You can feel hungry even without the calm and deliberated belief that it would be best for you to have something to eat now. And you can have such a belief without feeling hungry. The second is that appetite and reason can be positively at odds with one another. You can feel hungry even though you know that food now would be bad for you. This is the condition of many a dieter. And you can know that it would be best for you to eat even though your gorge rises at the very thought of food. This the the condition of many an anorexic. The third is that such disagreements between reason and appetite do not typically end with the conversion of one by the other to its own point of view. Your hunger may lead you to eat in spite of your knowledge that it would be best not to; but it will not typically do so by persuading you to believe that after all over-eating is not harmful. Likewise your knowledge that it would be best for you to eat no more may stop you eating in spite of a continuing hunger; but it will not typically do so by stopping you from feeling hungry.

Now are Republican reason and Republican appetite the only things that might move one to act? It seems not. Consider for instance an emotion such as anger. This emotion sets goals. For instance if you are angry with someone this might impel you to strike them. And the proof of this would be that if anger were the only force in operation unrestrained by any others then you would indeed strike. Now is anger to be identified with a calm and reasoned apprehension of what is good? No. For it is not calm and reasoned. Is anger then an appetite of the same kind as hunger and thirst? No. For conflicts between reason and anger are rather different from conflicts between reason and appetite. Suppose that you are angry with someone and inclined to attack. Suppose also that reason opposes this. You reflect for example that the person with whom you are angry with in fact neither meant nor did you any harm. These reflections may of course stop you *acting* as your anger would suggest. More important, they can stop you *being* angry, in a way that the reflection that drink would be bad for you cannot stop you feeling thirst. For one ingredient of your anger will be some sort of belief, for instance, that the object of your anger has wronged you. Such beliefs may be corrected by your calmer calculations, by your reason. If they are so corrected, then your anger fades away, for one of its essential ingredients has been removed. By contrast of course, thirst and hunger have no such ingredient. They do not consist even partly in the belief that drink and food would now be beneficial. And this is why realizing that drink and food would be harmful does not stop one feeling hunger and thirst.

There are other states that share these features with anger. Consider pride. This can lead to action. It can lead to actions other than those suggested by either reason or appetite. And pride leads to action via some sort of belief about good and harm, for instance, via the belief that something is a slight, or that something reflects well upon you. These beliefs may be corrected by reason; and when they are, one's pride may cease to urge actions contrary to those that reason suggests. Or reason may endorse these beliefs, in which case one's pride adds its weight to the side of reason in any dispute it may have with appetite. In other words, such a state as pride is particularly apt to play the role of an Auxiliary. It is therefore things like anger and pride that Plato meant by his talk of *thumos*; and he seems quite right to put such things together in a class of their own separate from either reason or appetite.

Of course, you may attempt to deal with these Republican contrasts between reason, *thumos* and appetite by arguing that there is less in them than meets the eye. All that is going on in such cases, you might say, is that one now has one appetite for one thing and a belief that the satisfaction of this one appetite now would mean the dissatisfaction of many future appetites for other things. So really, you might continue, there is here only one goal-setter, namely appetite present and future; and the only thing that reason does here is point out that the means of satisfying one appetite would frustrate some stronger ones. But that is simply to insist on the bipartite theory come what may. It is to reveal what Plato would call an oligarchic soul (*Rep.* 553–555).

Let us then accept the tripartrite soul, and turn to investigate how Plato uses it to define justice. The chief thing to bear in mind is that Plato, like other Greek moralists, works with a list of four cardinal virtues: wisdom, courage, discipline and justice. The first three virtues are each explained by reference to one of the three parts of the soul or of the city. You have wisdom when the part in supreme command—whether the intellect or the class of Rulers—has an accurate apprehension of good and harm. You have courage when the second part—anger or auxiliaries—is duly in harmony with and subordinate to the first, conforming itself to what the first part apprehends of good and harm, and throwing its own weight in on the side of the first part rather than rushing off to side with appetite or to act on its own unreasoned conception of good and harm. You have discipline when the third part—appetite or the lowest class—is duly subordinate to the first two and has its own way only when those first two permit it. Thus three parts of the city or of the soul are used to define three virtues. Since there is no fourth part the fourth virtue of justice has to be defined in a different way. And just about the only way left by the tripartite theories of soul and city is to define justice as that condition where each of the three parts does its own job without trespass upon the others.

This argument by elimination is obviously a powerful one. For instance, one obvious way to challenge it would be by finding some fourth part of the soul or of the city and showing that justice is especially associated with that part in the manner that the other three virtues are associated with each of the other three parts. Another obvious way to challenge it would be by finding some fifth virtue to go alongside wisdom, courage, discipline and justice and showing that since this fifth virtue cannot be handled by Plato's account, Plato must be mistaken in his handling of the other four. Plato's theory however does not seem vulnerable to either of these obvious lines of attack. I at any rate cannot think of extra parts of the soul or of extra virtues that belong with those that Plato mentions.

Nevertheless, though neither of the obvious ways to attack Plato are likely to succeed, there still seems to be some ground for doubt about his definition of what makes an individual just. It is simply this. What has justice so defined got to do with justice as we ordinarily understand it? What has this condition of the soul got to do with, say, not attacking other people? Is the Platonic justice of an individual in any sense a social virtue, governing the individual's behaviour towards others? Plato himself says not: 'The real concern of justice is not with external actions but with a man's inward self' (*Rep.* 443). But if it is only justice as so redefined that Plato undertakes to show is beneficial to its possessor, how can he answer the original question about why be just? Has he not simply changed the subject?

These questions are searching. But Plato does have some answer to some of them. We challenge Plato to show that his just person will not do the sort of thing that we originally would have thought unjust; will not, for instance, take other people's goods. Plato can then reply that our original conceptions of justice and injustice were in fact inadequate, as we ourselves can see. It is no good trying to define justice by some observable pattern of behaviour. Recall what happened when it was suggested that justice might be defined as truthfulness and returning what we have borrowed (*Rep.* 331). As soon as we think about it we realize that there can be cases where the just individual will not be truthful or will not return what he has borrowed. The same point applies quite generally, says Plato. Any attempt to define justice by some observable pattern of external behaviour will founder on the fact of which his Theory of Forms makes so much, the fact that no such pattern can be identified with justice; for no such pattern will be unambiguously just, just under all circumstances at all times and in all places (e.g. *Rep.* 476).

But if that is so, how can Plato connect the performance of just actions with the order in the soul whereby he defines justice? How can he handle the fact that justice has something to do with behaviour? Plato can answer this point. One cannot define just action by reference to any observable pattern of behaviour. But one can, he says, define it in some other way. An action is just, remember, if it conserves that order within the soul by which justice itself must be defined (*Rep.* 443). And on this definition it turns out to be a trivial and obvious truth that a just individual, i.e. an individual whose parts have a certain organization, will do just actions, i.e. actions which conserve that organization. Otherwise that individual would not be just for long. Thus Plato's theory does after all point to some connection between being just and doing just actions. And if the connection is trivial and obvious then that is no objection to him. For there should be a trivial and obvious connection between being just and behaving justly.

There remains however one grave problem. We should expect individuals who are just to work for, to preserve, and to fit happily into just social arrangements in the community to which they belong. And that just individuals have such a concern for the just society ought to be as trivial and obvious a truth as the truth that just individuals do just deeds. It ought in short to be true by definition. The trouble is that Plato's definitions of just individuals and just societies do not make this true by definition. Indeed, there is some difficulty how given his definition this will be true at all, let alone be truistic.

The difficulty stems from a point we mentioned earlier, Plato's principle that justice on the small scale in an individual must be defined so that it is exactly the same feature as justice on the large scale in a city. If the two sorts of justice had different definitions the concern of just individuals for justice in their city could be as trivial and obvious as the tendency of just individuals to do just actions. For example, we might define a just city as one whose parts are organized in a certain way, and then define just individuals as those disposed to play their part in such a city. Or instead, we might define a just individual as one whose parts are organized in a certain way, and then define a just city as one whose members are such individuals. Either way, there would be no problem of why just individuals should fit happily into the just city; they would do so simply by definition. But as things are, by defining just individuals and just cities in exactly the same way, Plato creates such a problem for himself. It is as if Plato had defined a just action as one with three parts of such and such a character organized in such and such a fashion. With that definition of just action it would no longer be obvious, and might not even be true, that a just individual will perform just actions.

There is then on the face of it a difficulty here for Plato. And we can see how this difficulty manifests itself in certain parts of his discussion. Consider what he says in *Rep.* 519–520, a very awkward and unsatisfactory discussion of why philosophers who have enjoyed the course of intellectual activity and development that culminates in knowledge of the Good itself should be expected to come back down into the cave and govern. Some remarks suggest that such a descent is required of the philosophers by their concern for justice. In particular, it would be unjust of them not to repay the city for their education by returning to rule over it. Other remarks suggest that in their concern for justice, for the undistracted domination of their intellects in the life that they lead, philosophers will prefer to remain outside the cave, and that the descent to the cave will provide happiness for the city at the expense of their own. In other words, Plato wants—as indeed he should want—the result that the just individual will have a concern for justice in society. But the way he has defined justice for cities and individuals makes this result difficult to reach.

Nevertheless, I suspect Plato can in fact do better than this awkward passage would suggest. It is a central feature of the Theory of Forms that when focused upon Forms the intellect operates in abstraction from any concern with particularity. Thus the philosopher loves beauty itself, rather than just one particular kind of beauty (*Rep.* 475–476). Moreover, the whole upbringing of philosophers in the ideal city has right from birth been calculated to rid them of any concern with particulars in their particularity and to focus them rather upon what is general. Recall the arrangements about property and the family. There is no piece of property of which one philosopher can say 'That's mine' without others of that class being able to say exactly the same thing; likewise, when I say 'I love my mother', I will not mean I as opposed to anyone else of my generation, or my mother as opposed to any other woman of hers (*Rep.* 461–466). If this is how my attitudes have been formed right from birth, then consider how I will feel once I have got out of the cave but am summoned back down to rule. I will no doubt want to continue with intellectual activity. But I am incapable any longer of desiring that I, Nicholas Denyer, as opposed to someone else, should continue to enjoy the intellectual life. My concern for justice and the dominance of the intellect will amount simply to a concern that there be intellectual activity going on, and that it go on as part of some order in which the intellectual rules over the appetitive and the thumoeidic. In short, my sole concern is now the thoroughly impersonal one that the life of the just city should continue. And so I can have no self-interest which would urge me not to play my proper role in the continuance of that city.

This or something like it is the way that Plato should, I think, have resolved the difficulties posed for him by his assumption that what makes both a city and an individual just is a single feature present in both cases. At any rate, this line of argument does in the end deliver the conclusion that just individuals will be concerned to promote justice in their city. And it delivers this conclusion without drawing on materials that are radically unPlatonic. Still, if this is the Platonic solution to our difficulty, we might wish that Plato himself had unambiguously put it forward.

We have examined Plato's definition of what makes an individual just. We have seen how after one or two difficulties this definition can be reconciled with the obvious facts that a just individual will do just deeds and in particular will foster and preserve the just society. But we have not yet examined the question: is it a good thing for me to have that order in my soul which defines justice? It is only in Books 8 and 9 that Plato offers any reasoned answer to this question. His answer is a clear-cut yes. His reasoning is a little more complex.

By far the bulk of his reasoning is in effect an argument by elimination. The tripartite theories of the soul and of the city enable Plato to set up a classification of alternatives to justice; namely tyranny, democracy, oligarchy, timarchy and their counterparts in the individual. The classification, he acknowledges, is not altogether exhaustive. But he claims that any further alternatives to the life of justice will simply be intermediates between the four pure cases that he discusses in detail (*Rep*. 544). So if Plato can eliminate these four as thoroughly unpalatable by comparison with justice, he will have proved that justice is the best thing possible. Like all arguments from elimination this raises an obvious difficulty. Just as the argument from elimination to show that justice is the order of the soul raised the difficulty that maybe there were other alternatives besides those explicitly considered, so too the current argument from elimination raises the difficulty whether there are other alternatives to justice completely distinct from the four that Plato mentions. Here, as in the previous argument, we can be sure that there are no other alternatives only if we can be sure that the tripartite theory of the soul is correct.

How then does Plato eliminate the alternatives to justice? In large measure his argument consists simply of vivid description (*Rep*. 545–580). We are presented with, for example, a vision of the tyrannical personality, in which all is enslaved to a single craving. And as soon as we grasp what such a personality is like we feel instantly repelled. There is nothing whatsoever invalid about such arguments by vivid description. But they have one feature that may make them less than universally persuasive. For all these vivid descriptions presuppose that if your intellect is subordinated to other parts of the soul, then your true self, that core of you which alone is fully human, has been subordinated to something less than fully human, something better compared to an animal. What you are most fully identified with has therefore been subordinated to a thing in some sense outside the real you (*Rep.* 588–589). These analogies are not the happiest way to make Plato's point. For when the intellect is compared with a human being, this invites uncomfortable questions about that human being in turn: Will not her soul too consist of three parts, intellectual, thumoeidic and appetitive? And will not the intellectual part itself be like a human being and thus consist of three such parts? And so on to infinity. (Such questions can be asked of any theory which identifies your true self with what it acknowledges is only a part of you.) Still, we can accept something of the point that these analogies try to make. We can see how someone whose life is organized round a single craving, for money, say, or alcohol, can be thought of as controlled by some sub-human force. But this will not be acceptable to any save those who already in some degree feel that Platonic justice is the best state of the soul. For to accept the identification of oneself with one's intellect is already to accept much of what Plato says about the benefits of what he defines as justice.

The elimination is not however simply by vivid description of a possibly contentious sort. For there is also argument of another kind. Thus Plato argues from the premises that philosophers opt for the life in which intellect predominates and that only philosophers are equipped with the wide experience and the intellectual powers that one needs for judging the different ways of life (*Rep.* 582). The form of the argument is fine. The chief trouble is being assured of the truth of its premises. How do we identify the philosophers whose judgment we are to regard as authoritative? What about people who certainly pass as philosophers but who just as certainly would not opt for the life that Plato recommends? After all, many of those employed as philosophers would favour the bipartite theory of the soul and say that reason is and can only be the slave of appetite present and future. Do we simply say that their judgment does not count? And that in the relevant sense they are not genuine philosophers anyway? If we identify our authoritative guides by their preference for the intellect, rather than by their readiness to follow appetite, have we not already made assumptions in favour of Plato? Must we not then already be partly persuaded of Plato's case before his current argument can get any grip on us?

Similar questions are raised by Plato's arguments about the genuineness of philosophical pleasures, culminating in the calculation that the philosopher king gets 729 times more pleasure than the tyrant (*Rep.* 583–588). I can neither follow nor take seriously the exact details of the final calculation. My hope and belief is that Plato did not take them seriously either. What Plato did mean seriously however is the earlier argument about the pleasures of the philosophic life. Pleasure consists in the replenishing of some depletion. Hunger, for instance, is such a depletion, and food is its replenishment. That is why you enjoy your food when you're peckish. Ignorance too is a depletion. The 'food' which replenishes it is truth; the 'eating' of this replenishment is knowledge. So far so good. There is nothing here that even the tyrannical personality need contest. But the argument is not yet complete. It is completed only by adding that truth and knowledge are things far more real than anything bodily such as food; and that since the satisfaction which they constitute is much more real, the pleasure that they provide is greater. But this final and essential step will succeed in persuading us only if we are already in some measure inclined towards Plato's conclusion. It will carry no conviction with those who have no inkling that the intellectual life offers something far more substantial than the life of sensual gratification.

In some sense then Plato's arguments seem to presuppose some prior acceptance of their conclusion. But are his arguments vitiated by this circularity? Are they rendered powerless by the fact that they appeal to some prior inkling that the life of justice and reason is the good life? Perhaps not. They do indeed appeal to some such inkling. But if what Plato argues elsewhere is correct, then some such inkling will in fact be possessed by everybody, even by those who are not yet full-blown Platonists. Recall the analogies of the Sun, Divided Line and Cave. The world that we perceive provides some intimation of the truer reality which becomes the sole concern of the philosopher. It is an image of that higher reality, albeit a defective one. Because of this, the world we perceive can stimulate a yearning that it cannot itself satisfy, and can point beyond itself to show how this yearning is satisfied in the realm of the Forms; much as cocktail nibbles can stimulate the appetite for a proper meal. All this is of course brief and obscure: and to elaborate on it properly would mean trespassing upon the areas reserved for Julia Annas elsewhere in this volume. But even in its brief and obscure form my description may indicate how Plato can escape the charge of reasoning with vicious circularity in his arguments that the life of justice and of intellect is indeed the best. For those who feel inclined to dispute his conclusion will do so out of a concern for the world of the senses. But such a concern will itself provide the makings of that concern for intellect and truth which Plato's arguments need if they are to carry conviction. There may then be a circularity in Plato's arguments for justice; but if his arguments about Forms are right, this circularity is not vicious.

Aristotle

Aristotle (384–322 BC) was born in Stagira, Macedonia. He went to Athens and entered Plato's Academy when he was eighteen. He remained there until Plato's death in about 347 BC, when he left Athens to spend the next five years at Assos in Asia Minor and at Mytilene on the island of Lesbos, working on philosophy and biology. In 343 he was invited to return to Macedonia to tutor the son of Philip II of Macedonia, the future Alexander the Great. This lasted three or four years. After a further period at Stagira, Aristotle returned to Athens where he opened a philosophical school at the Lyceum or Peripatos. On the death of Alexander in 323 there was anti-Macedonian feeling in Athens, and to avoid the same fate as Socrates, Aristotle took refuge in Chalcis on the island of Euboea, leaving the school in the charge of his pupil Theophrastus. He died the following year.

The works credited to Aristotle are probably lecture notes, not intended for publication, but collected and edited and arranged in some sort of order by other people, and first made generally available in about 60 BC, more than 250 years after he died.

In addition to two works on ethics, the better known of which is the *Nicomachean Ethics*, there were logical works, physical works, biological works and psychological works.

A slightly abridged one-volume collection of Aristotle's works is *The Basic Works of Aristotle*, edited and with an introduction by Richard McKeon (New York: Random House, 1941). A good pocket-sized collection of extracts from Aristotle's works, now hard to obtain, is *Aristotle Selections*, edited by W. D. Ross (Oxford University Press, 1927).

The edition of the *Nicomachean Ethics* prescribed by the AEB and JMB is *The Ethics of Aristotle*, translated by J. A. K. Thomson, revised with notes and appendices by Hugh Tredennick, with an introduction and bibliography by Jonathan Barnes (Harmondsworth: Penguin, 1976). The bibliography lists over 100 works on Aristotle, published up to 1975. Jonathan Barnes has since written a book, *Aristotle*, for the Oxford 'Past Master' series (Oxford University Press, 1982). It contains a useful chapter on Aristotle's ethics, as also does J. L. Ackrill, *Aristotle, The Philosopher* (Oxford University Press, 1981).

The standard work on the *Nicomachean Ethics* is still W. F. R. Hardie, *Aristotle's Ethical Theory* (Oxford: Clarendon Press, 1968). Aristotle's influence on recent ethical writing is evident in, for example, Philippa Foot, *Virtues and Vices* (Oxford: Blackwell, 1978).

Aristotle, *Nicomachean Ethics*[1]

ROSALIND HURSTHOUSE

Our understanding of the moral philosophy of Aristotle is hampered by a number of modern assumptions we make about the subject. For a start, we are accustomed to thinking about ethics or moral philosophy as being concerned with theoretical questions about actions—what makes an action right or wrong? Modern moral philosophy gives two different sorts of answers to this question. One is in terms of a substantial ethical theory—what makes an action right or wrong is whether it promotes the greatest happiness, or whether it is in accordance with or violates a moral rule, or whether it promotes or violates a moral right. The other sort gives a meta-ethical answer—rightness and wrongness are not really properties of actions, but in describing actions as right or wrong we commend or object to them, express our approval or disapproval or our emotions concerning them. But the ancient Greeks start with a totally different question. Ethics is supposed to answer, for each one of us, the question 'How am I to live well?' What this question means calls for some discussion.

The question can be expressed in a variety of ways; none is perfect, but one comes to understand it by grasping the variety.

<table>
<tr><td rowspan="3">'How</td><td>should</td><td rowspan="3">I live in order to</td><td>live the best life</td><td rowspan="3">?'</td></tr>
<tr><td>ought</td><td>flourish</td></tr>
<tr><td>must</td><td>be successful</td></tr>
</table>

The first comment which needs to be made is that one should not be misled by the presence of so-called 'value' words ('well', 'should', 'best', etc.) into thinking that these are specifically moral words. For then one will understand the question as 'How am I to live morally well?' 'What's the morally best life?' 'How should I live from the moral point of view?' And although, as we shall see, one would not be entirely wrong to do so,

[1] I am grateful to Gavin Lawrence for his detailed and helpful criticism of an earlier draft of this paper and for much discussion on the topics discussed herein over the years. All references to the *Nicomachean Ethics* have been given in terms of the so-called 'Bekker numbers' which are standardly used for giving exact references to Aristotle's writings. They also enable one to identify a passage on the page of any good translation, for instance the current Penguin edition of the *Ethics* introduced by Jonathan Barnes.

it is nevertheless not the proper understanding of the question. We should/must/ought not read in a 'morally' qualification, any more than we would at the beginning of this sentence. This point shows up particularly clearly in any versions of the question involving 'flourish' or 'be successful'. Compare 'How should this plant be treated in order that it will flourish?' and 'How ought I to study if I am to be a successful student?' where once again we wouldn't think that these were moral 'shoulds' or 'oughts'.

The next comment that needs to be made is also about these versions—about what is meant by 'flourish' and 'successful'. 'Flourishing' is one of the standard translations of the Greek word *eudaimonia*, a concept that beginning readers of Aristotle find hard to grasp. It is used in ways which lead us to translate it (when it is an abstract noun) as good fortune, happiness, prosperity, flourishing, success, the good/best life; where it is an adjective of a person as fortunate, happy, prospering, flourishing, successful, living well.[2] The extent to which any one of these is and is not an adequate translation can be seen by comparing what we say about them and what Aristotle says about *eudaimonia* in Book I. For a start, he tells us that it is what we all want to get in life (or get out of it); what we are all aiming at, ultimately (1094a1–26); the way we all want to be. And we all agree in one sense about what it consists in, namely, living well or faring well. But another truth about it is that we can disagree about what it consists in too, to the point where some of us can say it consists in wealth, others that it consists in pleasure or enjoyment and others that it consists of honour or virtue (1095a14–25).

What do we say about success and prospering? Well, 'succesful' and 'prosperous' have a materialistic sense in which they connote wealth and power; when we use them in this way it is obvious to us (a) that one can be happy and count oneself as fortunate without them and (b) that they do not necessarily bring with them happiness and the good fortune of loyal friends, loving relationships, the joys of art and learning and so on. So many of us will say that (material) success and prosperity is not what we want; that having it doesn't amount to faring well. But 'success' has a non-materialistic sense as well. Someone who possesses wealth and power may yet count her life to be not a success but a failure, perhaps because she finds herself to be lonely and lacking the conviction that anything she does is worthwhile. Similarly, someone who lacks wealth and power may still count their lives a success, thinking of themselves as rich in the things that matter. And it is the possibility of this non-materialistic sense of 'success' which makes it a suitable trans-

[2] Etymologically it means 'well (*eu*) demoned/genuised', i.e. blessed with a good genius or attendant spirit (*daimon*).

lation of 'eudaimonia'. Perhaps nowadays 'prosperous' can have only the materialistic sense—but the non-materialistic one still lurks in 'May you prosper', the wishes for a prosperous New Year, and indeed the non-materialistic use of 'rich' I just exploited.

My talk here of two different senses should not be taken to imply that the word 'success' is literally ambiguous. In describing the lives of many people as successful one would not necessarily be meaning 'successful in the one sense rather than the other'. For it is no accident that the word has these different senses, since so many people believe that wealth and power are things that matter, are things one is fortunate in having, because they bring happiness. Hence too the materialistic interpretation that can be given to 'the good life' or 'being well (or better) off'. This was as true of the ancient Greeks as it is of us; which is why some people say that *eudaimonia* consists in having wealth. And one of the constraints that Aristotle puts on an account of *eudaimonia* is that it should provide some explanation of this fact (NE1099a32–1099b8).

I said above that one of the truths that determines the concept of *eudaimonia* is that it is something everyone wants, the way everyone wants to be. Someone who said that she didn't want to be *eudaimon* would be incomprehensible. Some philosophers, for instance Mill, have maintained that this is true of happiness, and 'happiness' is certainly the most common translation that has been given. 'True (or real) happiness' would be better, since we tend to say that someone may be happy (though not truly happy) if they are living in a fool's paradise, or engaged in what we know is a fruitless activity, or brain damaged and leading the life of a happy child; whereas such people are not flourishing or leading successful lives and none of us would want to be that way.

But even 'true (or real) happiness' is not obviously something everyone wants—unless, as I am sure was true of Mill, one is already thinking of 'true happiness' *as eudaimonia*. For, thinking of (true) happiness as something like (well-founded) contentment or satisfaction or enjoyment one might intelligibly deny that one wanted to be happy. For surely one can think that happiness is not the most important thing in life—'We're not put on this earth to enjoy ourselves' people say. I might want not just to be happy, but to do great deeds, discover great truths, change the world for the better, no matter what it cost me in terms of happiness.

Of course, rather than saying 'no matter what it costs me in terms of happiness' I might say instead 'Then I would count myself as happy or content, no matter what it cost me'. This, I think, shows that 'happiness' does not have to connote bovine contentment or a life full of pleasure and free from striving and suffering, and, as with 'success' above, it is the possibility of this second sense—happiness despite a lot of striving, effort and suffering— which makes it a suitable translation of 'eudaimonia'. Once again, as with 'success', the word 'happiness' is not ambiguous. It is no accident that it has these different senses since so many people do want contentment and a life that is pleasurable and enjoyable without cost. And, as before, Aristotle recognizes as a constraint on the correct account of *eudaimonia* that it should provide an explanation of this fact (1099a6–1099a20).

Bearing all these points in mind, let us return to our question 'How am I to live well?' and its various versions—'How should/ought/must I live in order to flourish/be happy/successful?' We have seen that when 'success', 'happiness', etc., are construed in the intended way, this is a question any one of us is bound to be interested in because we all want to flourish/be happy/successful; the very idea that someone interested in life should not want to 'make a go of it' in this way is deeply puzzling.[3] This, one might say, contrasts with wanting to be *morally* successful or wanting to lead a morally good life—there is nothing puzzling about someone who doesn't want to do that. As we noted above, the 'should/ought/must' in the various versions of the question should not be given a particularly moral reading, any more than they would be in 'How should/ought I to live in order to be healthy?'

So much for the discussion of what the question means. But now we are clear about that a new difficulty arises. How can the question, understood in the right way, have anything to do with ethics? If we understand it as asking 'How am I to live morally well?' we can see why it counts as a question for ethics to (try to) answer. But this interpretation is the one that has just been ruled out. It now seems to be an entirely self-seeking or egoistic question which has nothing to do with ethics.

Another obstacle we have in understanding the ancient Greek view of ethics is that it does not clearly embody the contrast—between the moral and the self-seeking or egoistic—which this new difficulty relies on. But the obstacle may be surmounted by looking carefully at the answer Aristotle gives to this question that apparently has nothing to do with ethics. For his answer is: 'If you want to flourish/be happy/successful you should acquire and exercise the virtues—courage, temperance, liberality, patience, truthfulness, friendship, justice . . . .' Or, as we might say, be a morally virtuous person.[4] With this answer we are

[3] Though perhaps not incomprehensible, if we can understand a certain sort of neuroticism in which the person seems bent on misery and self-destruction. Aristotle appears not to recognize the existence of such people.

[4] The translation of some of Aristotle's terms for virtues makes them sound a little odd, and they are best understood by noting what vices they

clearly back in the business of doing ethics—but how could this have come about when we started with the self-seeking or egoistic question?

The claim that is basic to Aristotle's view is that it comes about because *qua* human beings we naturally have certain emotions and tendencies and that it is simply a brute fact (made up of a vastly complex set of other facts) that *given* that we are as we naturally are we can only flourish/be happy/successful by developing and exercising those character traits that are called the virtues—courage, justice, benevolence and so on. For reasons that I shall go into later, Aristotle does not in fact give the argument for each such character trait, but it is worth briefly considering some examples as an illustration of (roughly) how the argument goes and what sorts of facts are relevant.

Take one of the simplest cases for us—generosity. Here are some of the relevant facts; we are naturally sociable creatures who like to have friends and want to be loved by friends and family. We also like and love people who do things for us rather than always putting themselves first. We also are not merely sympathetic but empathetic—the pleasure of others is pleasurable to us. Given that this is how we are, someone who is mean and selfish is unlikely to be liked and loved and hence likely to be lonely and unhappy; someone who is generous is likely to enjoy the benefits of being liked and loved and, moreover, in the exercise of their generosity will find much added enjoyment, for the pleasures of those they benefit will be pleasures to them.

Take another—honesty. Amongst the relevant facts there are some similar to the preceding ones—that we want friends, want them to be trustworthy, want them to trust us—and some that are rather different, for instance that there are likely to be occasions in our lives when we

---

are opposed to. So, for instance, 'temperance' is not a matter of eschewing alcohol, but having the right disposition in respect of alcohol and food and sex—being neither an alcoholic, nor a glutton, nor sexually licentious. Of the virtue called, in translation, 'patience', Aristotle himself remarks that it doesn't really have a name, but we can readily grasp it by seeing that it is opposed to the vices of being bad tempered in various ways on the one hand, and poor spirited on the other. It is also important to realize that the term we translate as 'virtue' (*arete*) has not specifically moral overtones and is better translated as 'excellence'. So it should come as no surprise to us that Aristotle's list contains non-moral virtues or excellences such as wittiness. But we need not even take many of these very seriously as excellences, for in his other ethical work, the *Eudemian Ethics,* Aristotle makes a point of denying that they are excellences (of character) on the grounds that they do not involve choice (EE1234a25). Finally, we should note that Aristotle's list is open-ended—he nowhere claims that it is exhaustive—so it is open to us to add to it virtues with which we are more familiar, e.g. benevolence, compassion, honesty, kindness....

need to be believed—as the many fables on the theme of crying 'wolf' too often illustrate. Folk wisdom also contains the adage that 'honesty is the best policy' and the conviction that 'the truth will out' to the discomfort of those who have lied about it. The exercise of this virtue is not as immediately enjoyable as the exercise of generosity, but the honest person has the advantage of not having to keep a constant guard on her tongue and has peace of mind thereby. One should also note that the honest person can tell the truth effortlessly in circumstances in which doing so would be embarrassing, frightening, unpleasant or unfortunately impossible for the person who lacks the virtue. Literature abounds with scenes in which a character desperately needs to tell the truth for if she does not a profound relationship in her life is going to be destroyed—she will lose her lover, or her closest friend will feel betrayed, or her son will turn in bitterness from her, or she will put herself in the hands of the blackmailer or . . . to her subsequent irremediable regret and misery. But the truth in question is one of those truths it is hard to own up to—and she can't bring herself to do so. But had she armed herself with the virtue of honesty she would have been able to. Much more could be said here too about the harm one does oneself through self-deception and how difficult it is to be simultaneously ruthlessly honest with oneself but dishonest to other people.

Even more than honesty, courage is a character trait one needs to arm oneself with given that we are the sorts of creatures we are—subject to death and pain and frightened of them. It is not so much that we need courage to endure pain and face death as ends in themselves, but that we are likely to have to face the threat of pain or danger for the sake of some good that we shall otherwise lose. I read of someone who had the opportunity to save someone's life by donating bone marrow; one might see this as a wonderful opportunity but lack the courage to do it, to one's subsequent bitter regret. And how much worse the regret would be if one's cowardice led to the death of someone one loved. If I have managed to make myself courageous I am ready to save my child from the burning house at whatever risk to myself, to stand up to the terrorists who threaten my friends' lives and to my racist neighbours who are trying to hound me and my family from our home. In a society in which cancer has become one of the most common ways to die we also need courage to enable us to die well, not only so that we may not waste the last years or months of our lives but also for the sake of the people we love who love us.

All the above is schematic. I do not pretend to have shown conclusively that generosity, honesty and courage are necessarily part of flourishing or living well, and of course much of what I have said is open to detailed disagreement. I cannot go through many of the details here, but I will discuss one pair of objections that spring very naturally to mind, since the responses to them form part of the further exposition.

The two objections one wants to make are that, contrary to what has been claimed, the virtues are surely neither sufficient nor necessary for living well. Not sufficient because my generosity, honesty and courage (for example) might, any one of them, lead to my being harmed or indeed to my whole life being ruined or ended. Not necessary because, as we all know, the wicked may flourish like the green bay tree.

How do we envisage that my virtue might lead to my downfall? It is not quite right to say that it is obviously the case that, having the virtue of generosity I might fall foul of a lot of people who exploit me or find myself poverty-stricken. For built into each concept of a virtue is the idea of getting things *right*. (This is what distinguishes full virtue from natural virtue—see 1144b1–17.) In the case of generosity this involves giving the right things or amount for the right reasons on the right occasions to the right people. *The right amount,* in many cases, would be *an amount I can afford* or *an amount I can give without depriving someone else*. So, for instance, I do not count as mean, or even ungenerous when, being relatively poor, or fairly well off but with a large and demanding family, I do not give lavish presents to richer friends at Christmas. *The right people* do not include the exploiters for I do not count as mean or ungenerous if I refuse to let people exploit me; moreover generosity does not require me to help support someone who is simply bone lazy, nor to finance the self-indulgence of a spendthrift. Any virtue may contrast with several vices or failings and generosity is to be contrasted not only with meanness or selfishness but also with being prodigal, too open-handed, a sucker.[5]

Once this point is borne in mind, examples in which I may suffer because of my virtue are harder to find. Nevertheless, there are some; sudden financial disaster might befall many of us, leaving the generous in dire straits where the mean do much better. Just as, in the past, people have been burnt at the stake for refusing to lie about what they believed, so now, under some regimes, people are shut in asylums and subjected to enforced drugging for the same reason while the hypocrites remain free. My courage may lead me to go to the defence of someone being attacked in the street to no avail and with the result that I am killed or maimed for life while the coward goes through her life unscathed. Given these possibilities, how can anyone claim that the

[5] Cf. for example, 1106b1–22 and 1109a20–29. Note in the latter passage the comparison with finding the centre of a circle, which is a better image than finding a midpoint ('mean') between just two opposing vices.

question 'How am I to flourish?' is to be honestly answered by saying 'Be virtuous'?

There are two possible responses to this. The first is to grit one's teeth and deny that the virtuous person can be harmed by her possession of virtue. To be virtuous *is* to flourish, to be (truly) happy or successful. Nothing counts as being harmed except doing evil, and nothing counts as a genuine benefit, or advantage, or being better off than doing what is right. There is more than a grain of truth in this view, to which I shall return later on, but, on the face of it, it is, as a response to the sorts of examples we have envisaged, simply absurd. As Aristotle says, 'Those who maintain that, provided he is good, a man is happy (*eudaimon*) on the rack, or when fallen amongst great misfortunes are talking nonsense . . . ' (NE1153b17) (The point of these examples is that I become unable to exercise virtue, either because I am dead, or because I have become physically, mentally or materially incapable of doing so.)

The second response is to deny that the answer to the question was ever supposed to offer a guarantee. If I ask my doctor 'How am I to flourish physically/be healthy?' she gives me the right answer when she says 'Give up smoking, don't work with asbestos, lose weight, take some exercise . . . ' Even if, despite following her advice I subsequently develop lung cancer or heart disease, this does not impugn its correctness; I can't go back to her and say 'You were wrong to tell me I should give up smoking, etc.' She and I both know that doing as she says does not guarantee perfect health; nevertheless, if perfect health is what I want, the only thing I can do to achieve it is follow her advice. Continuing to smoke, work with asbestos, etc, is asking for trouble—even though, it is agreed, I may be lucky and live to be a hearty ninety.

Similarly, the claim is not that being virtuous guarantees that one will flourish. It is, rather, probabilistic—'true for the most part' (1094b21–22). Virtue is the only reliable bet; it will probably bring flourishing—though, it is agreed, I might be unlucky and, because of my virtue, wind up on the rack.[6] So virtue is not being made out to be guaranteed sufficient for flourishing.

But now we move to the second objection. Is it not being made out to be necessary? It was just said to be the *only* reliable bet, as if, as in the medical case, making no effort to acquire the virtues was asking for trouble. But don't the wicked, as we said above, flourish? In which case virtue can't be necessary. The two possible responses to this objection

[6] It is important to note that the only similarity I am claiming between the two cases is on this point. Giving up smoking, etc., is not constitutive of flourishing physically the way exercising the virtues is constitutive of flourishing as a human being, and there are other disanalogies too.

are elaborations on the two that were given to the other. The first denies that the wicked ever do flourish, for nothing counts as having an advantage or being well off or . . . except doing what is right. The second, continuing to pursue the medical analogy, still insists that virtue is the only reliable bet and, agreeing that occasionally the non-virtuous flourish, maintains that this is, like fat smokers living to be ninety, rare and a matter of luck. So, for instance, it is usually true that people who are entirely selfish and inconsiderate miss out on being loved—but such a person might be lucky enough to be blessed with particular beauty or charm, or by lucky chance come across someone else very loving who just fell for them in the mysterious way that sometimes happens. But, the claim is, we can all recognize that this *is* a matter of luck—one could never rely on it.

However, many people may feel that this response is implausible. Surely it is not simply by pure chance and luck that the non-virtuous flourish. Isn't power just as good a bet as virtue, if not a better one, for flourishing? If one has power, people do, as a matter of fact, love one for that; one is respected and honoured, people treat one with special concern and consideration—and all despite the fact that in order to get and maintain power one will undoubtedly have to be selfish, dishonest, callous, unjust . . . to a certain extent. So the answer to 'How am I to flourish?' should not be 'Acquire virtue' but 'Acquire power'[7]. This objection can be seen as a form of one of the oldest, and still current, debates in moral philosophy. In Plato's *Republic* it takes on a form specifically related to the virtue of justice—if injustice is more profitable than justice to the man of strength, then practising injustice is surely the best way of life for the strong. Its most modern version is entirely general—'What reason have I to be moral?' One very important question it brings up is whether morality, or moral judgments, give reasons for acting to everyone. If some action ought not to be done (because, say, it is dishonest or unjust) does this mean that everyone

[7] We might of course think of further alternatives—what for instance of the life of the entirely selfish but dedicated great artist? Aristotle does recognize an analogous alternative in Book 10. There he argues that the best life consists in intellectual activity (contemplation) not in the practical activity necessitated by the exercise of the (moral) virtues. And this apparently allows that, if I am to live well, I should *not* acquire and practise the virtues but acquire some other set of character traits which best armed me for becoming a successful contemplator. How this can be reconciled, if at all, with what has been said in the earlier books of the *Ethics* is a major problem in Aristotelian scholarship and raises questions that are interesting in their own right. Are there ways of flourishing which actually necessitate vice or must any flourishing human life resemble the fully virtuous one to some extent? (Cf. footnote 11 below.)

has a reason not to do it, or is it open to the powerful to say truly that there is no reason for them to refrain?

What then, should be said about this old, but still hotly debated issue? When we were considering how 'success' could work as a translation of *eudaimonia*, we noted that one could be successful in a materialistic sense—wealthy and powerful—while still counting one's life not a success but a failure, because, say, one felt lonely and unfulfilled. Now let us consider someone who is (a) successful in the materialistic sense, (b) non-virtuous—they have acquired their power by cheating and lying, ruthlessly sacrificing people when it suited them, but (c) perfectly happy—they don't feel guilty, or lonely, or unfulfilled or worried about what would happen to them if they lost their power, or that their life is a failure in any sense. The question we then ask ourselves is—do we find this person's life enviable or desirable? And part of the truth I said was contained in the view that nothing counts as a genuine advantage or being better off than doing what is right is that many of us are going to say 'No'. We may be hard put to explain *why* we say 'No'; perhaps we cannot say anything more than that we couldn't live like that, or that we wouldn't want to have cheated our friends or to have let our parents or children down. But our inability to say more than this does not matter; all that matters is that we can view a life containing every apparent benefit and advantage as one that we don't want because it contains having acted wrongly in various ways.

To anyone who thinks this way, Aristotle's answer to 'How am I to flourish?' is going to emerge as the only possible answer. 'Acquire power' was, in any case, an answer that could only recommend itself to the minority who thought they could achieve this, and it now appears that even if I count myself as part of this minority, I may still not regard the acquisition of power through the abandonment of virtue as something that will give me the sort of life I want.

But now we encounter a new difficulty. In what way is Aristotle's answer an answer to a question that anyone who thinks this way is genuinely open-minded about? If what you think already is that the wicked do not really flourish; that, viewed as calling for acting wrongly, power and its attendant benefits are not really desirable at all, of course you will reject the answer 'Acquire power'. And if, seeing the world this way, you already regard acting virtuously as incomparably rewarding of course you will agree with Aristotle's answer. But then he will have been preaching to the converted. And if he has, all along, been preaching to the converted then we may be seized with a qualm about whether his answer has any objective correctness about it. For what appeared to give it some claim to objectivity, namely its grounding in facts about the human condition, is now revealed to be strictly irrelevant. The virtuous do not need to consider facts about the human condition to convince them that living well is practising the virtues; they already think of living well in those terms—which is exactly why they say that the wicked do not really flourish.

Our difficulty can be highlighted by imagining what the wicked are likely to say about the virtuous. Would not some of the people depicted in *Dallas* and *Dynasty* for instance, regard the life of a fairly ordinary virtuous person as simply pitiable? For they are convinced in advance that living well involves as least being materially very well off, and hence that the modestly endowed do not really flourish. So they will no doubt reject Aristotle's answer as absurd.

Does it follow then that his answer works only for those who believe it already? No, because the virtuous and the wicked do not exhaust the field. The question was whether Aristotle's answer could recommend itself to someone who was genuinely open-minded about how to live well, i.e. someone who does not already have a settled conviction about what flourishing consists in, unlike the fully virtuous and utterly corrupt, who do.

What is it to have a 'settled conviction' about this? It is not simply to have a consciously held belief, for I may have theoretical convictions which an argument or a piece of counter-evidence might dislodge at any minute (cf.1095a24–27). It is for one's character to have achieved its *dernière consistence*, such that one habitually acts and thinks in certain ways—and, as Aristotle says 'to dislodge by argument habits long embedded in the character is a difficult if not impossible task' (1179b16–17). Viewed this way, having a settled conviction need not be having a consciously held belief about what flourishing consists in (which indeed not many people other than philosophers do have). Correspondingly, not having a settled conviction is, regardless of beliefs one may profess, having a character which is not (yet) settled into its final mould.

Who then are the non-virtuous-but-also-non-wicked—the 'unsettled' as I'll call them? Strictly speaking, children count as 'unsettled' in this sense but young children will not be asking themselves 'How am I to live well?' Paradigmatically, the 'unsettled' will be the students to whom Aristotle's lectures are addressed—people old enough to be interested in the question, but young enough to be not (yet) virtuous but not thereby vicious. It is important, Aristotle tells us, that such people have been well brought up for without such training they will not be able to grasp 'the starting-point' (1095b4–8). This amounts to his acknowledgement of the point I mentioned above—that his account of flourishing cannot be made out to those who have become so corrupt that they can see pleasures and benefits only in the lives of the very wealthy and self-indulgent. To have been well brought up is to have been trained in some way from infancy to find enjoyment and pain in the right things (1104b13). So, for example, we may take it that the well brought up unsettled do recognize some goods that the vicious do not—they know, for instance, what it is to enjoy a friendship with someone who is neither rich nor glamorous, but generous and to take pleasure in sharing their own possessions with such a friend. They know what it is to feel ashamed about lying to people who trust them and to find relief in confessing. But they also still feel the pull towards the lives of the wicked and are far from being fully virtuous—they still do lie and say cruel things and act selfishly.

So now our question is—can Aristotle's answer recommend itself not only to the fully virtuous but also to them? Can the life of the virtuous be represented to the unsettled as the flourishing life—i.e. as the most enjoyable, containing real benefits or advantages and the only one worth going for? Or are its pleasures and advantages only recognizable by the virtuous—from the inside as it were?

There is a charming Thurber cartoon which depicts a riotously drunk woman in a flowery hat and low cut gown (perhaps connoting somewhat loose sexual morals) who is clearly having a whale of a time; she is being contemplated with frosty disapproval by a dour man in a dog-collar who is saying 'Unhappy woman!' Now part of what makes this funny, I take it, is not so much that describing this obviously cheerful woman as unhappy is completely inappropriate, for it makes good sense to pity someone who habitually gets very drunk, no matter how much they may enjoy themselves at the time. What is inappropriate is that the man who calls her unhappy so obviously never enjoys himself in any way at all. If she may truly be described as unhappy, so may he. If it was the case that the virtuous were bound to be like Thurber's man—if virtue was so much a matter of suppressing or eliminating our natural desires and tendencies that the virtuous life did not characteristically contain much recognizable satisfaction—then it would indeed seem impossible for the virtuous to represent their lives as flourishing to anyone but themselves. But Aristotle's promise is that this is not how things are. Although virtue is about things that are difficult for man, we are constituted by nature to receive the virtues (1103a24–26). Our natural desires and tendencies are such that they can be brought into complete harmony with our reason, so that doing what we know to be right is doing what we enjoy doing (cf. 1099a15–22, 1102b12–29, 1166a13–15). And surely Aristotle's promise is met. The virtuous are not characteristically like Thurber's man; he is not a good example of a virtuous man at all. The virtuous, as they eat, drink and make love with healthy gusto, rejoice in the love, trust and support of their friends and families, cheerfully make the best of the sorts of bad jobs that befall anyone, look forward serenely to their futures, delight in their work and intellectual pursuits, are people who can be seen to be enjoying themselves and possessing advantages and benefits even by the unsettled who may as yet see the lives of the powerful and corrupt as enjoyable and containing advantages and benefits too.

Indeed, thinking back, we might wonder whether the alternative position is even intelligible. If there cannot be common agreement on the application of words such as 'benefit', 'advantage', 'pleasure', 'enjoyment', 'good' and 'harm', 'loss', etc., how can such words be taught? So why might anyone hold such a position—for it is held and expressed as the first responses to the two objections considered above. It seems that in part people are led into it by finding it necessary to make the first response rather than the second to the first objection. So, for instance, Phillips, responding to the point that my virtue may require me to lay down my life, insists that when this is so the virtuous 'see death as a good'.[8] He would presumably want to say the same about other 'evils', 'disadvantages' or 'losses' such as being tortured, or reduced to physical or mental incapacity, or being made destitute too, and indeed, generalizing his point in this way, McDowell maintains that the virtuous understand the notions of 'benefit, advantage, harm, loss and so forth' in such a way that no 'sacrifice' necessitated by virtue counts as a loss, and that the virtuous life cannot, even under such circumstances, contain any ground for regret.[9]

But here an important distinction seems to have been missed. Let us agree that there are cases in which the virtuous person may see her death or pain 'as a good', namely those cases in which some other good will be (or may be) achieved by them—say that others live or do not suffer. But these are not the only sorts of cases in which virtue may require me to die or suffer—what of the cases in which a tyrant tries to force me to do something wicked by threatening me with death or torture? As Aristotle says, there are some things we must sooner die (and, by implication submit to torture, destitution, etc.) than do, but this does not entail that the virtuous must see their death or pain in such circumstances as a good. Rather, they see it as the lesser of two evils—lesser, but a great evil all the same. Freedom from pain, health, modest possessions, the way of life, life itself, these are all goods and precious to the virtuous person; their loss is a real loss and she may regret them as such, regretting that circumstances made it necessary.[10]

[8] D. Z. Phillips, 'Does it Pay to be Good?', *Proc. Arist. Soc.* n.s. **65** (1964-65).

[9] John McDowell, 'The Role of Eudaimonia in Aristotle's Ethics', reprinted in *Essays on Aristotle's Ethics*, Amelie Rorty (ed.) (California: University of California Press, 1980), 369–370.

[10] Aristotle explicitly acknowledges the existence of such cases in his section on 'mixed' actions (Book 3, ch. i). The characteristic of these is that what is chosen—say death or torture or the enduring of disgrace—is something that considered 'in itself' is *not* a good, not the sort of thing that

Phillips seems to have overlooked this distinction, and been led to the position of the first response through a confusion over what Aristotle's answer is an answer to and hence over what it amounts to. It is an answer to the question 'How am I to live the best life, to flourish?' and the answer is 'Be virtuous, i.e. acquire and practise the virtues'. The question is not 'How should I act on this particular occasion?' nor is the answer 'Be virtuous', in its other sense, i.e. 'Act now in the way required by virtue because if you do you'll flourish'. Inevitably, if one takes the question and answer this wrong way the Aristotelian position becomes very peculiar. For a start, the probabilistic second response is ruled out as unintelligible. I ask 'How should I act on this particular occasion?' in circumstances in which virtue requires me to bring some great evil upon myself and the answer of the second response is made out to be 'Act in accordance with virtue because if you do you'll probably flourish, though of course you won't on this occasion', or 'Act in accordance with virtue because when other people less unluckily circumstanced than you are now act that way *they* flourish'. If this were what the second response amounted to, no wonder philosophers reject it and are drawn to the first. For if one takes the question and answer this wrong way something else seems attractive about the first response too. If I ask 'How should I act on this particular occasion?' in quite ordinary circumstances and am told that I should tell the truth, or share my cloak, i.e. be virtuous, because I will flourish if I do (and won't if I don't) I surely have not been given the right answer.

Acting virtuously, we want to say (as does Aristotle, cf.1105a26–1105b1, 1144a14–20), is an end in itself, something you do for its own sake, not because you have calculated that on this occasion it will pay off. If you think that each virtuous act is supposed to benefit you and is to be done for that reason you have missed the whole point of morality—unless, that is, you have become fully virtuous and respecified the concept of 'benefit' in such a way that for you to act virtuously, even when it brings evil upon you, *counts* as a benefit, as the first response holds. This leads people to say that virtue or morality 'can't be justified from the outside'. Its only justification comes from within morality, in terms of a concept of flourishing or living well which only the virtuous have. But if people arrive at this point only through misidentifying the question Aristotle answers, do we have any reason to continue to accept it?

Divorced from the background of the misidentification, the claim is open to two different interpretations. Is it that morality can't as a matter of fact be justified from the outside—that facts recognizable by the

---

anyone would go for. In so far as he takes something that he recognizes not to be a good but an evil the agent acts involuntarily and can be pitied.

virtuous and non-virtuous alike are not available? Or is the claim that necessarily it can't be justified from the outside—that any facts recognizable by the virtuous and non-virtuous alike must be irrelevant? I have heard people claim the second but we should note what an extraordinarily strong claim it is. Suppose that we were so constituted that virtue characteristically led to our dropping dead at thirty and vice characteristically led to our living to a hearty ninety—are people prepared to say that this would have no bearing at all on the claim of the virtuous that they flourish? Of course, the presently virtuous might say that even under such conditions they would rather die at thirty than lead the wicked life, or not live at all, but this seems to me expressive of the belief that if that were the sort of creature that we were there would be no such thing as flourishing for us. If we had been like that I would suppose that the concept of a virtue, and the whole history of moral philosophy would be unimaginably different, and I do not know of any argument that supports the view that it could just as well have been the same.

This example is instructive, for it shows what sort of fact would have to be available if virtue were to be justified 'from the outside' in a strong sense, as, I take it, it would be if, contrariwise, it was virtue that yielded long life and vice that was fatal. (One could regard hellfire religion as trying to provide a fact that served this purpose.) What conditions would such a fact meet? It would be a fact that connected virtue to something which, like life itself, is (i) a good to any human being and (ii) can be recognized as such. And it is important to acknowledge that such a fact (or facts) are not available.

On the first condition we must acknowledge that the virtues cannot truthfully be said to be goods to every human being, but only to the 'natural' ones who are social animals. 'Man is by nature a social animal' does not entail that every man is, for in the natural sciences as in ethics, many things, Aristotle says, are true only 'for the most part', not universally. If there are people who by nature do not enjoy the company of others and feel out of place sharing our communal life (it is thought possible that (some) psychopaths are such people) then perhaps the most that can truthfully be said to them is that they should assume virtue even if they cannot have it.[11] Moreover, as has already been conceded, the fact that is available, viz. that the virtuous characteristically flourish while the vicious do not, is not recognizable as such by the vicious. It is not a scientific fact about human nature like 'All

[11] Pending further specification of such people this *is* still a possibility; it is not obvious so far that what they should do is acquire and practise the vices. Cf. the question raised at the end of footnote 7 above.

men are mortal'. But is this simply because they have got themselves their peculiar concept of flourishing?

Just as the virtuous have to give some reason for saying that Thurber's woman is unhappy in the teeth of the fact that she is clearly enjoying herself so the wicked would (in theory) have to give some reason why the lives of the virtuous are pitiable. If such lives are manifestly being enjoyed and contain *some* things recognized to be goods to the sort of animal we naturally are, such as friends and family, love, respect, independence, leisure, enjoyment itself—some justification has be given for describing such lives, intelligibly, as pitiable. Presumably what could be said is that people enjoying such lives are content with too little, and that such goods as their lives contain have been bought at too high a price—as Nancy Mitford claimed that she valued independence as a good but not at the price of having to put away her own underclothes instead of having servants to do it. Just as the virtuous say of the wicked happy man that he is content with too little in friends bought with power and respect prompted by fear and that he has gained his (admitted) advantages at the intolerably high price of degradation, so the wicked may say of the virtuous that, for instance, they are degraded by having to cook for themselves and content with too little in always having sex with the same old partner. But is their disagreement solely about what counts as 'degradation' and 'a good friend' and 'the best sexual partner' and 'enjoyment' and . . . i.e. a disagreement about the application of 'value' terms which amounts to irreconcilable views of what flourishing consists in? If this were so, it would seem that the only really corrupting belief would be a false belief about what flourishing consists in. Is this so?

Aristotle says little about the role of belief in virtue. For him the role of the intellect in virtue is played by *phronesis*, usually translated not very happily as 'prudence' or (better) as 'practical wisdom'. This involves the ability to deliberate well—to figure out how to achieve what you want, but also (for so far this is mere cleverness, *deinotes* (1144b24–30)) getting the end *right*. If you think that flourishing consists in the life of pleasure instead of the life of virtue then your deliberations, however successful in getting you the pleasures you want, are not correct or good deliberations because they are misguided. It is only if you have correctly identified your end as the life of virtue that you can deliberate well in the full sense.

This does indeed suggest that there is only the one corrupting belief and hence that the only way to guide the unsettled into virtue would be to keep on telling them that flourishing consists in exercising virtue and to ensure somehow that they keep on acting in accordance with virtue in the way that, so Aristotle assures us, will eventually bring it about that they do so habitually and come to share the true conception. But in that 'somehow' lies the difficulty. *How* can the unsettled be convinced that the occasional black lie is not 'really' worth telling; that such 'advantages' as it might bring are not real advantages because secured at too high a price? Do we just keep on *saying* so? Unfortunately, Aristotle does not tell us, and we must work it out for ourselves.

I do not think that moral education does or should consist simply in insisting that wrong acts are not worth doing because they do not secure 'real' advantages and, correspondingly, I do not think that the (theoretical) disagreement between the virtuous and the vicious over whether the virtuous characteristically flourish while the vicious do not is simply a disagreement about what flourishing consists in. It is also a disagreement about the explanation of why the virtuous and vicious don't flourish when they don't. For each side attributes its own failures to bad luck or odd circumstances and the failures of the other side to being the way things were bound to fall out—it's a disagreement about how life works.

I should like to suggest that the belief that we are so constituted that the virtuous characteristically flourish (so the failures are due to bad luck) while the wicked do not (so their failures are just what was to be expected) is part of virtue itself. It used to be called the belief in providence, and to doubt it while still believing that one must do as virtue requires is to fall into the vice of despair. To doubt it while not yet believing that one must do as virtue requires (because one is unsettled and not yet virtuous) is to be (still) in the grip of a number of beliefs that are corrupting and to which the above belief is the proper corrective.

One is the belief that one can get away with certain things, that the occasional bare-faced lie or piece of cruelty won't come home to roost. Another is that one can have things both ways, reaping the advantages of virtue and vice simultaneously. Another very tempting thought is that one is particularly clever, and hence that even if most people can't manage this, one will be able to oneself, that although, as Foot says, people cannot be manipulated like household objects in general, nevertheless you will be able to manage being the manipulator but never the manipulated. Another is that one is blessed with some special characteristic like beauty or social position which will command love and respect from some and mysteriously guarantee that you won't find yourself wanting love and respect from anyone who is unimpressed.

Maybe these are all just versions of the same belief—a denial of the one I have claimed is part of virtue. In presenting it or them in different formulations I was intending to illustrate the ways in which they may be expressed by the unsettled. It is not that many people consciously hold such beliefs; rather they are expressed in reactions people have to events in their lives; the surprise and feeling of having been unfairly punished when just that one lie does come home to roost or when one reaps the whirlwind; the thought 'How can this have happened to *me*?'; the shock when one finds oneself the sucker; the difficulty in understanding how one's beautiful self can *not* be loved. They are expressed too in one's reactions to other people's lives be they real or fictional. Perhaps one of the most corrupting things about the lives that are portrayed in films and on television is the way in which they do show the wicked flourishing and the (token) good being tricked and victimized. One is encouraged to believe that this is realistic, and to the extent that one believes what one is shown, rather than reacting with sceptical scorn, one is settling towards vice rather than virtue.

I have been talking as if it were obvious that the unsettled were adolescents, as we assume Aristotle's students were. But the account he gives of full virtue—that perfectly harmonious state in which we always do what is right gladly and never knowingly fall into wrongdoing—sets the standard very high. Probably none of us has got there yet, and to the extent that we are still unsettled we still need to correct our tendency to think that we can get away with acting wrongly. It is true that, in line with the idea that to be virtuous is to have a view of flourishing according to which acting wrongly *cannot* count as securing one any benefit, we may sometimes correct this tendency by reminding ourselves that we won't be 'getting away' with anything, but rather throwing away something it is worth hanging on to. But let us frankly acknowledge that this doesn't always secure inner conviction. When it doesn't, reminding oneself of the corrective belief nevertheless may. I can't convince myself that I haven't got away with acting wrongly, but I can convince myself that I got away with running a great risk and might not be so lucky again. I can't convince myself that in acting rightly I haven't suffered a real disadvantage but I can convince myself that this was bad luck and shouldn't give me a reason to act otherwise next time. And in this way I may gradually settle into the belief that acting wrongly is never worth doing, serene confidence in which would be virtue indeed.

This debate that I have been going through is often discussed under the heading 'Must morality have a point?' I have maintained that, according to Aristotle, the fact of the matter is that it *does* have a point. If that is so, but it is nevertheless not true that it must have, this could only mean that virtue's constituting a flourishing life (in the sense of 'flourishing' that the unsettled can grasp) was a happy accident, something that is not necessarily so, but could be otherwise. But this seems to me to be a dangerous thought. If we allow our society to degenerate into a state in which it is extremely difficult for many of the people within it to exercise the virtues of honesty, generosity, courage and justice, because their best chances of minimal comfort and even survival lie in the opposing vices, and think that, since morality doesn't have to have a point, it will still be teachable, we may be in for a nasty surprise. And even if, under such circumstances, we were able to convince the next generation that there really is a concept of flourishing, grasped only by the virtuous, in terms of which one can flourish when too poor to be able to do anything for one's family and friends, even save them from starvation or hypothermia, and circumstanced in such a way that even the minimal physical pleasures are denied one, we would, I think, be offering them false coin. Aristotle recognises as a constraint on his account of *eudaimonia* that the flourishing life should contain the real advantages of (some) material wealth and pleasure to which the vicious attach such importance, and we should be honest enough to do the same.

René Descartes

René Descartes (1596–1650) was born at La Haye, near Tours in France. He entered the Jesuit School at La Flèche in 1606, where he studied Latin and Greek and the classical authors, and acquired respect for the certainty of mathematics and distaste for the theories of Aristotle as developed by medieval commentators. In 1616, he took a degree in law at the University of Poitiers. There followed a period during which he travelled, for some of the time as a gentleman-officer in the armies of Maurice of Nassau, Prince of Orange, and Maximilian, Duke of Bavaria. In 1625 he returned to Paris and renewed his acquaintance with Father Marin Mersenne, who was later instrumental in making his views known to many of the famous intellectuals in Europe. From 1628 to 1649 he lived in Holland and worked out in detail the scientific, philosophical and mathematical ideas that had engaged him during his travels. His main philosophical works are *Rules for the Direction of the Mind*, written in 1629–30 but not published until 1684, *Discourse on Method*, 1637, *Meditations*, 1641, *Principles of Philosophy*, 1644, and *The Passions of the Soul*, 1649. In 1649, Descartes accepted an invitation to visit the Queen of Sweden and instruct her in philosophy. He succumbed to the rigorous climate, and died in February 1650.

For a long time the most frequently quoted English translation of Descartes' work was *Philosophical Works of Descartes*, translated by Elizabeth S. Haldane and G. R. T. Ross (Cambridge University Press, 1911), but this has now been superseded by a new translation, *The Philosophical Writings of Descartes*, translated by John Cottingham, Robert Stoothoff and Dugald Murdoch (Cambridge University Press, 1985).

The edition of the *Meditations* prescribed by the AEB and JMB is *Descartes, A Discourse on Method, Meditations on the First Philosophy, Principles of Philosophy*, translated by John Veitch, introduction by A. D. Lindsay (Everyman's Library No. 1570; London: Dent, 1912). This translation of the *Meditations* was first published in 1853.

There are a great many books, and collections of articles, on Descartes' philosophy. Two that are not too difficult or technical are the following:

O. K. Bouwsma, *Philosophical Essays* (Lincoln, Nebraska: University of Nebraska Press, 1965). There are three entertaining and challenging essays on the *Meditations* in this book: 'Descartes' Skepticism of the Senses', 'Descartes' Evil Genius' and 'On Many Occasions I Have in Sleep Been Deceived'. H. G. Frankfurt, *Demons, Dreams and Madmen: the Defense of Reason in Descartes' Meditations* (Indianapolis: Bobbs-Merrill, 1970).

One that is difficult is Bernard Williams, *Descartes: the Project of Pure Enquiry* (Harmondsworth: Penguin, 1978). Reviewing it in *The Times Higher Education Supplement* (14 April 1978), Anthony Kenny wrote: 'But it is no criticism of Williams to say that his book is not easy reading for the non-philosopher. Philosophical books aimed at the non-philosopher which are easy to read, impressive, and convincing are almost always fraudulent. Beginning philosophy almost always involves a struggle to keep afloat, because philosophy has no shallow end. The gift of writing philosophical prose which can be followed effortlessly at first reading and which will yet repay the most minute scholarly research is a very rare one shared by not more than half a dozen writers in the whole of history: and one of the greatest of those half dozen was Descartes himself.'

Doubt, Knowledge and the *Cogito* in Descartes' *Meditations*

JOHN WATLING

Descartes published his *Meditations in First Philosophy* in 1641. A French translation from the original Latin, which he saw and approved, followed six years later. The words 'in First Philosophy' indicate that the *Meditations* attack fundamental questions, the chief of them being the nature of knowledge and the nature of man. I shall deal almost entirely with his treatment of the first, the nature of knowledge; even when the two questions become mixed up, as they notoriously do, I shall not encroach on to the second, the nature of man. The *Meditations* were intended to confirm Descartes' reputation as a philosopher (he was already pre-eminent as a mathematician and a scientist) and, to increase their impact, they were accompanied in their first publication by a series of comments solicited from notable theologians and philosophers together with Descartes' replies. These comments are called the *Objections* and numbered from one to six, but it is only an accident that there are six Meditations and six Objections. There are six Objections because there are six objectors (that is not quite true, the sixth Objection being a collection of comments from several people) and each Objection ranges over the whole work, although, of course, the different commentators focused upon the parts they found important or questionable. Many of the Objections, particularly those of Arnauld and Gassendi, contain acute and valuable criticisms. Descartes took exception to Gassendi's contribution and wished not to have it published. He maintained that Gassendi quite misunderstood him, but that doesn't seem true. It is true that Gassendi pokes fun at Descartes in addressing him first 'O Soul' and later, pretending to realize his mistake, 'O Mind', but no doubt the trouble was that Gassendi understood rather too well, fastening upon inconsequentialities in the argument and inconsistencies in the thought and finding, against both, formidable arguments. Inconsequentialities and inconsistencies there are, so much so that the work is a set of parts rested together to give the appearance of a construction, not fitted together really to make one. That did not prevent the *Meditations* having as great an influence on philosophical thought as any work from the day of its publication to our own, or prevent Descartes' ideas from occupying the minds of philosophers ever since.

Among Descartes' scientific opinions were many that he did not know to be true. He held that nature abhorred a vacuum and he certainly did not know that to be true. Nature does not abhor a vacuum. He held that there were ice crystals in the upper atmosphere and that the white halo to be seen around the sun in some atmospheric conditions was formed by refraction of the sun's light in those ice crystals, just as the rainbow is formed, men learnt from Descartes' celebrated theory, so much deplored by Keats, by the refraction of the sun's light in the water drops of a shower of rain or the spray of a waterfall. His explanation of the sun halo is accepted. It was a remarkable piece of anticipation on his part, but he had little indication that the ice crystals were there, other than the phenomenon he invoked them to explain. Nevertheless such opinions, the former opposed by eminent authorities of his own day, among them Galileo, the latter involving what must have seemed even to him to be a speculation, are not the sort of which Descartes first calls his knowledge into question. Indeed they are not the sort of which he ever explicitly, for more than a moment, calls his knowledge into question, when, at the beginning of the *Meditations*, he proceeds to withdraw his assent, or, better, to explore what would remain if he were to withdraw his assent, from every one of his opinions that he does not know for certain to be true. He applies his rigorous test to his knowledge of opinions of a sort that, before he started meditating, he would have said he knew for certain to be true and which everyone, before reading his discussion and probably afterwards too, would say he knew for certain. He investigates whether he knows that he is sitting in front of the fire, not whether he knows that there are ice crystals in the upper atmosphere, whether he knows that two and three makes five, not whether he knows that nature abhors a vacuum. Such a procedure, which avoids the things we genuinely find dubious and which never examines the difference between them and the things we find certain, cannot but seem unsatisfactory. Descartes sought a different dividing line and by his rigorous test he hoped to discover opinions of which his knowledge was perfect and to demonstrate the nature of that perfect knowledge. What these were we shall soon see; they were not at all what most people take them to be.

In the course of the first Meditation, Descartes finds several different reasons for refusing to accept as certain things that are universally taken to be so. He has the evidence of his senses for many things, yet he has found before that his senses have deceived him: he should not put complete trust where he has once been deceived. That is not such an obviously sensible maxim and he admits that there may be favourable circumstances in which his senses never deceive him. Unfortunately, he argues, he does not even know for certain whether he is using his senses. He has often dreamt that he was sitting by the fire, writing, when he was actually asleep in bed. There is no certain mark to distinguish waking from sleeping. His senses may never deceive him and yet, because he can dream and form opinions that do not arise from the use of his senses but seem to do so, he can be mistaken even about those matters on which the senses are perfectly reliable, even about whether he is sitting by the fire. In sum, he refuses to accept as certain his opinions about the physical world around him on the grounds that he is sometimes mistaken about them, even about those that seem most evidently true. Further, his fallibility arises from his being a man: it is part of men's nature that they fall asleep and dream.

However, his consideration of dreaming points, he feels bound to admit, towards some things common to dreams and reality. The fact that he regularly falls asleep and dreams does not show that he ever makes mistakes about features common to both states. Things in dreams are coloured, just as they are in waking life, they have some shape, some length and breadth, they are few or numerous, near to or far away from each other and the events that happen to them occur in one order or another. In all these ways dream things are like waking things, therefore the fact that he dreams quite fails to establish that his opinion that there are colours, shapes, numbers, space and time is ever mistaken. What is more, the fact of dreaming, he says, fails to show that he is ever wrong in his opinions on simple matters concerning those things since, 'whether I am awake or asleep, two and three always make five and squares never have more than four sides'. These assertions raise difficulties which are not important for the progress of Descartes' discussion, since he soon finds means of setting aside the apparent certainties, but do have an interest of their own. Although it is impossible to depict to oneself, in a dream or otherwise, a bodily thing without shape or surface character, or a square facet with more than four sides, it is not impossible to dream that bodily things have no shape and that squares have more than four sides. To dream something that in waking life we know to be untrue, we need not depict or behold it, we may merely dream it, take pleasure in it or fright at it, and, in one way and another, reflect upon it. Squares we behold in dreams must have four sides, but we can dream that they do not; we can dream that squares never do have. The common features of dreams and waking life do not establish that Descartes could not be misled, in a dream, into the opinions that bodily things have no shape or colour, that squares have more than four sides or that two and three make six. However, Descartes' confusion here, if I am right and it is a confusion, has no effect upon the course of his argument. He wonders for a moment whether he should not rest certain with arithmetic and geometry, sciences which deal, he says, only with simple things like number and shape, and reject physics, astronomy and medicine, which look beyond such simplicities, but he immediately finds reason to reject them all.

He observes that he himself often considers other people to be mistaken in arithmetic and geometry, the sciences of the simple things. He sometimes thinks them mistaken when they themselves are most confident. May it not be that he himself is mistaken in his opinions in those sciences, even in those that seem to him most simple and obvious? Actual mistakes by others, on difficult matters that seem easy to them, point to the possibility of mistakes on his own part on matters that seem easy to him. Again, a man's capacity to arrive at correct opinions in arithmetic and geometry depends upon his constitution, upon how he is made. Descartes does not speculate upon what features of his make-up enable him to recognize mathematical truths, nor point out that they are very much more mysterious than the organs and nerves of his sensory apparatus upon which his capacity to perceive what lies around him depends. He emphasizes only that his mathematical capacities do depend upon his constitution and, to discover what reason he has to believe that his constitution is not faulty and fallible, enquires how he may have come by it, not what it is. He believes himself to have been created by an all-powerful god. Such a god could have brought it about that the sky and the earth did not exist while, at the same time, making Descartes believe, just as he does believe, that they do. If such a god could do that, could he not also ensure that Descartes makes a mistake every time he adds two to three or counts the sides of a square? The god who created the world is said to be good as well as powerful, so he should not have wished so to deceive him, but Descartes knows that, if there is such a god, he sometimes allows him to be deceived.

This argument by which Descartes extends his doubts to the simplest questions of mathematics seems to require that an all-powerful god, or demon, should have power over the truths of mathematics. He argues that, since such a god could have arranged that there is no world and arranged, too, that Descartes seemed to see one, so he could have ensured that Descartes held erroneous opinions on simple mathematical questions. The implication is, presumably, that he could have done so by arranging that two and three do not make five and arranging, also, that to Descartes they seemed to do so. To be able to arrange that two and three do not make five and that squares have more than four sides is to have power over arithmetic and geometry, or, perhaps it would be better to say, arithmetic and logic. It is, of course, absurd to suppose that two and three could have had some other sum than five or that squares could have had some other number of sides than four. Since that is absurd, it is absurd to credit any being with the power of bringing it about. In arguing as he does, Descartes seems to embrace this absurdity and, since it is an absurdity, his argument seems invalid. It does not seem to justify doubts about these simple truths.

There is, however, good reason to think that Descartes did not attribute power over such truths to however powerful a god or demon. At the beginning of the second Meditation he explicitly asserts that, in the case of one such truth, the most powerful deceiver would be powerless. What is more, there is an argument, very like his, but not requiring the attribution of such power, which Descartes could have employed to justify his doubts. Very likely it is what he intended. The arguments are, indeed, easily confused. To deceive us about the world, a god needs power over us; he does not need power over the world. If he finds that the world exists, he exerts his power to ensure that it seems to us not to. If he finds that the world does not exist, he exerts his power to ensure that it seems to us that it does. In just the same way, if he finds that two and three make five, he need only work on us to make them seem to us to make six. If he finds them to make six, he need only work on us to make them seem five. If you have enough power over a man, you can deceive him. You don't need power over the matters he is to be deceived about. That argument shows that an all-powerful god could mislead Descartes and, if it is possible that such a god exists, it shows that Descartes could have formed and could form erroneous opinions about even the simplest mathematical truths. It shows that Descartes' mathematical opinions are liable to error, just as his earlier arguments showed that his opinions about the world around him were. However, it does not show quite what Descartes argues for. It shows that Descartes could hold mistaken opinions in mathematics, it does not show that he could be mistaken in the opinions he holds. Now the former, that he could reach mistaken opinions, shows him fallible in mathematics and so shows that he cannot be certain of the opinions he holds, but it is the latter that Descartes asserts. He writes: 'it may be that he has decided that I make mistakes every time I add two and three or count the sides of a square' and, later on, at the end of the first Meditation, when he decides to guard against the possibility that he is in the hands of an ill-intentioned deceiver, he decides to reject all these old opinions that he has discussed as deceptions. Evidently, the suggestion is that he should hold all his opinions to be deceptions until he discovers one that cannot be a deception. Now, it cannot be that a god is deceiving him about the sum of two and three, for Descartes believes it to be five and it could not be anything else. It is not possible that his opinion that two and three make five is a deception. If that is the policy he is to adopt, he should admit that, in two and three make five and squares have four sides, he has found what he is seeking.

My point is that, towards the end of the first Meditation, Descartes is led astray. An opinion that cannot be a deception is not the same thing as an opinion on a matter about which he cannot be deceived. What is more, being the former, the one Descartes comes to think important, does not imply that an opinion is something he knows for certain to be true, or even that it is something he has any knowledge of at all. A little child who knows next to nothing about arithmetic may pick up the idea that two and three make five. That would be an opinion that cannot be a deception, but there is no reason to suppose that the child knows it for certain, or in any way at all, to be true. On the other hand, if there is some matter on which the child couldn't be deceived, such as whether its parents love it or not, that, surely, is something about which the child has certain knowledge. Of course, the words 'So two and three may not make five' could be used to express the conclusion that that is something we do not know for certain. The words 'may' and 'possibly' are often used to express lack of confidence in the opposite opinion or imperfect knowledge of it, so it is not unreasonable to say 'I am liable to error in mathematics, even on the simplest questions, so two and three may not make five'. However, Descartes introduces the all-powerful deceiver in order to demonstrate that error is possible over the simplest questions in mathematics, just as, for the same purpose, he points to the mathematical errors of other people. From that possibility of error, once established, he argues to his uncertainty, his lack of knowledge, even about the simplest matters. There would not be an argument here, if he were merely using the words 'It is possible that I am mistaken in my opinions' to mean 'I do not know for certain that my opinions are true'.

The bogy of an all-powerful deceiver is Descartes' final argument for doubt. He decides to reject as uncertain every one of his opinions that may be the deception of an all-powerful being. He admits that he does not know that he was created and made as he is by such a god, but he argues that upon any other supposition of his origin, that he came to be as he is by fate, or by chance, or by the sequence and linking of events, he is even more likely to have a faulty constitution that leads him into error. Descartes, of course, had no inkling of the explanation that Darwin was to give in his theory of natural selection of how the linking of causes and effects might have provided human beings with faculties adapted to their needs. Awareness of the theory of natural selection should have removed his doubts, since he argues for them from the probability that his constitution and circumstances derive from an all-powerful deceiver, or from something worse, and natural selection takes away that probability by providing a plausible alternative. I think, however, that the argument Descartes gives here is not quite the one he intended. Consider his reason for doubting, earlier in the Meditation, that he is sitting by the fire writing. It is that he cannot tell whether he is dreaming or awake, not that the probability is that he is dreaming. Why then should he need more reason for his new doubts than that he does not know enough about his origins to be sure that his faculties are reliable? The process of natural selection, even if it could be proved to be the process by which Descartes came to be as he was, does not guarantee that. A sudden change in the environment, a short time before, might have rendered his slowly developed faculties useless.

Descartes argues from his great ignorance concerning his own nature and origins and concerning many things about the world around him, that he possesses knowledge only when, however he is made and whatever the world is like, his opinions will be correct. In his fanciful image, the all-powerful, possibly ill-intentioned god represents his own unknown and possibly defective make-up and the world's only partially known and possibly hostile nature. I have already pointed out the ambiguity in this conclusion. It may mean that he has knowledge of those, and only those, matters about which, however he is made and whatever the world is like, he will form a correct opinion. It may mean that he has knowledge of those, and only those, of his opinions which, however he is made and whatever the world is like, he will be correct in holding. The former focuses on the matters in question and requires the impossibility of his being wrong about them. The latter focuses on the opinions he holds and requires the impossibility of his being wrong in holding them. This conclusion or, as I think, one or other of these conclusions, provides Descartes with the rigorous test for his opinions that he has been developing throughout the first Meditation. It is the application of this test that he speaks of as his method of doubt. Where did it lead him?

When, at the beginning of the second Meditation, Descartes starts to test his opinions by the method he has perfected in the first, rejecting as false, or, at least, suspending judgment upon, everything that may possibly be a deception, it seems to be the second of the two ways of guarding against deception that he adopts. He begins to run through his opinions, discarding them if he finds that they could be deceptions. He fears, not unreasonably you may think, that he may be left with nothing. He sacrifices his beliefs in the existence of bodily things, the existence of his own body among them. He almost relinquishes his belief in his own existence, but stops, for he realizes that that cannot be a deception.

> No, certainly, there is no doubt that I exist, if I am convinced, or even if I think anything. But there is a very cunning and very powerful deceiver who employs all his efforts to deceive me about everything. There is, then, no doubt that I exist, if he deceives me; and, deceive me as much as he will, he will never find a way of making me nothing, while I think that I am something. So that,

> having thought well about the question, and carefully considered everything, I cannot but conclude, and henceforth hold, that this proposition: *I am*, *I exist*, is necessarily true, every time I affirm it or conceive it in my mind.

So he concludes that there is at least one of his opinions that survives his rigorous test, when it seemed only too likely that nothing would survive it, his belief that he himself exists. He could have found another by an exactly similar argument, although he doesn't explicitly do so. It is the belief he sometimes had that he holds a belief. If he ever believes that he holds a belief, that cannot be a deception, since the deceiver could never find a way of making him beliefless when he believes himself beliefful.

This is the passage in the *Meditations* in which Descartes presents the thought known as the *cogito*. That name comes, of course, from the first word of the Latin for 'I think, therefore I am', '*Cogito*, *ergo sum*'. Descartes did not sum up his thought in that formula in the *Meditations*; he did use it, but in French, in an earlier work, *The Discourse on Method*. The account of the *cogito* in the *Meditations* is clearer and better than that in the *Discourse*. The passage, the one I have just quoted at length, is persuasive but very mysterious. It certainly seems to present an argument, and it is rather surprising to find Descartes' first discovery of an opinion that survives his rigorous test identified by an argument. If an opinion that passes his test is recognized by proving it, then he must already have found an opinion that passes it, upon which the proof rests. In the first Meditation, before he formulated his rigorous test, the opinions that he considered to be most obviously beyond doubt were ones that required no proof: 'I am sitting by the fire' and 'Two and three make five'. Unless Descartes is very much misled, it cannot be that he offers a proof that he exists from the fact that he thinks in order to show that he is certain, if of nothing else, of his own existence.

Apart from the inappropriateness of such a proof, there is another reason why that cannot be what the *cogito* passage presents. I have pointed out that the argument would work as well for 'I believe', as it does for 'I exist'. For 'I exist' the argument, very much compressed, would go: 'No one could make me think I existed when, at that very time, I didn't, therefore "I exist" is necessarily true'. If, in that argument, Descartes were proving his existence from his thinking, then, in the parallel argument for belief, or thinking, which would go: 'No one could make me think I thought when, at that very time, I did not, therefore "I think" is necessarily true', he would be proving that he thought from the fact that he thought. Now, the argument is persuasive, and it is as persuasive for 'I think' as it is for 'I exist'. It cannot be as silly and empty as 'I think, therefore I think'.

I seem now to be admitting that the passage does present an argument and, indeed, I think it does. If it is not the argument 'I think, therefore I am', what argument is it? The premise, at least, is not difficult to identify. It is the fact upon which Descartes insists, that however an all-powerful deceiver exerts himself, he will never bring it about that Descartes believes that he exists when, at that very time, he does not. His premise is: whatever the deceiver does, if I think I exist, then I exist. When I said, earlier, that Descartes did explicitly deny that an all-powerful god would have power over a simple truth it was this passage that I was thinking of. He can hardly have thought it less necessary that if I am square I have four sides than that if I think I exist then I exist. Now, from that premise, it follows at once that Descartes could not be mistaken in his opinion that he exists. Whatever the deceiver does, Descartes will not be mistaken in holding that he himself exists. Since that is exactly what must be true of an opinion of his, if it is to pass his rigorous test and be counted as known for certain, or, at least, if it is to pass one of the two tests his words ambiguously express, Descartes can consistently conclude that his opinion that he himself exists passes his test and can be counted as one thing that he knows for certain to be true. The parallel argument in which 'I think' replaces 'I exist' proves, just as validly, that he cannot be mistaken in his opinion that he thinks. The arguments are not proofs of the propositions 'I exist' and 'I think' that pass the test; it would be absurd to offer such a thing: they are proofs that they do pass it.

It is that fact, that the arguments are not proofs that he exists and thinks but proofs that, in believing that he exists and that he thinks, he knows that he exists and that he thinks, that explains why it does not matter that the premises of the arguments, that he cannot, without existing, believe himself to exist or, without thinking, believe himself to think, are simple truths of logic, less obvious, if anything, than 'squares have four sides' that Descartes admits that he may be mistaken about. Descartes' knowledge that he exists and that he thinks arises, if the *cogito* argument is correct, from the simple logical facts. It does not arise from his knowledge of those facts. Everyone who believes that he exists, knows that he exists, whether or not he knows that he knows it. Knowledge must, if Descartes' strict conditions are to be fulfilled, arise from facts of logic. It cannot arise from men's intelligence, powers of reasoning or perceptual faculties, for all of those may be disturbed by illusions, emotions or drugs, and may have built-in defects. Only a logician, probably, will notice the simple logical fact that a man cannot, without existing, believe himself to exist, so only a logician will know that he and everyone else know themselves to exist. Nevertheless, everyone will know the fact, that he himself exists, that only the logician, Descartes, knows he knows. No knowledge of logic or power of reasoning is required for that. If the *cogito* is correct, everyone who believes he himself exists, knows it.

The *Meditations* show clearly how the formula 'I think, therefore I am' should be modified to provide a less misleading short-hand for the *cogito* argument. Expand 'I think' to 'I think I am' and replace 'therefore' by 'If . . ., then . . .': 'If I think I am, I am', a formula which brings out the peculiar feature of thinking that you exist: the truth of what you think is implied by your thinking it. If you think you exist, you do exist, because if you think anything, you exist. If you think that you think, you do think, because if you think anything, you think. If you think that you are a being with an understanding, then you are a being with an understanding, because if you think anything, you are a being with an understanding. Gassendi commented that Descartes might as well have employed any of his actions to prove his existence, since he could not walk without existing or see without existing: 'it being manifest by the natural light that everything that acts is or exists'. 'If I think, I am' leads on to 'If I think I am, I am' and to the impossibility of mistake. It is true that if I walk, I exist but, since there is no such thing as walking that I exist, it leads nowhere. Bertrand Russell was misled into supposing that Descartes' argument relied upon the immediacy of thought whereas it establishes both the logical immediacy of thought and the logical immediacy of existence. Russell allowed that, when he himself was thinking, he knew that a thought existed but questioned the inference to the existence of a thinker of that thought. The *cogito* argument would work for thoughts, since if there were no thoughts, no one could think there were, but Descartes had no need to argue from thoughts to a thinker. He could deal with 'I think' and 'I exist' directly.

In Descartes' proof logic, not psychology, is fundamental. That is entirely in accordance with his philosophy, since his rationalism puts what can be discovered by reason at the foundation of everything, but for others it cannot but serve as a warning that something, somewhere, is wrong with the argument. It can hardly be that there is an item of knowledge which humans owe solely to a logical truth. Where does the mistake lie?

The argument builds two conclusions, one upon the other. The first is that I cannot be mistaken in believing that I exist; the second, that if I believe I exist, I know that I do. The first conclusion, as I have already shown, is sound. The second is unsound. I pointed out the mistake and how it arises when I pointed out the ambiguity of 'Mistake here is impossible'. The way that ambiguity applies to the second step of the *cogito* can be easily seen by considering a parallel argument with the same two steps.

First, two and three cannot but make five, therefore no one can be mistaken in believing that two and three make five. Second, no one can be mistaken in believing that two and three make five, therefore everyone who believes that two and three make five knows that two and three make five. In this argument, as in Descartes' *cogito* argument, the first step is sound. No one can be mistaken in believing that two and three make five. The reason for the impossibility of mistake is not the same as in Descartes' argument: here it is the impossibility of two and three not making five, there it was the fact that, unless you exist, you cannot believe that you exist, but the impossibility is present just the same. Since every mathematical fact is as necessary as 'two and three make five', the same manner of argument would show that anyone who believes any arithmetical fact knows that fact to be true, yet, as Descartes himself affirms, people are notoriously liable to be mistaken about difficult questions in arithmetic. Evidently, the fact that you cannot be mistaken in believing something does not at all show that when you believe it you know it to be true. You might, for example, have arrived at your belief by making two mistakes, one cancelling out the other, or you may have taken the word of some quite unreliable or deceitful source who wished to misinform you but has miscalculated and unwittingly given you the right answer. The fact that you cannot be mistaken in believing something seems to show that you know it because it seems to show that it is impossible that you should have been mistaken about the question to which it is an answer. In fact, you could very easily have been mistaken about whether two and three make five. How? By believing them to make six.

Compare the consequences of the fact that two and three cannot but make five with those of the fact that it is a ridiculously simple arithmetical proposition that two and three make five. The first has the consequence that you cannot be mistaken in believing it, the second that you cannot be mistaken about it. The simplicity of a proposition of arithmetic has the effect that, if it is true, you believe it true, if false, you believe it false. That is why you are right to claim knowledge of the simple arithmetical truths. Of course, your knowledge does not come up to Descartes' requirements, it depends upon your make-up and an evil god could deceive you, but your immunity from error, both less and more than Descartes required, is very close to knowledge. Certainly, it is closer than the Cartesian immunity of anyone, even a complete idiot, who believes that two and three make five. The strange thing is that Descartes saw this about the simple truths of arithmetic. He saw that forming a correct opinion about them, and being able to learn to form a correct opinion about them, depended upon how he was made. For that reason he did not count them as truths known for certain. How did he miss the fact that the opinion he formed about whether he existed also depended upon how he was made and should, likewise, have not been counted as known for certain? It may have been because, although Descartes approached the question 'What do I know for certain?' by enquiring into his own powers, not by enquiring into the matters he held opinions about, passing events, mathematics, mechanics and meteorology, he did not succeed in keeping to his method. He fell into something between the two enquiries and mistook a dead end for a way out. Had he held his line, he might have found no way out and come to suspect that the trouble lay, not with his own powers, but with the over-rigorous demands he was making upon them. Such a suspicion does indeed begin to dawn upon him at the beginning of the third Meditation. There he suggests that his doubts have been rather unreal, his actual words are 'bien légère, et pour ainsi dire, métaphysique', 'very light, and so to speak metaphysical', since he hasn't any reason to believe that a deceiving god does exist. However, it is not doubts about the validity of his *cogito* argument that inspire his retraction, it is the hopelessness of building upon the certainties that he exists and thinks to restore the sensory knowledge he cannot get on without. As we shall soon see, he does build a good deal upon them, a good deal more than they can stand.

You might be tempted to think, faced with the refutation of the *cogito* argument as I have interpreted it, that my interpretation is wrong. Perhaps what Descartes does, you might say, is to derive from the simple truth that, if I think I am, I am, a policy for forming a true opinion about my existence. 'I don't know whether or not I exist', he says to himself, 'but I do know that if I believe that I exist, I exist, so I will adopt the opinion that I exist. I will adopt it, not because there is any reason to think it true, but because, if I adopt it, it will be true.' Now, I don't myself think that anyone who adopts a belief solely out of policy, even with the best motives, knows that belief to be true; but, however that may be, if Descartes argued in this way, he would have had no excuse for thinking that he had escaped the deceiver's powers. He would not because, although he would not be deriving his existence from a premise about which he might be deceived, he would be justifying his policy by such a premise. It is a simple truth that if he thinks he exists, he exists, but he might have been so made that he didn't see its truth, thinking benightedly instead that if he thought he existed, he would not exist, and so adopting a policy of believing he didn't exist. That would be, obviously enough, a policy that would lead him into error.

The fairy-tale malicious god makes Descartes' doubts seem frivolous. In fact, they are a natural extension of quite ordinary doubts about our senses and our minds. We can be deceived by concealed mirrors, our thinking can be set astray by nervousness or by drugs. The insistence that, unless we know that such factors are not operating, we cannot be certain of the things we seem to see and the things we seem to prove is a compelling one. It demands an answer. Descartes' claim that there is knowledge owed solely to a simple logical fact would, if it were correct, provide such an answer. It meets the problem squarely and, however implausible it now seems, it had to be explored, if only to be put aside. It was not the only answer he gave in the *Meditations*. The knowledge that he existed and thought proved too limited, exploit it as he might.

One of the ways in which he does so is to argue, at the beginning of the third Meditation, that there is nothing peculiar in his having the knowledge the *cogito* has shown him to have, except his clear and distinct perception of the fact he knows. Such a perception could not yield knowledge if it could ever lead him astray, therefore everything that he perceives very clearly and distinctly is true. Here, he argues back from the fact that he knows that he exists, to a conclusion about his manner of reaching that opinion. It must have been reliable, or it would not have led him to an opinion he knows for certain to be true. This argument is outrageous. It quite ignores the fact that he proves his certainty of his own existence by proving the impossibility of his being mistaken in believing it, an impossibility which has nothing to do with his manner of arriving at the belief, would be present however he arrived at it and arises solely from the fact that he cannot, without existing, believe that he does exist. The truth is that, far from validating clear and distinct perception as a route to knowledge, the *cogito* argument, in Descartes' hands, discredits it, for the argument separates the things he perceives clearly and distinctly into two sorts: those, such as 'I exist', that are beyond doubt and those, such as 'two and three make five', that are not.

Nevertheless, Descartes does, henceforward in the *Meditations*, accept that he knows those facts of which he has a clear and distinct perception. When speaking of perception, he is certainly using the term to cover an intellectual faculty and almost certainly using it for an intellectual faculty alone, since, in the argument I have just been complaining of, he speaks sometimes of perception and sometimes of conception without, apparently, intending anything different. Of course, it is common to speak of perception when the senses are not involved as when we say such things as 'I saw at once that the argument was valid' or 'I saw that it was no use reasoning with him any longer'. Descartes' conclusion, in the argument I have been complaining of, that nothing that he clearly and distinctly conceives can be false shows, too, that the intellectual perception he has in mind is a clear grasp, or understanding, of a fact. He has reached the conclusion that a clear understanding of a question is enough to reveal the answer to it. That conclusion enables him, in his later meditations, to accept that he does know the simple truths of mathematics and logic.

Even that retraction leaves him in doubt concerning the evidence of his senses. He needs some way of setting a limit to the frailty of his sensory faculties. There would be such a limit, he considers, if there was no possibility that they were not the gift of a well-intentioned all-powerful being. That would mean, of course, that what he supposed possible in the first Meditation, that there could exist an ill-intentioned all-powerful being, was not possible. An ill-intentioned creator cannot be a possibility, if a well-intentioned one is a necessity. His argument in the fifth Meditation is intended to show, not merely that there is a god, a benign, omnipotent being, but that it is a logical necessity that there is. That can be seen, he thinks, by understanding clearly the implications of being perfect. A non-existent being is less than perfect. Since man is the creature of a perfect being, he cannot but have faculties that, rightly used, lead him to truth rather than falsehood. I shall barely enter into a discussion of that argument; I have outlined it only to point out that here, as with the *cogito*, Descartes sets out to establish that our holding a false opinion, provided in this case we take certain precautions, is a logical impossibility. It is not such a simple and obvious impossibility as not existing but thinking that we do exist, but it was nevertheless, so Descartes thought, an impossibility: not existing but being perfect. This argument has been much criticized, notably by Immanuel Kant in *The Critique of Pure Reason*. His simplest, but very effective, criticism was that Descartes' impossibility is no more than the necessity that if any being is perfect, it exists, from which it does not follow that there exists a perfect being. However that may be, this argument of Descartes' founds all our knowledge upon a simple logical truth. In his metaphysics, his view of the fundamental nature of the world, God stands high but the simple logical truths stand higher. Remember what he says at the beginning of the second Meditation, that no powerful and cunning deceiver can bring it about that he is nothing while he believes that he is something. If the logical truth that if he thinks he exists, he exists cannot be subverted by an all-powerful being, neither could it have been created by one and neither could the truth that to be perfect, a being must exist, the truth, if Descartes is right, that implies that there must be a god. It is the logical necessity of there being a benign god that upholds our knowledge. The god that there must be is not responsible for that logical necessity. No doubt that explains why Descartes' hope that his philosophy would be adopted by the Catholic church came to nothing. The church, understandably enough, was not prepared to see God playing second fiddle to squares have four sides.

I have sought to show that, in one way or another, Descartes bases our possession of any knowledge at all upon a logical fact: in one argument upon the fact that to think he exists implies existing, in another, upon the fact that to be perfect implies existing. I have argued in some detail that the former can provide no such basis but have only indicated an argument that the latter can do no better. Once Descartes had accepted that his doubts were justified, only faulty reasoning enabled him to avoid the conclusion that he knew no single thing. Had he argued correctly and reached that conclusion, then, to say the very least, he should have returned to re-examine the justification for his doubts. Now his justifications were of different kinds, but, since his conclusions were reached by accepting his most extreme doubt, it is the justification for that extreme doubt that must be re-examined. As I pointed out, his stated justification is the probability that he was made by a god who may be a deceiver or in some worse way. That contention never carried much conviction, as he himself comes to admit, and, once seen to have the fearful consequences it does have, will carry even less. I suggested that it was not his real justification, which was the one implied by the test to which he subjects his opinions: would it be possible for me to be mistaken about this matter? His justification for his most extreme doubt is that the matter is one for which the possibility of his forming a wrong opinion exists. What should we think of that?

I don't know that I can prove it, but my own opinion is that we should think it worthless. Far from being a reason for thinking that we do not know something, the possibility of forming a wrong opinion is a reason for thinking that perhaps we do know it, since one requirement for knowledge, that here is a matter on which our choice can be right and can be wrong, is fulfilled. Consider an example where it is not fulfilled, a novelist's writings, in his novel, concerning the doings of his characters. If he writes that the hero won through, then the hero did win through; if he writes that he did not, then he did not. The author cannot possibly be mistaken. Here are statements for which Descartes' rigorous condition is fulfilled, yet here there is no question of knowledge. The statements in a novel do not express knowledge of anything. They have quite another function. Of course, one such example proves nothing. All I can do is to suggest that, for knowledge, the possibility of a wrong choice must have existed but the one who knows will have been clever enough to avoid it.

Descartes, *Sixth Meditation*: The External World, 'Nature' and Human Experience

JOHN COTTINGHAM

The Sixth Meditation deals, as its title proclaims, with 'the existence of material things, and the real distinction between the mind and body of man'.[1] In this paper, I want to start by examining Descartes' argument for the existence of material things—for the existence of an 'external', physical world around us. Next, in section two, I shall use this argument concerning the external world to bring out an important general point about the 'dialectical' way in which Descartes presents his reasoning in the *Meditations*. This will lead me on to the third section of the paper, which will analyse the concept of 'nature' and the role it plays in Descartes' reasoning, particularly in the Sixth Meditation. And this in turn will bring me to the fourth and final part of the paper, which will focus on what is by general consensus the most fascinating part of the Sixth Meditation—Descartes' account of the relation between mind and body. What I shall try to do in this final section is to highlight a curious tension between Descartes' recognition of the facts of human experience on the one hand, and on the other hand his doctrine that we are essentially incorporeal or non-physical substances.

[1] E 127 (AT VII 71; CSM II 50). References to 'E' are to page numbers of the Everyman edition of Descartes which is the prescribed A-level text: *Descartes, A Discourse on Method, Meditations and Principles*, trans. J. Veitch (London: Dent, 1912). All quotations are taken from this edition. For the reader's convenience, I have added, in brackets, cross-references to the standard twelve-volume edition of Descartes known as 'AT'—*Oeuvres de Descartes*, C. Adam and P. Tannery (eds), rev. edn (Paris: Vrin, 1964–76), and to the new two volume English translation 'CSM'—*The Philosophical Writings of Descartes*, trans. J. Cottingham, R. Stoothoff and D. Murdoch, (Cambridge University Press, 1985). Veitch's translations, though first issued by Everyman in 1912, originally appeared in 1850–53; they are tolerably accurate, if sometimes rather stilted. Readers should, however, be warned that Veitch sometimes follows Descartes' original Latin text of the *Meditations* (1641) and sometimes (often without indication) follows the later French version of 1647 which was not by Descartes. Thus in the title of the Sixth Meditation quoted above, the phrase 'of man' is not in the original Latin.

1. The proof of the external world

The flow of argument in the *Meditations* is from self to God to the external world. Having established first that he exists as a thinking thing, then that God exists, Descartes finally, in the Sixth Meditation, arrives at the conclusion that the external world exists. There are indeed, he decides, 'corporeal' (i.e. physical) things: these include his own body and numerous other physical objects all around him.

This is not perhaps a very surprising or spectacular result to reach after six days of intense meditation. As Descartes himself admits in the Synopsis to the *Meditations*, facts such as the fact 'that there is in reality a world, that men are possessed of bodies, and the like' are ones which 'no one of sound mind ever seriously doubted'.[2] But for Descartes, even these seemingly obvious and elementary truths are less certain, and more complicated to establish, than the knowledge of our minds and of God. 'So that the latter [truths] are of all which come under human knowledge, the most certain and manifest—a conclusion which it was my single aim in these Meditations to establish'.[3]

The proof of the existence of an external world in the Sixth Meditation is in fact quite difficult to isolate on a first reading. There are several seemingly false starts—apparently promising lines of reasoning which are eagerly taken up only to be discarded. To begin with, Descartes notes that he has the power to imagine, or picture, corporeal objects; such a power could easily be accounted for, suggests Descartes, if his mind is united to a body, and can somehow make use of that body in order to form images of things.

This is somewhat mystifying as it stands, and Descartes says little to explain just what he has in mind. But some years later, when he was questioned about this passage by the young Dutchman Frans Burman, he supplied a fuller explanation. Imagination, he tells us, differs from pure 'intellection' or understanding in so far as it involves actually 'picturing' an object in the mind's eye. For example, I can understand that a thousand-sided figure has a thousand angles without being able to picture the figure (except perhaps in a very confused way). But if we take the proposition that a triangle has three angles, I not only understand this to be true, I can also vividly picture the triangle: I 'see' the three lines 'there in front of me' as if they were actually, physically present. Now this vivid process of 'imaging' or 'depicting' objects could easily be accounted for, Descartes suggests, if there is a physical organ, the brain, where the three lines are actually, physically traced out, so

[2] E78 (AT VII 16; CSM II 50).
[3] Ibid.

that the mind can directly 'contemplate' or 'inspect' the resulting picture.[4]

The argument, in sum, is that imagination requires a brain for the forming of physical images; therefore at least one physical object—the brain—exists. The modern reader is unlikely to be very impressed by the details of this argument. Indeed, to anyone even remotely familiar with the neurophysiology of the brain, the bizarre notion of images being actually, physically traced out there will sound quite absurd. Fortunately, however, we do not have to spend further time on this curious argument since from the standpoint of the *Meditations* Descartes is of course committed to supplying absolutely firm and unshakeable reasoning to support his conclusions. And he has to admit here in Meditation Six that his conjecture about the physiological basis for imagining does not have the status of a watertight argument. His reflection on the power of imagining entitles him, he says, to make a 'probable conjecture' that material objects exist, but, he does *not* find here an argument from which he can 'necessarily infer the existence of any body'.[5]

Next, Descartes considers the faculty of 'sense-perception'—though it is worth noting right away that there is a slight awkwardness in the Everyman translation here. The term 'sense-perception' as used in modern English already implies the existence of the body: sense-perception is what one does with the five senses—sight, hearing, taste, smell and touch—and these senses of course involve the use of bodily organs. Furthermore, 'perception', as ordinarily used, is an 'achievement' concept: that is, to say that someone perceives X implies that there really exists an X which is perceived. But as Descartes uses the term 'sense-perception' (in the original Latin *sentire*, literally 'to sense') it does not imply the existence either of external objects of perception or of any bodily organs of perception. By *sentire* Descartes means merely the having of sensory 'ideas' (what Hume was later to call 'impressions'); that is, Descartes is talking merely of the subjective consciousness of certain kinds of visual, auditory, gustatory, olfactory and tactile data. 'Sense-perception' construed in this narrow sense is simply a characteristic kind of conscious awareness; and its use at this stage does not commit Descartes to any implications either about external objects or about the possession of a body, or bodily sense organs.

Descartes proceeds to note that in virtue of this faculty of sense-perception (or sensory awareness), certain sensory ideas are presented to him. I am aware of certain sensory ideas being presented to my

[4] AT V 154 and 162/3. Cf. J. Cottingham (ed.), *Descartes' Conversation with Burman*, 14, 23 and 74ff.
[5] E129(ATVII73;CSMII51).

consciousness (I do not yet know their cause)—ideas of 'hardness, heat and the other tactile qualities, and in addition, light, colours, odours, tastes and sounds'.[6] Let us call this 'proposition one':

(1) I have sensory ideas.

The next point Descartes makes is that these ideas are apparently caused by something outside me. The main reason for supposing this is so is that the ideas in question do not depend on my will: they are 'presented to me without my consent being required'.[7] What Descartes means by this, is, I think, quite straightforward. For example, as I sit composing this paper, the visual impressions of my typewriter, books, papers and so on, come to me whether I like it or not. I cannot conjure them into existence or make them go away at will.[8] So now we have proposition number two:

(2) Sensory ideas are caused by something other than myself.

But if sensory ideas are caused by something external to me (or my mind), then the most obvious supposition to make, says Descartes, is that they are caused by real external objects which resemble the ideas: 'As of those objects I had no knowledge beyond what the ideas themselves gave me, nothing was so likely to occur to my mind as the supposition that the objects were similar to the ideas which they caused'.[9] So we arrive at our conclusion, proposition number three:

(3) Sensory ideas are caused by objects resembling my sensory ideas.

So far so good. Or rather so far not so good. For in case anyone should suppose that the reasoning just sketched settles the question of the existence of external objects, Descartes now proceeds to make it clear that such reasoning will not do. Indeed, it emerges that what he has so far given us is merely a kind of résumé of the train of thought of an ordinary person who has not subjected his beliefs to philosophical

[6] E 129 (AT VII 75; CSM II 52). Descartes first of all talks of the perception of *qualities*; later (E 130, line 2) he says that it is the *ideas* of these qualities 'which alone I properly and immediately perceive'. For a useful discussion of the origins of this use of 'idea' see P. Alexander, *Ideas, Qualities and Corpuscles* (Cambridge University Press, 1985), 97ff.

[7] E 130 (AT VII 75; CSM II 52).

[8] Cf. Berkeley, *The Principles of Human Knowledge* (1710) Section 29: 'When in broad daylight I open my eyes, it is not in my power to choose whether I shall see or not, or to determine what particular objects present themselves to my view . . . The ideas imprinted on [the senses] are not creatures of *my* will.'

[9] Loc. cit., note 6.

scrutiny. The easy three-step argument just sketched represents merely the thinking of the typical 'pre-philosophical man'—the person who has not done any Cartesian meditations.[10] Such a man has sensory impressions or 'ideas' of trees and mountains, tables and chairs, and he takes it as just obvious that these sensory impressions are produced by objects which more or less resemble the ideas—which are more or less the way he perceives them to be.

In order to undermine this naive pre-philosophical view, Descartes reminds us of the systematic doubts introduced in the First Meditation. Can we really trust the senses? Are they not subject to illusions? 'The senses sometimes mislead' warned the First Meditation.[11] Now, in the Sixth Meditation, Descartes reinforces the point with an example: 'I frequently observed that towers which at a distance seemed round appeared square when more closely viewed'.[12] And it is not just the external senses which can be convicted of deception. Even the 'internal' senses—those which seem to tell me about my own bodily condition—can provide misleading information. Descartes' example—one that particularly interests him as a student of physiology—is the curious phenomenon of the 'phantom limb': 'I have sometimes been informed by parties whose arm or leg had been amputated that they still occasionally seemed to feel pain in that part of the body which they had lost—a circumstance that led me to think that I could not quite be certain even that any one of my members was affected when I felt pain in it.'[13]

After this recapitulation of, and expansion of, his earlier doubts about the senses, Descartes—still speaking with the voice of the philosophical meditator who will take nothing for granted—specifically addresses the naive argument for the existence of external objects which he has just sketched out a moment ago. To the pre-philosophical man it may seem just obvious and 'natural' to suppose that sensory ideas are caused by external objects; but 'as nature seemed to incline me to many things from which reason made me averse, I thought that I ought not to confide much in its teachings'.[14] And here Descartes reminds us of the extreme or 'hyperbolical' doubt he had raised in the First Meditation: 'I saw nothing to prevent my having been so constituted by nature as that I should be deceived even in matters that appeared to me to possess the greatest truth.'[15]

[10] For the 'pre-philosophical' man, cf. *Descartes' Conversation with Burman*, AT V 146; Cottingham (op. cit. note 4), 3.

[11] E 80 (AT VII 18; CSM II 12).

[12] E 131 (AT VII 76; CSM II 53).

[13] Ibid.

[14] E 132 (AT VII 77; CSM II 53).

[15] Ibid. Cf. Meditation One: E 82 (AT VII 21; CSM II 14).

At this point, however, the argument enters yet another phase, and Descartes now proceeds to allay the doubts he has just raised. We are, he reminds us, no longer in the morass of doubt characteristic of the earlier Meditations. God's existence has been established (at least, Descartes takes it to have been established) by the arguments of the Third and Fifth Meditations. And God, being defined as the supremely perfect being, is necessarily benevolent and incapable of malicious deception. 'It is impossible for him ever to deceive me', Descartes had observed in the Fourth Meditation, 'for in all fraud and deceit there is a certain imperfection . . . The will [to deceive] testifies without doubt of malice and weakness and such, accordingly, cannot be found in God.'[16]

With this in mind, Descartes returns to his sensory ideas. 'I cannot doubt', he resumes, 'that there is in me a certain passive faculty of perception, that is of receiving . . . the ideas of sensible things.'[17] Clearly *something* must produce these ideas. And while it is theoretically possible that the ideas could be produced directly by God himself or by some intermediate cause other than a physical object, nevertheless God has given us 'a very strong inclination to believe that those ideas arise from corporeal objects'. And so, finally, Descartes is able to arrive at his long-sought conclusion: 'I do not see how God could be vindicated from the charge of deceit if in truth [these ideas] proceeded from any other source, or were produced by any other causes, than corporeal things; *and accordingly it must be concluded that corporeal objects exist*'.[18]

2. Descartes as Dialectician

It is, then, not until the point we have just reached, halfway through the final Meditation, that Descartes actually reaches the firm result that physical (or 'corporeal') objects exist. I hope I have brought out how many twists and turns the argument has taken along the way, and how Descartes' reasoning is divided into successive phases. The starting point (phase one) is the thought that it is natural or 'obvious' to suppose that external objects exist in a way that matches our sensory ideas of them. Next (phase two) cold water is thrown on this: the senses are often unreliable; and in any case the fact that I am naturally strongly inclined to believe something is no guarantee of its truth. But then, finally, (phase three) these doubts are swept away as we are reminded of

[16] E 111/2 (AT VII 53; CSM II 37).
[17] E 133 (AT VII 79; CSM II 55).
[18] E 134 (AT VII 80; CSM II 55). Italics supplied.

the existence of a benevolent God who would not allow us to be subject to systematic deception. And in the light of this I can conclude that my inclination to believe in corporeal objects must have some foundation in reality.

But even now Descartes' twisting argument has not exhausted itself. Although I can conclude that physical objects exist, there is a qualification: 'they are not perhaps exactly such as we perceive them by the senses, for their comprehension by the senses is in many instances very obscure and confused'.[19] And the rest of the Meditation is taken up with examining exactly how far I am justified in concluding that the world conforms to my sensory perception of it (and whether, if it does not, this fact can be reconciled with the benevolence of God).

This twisting and turning of argument and counter-argument—the setting up of one position which is immediately knocked down, the reaching of a conclusion which immediately needs modifying—is extremely characteristic of Descartes' style throughout the *Meditations*. Indeed, it is a feature of a great deal of philosophy, from Socrates onwards, that it proceeds in 'dialectical' fashion. A proposition or a definition is put forward only to be attacked; as a result of the attack, it is revised, and then the revision is in turn criticized and subsequently modified. In Plato's writings, this cut and thrust of refutation and counter-refutation is especially vivid, because the train of the argument is presented in dialogue form: we actually see character *A* setting up a position and character *B* knocking it down. This is of course not the case in Descartes (though Descartes did embark on—but unfortunately never finished—a presentation of the arguments of the *Meditations* in dialogue form, which he called *La Recherche de La Vérité*, or *The Search for Truth*).[20] But although the *Meditations* themselves are not explicitly cast in dialogue form, the presentation of successive arguments and counter-arguments is highly 'dialectical', and to interpret a given passage correctly we need constantly to ask ourselves who is speaking, as it were. In the case of any given passage we need to ask: are we dealing with the views of the ordinary 'pre-philosophical' man; or are we dealing with the exaggerated sceptic of the early *Meditations* who is prepared to take nothing whatever for granted; or are we at the stage where the existence of a benevolent creator has been established? Context is all important; and it follows that it is often disastrous to lift a given proposition or conclusion out of the *Meditations* and quote it as if it represented Descartes' final and considered philosophical view. We

[19] Ibid.

[20] This unfinished dialogue was found among Descartes papers on his death in Stockholm in 1650. Its date is uncertain, but it may well have been compiled at roughly the same time as the *Meditations*. See CSM II 399.

must always ask which Meditation we are dealing with, and be aware of which stage the dialectic has reached. What is more, as we have just seen in the case of Meditation Six, even within a single Meditation the dialectical process continues to develop constantly, with new twists and turns from paragraph to paragraph. Descartes refers back to previous trains of thought; arguments are recapitulated and elaborated, conclusions reinforced or modified. Nowhere in the *Meditations* do we find a static exposition of finished results. The work, as its name implies, is not a set of finished doctrines, but a series of mental exercises which have to be *worked through*. And it is all-important to keep track of the precise stage of the workout which we have reached.

3. 'Nature' and Knowledge

Having established, to his satisfaction, the existence of an external world of physical objects independent of himself, Descartes proceeds, in the remainder of the Sixth Meditation, to develop an account of how we gain information about this external world (including information about what is happening to our own bodies).

In this third section of the paper, I want to focus attention on a concept which plays an important role in Descartes' account of how we gain knowledge of the external world: the concept of 'nature' and what it is 'natural' to believe. As we have seen, the argument for the existence of external objects started from the thought that when I consider what causes my sensory ideas, the natural and obvious supposition for me to make is that they are caused by physical objects. As Descartes expresses it, I have a 'very strong inclination to believe that sensory ideas arise from corporeal objects'.[21]

Human beings it would appear, are *naturally inclined* towards certain beliefs and suppositions. But now an important question arises: if, as Descartes firmly believes, God created me and gave me the nature which I have, does it not follow that *whatever* I am naturally inclined to believe is true?

At first Descartes seems to answer unambiguously in the affirmative:

> On the ground that God is no deceiver . . . I may with safety conclude that I possess in myself the means to arrive at the truth. And . . . it cannot be doubted that in each of the dictates of nature there is some truth . . .[22]

The three ensuing paragraphs all begin with the Latin phrase *Natura docet* (or its close equivalent): *'nature teaches'*. First, nature expressly

[21] E 134 (AT VII 79; CSM II 55).
[22] Ibid.

teaches me that I have a body. Second, nature teaches me that I am not just lodged in my body (like a pilot in a vessel) but 'intimately conjoined and intermingled with it'. And third, nature teaches me that my body is surrounded by many other bodies—some beneficial to me, others harmful.[23]

What exactly does this talk of nature's *teaching* mean? Rather too helpfully for comfort, Descartes initially provides no less than three explanations of the term 'nature'. By nature considered in general, he says, I understand nothing other than (i) God himself, or (ii) the order and disposition established by God in created things. And he goes on to say that by *my* nature in particular I understand (iii) the assemblage of all that God has given me.[24] The first two glosses, which deal with 'nature in general' can be made sense of fairly easily. When Descartes equates nature with God himself, he is following the traditional theological account of God as 'pure being'—the supreme reality, everything that is. Since God comprises the whole of nature, everything in the natural world is (a part of) God: every natural thing partakes of and reflects the divine being.[25] The second gloss—nature is the 'order and disposition established by God in created things'—is also standard orthodoxy: the natural world is a set of divinely ordained structures and patterns of events initiated and sustained by God's creative *fiat*. But it is the third gloss, dealing with 'my nature in particular' that is of special interest for the present discussion. Nature, my nature as a human being, is, says Descartes, the totality of what the creator has given me. Since God is the sole source of being, everything positive which I have, I have from God.

But this result seems too strong for Descartes' purpose. If everything I have, I have from God, then all my natural inclinations would seem to have their source in the creator; and it appears to follow from this that anything I am naturally inclined to believe can be thought of as involving a God-given impulse, and will therefore be true. I say this result is 'too strong' for the obvious reason that in past ages, and no doubt today as well, very many human beings have been strongly inclined to believe things that are false. What is more, Descartes' own method of philosophizing seems to acknowledge this; for his starting point in philosophy is the idea that all of us since early childhood have been in the grip of 'prejudices', or preconceived opinions which are often confused, and may very well be quite false. As Descartes puts it in the

[23] E 134/5 (AT VII 81/2; CSM II 56).

[24] E 134 (AT VII 80; CSM II 56).

[25] 'God cannot incline to nothingness, since he is supreme and pure being', *Conversation with Burman*, AT V 147; cf. Cottingham (op. cit., note 4), 5 and 56ff.

opening article of his *Principles of Philosophy*, these preconceived opinions 'stand in the way of our arriving at knowledge of the truth'.[26]

Some examples of these preconceived opinions are listed towards the end of Book One of the *Principles*. One case mentioned concerns the shape and movement of the earth. Most children until they are taught otherwise, are inclined to suppose that the earth is immobile and its surface flat.[27] (I suspect that this is just as true of children today as it was in the seventeenth century. The majority of parents, I think, would testify that the average five or six year old tends to be highly sceptical when told that the earth spins on its axis.) But the problem for Descartes now seems more serious than ever: do we not have a clear example here of a 'natural' belief that is none the less false?

Descartes has an answer to this—or an answer of sorts. 'Such beliefs', he says in the Sixth Meditation, 'though *seemingly* the teachings of nature are not in reality so, but obtained a place in my mind through a habit of judging inconsiderately of things'.[28] But how on earth are we supposed to distinguish the 'genuine' teachings of nature from such 'seeming' teachings, or pseudo-teachings? A clue finally emerges when Descartes proceeds to discuss another favourite example, that of the size of the stars. Most children (and uneducated people) tend to suppose that the stars are very small (compare the nursery rhyme 'Twinkle twinkle, *little* star'). But the belief that the stars are small is not, says Descartes, the result of the genuine teaching of nature:

> Although the impression a star makes on my eye is not larger than that from the flame of a candle, I do not, nevertheless, experience any real or positive impulse determining me to believe that the star is not greater than the flame; the true account of the matter being merely that I have so judged from my youth without any rational ground.[29]

The key phrase here is 'rational ground'. It turns out that, for Descartes, my *nature* is a reliable guide to the truth only is so far as I am endowed with a faculty of *reason*. Human beings may believe all sorts of things, but it is the human power of reasoning, the God-given *lux rationis* ('light of reason') as Descartes terms it elsewhere, that enables them to sort out the true from the false. So Descartes' talk of 'nature', and of our strong inclinations to believe in certain things, turns out, in the end, to be rather misleading. A strong impulse to believe something

[26] *Principles of Philosophy* (1644) Book I, art. 1: E 165 (AT VIII 5; CSM I 193).

[27] *Principles* Book I, art. 71: E 195 (AT VIII 36; CSM I 219).

[28] E 135 (AT VII 82; CSM II 56). Italics supplied.

[29] E 136 (AT VII 83; CSM II 57).

is, it emerges, no guarantee of its truth. For the impulse counts as 'natural' in Descartes' special sense only if the inclination to believe is a result of clear and distinct intellectual perception and rational deliberation. It is no accident that Descartes uses the phrases *lux rationis* ('light of reason') and *lumen naturae* ('light of nature') more or less interchangeably. Both refer simply to the innate faculty of reason.[30]

But what then, is the connection, if any, between the use of reason, and the impulse to believe something? In the Fourth Meditation Descartes makes the point that transparent rational understanding generates assent: we cannot but judge that what we clearly and distinctly perceive is true, since 'great clearness of the understanding' naturally gives rise to 'strong inclination of the will'.[31] This little piece of introspective psychology is surely sound enough. Once I have clearly understood a proposition like 'Two plus two equals four', once I have clearly perceived what is being asserted, then I have a strong (indeed irresistible) impulse to assent to the truth of the proposition in question. When the light of reason has been shed on some simple and self-evident proposition, there follows a strong inclination to assent to its truth. But it is very important to note that the converse does not hold. The fact that I am strongly inclined to believe something does not show that its truth has been established by the light of reason: a strong inclination to believe is a necessary, but *not* a sufficient condition of clear and distinct intellectual perception. For my inclination to assent to a proposition may be the result not of rational scrutiny but of habitual and unthinking acceptance of something that 'seemed plausible' when I was young. My acceptance may ultimately be due to nothing more than unthinking prejudice.

The upshot is that Descartes' talk about the 'teachings of nature', and his admission that some of the things we are inclined to believe are only the 'seeming' teachings of nature, is not very happily expressed. What he might better have said (and what he comes near to saying elsewhere) is: be on your guard against an apparently spontaneous inclination to believe something. Such an inclination is to be trusted only when it directly results from a previous clear and distinct perception of the

[30] *Lumen naturale* or *lumen naturae* ('natural light', 'light of nature') are the phrases most commonly found in the *Meditations* and *Principles*. For the phrase *lux rationis* ('light of reason'), cf. *Rules for the Direction of the Understanding* (1628): AT X 368; CSM I 14. Commenting on the 'light' metaphor Descartes observed to Hobbes: 'As everyong knows, a "light" in the intellect means transparent clarity of cognition' *(Third Set of Objections and Replies)* AT VII 192; CSM II 135). (The *Objections and Replies* were published with the *Meditations* in 1641.) For the innateness of the natural light see *The Search for Truth*, AT X 495; CSM II 400.

[31] E 116 (AT VII 58; CSM II 41).

intellect. If the matter is put this way, then we have the classic Cartesian formula for the avoidance of error: 'restrain your will, and give assent only to what your intellect has clearly and distinctly perceived'.[32]

4. Sensory information and the body

Strict adherence to the Cartesian formula just quoted ('assent only to what is clearly and distinctly perceived by the light of reason') would result in a very austere picture of the world. According to Descartes, the light of reason enables me to perceive clearly and distinctly two principal kinds of things: firstly, I can achieve knowledge of the nature of intellectual essences, or minds (e.g. myself *qua* thinking thing, and also God and other intellectual natures); and, secondly, I can achieve knowledge of the nature of corporeal objects—but only in so far as these can be characterized in terms of pure mathematics.

> I possess the means of acquiring a perfect knowledge as well relative to God himself and other intellectual objects as to corporeal nature, in so far as it is the object of pure mathematics.[33]

But of course the world as we actually experience it is strikingly different from this. We do not apprehend the world as consisting on the one hand of pure intellectual essences, and on the other hand of mathematical objects such as spheres and triangles. Indeed, both these kinds of items seem more like abstractions than real inhabitants of the world (I have certainly never encountered either a pure incorporeal mind or an object of pure mathematics, and I am not sure I would count either of these items as real things, in the ordinary robust sense of 'real').

Consider how we actually experience first, the external world and second, the inner world of our own consciousness. The world 'out there' is not perceived by us in pure geometrical terms; rather, what we characteristically perceive are collections of objects possessing various sensible qualities. In other words, the world around us, as we ordinarily experience it, consists not of abstract geometrical essences, but rather of things having colours and textures and smells and tastes and sounds. What we are aware of is (to quote Wordsworth's famous list) 'the light of setting suns, and the round ocean, and the living air, and the blue sky'[34] . . . and much else besides. Secondly, as for our own inner life, our awareness of ourselves as conscious beings, what we are aware of is,

[32] Cf. Fourth Meditation: E 119 (AT VII 62; CSM II 43).
[33] Fifth Meditation: E 126 (AT VII 71; CSM II 49).
[34] W. Wordsworth *Lines written above Tintern Abbey* (1798).

pretty clearly, not just a series of modes of thought or modifications of a pure 'intellectual substance'. When Claudio in *Measure for Measure* talks about the horror of death:

> Ay, but to die, and go we know not where
> To lie in cold obstruction and to rot
> This sensible, warm motion to become
> A kneaded clod[35]

what he fears is not primarily the cessation of *thought* (indeed the rest of the speech makes it clear that he believes this will continue in some spiritual form); what he fears is the cessation of 'this sensible warm motion'—the rich and vivid sensuous experience that constitutes the conscious life of an embodied, warm-blooded human being.

Thus there is a striking gap between the Cartesian clear and distinct perception of the outer world (in terms of pure geometrical essences) and our ordinary experience of it. And there is, secondly, a striking gap between the Cartesian clear and distinct perception of ourselves (as necessarily incorporeal, non-material, intellectual substances) and our sensory awareness of ourselves as physically embodied beings.

With respect to the first gap, Descartes is fully prepared to defend his position that the real external world should be characterized purely in terms of the sizes, shapes and motions of particles; the grasp of the senses is, he says, 'very obscure and confused', and sensory information about colours, sounds, odours, tastes and so on should not be taken as providing a reliable guide to what really exists in nature.[36] Whether Descartes' position here is tenable is a complicated question that is the subject for a separate discussion.[37]

With respect to the second gap (between our conception of ourselves as pure thinking substances and our sensory awareness of ourselves as embodied beings) Descartes certainly acknowledges—in a famous passage to which we have already referred above—how strongly our inner experience testifies to the fact that we are physically embodied beings:

> There is nothing that nature teaches me more expressly than that I have a body which is ill affected when I feel pain, and stands in need of food and drink when I experience the sensation of hunger and thirst. ... Nature likewise teaches me by these sensations of pain, hunger, thirst, etc., that I am not only lodged in my body as a pilot in

[35] W. Shakespeare *Measure for Measure* (*c*. 1604), Act III, Scene 1.

[36] E 134, 135, 137 (AT VII 89–83; CSM II 55–58).

[37] For a stimulating treatment of this issue see B. Williams, *Descartes, The Project of Pure Inquiry* (Harmondsworth: Penguin, 1978) Ch. 8.

> a vessel, but that I am intimately conjoined and as it were intermixed with it.[38]

On reflection, however, there is something very curious about this. A strong impulse to believe something is, as we have seen, no guarantee of its truth. Descartes will normally allow that the voice of 'nature' is speaking only when the light of *reason* is involved. But now there seems to be a direct conflict between what reason establishes about my essence, and what my own inner experience tells me. The voice of reason has quite clearly established—only four paragraphs before the passage just quoted—that I am purely a thinking thing—entirely distinct from the body: 'my essence consists *only* in my being a thinking thing'.[39] As Descartes puts it in the *Discourse on the Method*, where he summarises his rational conclusions about the distinctness of mind from body:

> I concluded that I was a substance whose whole essence or nature consists only in thinking, and which, that it may exist, has need of no place, nor is dependent on any material thing; so that 'I', that is to say the mind by which I am what I am, is wholly distinct from the body, and . . . is such that, although the latter were not, it would still continue to be all that it is.[40]

So on the one hand there is the voice of nature as reason telling me that I am wholly distinct from my body; yet on the other hand there is the voice of nature as experience telling me that I am 'intimately conjoined and intermixed with the body'—so much so, indeed, that 'my mind and body compose a certain unity'.[41]

The teachings of 'nature' would thus appear to be nothing less than contradictory. And the contradiction seems to be highlighted later on in the Sixth Meditation when Descartes reflects further on what he means by the term 'nature'. As initially introduced, my 'nature' was supposed to mean the totality of what God has given me. This, says Descartes, comprises everything that belongs to the mind, including 'all the truths I discern by the aid of the natural light'. But 'nature' in the present context (i.e. when associated with the experiences of hunger, thirst, pain, etc.) is, says Descartes, to be taken in a different sense, 'to designate the things which God has given me as [a composite being or] a being composed of mind and body.'[42] What this boils down to is that firstly I possess clear and distinct perceptions of the natural light,

[38] E 135 (AT VII 81; CSM II 56).
[39] E 132 (AT VII 78; CSM II 54). Italics added.
[40] *Discourse on the Method* (1637) Part IV: E 27 (AT VI 33; CSM I 127).
[41] Loc. cit., note 37.
[42] E 136 (AT VII 82; CSM II 57).

which are attributable to me *qua* thinking thing, and which tell me that I am a non-corporeal, purely thinking substance; and secondly I have 'natural' feelings and sensations (e.g, of pain, hunger and thirst) which are attributable to me *qua* compound of mind and body, and which tell me that I am (at least partly) corporeal.

The problem is now all too plain. If the true me ('I, that is to say the mind by which I am what I am') is wholly distinct from the body, how can it be that experience tells me that I am united with the body? It appears that I am two incompatible things: (i) I am a pure incorporeal mind—this the light of reason tells me; and (ii) I am a psycho-physical being, a compound of mind and body, and this my experience tells me.

When Frans Burman interviewed Descartes in 1648, he picked up this contradiction. Quoting the passage from the Sixth Meditation about the mind and body being 'very closely joined and intermixed' so as to form a unity, he asked 'how can this be, when [according to you] their natures are so completely different?' Descartes lamely replied

> This is very difficult to explain; but here our experience is sufficient, since it is so clear on this point that it just cannot be gainsaid.[43]

The reply is lame because although the evidence of my inner sensory experience may, as Descartes says, be undeniable, the result it seems to lead us to (that I am an embodied creature) is incompatible with Descartes' central claim that I am essentially incorporeal.

Those inclined to defend Descartes here may be asking why Descartes cannot maintain both positions. Why cannot he say something like this: 'Yes, I am essentially and necessarily a pure, incorporeal mind. But for the duration of my life on earth, I am also equipped with a body. (In theological terms, God has conjoined a body to my soul.) Thus, though my experience does indeed inescapably testify to my possession of a body, this body is "mine" only in a contingent sense. It is not essential to what makes me *me*; I could do without it—and perhaps will do without it in the next world'. Incidentally, the theological overtones of this imaginary defence of Descartes fit quite well with some of the things Descartes himself says about life after death. In the first edition of the *Meditations*, it is claimed on the title page that the work includes a demonstration of the immortality of the soul. And in the Synopsis to the *Meditations*, Descartes says that his distinction between mind and body is 'sufficient to show that the destruction of the mind does not follow from the corruption of the body, and thus to afford to men the hope of a future life'.[44]

43 AT V 163; Cottingham (op. cit., note 4), 28.

44 E 76 (AT VII 13; CSM II 10). Note that 'mind' *(mens, esprit)* and 'soul' *(anima, âme)* are used interchangeably by Descartes.

Unfortunately, however, this way of defending Descartes will not work; and part of the reason why it will not work emerges in the crucial passage from the Sixth Meditation to which we have already referred more than once. If I were just a mind, temporarily lodged in a body like a pilot in a ship, then, Descartes has to admit,

> I should not feel pain when my body is hurt, seeing I am merely a thinking thing, but should perceive the wound by the understanding alone, just as a pilot perceives by sight when any part of his vessel is damaged.[45]

The point about the damage to a ship is that whether the pilot sees it for himself or merely hears it reported ('Damage to the starboard bow, sir!'), he is aware of it as something as it were *external* to himself. The ship in which he is sailing is damaged, but *he* is still intact. Perhaps the damage can be repaired; perhaps he can take to the lifeboats, or get a new ship. But, at all events, what has happened affects him only, so to say, contingently and indirectly. By contrast, when a steam roller goes over my foot, I do not merely receive a report from the nervous system ('damage to the right foot!') I am aware of something's being wrong in a peculiarly intimate way—I feel pain. The inescapable fact, moreover, and this is the crucial point for the present purpose, is that I feel it as *my* pain. It is not just that the body to which I am attached is damaged; rather *I* am injured, *I* have been hurt. (Compare the soldier wounded on the battlefield: he does not say 'My foot's been damaged' but rather 'I've been hurt'.) In such cases, to insist on the mutually exclusive categories of Cartesian mind/body dualism—e.g. to ask 'is the pain a mental or a physical event?'—really does not work. For the pain belongs not to my mind or to my body but to *me* qua embodied creature, human being composed of flesh and blood.[46]

It is perhaps remarkable that, despite such clear acknowledgement of this inner experience of himself as an embodied being, Descartes never retracted or modified his official arguments to the effect that his 'true nature or essence' was wholly incorporeal and independent of the body. It has not been part of my purpose in this paper to expound those official arguments. Just to summarize them: the groundwork is laid in the Second Meditation (where Descartes observes that he can doubt that he has a body);[47] the bulk of the argumentation is in the Sixth Meditation, where Descartes claims he has a clear and distinct percep-

[45] Loc. cit., note 38.

[46] For further discussion of the problems which sensations pose for mind/body dualism, see J. Cottingham, 'Cartesian Trialism' *Mind* **XCIV**, No. 374 (April 1985).

[47] E 88 (AT VII 28; CSM II 19).

tion of himself as a thinking and unextended thing (in contrast to body which he clearly perceives to be unthinking and extended);[48] and later on Descartes bolsters his position by claiming first that mind is always indivisible while body is divisible, and second, that the removal of any part of the body leaves the mind intact.[49] One reason why I have not examined these classic arguments is that they have been analysed and evaluated *ad nauseam* by almost every commentator on Descartes. Suffice it to say that I accept the consensus view that the arguments are invalid. The fact that I can doubt that I have a body does not entail that the body is a non-essential part of me (any more than the fact that I can doubt that a triangle has some property F entails that F is a non-essential property of the triangle).[50] Further, the alleged clarity and distinctness of the perception that the mind is unextended and indivisible is open to question. Finally, the claim that any part of the body (including the brain!) can be removed, while leaving the mind intact, is unsupported and—to the modern ear—preposterous.

So at the end of the day it was the 'light of nature' in the sense of the processes of rational argument that led Descartes astray. The arguments supposed to establish the real distinction between mind and body are flawed. But alongside the voice of nature as reason, Descartes is, to his credit, prepared to acknowledge the conflicting voice of nature as experience. And this voice tells a different story: that we humans are not incorporeal minds attached to bodies, we are creatures of flesh and blood, physical beings. To acknowledge the physicality of man is of course not at all to deny the rich intellectual life that our species enjoys. The Aristotelian definition of man as a *rational animal* acknowledges our physical nature while also stressing, quite rightly, our ability to think and reason. So to say that we are 'thinking things' is in a sense quite correct, provided we do not follow Descartes in making the further, illegitimate, move of saying that what *does* the thinking is something incorporeal—a pure, non-extended mind or soul. Rather what does the thinking is a *person*, and a person is, necessarily, something with a body.

[48] Loc. cit., note 39.

[49] E 139 (T VII 86: CSM II 59).

[50] Cf. Antoine Arnauld's criticisms of Descartes in the *Fourth Set of Objections*: AT VII 201; CSM II 141.

David Hume

David Hume (1711–1776) was born in Scotland and attended Edinburgh University. In 1734, after a brief spell in a merchant's office in Bristol, he went to France to write *A Treatise of Human Nature*, published anonymously in 1739 (Books I and II) and 1740 (Book III). An *Abstract*, also anonymous and written as if by someone other than the author of the *Treatise*, appeared about the same time, and provides an invaluable account, in a brief compass, of what Hume thought most important about the *Treatise*. The *Treatise* was not well received, and Hume was unsuccessful in his candidature for the chair of moral philosophy at Edinburgh. He rewrote Book I of the *Treatise*, adding a controversial discussion of miracles and providence; and a revision of this was published as *An Enquiry Concerning Human Understanding* in 1748. His *Enquiry Concerning the Principles of Morals*, which was a rewriting of Book III of the *Treatise*, was published in 1751, and his *Dissertation on the Passions*, corresponding to Book II of the *Treatise*, but with significant omissions, such as the account of the psychological mechanism of sympathy, in 1757. In 1752 he had been made keeper of the Advocates' Library at Edinburgh, and wrote his *History of England* which, at the time, brought him more approbation than his philosophy. During this time, he wrote the *Dialogues Concerning Natural Religion*, published posthumously in 1779. In 1763 he became secretary to the British Embassy in Paris. He returned to London in 1766, and a year later was Undersecretary of State. In 1769 he returned to Edinburgh and worked on final editions of his writings, and on an autobiography, dated 18 April 1776, a few months before his death.

The edition of Hume's first *Enquiry* prescribed by the AEB and the JMB is in David Hume, *Enquiries Concerning Human Understanding and Concerning the Principles of Morals*, reprinted from the 1777 edition with Introduction and Analytical Index by L. A. Selby-Bigge, third edition with text revised and notes by P. H. Nidditch (Oxford: Clarendon Press, 1975).

The following may be useful:

N. Kemp Smith, *Philosophy of David Hume*: a critical study of its origins and central doctrines (London: Macmillan, 1941)

D. F. Pears (ed.), *David Hume, A Symposium* (London: Macmillan, 1966).

J. Passmore, *Hume's Intentions* (London: Duckworth, 1968)

A. G. N. Flew, *Hume's Philosophy of Belief* (London: Routledge and Kegan Paul, 1971)

J. C. A. Gaskin, *Hume's Philosophy of Religion* (London: Macmillan, 1978)

Hume on Thought and Belief

EDWARD CRAIG

I. Two topics given prominence in the early sections of Hume's *Enquiry Concerning Human Understanding* are those of thought and belief. Of each Hume asks two questions. One, which we might call the *constitutive* question: what exactly is it to have a thought, or to hold a belief?—and another, which we may call the *genetic* question: how do we come by our thoughts, or our capacity to think them, and how do we come to believe that certain of these thoughts are true? In this lecture I shall be considering the detail of Hume's answers to these questions; but first I want to say a little about why they should have loomed large for him at all.

The hundred or so years before the appearance of Hume's work had seen an intense philosophical interest in Reason, and a mood of great optimism about its powers. Reason, it was thought, was the divine spark in Man, one of the links which entitles us to say that we are made in God's image. Reason, properly used, would issue guarantees for our beliefs, or rather for such of them as really were true; and that was the way in which belief could, and should, be attained. Many of you will be acquainted with Descartes' *Meditations*, a seminal work of its epoch. In it, we are allowed to follow the (allegedly successful) fortunes of an individual inquirer who seeks within his own thought a rational guarantee of the truth of at least his most carefully formed beliefs.

To this estimate of the powers of human reason, and the theological metaphysic that lay behind it, Hume was implacably opposed. For him, Man was a part of nature, not some semi-divine spectator of it. Reason, as his predecessors understood it, was capable of providing a secure foundation for only a tiny fraction of our beliefs, almost all of them lying within pure mathematics. As regards a whole range of beliefs so basic that one can hardly think of human life without them, reason was powerless. The belief that there is an external world which exists whether we perceive it or not, the belief in the simplest inferences from our experience to predictions about the immediate future, the belief that some events are caused by other events, the belief that we are in any sense the same person today that we were yesterday—these beliefs not only are not, but could not be, the product of reason. Rather they are produced by a psychological mechanism, fixed within human nature, which works in accordance with certain specifiable natural laws. What laws govern the physical, Newton had recently told us—or so it seemed to Hume's generation; it was now a question of formulating the corresponding laws governing the mental.

This Hume sets out to do. Accordingly, his normal procedure has two parts, one negative and one positive. Typically, he will take some class of especially basic beliefs, such as those just mentioned, and argue first that it is not our reason which brings us to hold them, because there is no rationally cogent argument for their truth. It is the prominence of this negative aspect which makes us think of Hume primarily as a sceptic, which indeed he is—a sceptic about the powers of reason. But we should not so emphasize this aspect as to lose sight of the other: he is equally keen to provide the true account of the origin of these beliefs. They originate not in reason but rather in the mechanics of human nature; it is here that his Newtonian ambitions come to the fore. The negative claims are required if the positive claims are to obtain a hearing; the positive claims bolster the negative by offering an answer to the response: 'But if reason didn't lead us to these beliefs, how do we come to have them?'

Well, there's potted history of philosophy for you. Indeed, I imagine that 120 years have rarely been forced into a smaller pot—I rather hope not. But I also hope that it is enough to give you some idea of why the question about the origins of our beliefs should have been of such fascination to Hume, and how it came to be so near the centre of his philosophical endeavours.

The fact that it did so has consequences of immediate relevance to our topic. First, someone who is interested in what I called the genetic question about belief—how do beliefs arise?—can hardly avoid the constitutive question—what is a belief? If we are asked how watches are produced we might casually reply, 'Oh, by watchmakers' and so duck out of giving any account of what a watch is; but it is clear that an attempt to say in any detail how they are made will have to offer a fairly specific view of what a watch is, even if not, perhaps, of what it is for. It can come as no surprise, then, that Hume spends a good deal of time on the question, just what the state of believing may be.

Given that, nor can it come as a surprise that he is interested in the parallel question, 'What is a thought?' For it is natural to suppose that believing that today is Thursday consists in thinking the thought that today is Thursday plus doing something else, such as accepting it, or feeling convinced by it. If that is right, then what a thought is ought to be an important part of the answer to the question what a belief is. Thus the two topics, thought and belief, and the two approaches, constitutive and genetic, hang together.

Besides, there was another very good reason, coming from outside his own philosophical concerns, why Hume should have been much exercised about the investigation of thought, or as he would have put it 'the nature and origin of ideas'. John Locke's masterpiece, *An Essay Concerning Human Understanding*, had started from this very question, and Locke's answer to it was the source of much that was new and exciting about his philosophy. Hume was in this regard very much a Lockean—with minor modifications he simply took the doctrine over and treated it as the foundation of his own work. Let us now see what that doctrine was, forgetting about Locke, and looking at Hume's version directly.

II. The first thing to be said is that *ideas*, or thoughts as Hume sometimes calls them,[1] are copies of *impressions*. But although copies of them, they are not indistinguishable from them, so we need to know how they differ; and in any case, what are *impressions*? Hume tells us:

> By the term *impression* . . . I mean all our more lively perceptions, when we hear, or see, or feel, or love, or hate, or desire, or will.[2]

That is a pretty mixed bag, so let us take the first three to start with, the main senses by which we perceive external objects. Think now of seeing a tree—not the tree itself, but what it is like to see the tree. You *could* have this experience if there were no tree there, but, for instance, a very accurate hologram of a tree; or maybe if you were ill and had a very life-like hallucination of a tree. In common to all these situations would be the impression of a tree. For another example, think of hearing a violin, once live, once in an excellent reproduction. In each case there is a certain characteristic experience of perception: in Hume's words an (auditory) impression. The second group, love, hate, desire and will is not so perspicuous; but the point must be that, in Hume's opinion, there are again certain characteristic experiences connected with each, experiences that we can have by introspecting when we feel these emotions or perform these acts of mind. The experience of perceiving one's own inner state is once more an impression. Ideas, we are told, are like impressions. They differ from them only in point of 'force and vivacity'.[3] How are we to understand that?

To grasp this, think not of actually *seeing* a tree, but of forming an image of a tree in your mind's eye, as we say. Hume's thought, I believe—and it is quite plausible, though not every philosopher nowadays would agree with it—is that the experience of having that image is

[1] *An Enquiry Concerning Human Understanding* (hereafter ECHU), 18 (page numbers relate to L. A. Selby-Bigge's edition, revised by P. H. Nidditch, (Oxford: Clarendon Press, 1975)).

[2] ECHU, 18.

[3] E.g. ECHU, 18.

in an obvious way similar to the experience of seeing the tree. It is, if you like, a sort of faint reproduction of what it is like to see the tree; conversely, the seeing is a brighter, more vivid version of the mental image. This, surely, is what Hume has in mind: the seeing of the tree furnishes an impression, the image of it is what he calls an *idea*. In his larger and earlier work on this subject, *A Treatise of Human Nature*, he actually said as much, and explicitly identified *ideas* with images:

> Those perceptions, which enter with the most force and violence, we may name *impressions* . . . By *ideas* I mean the faint images of these in thinking and reasoning.[4]

So I think that we may take it that impressions are what we call perceptions, and that ideas are what we call images. But notice in passing that this isn't Hume's terminology—he calls[5] all these things *perceptions*, and then says that impressions are the more forceful and lively, ideas the fainter.

I hope that this comparison between seeing a tree and forming an image of a tree gives you some feeling for what Hume means when he uses the terms 'forceful, lively' on the one hand and 'faint' on the other, to distinguish between impressions and ideas. Notice now that Hume commits himself to two important claims: that this different level of 'force and vivacity' is the *only* difference between impressions and ideas; and that ideas are the building blocks of thought.[6] For the purpose of this lecture I shall simply accept the thesis that impressions and images differ only in point of force and vivacity. But I shall now simply accept the thesis that thoughts are images, or even combinations of images. This is Hume's answer to the constitutive question about thought, and it certainly calls for critical discussion.

First, however, let us look at some more of Hume's views. What of the genetic question, that one about the *origin* of ideas? Where does he think we get them from? He is certainly ready to give a straight answer: we get them by copying them from impressions. So they are not just 'copies of impressions' in the sense of resembling them—they actually are copied from them. The thought of the colour red is an image of something red; and you can produce that image, which is to say have that thought, only because you have had the experience of seeing a red thing and your mind has retained the character of that experience. A man blind from birth couldn't have that image, and hence couldn't think that thought.[7]

[4] *A Treatise of Human Nature* (hereafter THN), Book I, Pt I, Sect. I.
[5] E.g. ECHU, 18.
[6] See the above quotation from THN, and also ECHU, 18.
[7] ECHU, 20.

This principle, that all our ideas are copied from impressions, cannot be held in quite so direct a form, as Hume was well aware. After all, we can think of, or have the idea of, a unicorn; but we have never seen, or had the impression of a unicorn. To take one of Hume's examples,[8] we can think of a golden mountain, but we have never experienced one. To meet this problem, Hume introduces a distinction which is in fact taken over unaltered from Locke, namely that between simple and complex ideas. The thought is not difficult to grasp: the idea of a golden mountain is composed of the idea of gold and the idea of a mountain, either of which you could have without having the other. But the idea of red cannot in that way be separated out into two ideas of which it is composed. So the idea of a golden mountain is a complex idea, whereas that of red is simple.

Having made that distinction, we are in a position to state the principle about the relationship between impressions and ideas more accurately. Only of simple ideas is it strictly true that you cannot form them unless you have already had the corresponding impression. A complex idea you *may* have copied from a corresponding impression, but it is not necessary to have done so. For we possess a faculty of imagination, and we are entirely free to combine any ideas which will go together without logical contradiction. Our impressions set limits to our stock of simple ideas, therefore; what complex ideas we build out of them is up to us.

To this rule Hume admits one famous exception.[9] Consider some particular shade of blue, and imagine someone who has experienced all other shades of blue, but by chance not yet this one. Would he not be able to supply it from his imagination by so to speak 'joining up' the shades that lie either side of it in the colour spectrum? Hume thinks that there will be widespread agreement that he could. Yet the idea of a particular shade of blue is certainly a simple idea, on Hume's definition, if anything is. So there are exceptions to the principle that there is no simple idea not preceded by the corresponding impression; evidently they can occur when, as in the case of colours, impressions form some kind of continuous series. But Hume isn't worried:

> . . . this instance, is so singular, that it is scarcely worth our observing, and does not merit that for it alone we should alter our general maxim.[10]

III. All this may sound fairly straightforward—I hope it does. But it raises a number of tricky problems which we should now start to

[8] ECHU, 19.
[9] ECHU, 20–21.
[10] ECHU, 21.

consider. One way in is this: is Hume justified in dismissing quite so glibly the matter of the missing shade of blue? After all, don't most impressions fall into some kind of continuous series? Impressions of shape do so. Impressions of sounds do so as well, as regards volume, pitch and tone-colour. Impressions of temperature do so, and impressions of pressure. Most of us, not being dogs, aren't very sensitive to the properties or impressions of smell, nor, unless professional wine-tasters, to those of taste, but surely these also form continuous series? And aren't we now getting very close to saying that *all* impressions fall into some such series or other? To make matters even worse, consider this: if Hume thinks we could supply, from our imagination, one shade that was missing from our experience, why shouldn't we supply two or three? Why is he so confident that it is impossible (as opposed to just difficult) for a human being to supply *most* of the shades of the spectrum from having had experience of just a few of them? And if we are right in thinking that all impressions fall into such continuous series, doesn't this mean that Hume's principle is shot to pieces, by his own admission? How can he then allow himself to treat the case of the missing shade of blue so lightly?

To begin to answer that question, in so far as it can be answered, we need to ask another question first: what exactly does Hume want this principle for? What work is it called upon to do in his philosophy? He tells us this immediately: it is to be an instrument for testing the credentials of the concepts occurring in philosophical discussion.

> When we entertain, therefore, any suspicion that a philosophical term is employed without any meaning or idea (as is but too frequent), we need but inquire, *from what impression is that supposed idea derived*? And if it be impossible to assign any, this will serve to confirm our suspicion. By bringing ideas into so clear a light we may reasonably hope to remove all dispute, which may arise, concerning their nature and reality.[11]

Let us illustrate this by going straight to an example in which Hume was especially interested, and which is the subject matter of one of his most famous chapters:[12] the idea of *causality*. Just what is the content of this idea? Given Hume's principle about ideas needing corresponding impressions, a serious problem arises. Think of two events, perhaps the movement of one billiard ball, and then the subsequent movement of another billiard ball.[13] The former, we say, *causes* the latter. What

[11] ECHU, 22.
[12] ECHU, Sect. VII.
[13] Hume's own example, ECHU, 63.

does that mean? Hume's principle tells us to look for the corresponding impression. But there isn't one. There is an impression of the movement of the first ball, then an impression of the movement of the second; but there is no third impression which could be called the impression of the *connection* between the two, or the *bringing about* of the second by the first. I can't now go into Hume's solution of this problem; I am just trying to make it clear that the principle, once accepted, does cut some ice—philosophers who have been talking blithely about the idea of causality as if it were the clearest thing in the world had better think again.

Notice now that this kind of point is completely unaffected by the difficulties that arise out of the 'missing shade of blue' example. For one thing, the idea of a cause doesn't look at all as if it might form part of a 'spectrum' of closely resembling ideas. And secondly, what gets the problem going is the observation that there simply *isn't* a corresponding impression;[14] not, as with the shade of blue, just that certain persons might, as an accidental matter of their own experience, never have had one. Even if none of us had had that experience, because nothing was of that particular shade, it would still remain an accident, and perfectly possible that there should be such an impression tomorrow, when some artist mixes his paints slightly differently. But that there is no impression of the *causing* between two events isn't, it seems, an accident at all. Without investigating the details of anyone's biography Hume can confidently state that no one has had such an impression. He is therefore in a position to distinguish the former type of case from those cases in which he really wants to put his principle to work. And it would be nice to think that this is why he is not too bothered about the issues raised by the missing shade of blue.

There is another critical question that we ought to be at least aware of: what evidence does Hume have for his principle in the first place? Granted, it seems quite natural to suppose that all our ideas are formed from materials given in perception; but there have been plenty of philosophers who have denied it,[15] and what has Hume to say to them? In the *Enquiry* he offers two pieces of evidence. Firstly,[16] he claims that any of our ideas which we care to examine will be found to conform to the principle. Secondly,[17] if we consider cases in which a person has no access to the relevant impressions, as for instance a blind man has no access to colours, then 'we always find' that he does not have the corresponding ideas either.

[14] Not, at least, in the place where one would most naturally look for it.
[15] To deny it is an important feature of the Platonic tradition for instance.
[16] ECHU, 19.
[17] ECHU, 20.

Neither of these points is really decisive. Let us consider the first one, remembering that Hume wants to use the principle to cast light, and sometimes to cast doubt, on central philosophical concepts. Some of these concepts, like that of cause (or, to give another example, that of substance) seem at first sight to fail the test. And on those grounds Hume wants either to dispense with them as being bogus, or to retain them but give a radically new account of them. But suppose the question is raised (as it soon was—by Kant) whether these may not be concepts to which the principle does not apply, concepts which are as it were innate, or generated from within by the mind, rather than being given to us in experience, what can Hume reply? Not that all our ideas conform to his principle, for that he can hardly assert until he has given reason to think that *these* conform to it, which *prima facie* they seem not to. It is perfectly possible that there are certain 'framework' concepts which are supplied by the mind for the organization of our experience, not copied from experience itself; and if there are they might well be such as to attract philosophical interest. To argue as if one already knew that there are no such things is merely dogmatic. Hume cannot rule out an idea, or subject it to radical surgery, because it does not conform, without better evidence that all healthy ideas *must* conform. Otherwise he has no comeback to the opposition's equally dogmatic assertion, that since (for instance) 'cause' and 'substance' don't conform, it follows that not all acceptable ideas do conform and so the principle is not universally true.

As to the second point, there are two things to be said. Why are we so sure that 'a blind man can form no notion of colours'? If by that Hume means an idea, as he must, and if an idea is a mental image, then being sure what 'notions' a blind man has won't be any too easy. It isn't, after all, very easy for me to be sure just what mental imagery you have, since it isn't something I can see or hear, as I can hear words and see your facial expressions. And a blind man, being blind, wouldn't know what to call these images, even if he had them, and so couldn't with any confidence tell us about them, which would make it even harder. Furthermore: suppose we were somehow quite certain that a blind man has no idea of colour, or a deaf man of sounds. Would it follow generally, that for *any* idea, call it X, we can't have the idea of an X without having the impression of an X, or at least of its simple components? No. To think it did would be simply to overlook the possibility we were considering a moment ago, namely that there may be certain concepts which are so to speak built into our minds and not experientially acquired. The outcome, I think, is that we had better regard Hume's principle as more postulated than proved.

We now arrive at a key issue to which I have not yet addressed myself. Does thinking consist in the inward manipulation of mental imagery?

We saw that Hume held that it does, since he equates ideas and thoughts, and takes them to differ from impressions only in respect of 'force and vivacity'. Can he be right about this?

First, let us be sure that we know what Hume has committed himself to. He is not just saying that some of us sometimes have mental imagery while we are thinking. He is not even saying just that *all* of us have mental imagery *whenever* we think. He is saying that thinking just *is* having mental imagery—that this is what *constitutes* thought. And that is almost certainly false. One reason is that if thinking just is having mental imagery then anybody who is thinking must at that time have images before his mind; which, surely, simply isn't the case. In so far as you are following what I have been saying, and not just sitting there, you have been thinking thoughts since I began to speak. But have you really had a constant stream of imagery going on in your heads all that time? If you are inclined to say that although you haven't been aware of it, it nevertheless must have been there, then please pause for a moment, and reflect that you wouldn't say that unless you believed that this theory about what it is to think just had to be right. And why should it? Indeed, how *could* it be right? There may be some thoughts, of a fairly concrete kind, which we can conceive of as being portrayed in imagery—though in a moment I shall raise doubts even about that—but what imagery could constitute the thinking of some highly abstract thought like (I purposely choose one that we recently have been thinking) the thought that what Hume says in favour of his principle about ideas needing corresponding impressions doesn't suffice to prove it? One might, with a little effort, think of imagery which can serve as a sort of feeble illustration of that thought, as a picture of a horse and jockey might illustrate the thought of going to Newmarket races; but surely one couldn't find any sequence of images which would even come near to conveying its whole content? Yet that is what there would have to be if thinking is just to *consist* in the mental manipulation of imagery.

Even so, I probably conceded too much just now in allowing that at any rate *some* thoughts might just consist in the occurrence of imagery. For take, say, an image of a cat sitting on a mat. The suggestion is that the image is a thought—not that it naturally *accompanies* a certain thought, but that it actually *is* the thought. If so, it must be some particular thought; for if an image, by itself, can't be a particular thought, and there is nothing more to thinking than entertaining images, then we couldn't have particular thoughts at all. So, what particular thought would our image of a cat sitting on a mat be? Would it be the thought that the cat is sitting on the mat? It might be, but surely that would depend on how the person entertaining it *understood* it—it would be possible to understand it as 'The cat was (or will be, or might be) on the mat', to take just a few examples. And this means that if an image is to be associated with a determinate thought there must be something else, not actually in the image, which determines how the image is to be taken; so the activity of thinking cannot be embodied wholly in images, with no remainder.[18]

It seems, then, that Hume's theory about the nature of thought is in some disarray. His opinion that thinking differs from perceiving (as we would nowadays call it) *only* in point of the 'force and vivacity' of the experiences involved, cannot be maintained, and we are left with no satisfactory view of what thinking consists in. His theory about where the ability to think comes from, and hence what its limits are, *might* still be true, that is, he might still be right to say that in order to think of X's, we must previously have experienced them, or at least their components—this thesis does not depend essentially on the discredited claim that a thought of an X is an image of an X. But even here we have to admit that, although the idea is quite attractive, and has found a good deal of support in the subsequent history of philosophy,[19] not all philosophers have been attracted by it, and Hume has not given any very compelling reason for thinking them wrong.

IV. I couldn't blame you if at this stage you concluded that Hume's theory of belief can't be in very good shape either. Haven't we said that *believing* something looks very much like *thinking* it, plus some further component? Then won't a theory of belief include a theory of thought, with the result that if the theory of thought is bad, the theory of belief will be dragged down with it? One might try to avoid that conclusion by denying that believing is thinking plus an extra factor. That line isn't altogether hopeless, but I cannot go into it now; in any case, it is definitely not the line chosen by Hume. But there may be quite a lot one can say about the nature of belief, and how we come to believe what we do, without relying on any very specific theory about what it is to think a thought. And interestingly enough, that is how it turns out. Hume's views about belief are quite detailed, but they are compatible with a wide range of theories about what a thought is; in particular, they do not require it to be true that thoughts are images, or sequences of images. I shall go on using Hume's terms; but when I speak of 'the idea of an X' I shall not be thinking of anything so specific as a mental image, but simply of whatever state of mind one is characteristically in when thinking about X's, without trying to describe it any more closely.

There is, obviously enough, a difference between on the one hand merely thinking something, just entertaining the thought, and on the

[18] The reader may find it interesting to compare: Ludwig Wittgenstein, *Philosophical Investigations*, para. 139 and note.

[19] Notably in Logical Positivism.

other hand believing it to be true. We can think the thought that Gordon Square is full of camels, in fact we are now thinking it—but we don't believe it. We can think the thought that there was once a detective called Sherlock Holmes, who had a friend named Dr Watson, and so on—but without believing any of it. So Hume begins by posing the famous question:

> Wherein, therefore, consists the difference between such a fiction and belief?[20]

One possible answer which quite naturally suggests itself is this: to think a given thought is to have before one's mind a certain sequence of ideas. To believe it is to have before one's mind that sequence of ideas, plus another idea, namely the idea of believing. But this Hume disposes of with a neat and powerful argument. When it comes to combining ideas, he points out, the imagination can do virtually what it likes. Provided two ideas are consistent, don't actually contradict each other, we can always put them together. For instance, we can juxtapose the ideas of being a horse and of having wings to give that of a winged horse, or of a man's head and a horse's body to give that of a centaur.[21] If belief were just another idea, we could attach it at will to any collection of ideas that was merely consistent with it, and so generate instant belief in anything we wanted to believe. Which of course we can't; there is no difficulty in thinking the thought that the square is full of camels, but just try to believe it! So this theory, which implies that we can, must be wrong.

There is another point which Hume could have made here: adding the idea of believing to the original thought wouldn't produce a belief, but just the more complex thought 'I believe that the square is full of camels'. Notice that I can *think* that thought without it having to be true, that is, without *believing* that the square is full of camels. What we need to add is *belief*, whatever that may be, not the *thought of believing*. And even if the addition of a further thought could produce belief, adding it would alter the content of what was being thought, so that it would not be possible to believe exactly the same thing as was previously being merely considered, which is surely a very uncomfortable consequence. For all these reasons, the theory has to be rejected.

What can we put in its place? Well, since believing something doesn't involve adding a further idea to the idea of the original something, it can only consist in the way in which that original idea is entertained, or how it strikes the mind. And now some of you will already be anticipating Hume's answer. According to his theory, the only way in which an idea

[20] ECHU, 47.
[21] Hume's own example, ECHU, 48.

can change without changing its content and so becoming the idea of something else, a different thought, is in respect of its degree of 'force and vivacity'. That must therefore be the solution: believing something is having the ideas you would have if just thinking it, but presented with greater force. That looks like being the only option that Hume has left himself, and there is no reason to think that he would find it unwelcome, especially as it helps him account for the fact that what we believe is largely involuntary; for though he makes the *combination* of ideas subject to the control of the will, he does not make it a voluntary matter just how forcefully a given idea strikes us. So increased force and vivacity is well suited to be the feature that differentiates a belief from a mere thought.

In *A Treatise of Human Nature* Hume said exactly that.[22] In the later and somewhat more cautious *Enquiry* he havers and wavers, comes very close to saying it, and ends up saying that whereas we all know that familiar feeling that attaches to an idea when we believe in its object, we have no words that satisfactorily describe it other than 'belief' itself. So here we see Hume withdrawing from his former position, according to which all our mental states lie on this one-dimensional scale of force and vivacity; though he withdraws with some reluctance, and without telling us anything very precise about the position he intends to occupy instead. That is not to say that he tells us nothing, however. Admittedly, he doesn't have much to say about what the 'manner . . . of conception' or 'feeling to the mind' is *in itself*, but he does say something about the sorts of effect it has, and how they differ from those in which a thought is merely entertained, though without belief. What is believed, he says, has 'more weight and influence'; it 'becomes the governing principle of our actions', and it has 'a much greater influence of every kind, either to give pleasure or pain, joy or sorrow'.[23]

In saying this, incidentally, Hume is doing little more than giving clear expression to what everyone recognizes from common-sense. We all know that just thinking the thought 'it is now raining' won't produce any tendency to put on a raincoat, whereas believing that it is raining will; hearing (and so coming to believe) that you have scored a big win on the premium bonds will have a much greater effect on your emotional state than just thinking about winning—or so I imagine. This, then, is hardly controversial. More controversial is Hume's account of the way in which belief arises.

[22] THN, Bk I, Pt III, Sect. VII.

[23] ECHU, 49–50. Hume had also said something very similar in the Appendix to THN, see p. 629 in *A Treatise of Human Nature*, L. A. Selby-Bigge (ed.), 2nd edn rev. by P. H. Nidditch (Oxford: Clarendon Press, 1978).

First we need to look at Hume's doctrine of the association of ideas.[24] The basic idea is nowadays part of the currency of thought, though in Hume's time it was only beginning to get a grip: certain thoughts, or certain experiences, regularly call up certain other thoughts; the succession of ideas in our minds is not random, but subject to rules. As Hume says,

> It is evident that there is a principle of connection between the different thoughts or ideas of the mind, and that . . . they introduce each other with a certain degree of method and regularity.[25]

The same principle, Hume suggests, is also responsible for the fact that the meanings of words in different languages correspond to one another to a high degree; if we take some concept, even quite a complex one, in one language, it is remarkable with what consistency we find in other languages words that are tolerably good translations of it. The explanation is that the contingencies of life tend to cause us to associate ideas in much the same groups, hence to have similar concepts, and hence to operate vocabularies that are approximately parallel. In the *Treatise*, Hume had called the principle of association

> . . . a kind of ATTRACTION, which in the mental world will be found to have as extraordinary effects as in the natural . . .[26]

—thereby hinting at his ambition to rival in psychology Newton's achievement in the science of matter; for surely this is an intentional allusion to the prominence of gravitational attraction in physics.

Under what circumstances, then, do we come to associate one idea with another? There appear to be, Hume boldly proclaims,

> . . . only three principles of connection among ideas, namely *Resemblance, Contiguity* in time or place, and *Cause* or *Effect*.[27]

Thus the perception, or the thought, of something tends to make us think of other things we know that resemble it, as for instance a portrait leads our thoughts to the person portrayed. The thought of an object or event leads our thoughts to other things nearby, or to events that happened at the same time. Finally, the thought or perception of something tends to give rise to the thought of its causes, or its effects. I shall concentrate attention on the third of these, since it is the type of association that is active in generating belief.[28] (Why the others aren't so

[24] ECHU, Section III.
[25] ECHU, 23.
[26] THN, Bk I, Pt I, Sect. IV.
[27] ECHU, 24.
[28] See ECHU, 26–27.

active in this respect Hume doesn't tell us—certainly a defect of his theory.)

Hume points out[29] that for all three principles of association, an idea is not only called to mind but also *enlivened* by the occurrence of a sensory perception, or of a memory, with which it is associated. Take resemblance, for example: if we see a picture of a friend our idea of him and feelings about him acquire as it were a fresh impetus, 'new force and vigour'. But Hume needs to be careful here—this 'force and vigour' had better not be too much like that 'force and vivacity' which turns ideas into beliefs. That would mean that seeing my friend's picture was what made me, via the associative link with the thought of him, believe in his existence. And that, as Hume is well aware,[30] isn't the case at all. I do believe that he exists, but not because I am looking at his picture. To see that, consider a slightly different case, in which I am looking at a picture of Sherlock Holmes. It resembles, let us suppose, Sherlock Holmes as I think of him; so it makes me think of Sherlock Holmes, perhaps brings some of the details of Conan Doyle's stories to mind, and so on. But one thing which beyond any doubt it *doesn't* do is make me believe that Holmes exists or existed.

Where the principle of association involved is that of cause and effect, things are different. When we see a piece of dry wood being put on a fire,[31] we not only think of the fire's burning more brightly rather than being dampened down, we also believe that this is going to happen. Likewise, if I hear a voice, I don't just think of a human being as its cause, I believe that there is someone there. This belief, Hume tells us,[32] referring to his preceding discussion of the effects of *Resemblance* and *Contiguity*, 'arises from similar causes'. That leaves him open to the question I mentioned a little earlier: why, if the causes are similar, don't resemblance and contiguity produce belief too?

A further point is clearly playing a role in Hume's thought. If I have an impression, and associate an idea with it, then that idea will derive force from it; if the association is based on cause and effect, the idea will become a belief. If however I had had instead of that impression only an idea, that is, if I had only thought of wood being put on the fire rather than seeing it happening, then I would still have had the associated idea of the flames burning higher and brighter, but not the belief that they really were about to do so. So if, to put it in general terms, the idea B is associated with A, the occurrence of A will tend to produce the *belief* in

[29] ECHU, 50–52.
[30] ECHU, 53–54.
[31] Hume's own example, ECHU, 54.
[32] ECHU, 54.

B only if A itself has a high degree of force and vivacity—it will have to be an *impression* of A, or at least itself a belief in A.

This result is more or less forced upon Hume by the everyday observation that the *thought* of clouds won't induce the *belief* in impending rain, whereas the *sight* of clouds, or the *belief* that they are gathering, may very well induce it. But forced or not, it would surely have been welcome to him. Recall his neo-Newtonian ambitions, and the evidence that he was pleased when his theory of mind showed affinities with Newton's physics. Recall also how believing something, on Hume's view, differs from merely entertaining the thought of it: the belief has more 'weight and influence', it is capable of guiding our actions. Now a belief, whatever state that may be exactly, will need *energy* if it is to be productive of action, and this energy will have to come from somewhere—so much is good Newtonianism. What sources are available? The mental states that have high energy, that is high 'force and vivacity', are for Hume impressions of the senses, memories, and beliefs themselves. So that an idea which arises by association with one of *these* states has the right sort of ancestry, and can acquire from it force and vivacity of its own. We can think, if we like, of energy flowing through the associative link and energizing the associated idea, so giving it the status of a belief and the capacity to play a vital role in the direction of action.

The analogy with physics is enjoyable, and would almost certainly have been enjoyable to Hume, but it wouldn't do to push it too hard. For one thing, nothing in Hume's system corresponds to the principle of conservation of energy—an impression doesn't become any the less forceful itself when it imparts force to an associated idea. Nor is there any reason to think that Hume regarded an exactness of parallel with Newtonian physics as an important aim.

V. This, then, is Hume's doctrine of the nature of belief and the way in which beliefs arise. Notice that it does not depend on acceptance of the view that thoughts are mental imagery. What is essential is only that a thought should be some state of mind capable of different levels of 'energy', or the capacity to affect decision and action. It would therefore be wrong to dismiss Hume's theory of belief solely on the grounds that his imagist theory of thought is untenable.

That does not mean that no criticisms can justly be made of it. Indeed, it would be amazing if the theory were not open at some point to serious objections. To give an account of the origin of belief that would work quite generally, for all kinds of belief and all circumstances, would be an enormous achievement. I doubt whether any modern psychologist would seriously contemplate attempting it; only when that science was in its infancy could anyone have approached the task with the confidence shown by Hume. His efforts are heroic, but the problem is surely far more complex than he allowed for. I shall briefly discuss just one general type of difficulty which it faces.

You will have noticed that Hume's theory is highly deterministic—he presents the process of acquiring belief as one to which we make little conscious contribution. What we associate with what, is fixed by the past course of our experience; our present impressions then trigger off these associations and transform the resulting ideas into beliefs by raising their 'force and vivacity'. All is automatic: impressions in, mechanism whirrs, beliefs out. But surely a theory of belief with any claim to be realistic, let alone comprehensive, has to find room for a little more than this? What about, for instance, the disturbance caused by emotional factors, like being unwilling to believe X, though objectively speaking the evidence suggests it, or desperately wanting to believe Y, though impartial judges would find the evidence heavily against it? There seems little doubt that such factors do have an influence upon what people believe. Again, turning now to the more rational aspects of our make-up, we sometimes deliberate, weigh evidence, and form an opinion on the matter in hand only after a good deal of thought. Where would such procedures find a place in Hume's scheme of things? He makes it sound as if belief were something that just happens to us, rather than something that we (occasionally, at any rate) consciously strive to attain.

There is another, closely related, phenomenon with which Hume's theory cannot easily cope. This is the case in which, without obtaining any *fresh* evidence, I review all the evidence available to me and come to a different conclusion from that which I had previously drawn. If this is possible, Hume faces problems. For his view surely implies that, given any particular set of associative links, only the occurrence of new and relevant impressions, or of some memory which I had not previously considered, could allow a new belief to be formed. Unless that happens, my belief must stay put. The possibility that on the basis of exactly the same evidence I might arrive at a different result seems excluded. Our best line, defending Hume, might be to claim that this phenomenon, in the pure form which causes the difficulty, just doesn't exist—if you come to a different conclusion there is always some difference, however slight, in your evidence—but whether we can really say that with a good conscience seems to me very doubtful.

Before we write Hume's theory off, however, there is one very important aspect that should not be allowed to escape us. If what I said at the beginning is correct, Hume approaches the topic of belief with a sceptical eye fixed on the Cartesian question, what reason we have for holding our factual beliefs. This concentrates his attention on those main types of belief which in everyday, or scientific, investigation we simply take for granted: that there are physical things which exist independently of whether we are at the time perceiving them, and suchlike. Now for this kind of belief some kind of quasi-mechanical theory looks much more promising. They do seem to be automatic, we do seem to be just 'landed' with them. They do not seem to have much to do with reason: children soon come to hold them, but they surely don't reason them out. If, on review, we conclude with the philosophical sceptic that we don't have *good reason* to believe them, we still go on believing. When Bishop Berkeley argues that there couldn't be such a thing as an independent material world,[33] we still go on believing in it even if we cannot answer him. Berkeley's arguments, Hume wrote

> . . . admit of no answer and produce no conviction.[34]

Whether they really 'admit of no answer' may be questioned. But Hume's point would remain, that these beliefs have the feel of a product of non-rational factors; our reason, it seems, neither produces nor sustains them. It can attack them, but the attack bounces off, and the beliefs remain. There are, of course, plenty of beliefs which one can argue one's way into, or out of. But on the other hand there do seem to be certain very basic types of belief which are the outcome of our animal constitution. Although it cannot be denied that Hume speaks as if he were giving a theory valid for all beliefs, it is understandable, in the light of his over-arching philosophical aims, that he should have had these primarily in mind. They are after all in a sense the foundation of nearly all our beliefs—if reason cannot justify *them*, it can scarcely justify anything—so it was on them that the sceptical attack on the powers of reason naturally focused.

We can now see, perhaps, that Hume's central philosophical contribution does not really depend upon the admittedly shaky detail of his somewhat primitive psychological theory. He is painting a new picture of Man and Man's position in the universe. Most major thinkers of the previous hundred years had portrayed the human being as a semi-divine creature which shared, in part, the attributes of God; they had stressed especially the powers of reason and the ability to acquire insight into the nature of reality. This proud self-vision was what Hume sought to overthrow. For him the more pressing comparison was not with God, but with the animal kingdom.[35] We are a part of the natural world, and subject to natural laws; that is true of our beliefs just as it is true of our emotions. So long as one does not try to push the analogy too far, or think too much in terms of actual historical influence, it is

[33] See George Berkeley, *Three Dialogues between Hylas and Philonous*.

[34] ECHU, 155, footnote.

[35] See ECHU, Sect. IX.

illuminating to regard Hume as a precursor of the intellectual movement which culminated rather more than a hundred years later in the triumph of Darwinism. Not that Hume thinks in terms of evolution, let alone natural selection. But he does make us continuous with nature, rather than with God, and the fulcrum on which he levers this new philosophy into place is his theory of belief.

Hume on Liberty and Necessity

GODFREY VESEY

1. Introduction

David Hume (1711–1776) described the question of liberty and necessity as 'the most contentious question of metaphysics, the most contentious science' (Hume [1748] 1975, p. 95). He was right about it being contentious. Whether it is metaphysical is another matter. I think that what is genuinely metaphysical is an assumption that Hume, and a good many other philosophers, make in their treatment of the question. The assumption is about language and reality. I call it 'the conformity assumption'. But more about that shortly. Let us begin at the obvious beginning, by considering what the terms 'liberty' and 'necessity' mean in the expression 'liberty and necessity'.

'Liberty' does not mean political liberty. It means what René Descartes (1595–1650) meant when he said that man is 'in a peculiar way . . . the author of his actions' (Descartes [1644] 1912, p. 179 (*Principles of Philosophy*, I, Sect. 37)). Man would not be the author of his actions if they happened by *chance*. And he would not be the author of his actions if he acted under *compulsion*; that is, if he were either externally compelled by someone bodily forcing him to do something, or internally compelled by some irresistible urge, such as kleptomania, the urge to steal. As a rule, man is not compelled to act as he does. He can act as he chooses. He can act 'freely'. That is liberty.

Now for 'necessity'. It is a term that has been used, in connection with causation, for a very long time. In ancient philosophy one kind of causation, involving necessity, was usually opposed to another, not involving necessity. Plato (428–348 BC), for instance, opposed two kinds of causes: 'things which are endowed with mind and are the workers of things fair and good' and 'things which being moved by others are compelled to move others', the latter being the kinds of causes that operate with necessity (*Timaeus*, 46c–48c). And Aristotle (384–322 BC) opposed two ways in which things happen. They may happen 'for the sake of something' or they may happen 'just as the sky rains, not in order to make the corn grow, but of necessity. What is drawn up must cool and what has been cooled must become water and descend, the result of this being that the corn grows' (*Physics*, 198b17). Connected with this is a distinction Aristotle made between 'final causes' and 'motor causes' (*Parts of Animals*, 639b12). If something happens for the sake of something, it has a final cause; if it happens of necessity, it has a motor cause. Aristotle held that, with some exceptions, such as the colour of people's eyes, everything in nature has a final cause.

Hume differed from Plato and Aristotle in *not* opposing one kind of causation, involving necessity, to another, not involving it. He said that all mankind have always 'without hesitation acknowledged the doctrine of necessity in their whole practice and reasoning' (Hume [1748] 1975, p. 95). He was, of course, wrong. Plato and Aristotle belong to mankind, and they did not acknowledge necessity in their whole practice and reasoning.

This difference between Hume, and Plato and Aristotle, is significant. It explains why there is a 'question of liberty and necessity' for Hume. If the causation of human actions is the same as the causation of drops of water—that is, the causes of both are what Aristotle called 'motor causes'—and if events caused by motor causes occur of necessity, then surely there is a problem. Does not necessity mean compulsion? How can human actions be both compelled and not compelled? On the face of it, necessity is not compatible with liberty.

Hume's answer to the question of liberty and necessity was what has come to be known as a 'compatibilist' answer. He himself described his treatment of the question as a 'reconciling project' (p. 95). The key to the reconciliation lay in his account of the meaning of the word 'necessity' in talk of causal necessity. It was to be an account which would make the causation of actions compatible with liberty, the latter being defined as the agent's having 'a power of acting, or not acting, according to the determinations of the will' (p. 95).

You may be thinking: anyone can show two things to be compatible if he is allowed to give whatever sense he likes to the terms. But Hume claimed that there is something special about the sense he attached to the term 'necessity'. It is, he held, the only reasonable sense we can attach to it (p. 81).

When philosophers talk of only one sense of a term being reasonable it is usually because they subscribe to some general philosophy of language. This was undoubtedly so in the case of Hume. He subscribed to the so-called 'way of ideas'.

The way of ideas combines three different assumptions or views about language. I shall call them 'the thought-signifying assumption', 'the conformity assumption', and 'empiricism'.

2. The Thought-signifying Assumption

Consider thinking and discourse. How are they related?

One possible view is that 'thinking and discourse are the same thing, except that what we call thinking is . . . the inward dialogue carried on by the mind with itself without spoken sound . . . whereas the stream which flows from the mind through the lips with sound is called discourse' (Plato, *Sophist*, 263e). Roughly, thinking is soundless discourse, talking to oneself.

But is talking to oneself enough, for there to be thinking? Is it not necessary for the talker-to-himself to *understand* what he says? And does not this mean that he must be conscious, not only of what he says to himself, but also of what he *means* by it; not only of soundless sentences, but also of what we might call 'sentence meanings'? And since sentences are made up of words, does not this mean that the talker-to-himself must be conscious of 'word meanings' ('ideas'), and of how ideas are associated in the sentence-meaning?

Such may have been the thought that led Descartes to say: 'I can express nothing in words, when I understand what I say, without making it certain, by this alone, that I possess the idea of the thing that is signified by those words' (Descartes, 1912, p. 229). Notice the word 'certain' in that quotation from Descartes. He was prepared to question most things, but not that understanding requires the existence of ideas. That seemed to him to be beyond question.

Thomas Hobbes (1588–1679), in *The Leviathan*, published ten years after Descartes' *Meditations*, was, I think, the first philosopher actually to spell out the thought-signifying view of language:

> The most noble and profitable invention of all other was that of SPEECH, consisting of *names* or appellations, and their connection; whereby men register their thoughts; recall them when they are past; and also declare them one to another for mutual utility and conversation; . . .
>
> The most general use of speech is to transfer our mental discourse into verbal; or the train of our thoughts into a train of words; and that for two commodities; whereof one is the registering of the consequences of our thoughts; which being apt to slip out of our memory, and put us to a new labour, may again be recalled by such words as they were marked by. So that the first use of names is to serve for *marks* or *notes* of remembrance. Another is, when many use the same words, to signify (by their connection and order) one to another what they conceive or think of each matter; and also what they desire, fear, or have any other passion for. And for this use they are called signs (Hobbes [1651] 1914, pp 12–13).

Nearly forty years later, John Locke (1632–1704) said much the same in Book III of his *Essay Concerning Human Understanding* (1690). In brief:

> So far as words are of use and signification, so far is there a constant connection between the sound and the idea, and a designation that the one stands for the other; without which application of them, they are nothing but so much insignificant noise (III.ii.7).

One interesting difference between Locke and Hobbes was that Locke thought that people might object that when they reflect (introspect) they do not encounter the non-verbal things they should encounter according to the theory. Why is it not generally recognized that there are mental propositions as well as verbal ones? He had an answer:

> . . . it is very difficult to treat of them asunder. Because it is unavoidable, in treating of mental propositions, to make use of words; and then the instances given of mental propositions cease immediately to be barely mental, and become verbal (IV.v.3).

Locke need not have worried. The thought-signifying assumption had too powerful a hold on the minds of people who philosophized about language to be dislodged by the consideration that we can identify non-verbal propositions only in terms of their verbal equivalent. Hume certainly had no qualms on this score. He felt no need to repeat what Hobbes and Locke had said about the use of speech. Obviously it is to express thoughts. The assumption acquired the status of a truism. George Campbell (1719–1796), in his *Philosophy of Rhetoric* (1776) wrote: 'There are two things in every discourse which principally claim our attention, the sense and the expression; or in other words, the thought, and the symbol by which it is communicated' (Campbell, 1823, p. 47). This was the book that James Boswell (1740–1795) said Hume had before him when he visited the dying philosopher 'on Sunday forenoon the 7 of July 1776, being too late for church' (Weis, 1970, p. 11). To Hume, Campbell's remark must have seemed so obviously true as hardly to be worth making. Is it not obvious that the sense of a sentence, whether uttered or not, is the thought it expresses? And that thoughts are ideas associated together?

The thought-signifying assumption is the first of the three assumptions or views about language that combine to make up 'the way of ideas'. The second, the conformity assumption, is the one I warned you about at the beginning of this lecture. It is metaphysical: it is about language and 'reality'.

3. The Conformity Assumption

For a sentence to be true is for it to correspond to a fact. That is the so-called 'correspondence theory' of truth. The conformity assumption is not about sentences in a language, but about the language itself. It is the assumption that for the language to be one in which true or false statements can be made, *the language* must correspond, or conform, to something. Philosophers who make the conformity assumption call that to which language is said to conform 'reality'. The conformity assumption, then, is the assumption that language, unless it is nonsense-language (in which nothing true or false can be said) conforms to something, called 'reality', in much the same way as a true statement *in* the language corresponds to a fact.

Now, if the conformity assumption is combined with the thought-signifying assumption, part of which is the notion that thoughts consist of ideas associated together, then the product is a view about ideas being either 'real' or 'fantastical'. Those are the terms Locke used. He wrote as follows:

> By *real ideas*, I mean such as have a foundation in nature; such as have a conformity with the real being and existence of things, or with their archetypes. *Fantastical* or *chimerical*, I call such as have no foundation in nature, nor have any conformity with that reality of being to which they are tacitly referred as to their archetypes (II.xxx.1).

It may help to have an example. We have the practice of making, and normally keeping, promises. I may say 'I promise to return your copy of the *Enquiry*'. In saying this I am not stating a fact, but making a commitment. Suppose, now, that anthropologists arrive in a spacecraft from some alien civilisation. In their community language has only a fact-stating function. Accordingly they assume that in saying 'I promise' I must be stating some fact. But they cannot discover what it is. To them the promise-making language seems to have 'no foundation in nature'. In other words, the idea of a promise seems to them to be '*fantastical* or *chimerical*'.

4. Rationalism and Empiricism, about Necessity

Anyone who takes the view that language should conform to 'reality'—or, in Locke's terminology, who holds that ideas are either real or fantastical—cannot rest content with that view. He is inevitably faced with the question: how do *I know* whether some idea I have is real, in Locke's sense, or not?

Philosophers who regard this as a sensible question to ask—that is, philosophers who make the conformity assumption—give one or other, or a bit of both, of two answers. The two answers are 'by reasoning' and 'by experience'. Someone who gives the answer 'by reasoning' is called a 'rationalist'. Someone who give the answer 'by experience' is called an 'empiricist'. (The word 'empiricism' comes from the Greek *empeiria*, of which the Latin translation is *experientia*, from which we get the word 'experience'.) The distinction between reasoning and experience goes back at least to Plato. Plato himself came down firmly on the side of saying that we know about reality (for him, the 'Forms' of things) by reasoning. He called the sort of reasoning involved 'dialectic'. Most philosophers who make the conformity assumption are not pure rationalists or pure empiricists. But certainly some are more one than the other. If you compare, say, René Descartes and Nicolas Malebranche (1638–1715) with John Locke and David Hume, then there is a good case for describing the first two as rationalists and the second two as empiricists.

I mention Malebranche because he is one of two philosophers (the other is Locke) whose views on causal necessity Hume explicitly rejected. Malebranche's reasoning went something like this. If some being were omnipotent then he (or she, or it) would only have to will something to happen for it to happen. Omnipotence is such that if he willed something to happen it could not but happen. In other words, if 'X' is an omnipotent being, and 'Y' is the event in question, then 'X wills Y' entails (that is, logically necessitates) 'Y happens'. Now, God is omnipotent, and is the only omnipotent being. So in the case of God, at least (and at most), there is a hard (in the sense of logical) necessary connection between a cause (God, or God willing) and an effect (whatever God wills). We think of there being a necessary connection between causes and effects, and in the case of God the thought applies. In fact, it applies only in the case of God. He is the only true cause. What we ordinarily think of as causes are merely the *occasions* on which God exercises his omnipotence. They are what may be called 'occasional' causes (Malebranche [1674–1675] 1980, pp. 448–450).

Malebranche's theory had the benefit of providing an analysis of causal necessity, but Hume rejected it on both rationalist and empiricist grounds. Rationalist, first. 'Though the chain of arguments which conduct to it were ever so logical, there must arise a strong suspicion, if not an absolute assurance, that it has carried us quite beyond the reach of our faculties, when it leads to conclusions so extraordinary, and so remote from common life and experience. We are got into fairy land, long ere we have reached the last steps of our theory; and *there* we have no reason to trust our common methods of argument, or to think that our usual analogies and probabilities have any authority' (p. 72).

The objection on empiricist grounds was what one would expect. We do not experience God exercising his omnipotent will. So we cannot properly claim to have any idea of it, since all our ideas come from experience (cf. Locke, 1690, II.i.1–2). We can no more comprehend the operations of God than we can those of the grossest matter (p. 73).

Hume rejected Malebranche's theory in favour of an empiricist theory of his own. It is to be found in Section VII of the first *Enquiry* (pp. 60–79), the section entitled 'Of the idea of necessary connection'. There is a useful recapitulation at the end of the section (pp. 78–79). Instead of quoting it I shall quote two paragraphs from a section—Book 1, Part III, Section XIV—of Hume's earlier work, *A Treatise of Human Nature* (1739). The section in the *Treatise* has the same title as that in the first *Enquiry*: 'Of the idea of necessary connection'.

> *What is our idea of necessity, when we say that two objects are necessarily connected together*. Upon this head I repeat what I have often had occasion to observe, that as we have no idea that is not derived from an impression, we must find some impression that gives rise to this idea of necessity, if we assert we have really such an idea. In order to do this I consider in what objects necessity is commonly supposed to lie; and finding that it is always ascribed to causes and effects, I turn my eye to two objects supposed to be placed in that relation; and examine them in all the situations of which they are susceptible. I immediately perceive that they are *contiguous* in time and place, and that the object we call cause *precedes* the other we call effect. In no one instance can I go any farther, nor is it possible for me to discover any third relation betwixt these objects. I therefore enlarge my view to comprehend several instances; where I find like objects always existing in like relations of contiguity and succession. At first sight this seems to serve but little to my purpose. The reflection on several instances only repeats the same objects; and therefore can never give rise to a new idea. But upon farther enquiry I find that the repetition is not in every particular the same, but produces a new impression, and by that means the idea, which I at present examine. For after a frequent repetition, I find that upon the appearance of one of the objects, the mind is *determined* by custom to consider its usual attendant, and to consider it in a stronger light upon account of its relation to the first object. It is this impression, or *determination*, which affords me the idea of necessity . . .
>
> This therefore is the essence of necessity. Upon the whole, necessity is something that exists in the mind, not in objects; nor is it possible for us to form the most distant idea of it, considered as a quality in bodies. Either we have no idea of necessity, or necessity is nothing but that determination of the thought to pass from causes to effects and from effects to causes, according to their experienced union (Hume [1739] 1888, pp. 155–156, 165–166).

It is tempting to put this as follows. The impression from which we get the idea of necessity is an inward impression, an impression of the mind being determined, on the perception of one object, to expect another. It is not an outward impression, and so does not justify us in talking of one object *really* necessitating another. This, I think, would be the straightforward way of putting it. But Hume, in the first *Enquiry*, prefers a different formulation. There *is* necessity in causation, but all we can mean by it is the constant conjunction of objects, and the consequent inference of the mind from one to another (pp. 82, 92–93, 96 incl. fn.).

5. Application of Hume's Theory of Causation to the Causation of Actions: Motives as Causes

Liberty, as I remarked earlier, means a man being the author of his actions. He would not be the author of his actions if they happened by chance. Equally, he would not be their author if he were compelled to act as he does. What was worrying about causal necessity was the thought that it implies compulsion. But if causal necessity means nothing but constant conjunction, that worry is removed. It still needs to be shown, however, that actions do not happen by chance. That would make a mockery of liberty. For Hume this means demonstrating that 'the uniformity observable in the operations of nature' (p. 82) is as observable in the operations of *human* nature as it is in the rest of nature.

He finds the key to this demonstration in the concept of *motive*.

Motives are such things as ambition, avarice, self-love, vanity, friendship, generosity, and public spirit (p. 83). They qualify as causes by virtue of the uniformity with which particular sorts of actions are observed to follow from particular motives. Take ambition. It qualifies as a cause, on Hume's theory of causation, because of the observable uniformity among the actions of ambitious people. And the same is true of the other motives. Avarice, for example. People motivated by avarice typically behave avariciously.

Hume devotes six pages (pp. 83–88) to illustrations of this, and concludes: 'Thus it appears, not only that the conjunction between motives and voluntary actions is as regular and uniform as that between the cause and effect in any part of nature; but also that this regular conjunction has been universally acknowledged among mankind, and has never been the subject of dispute, either in philosophy or common life' (p. 88).

In short, (a) motives cause people to act as they do, so their actions do not happen simply by chance. And (b) the necessity with which motives cause actions is nothing but the regular conjunction of motives and actions, so people are not compelled, by their motives, to act as they do. Liberty has been shown to be compatible with necessity, without being reduced to chance. The reconciliation is achieved.

This is what Hume thought. What did other philosophers think? It is time to consider the reception of Hume's reconciling project by other philosophers.

There are two main questions to consider. First, what did other philosophers think of what Hume said about motives as causes of actions? Secondly, what did they think of the empiricist account of causation as nothing but constant conjunction?

6. Motives as Causes: Criticism

Hume's treatment of motives as causes of actions had a mixed reception. Some philosophers approved. Others disapproved.

One who approved was David Hartley (1705–1757). Hartley's *Observations on Man* was published in 1749, the year after the publication of Hume's first *Enquiry*. Hartley closely followed Hume in what he said about motives. Hume said: 'the same motives always produce the same actions' (Hume [1748] 1975, p. 83). Hartley said: '. . . motives seem to act like all other causes . . . so that where the motives are the same, the actions cannot be different; where the motives are different, the actions cannot be the same'. Pursuing the theme that motives are like all other causes, Hartley described them as 'the mechanical causes of actions' (Brown, R., 1970, pp. 85–86).

Another philosopher who approved was John Stuart Mill (1806 1873). In his *System of Logic* (1843) Mill said that 'given the motives which are present to an individual's mind, and given likewise the character and disposition of the individual, the manner in which he will act might be unerringly inferred' (Mill [1843] 1974, VI.ii.2), and went on to say that those who think that this causation of actions by motives means that we are 'compelled, as by a magic spell, to obey any particular motive' have missed their way because they have rejected 'Hume's and Brown's analysis of Cause and Effect'. (Brown was Thomas Brown (1778–1820), author of *Observations on the Nature and Tendency of the Doctrine of Mr Hume Concerning the Relation of Cause and Effect* (1805).)

The chief eighteenth-century philosopher who disapproved of Hume's treatment of motives was the 'Montaigne of metaphysics', Abraham Tucker (1705–1774). Tucker began his only substantial work, *The Light of Nature Pursued* (1768) in about 1756, only a few years after the publication of Hume's first *Enquiry* and Hartley's *Observations on Man*. In Chapter 5, on 'Motives', he distinguished between what, following Aristotle, he called 'final causes' and the sort of causes that billiard balls are ('motor causes', in Aristotle's terminology). Suppose someone goes for a walk. The final cause is some end he proposes to himself, such as health. 'This final cause', Tucker says, 'we commonly style the Motive, by a metaphor taken from mechnical engines which cannot play without some spring or other mover to set them at work' (Brown, R., 1970, p. 103). Misled by the metaphor, we make the mistake of thinking of a motive as a 'motion, force, or impulse imparted to [the mind] . . . as there is to one billiard ball from another upon their striking'. We make such mistakes 'for want of first settling accurately with ourselves what they be'. 'A motive', Tucker says, 'is the prospect of some end actually in view of the mind at the time of action and urging to attain it' (p. 105).

If Tucker is right then Hartley was wrong when he said that motives 'act like all other causes'. The person who acts from some motive—ambition, for example—is not made to act by ambition in the way a billiard ball is made to move by another billiard ball striking it; he acts as he does because he wills some ambitious end; perhaps he wants to be Prime Minister one day. In Aristotelian terminology, motives are 'final' causes, not 'motor' causes.

Is this of any significance for the question whether our actions being caused is compatible with our acting freely? I think it is. If it is said that

(a) our actions are caused by motives,
(b) acting from a motive is acting as one does because one wills some desired end,

and

(c) being a free agent is being able to act as one wills,

then

(d) our actions being caused is compatible with our acting freely.

And in that case there is no need for a reconciling project involving an empiricist theory of causation.

7. Causation as Constant Conjunction: Criticism

Hume's theory of causation was the theory that 'we know nothing farther of causation of any kind than merely the *constant conjunction* of objects, and the consequent *inference* of the mind from one to another' (p. 92). The theory was a product of two things: first, Hume's non-recognition of kinds of causation which do not involve necessitation (Plato's causation by 'things which are endowed with mind and are the workers of things fair and good', and Aristotle's causation 'for the sake of something'), secondly, Hume's following the way of ideas, with all that that implies, including the empiricist version of the conformity assumption.

We have seen that if Hume had been prepared to acknowledge that motives are final causes, which do not necessitate, he could have saved himself the trouble of bringing his empiricist theory of causation to bear on the question of liberty and necessity. (He brought it to bear because he thought he needed to show that while motives necessitate (pp. 83, 87, 91, 92), they do not *compel*, since the necessitation is nothing but constant conjunction (pp. 82, 92–93, 96).)

Now let us consider Hume's theory, not as a means of reconciling liberty and necessity, but simply as a theory of causation.

The main question to be asked of any theory based on the conformity assumption is: does it do justice, or injustice, to our actual use of the word 'cause'? On this score there are two major criticisms that can be made of Hume's theory.

The first is that the theory does not cover the use of the word 'cause' in talk of *people* causing things to happen. We have already noticed that Hume turned a blind eye to Plato's talk of 'things endowed with mind' being causes. He turned the same blind eye to Descartes' talk of the *soul* as something within us 'which both moves the body and thinks' (Descartes [1649] 1970, p. 243), to Locke's talk of *agents*, with power to produce, continue or stop actions, and to his talk of liberty as a power that belongs to agents (Locke, 1690, II.xxi.14–15), and to Berkeley's talk of a *spirit* as a substance that 'acts, causes, wills, operates' (Berkeley [1707–1708] 1975, p. 331 (*Philosophical Commentaries*, 829)). That Hume should turn a blind eye to talk of souls or spirits causing bodily motions is understandable. He followed the way of ideas, and Berkeley had remarked that 'there can be no idea formed of a soul or spirit: for all ideas whatever, being passive or inert, they cannot represent unto us, by way of image or likeness, that which acts' (Berkeley [1710] 1975, p. 85 (*Principles of Human Knowledge*, 27)). Berkeley himself was prepared to talk of our having 'notions' of spirits, but evidently Hume was not.

The notion that people, as opposed to objects or events, cause things to happen is one that received a lot of attention in the 1960s. There were a great many papers, and chapters of books, on the subject (Vesey, 1961; Black, 1961; Chisholm, 1964; Kolnai, 1966; Taylor, 1966; Yolton, 1966; Thalberg, 1967; Davidson, 1968). Philosophers started talking, as Plato had done, of two kinds of causation. They called them 'agent causation', and 'event causation'. Roughly, agent causation is characterized by liberty; event causation, by necessity. Hume, it might be said in this new terminology, construed all causation as event causation.

The second major criticism that can be made of Hume's theory is that it grossly misrepresents our actual cause-finding practices. It suggests that we find out what causes what by passively registering sequences of events and allowing them to form habits of expectation in our minds.

There is, however, a complication. Hume, in the *Treatise* and *Enquiry*, provides various definitions of 'cause', mostly in line with his theory that the impression of which the idea of necessary connection is a copy is an internal impression. But part of one of his definitions is certainly not in line with that theory. It is the part that comes after the phrase 'or in other words' at the bottom of page 76 of the *Enquiry*. This is the passage:

> . . . we may define a cause to be *an object, followed by another, and where all the objects similar to the first are followed by objects similar to the second*. Or in other words *where, if the first object had not been, the second never had existed*.

There are three things to notice about the last part of this definition.

The first is that it is not equivalent to the first part. Whereas the first part suggests that we would call day the cause of night, because days *are* always followed by nights, the second part suggests that we would call the revolution of the earth on its axis the cause of the succession of day and night, because if the earth had *not* revolved on its axis the succession would *not* have existed. The second part points to a feature of our practice with the word 'cause' that is not pointed to by the first part. It is the feature of which Mill gave an example in his *Logic* nearly a hundred years later: 'if a person eats of a particular dish, and dies in consequence, that is, would not have died if he had not eaten of it, people would be apt to say that eating of that dish was the cause of his death' (Mill [1843] 1974, III.v.3).

The second thing to notice is that one cannot find out that so-and-so would *not* have happened if such-and-such had *not* happened by passively registering things that *do* happen. One needs to be active: to think up possible causal explanations, devise experiments to test them, conduct the experiments, and draw conclusions from the results.

The third thing to notice is that if one were asked 'What feature of our linguistic practice with the word "cause" is referred to by saying that there is a necessary connection between causes and effects?' it would at least be a start to say: 'It is part of what we mean when we say that X causally necessitates Y that *if* X *were* to happen Y *would* happen'.

8. Soccer or Rugger?

Recapitulation. We have seen what assumptions about language lie behind Hume's theory that causation is 'merely the *constant conjunction* of objects, and the consequent *inference* of the mind from one to another'. Hume concludes from his theory of causation that since motives are constantly conjoined with actions, they cause them; and that causes do not necessitate effects in a sense of 'necessitate' that involves compulsion. He concludes that necessity is compatible with liberty. And we have seen how some of Hume's views have been criticized. Abraham Tucker objected that motives are not motor, but final, causes of actions. And to Hume's theory of causation it has been objected that it does not do justice to the variety of our uses of the word 'cause'; and that it gives a false impression of what is involved in finding out what the cause of some phenomenon is: it is not a matter of passively registering sequences of events and allowing them to form habits of expectation; it is a matter of actively thinking up possible explanations, devising experiments to test them, conducting the experiments, and drawing conclusions from the results.

What further questions, if any, remain to be considered?

Given what I said about the assumptions about language that underlie Hume's theory of causation I can imagine you asking three questions: (i) What do present-day philosophers think of the thought-signifying assumption? (ii) What do they think of the conformity assumption? (iii) What would follow, for the question of liberty and necessity, if the assumptions were rejected?

(i) For quite a while after Hume the thought-signifying assumption was not questioned by philosophers. As I said earlier, it was regarded as a truism. The first bit of it to be questioned was the bit about ideas. F. H. Bradley (1846–1924), in his *Principles of Logic* (1883), attacked the notion that ideas are 'psychical particulars' that have some sort of permanence and can be recalled and resurrected to be associated with other ideas in thoughts. Such notions, Bradley said, are mere nonsense: 'These touching beliefs of a pious legend may babble in the tradition of a senile psychology, or contort themselves in the metaphysics of some frantic dogma, but philosophy must register them and sigh and pass on' (p. 280).

Philosophy notoriously takes its time about sighing and passing on. Old dogmas die hard. The dogma of the thought-signifying assumption is still very much with us. The *Philosophy of Rhetoric* (1776) of George Campbell is replaced by *The Philosophy of Language* (1966) of Jerold J. Katz. The terminology is more technical, but the assumptions are the same (Katz, 1966, pp. 98, 103).

The best place to find the thought-signifying assumption criticized is in the later works of Ludwig Wittgenstein (1889–1951). We make the mistake, Wittgenstein says, of 'looking for the use of a sign . . . as though it were an object *co-existing* with the sign' (Wittgenstein, 1958, p. 5; cf. 1980, Vol. II, sections 200–266). Wittgenstein's view, that 'if we had to name anything which is the life of a sign, we would have to say that it was its *use*' (1958, p. 4), is, I think, what lies behind the criticism of the thought-signifying assumption to be found in recent commentaries on Hume, such as Jonathan Bennett's *Locke, Berkeley, Hume* (1971 , pp. 1–11). I know it lies behind my own criticism of the assumption (Vesey, 1982).

(ii) What do present-day philosophers think of the conformity assumption?

The answer is that most present-day philosophers do not think of it at all. They *make* it, but are quite unaware of the possibility of not making it. It is a deep metaphysical assumption that is rarely articulated. It expresses itself in common philosophical responses to challenges of the form 'What justifies you in such-and-such a linguistic practice?' Suppose, for example, we are asked 'What justifies you, in general, in talking of people being responsible for their actions?' Instead of giving the common-sense response 'What are you suggesting? That we should stop doing so? If so, why?', we give the philosophical response 'We are justified by people's wills being free'. Similarly, if the question is 'What justifies you, in general, in looking for the causes of unexplained phenomena?', instead of giving the common-sense response 'What are you suggesting? That we should give up? If so, why?', we give the philosophical response 'We are justified by the fact that every event has a cause'.

This is the conformity assumption at work, producing the 'philosophical theories' we call 'libertarianism' and 'determinism'.

Many philosophers have qualms about declaring themselves to be libertarians or determinists, but only a few recognize and reject the assumption that leads to such philosophical theories. One who did reject the conformity assumption is Wittgenstein. Having said that it is the *use* of signs that give them life, he went on to assimilate different ways of talking to different games. He talked of *language-games*, to make the points (i) that the speaking of language is part of our life's activities (1953, Pt 1, Sections 23, 25), (ii) that just as there are any number of games so there are any number of uses of signs (1953, Pt 1, Section 23), (iii) that just as there are rules of games so there are rules of language (or, as he preferred to put it, *rules of grammar*) (1953, Pt 1, Sections 31ff.), and (iv) that just as it does not make sense to ask whether the rules now followed in some game, such as chess or soccer, are the right ones, so it does not make sense to ask whether certain rules of grammar are the right ones (1967, Section 320; cf. Rhees, 1982). The rules of grammar are arbitrary, Wittgenstein said; the use of language is in a certain sense autonomous:

> One is tempted to justify rules of grammar by sentences like 'But there really are four primary colours'. And the saying that the rules of

> grammar are arbitrary is directed against the possibility of this justification, which is constructed on the model of justifying a sentence by pointing to what verifies it (1967, Section 331).

Wittgenstein rejected the conformity assumption.

(iii) What would follow, for the question of liberty and necessity, if the conformity assumption were rejected?

Let it be granted that libertarianism and determinism are incompatible. Libertarianism is what, on the conformity assumption, justifies our treating people as responsible for their actions. They have 'free will': their acts of will are uncaused. Determinism is what, on the conformity assumption, justifies our treating phenomena as things to be explained causally. It says that events are causally determined. Now, if acts of will are free—that is, not caused—then it is false that all events are causally determined. And if all events are causally determined then it is false that some are not. There is no getting away from it. Libertarianism and determinism are incompatible.

Suppose, however, that the conformity assumption is rejected. Then we can forget about libertarianism and determinism. We are left with our practice of treating people as responsible for their actions, on the one hand, and our practice of treating phenomena as things to be explained causally, on the other. Are *they* incompatible?

Suppose you are a psychotherapist, and someone comes to you in a depressed state. At first you are not quite sure how to treat him. There are two possibilities. People can be treated as morally responsible agents; that is, as beings to whom attitudes such as resentment, gratitude, forgiveness, anger and love, are appropriate. P. F. Strawson (1962) calls this taking an attitude of involvement or participation towards people. Taking such an attitude you might *reason* with the depressed person, trying to get him to look on the bright side. Alternatively you might conclude, perhaps from the ineffectiveness of your reasoning therapy, that a quite different sort of approach is called for. You might suspect that the depression is due to an excess, or a deficiency, of some chemical substance in the person's brain. In that case you might resort to physical methods of treatment—drugs and so forth. That would mean treating him, not as a responsible agent, but as an *object*.

Now, is treating a person as a responsible agent incompatible with treating him as an object? Is there an incompatibility at this practical level?

There is certainly some sort of incompatibility here. I once had a friend with schizophrenia. Sometimes I was able to take the attitude of involvement or participation towards him; at other times I had to distance myself from him and virtually treat him as an object. One cannot take both attitudes at the same time. But I do not see this as a *philosophical* problem. One cannot play soccer and rugger at the same time, either.

Bibliography

Aristotle (1941) *The Basic Works of Aristotle*, edited and with an introduction by R. McKeon (New York: Random House).

Bennett, J. (1971) *Locke, Berkeley, Hume: Central Themes* (Oxford: Clarendon Press).

Berkeley, G. [1707–1710] (1975) *Philosophical Works*, introduction and notes by M. R. Ayers (London: Dent).

Black M. (1961) 'Making Something Happen', in S. Hook (ed.), *Determinism and Freedom in the Age of Modern Science* (New York: Macmillan).

Bradley, F. H. (1883) *The Principles of Logic* (London: Kegan Paul, Trench & Co).

Brown, R. (ed.) (1970) *Between Hume and Mill* (New York: Random House).

Brown, T. (1805) *Observations on the Nature and Tendency of the Doctrine of Mr Hume Concerning the Relation of Cause and Effect* (Edinburgh: Mundall and Son).

Campbell, G. [1776] (1823) *The Philosophy of Rhetoric*, 7th edn (London: William Baynes).

Chisholm, R. M. (1964) 'Human Freedom and the Self', in G. Watson (ed.) (1982) *Free Will* (Oxford University Press).

Davidson, D. (1968) 'Agency', in R. Binkley, R. Bronaugh and A. Marras (eds) (1971) *Agent, Action and Reason* (Oxford: Blackwell) and in D. Davidson (1980) *Essays on Actions and Events* (Oxford: Clarendon).

Descartes, R. [1641] (1912) *A Discourse on Method, Meditations on the First Philosophy, Principles of Philosophy*, translated by J. Veitch, introduction by A. D. Lindsay (London: Dent).

Hartley, D. [1749] (1834) *Observations on Man, His Frame, His Duty and His Expectations*, 6th edn (London: Thomas Tegg and Son).

Hobbes, T. [1651] (1914) *Leviathan*, introduction by A. D. Lindsay (London: Dent).

Hume, D. [1739] (1888) *A Treatise of Human Nature*, L. A. Selby-Bigge (ed.) (Oxford: Clarendon).

Hume, D. [1748] (1975) *An Enquiry Concerning Human Understanding*, in *Hume's Enquiries*, L. A. Selby-Bigge (ed.) with revisions by P. Niddich (Oxford: Clarendon).

Katz, J. J. (1966) *The Philosophy of Language* (New York: Harper & Row).

Kolnai, A. (1966) 'Agency and Freedom', in G. N. A. Vesey (ed.) (1968) *The Human Agent*, Royal Institute of Philosophy Lectures, Vol. 1, 1966/7 (London: Macmillan).

Locke, J. [1690] (1961) *An Essay Concerning Human Understanding*, edited with an introduction by J. W. Yolton (London: Dent).

Malebranche, N. [1674–1675] (1980) *The Search After Truth*, translated by T. M. Lennon and P. J. Olscamp (Ohio State University Press).

Mill, J. S. [1843] (1974) *A System of Logic Ratiocinative and Inductive*, J. M. Robson (ed.), introduced by R. F. McRae, in *Collected Works of John Stuart Mill* (Toronto: University of Toronto Press; London: Routledge and Kegan Paul).

Plato (1961) *The Collected Dialogues of Plato*, E. Hamilton and H. Cairns (eds) (New York: Pantheon).

Rhees, R. (1982) 'Language and Reality', *The Gadfly* **5,** No. 2.

Strawson, P. F. (1962) 'Freedom and Resentment', in P. F. Strawson (ed.) (1968) *Studies in the Philosophy of Thought and Action* (Oxford University Press), P. F. Strawson (1974) *Freedom and Resentment* (London: Methuen) and in G. Watson (ed.) *Free Will* (Oxford University Press).

Taylor, R. (1966) *Action and Purpose* (New Jersey: Prentice-Hall).

Thalberg, I. (1967) 'Do We Cause Our Own Actions?', *Analysis* **27.**

Tucker, A. [1768] (1834) *The Light of Nature Pursued*, 3rd edn (London: Thomas Tegg and Son).

Vesey, G. N. A. (1961) 'Volition', *Philosophy* **36**, and in D. F. Gustafson (ed.) (1967) *Essays in Philosophical Psychology* (London: Macmillan).

Vesey, G. (1982) 'Is Talk a Mode of Transport?', *The Gadfly*, **5**, No. 4.

Weis, C. M. (ed.) (1970) *Boswell in Extremes 1776–1778* (New York: McGraw-Hill).

Wittgenstein, L. (1953) *Philosophical Investigations*, translated by G. E. M. Anscombe (Oxford: Blackwell).

Wittgenstein, L. (1958) *The Blue and Brown Books* (Oxford: Blackwell).

Wittgenstein, L. (1967) *Zettel*, G. E. M. Anscombe and G. H. von Wright (eds), translated by G. E. M. Anscombe (Oxford: Blackwell).

Wittgenstein, L. (1980) *Remarks on the Philosophy of Psychology*, G. H. von Wright and Heikki Nyman (eds), translated by C. G. Luckhardt and M. A. E. Aue (Oxford: Blackwell).

Yolton, J. (1966) 'Agent Causality', *American Philosophical Quarterly* **3**.

Hume's Philosophy of Religion

ANTONY FLEW

I shall be dealing with not only Sections X and XI but also Part II of Section VIII and Part III of Section XII. Of all this material we have, anywhere in the originally anonymous and later emphatically disowned *Treatise of Human Nature*, Hume's first book, nothing more than at most hints. But in a surviving letter, written while he was still working on the manuscript of that *Treatise*, Hume wrote: 'I am at present castrating my work, that is, cutting off its nobler parts; that is, endeavouring it shall give as little offence as possible, before which I would not pretend to put it in the Doctor's hands'.[1] Enclosed with this letter were some 'Reasonings concerning Miracles', which must have anticipated what became Section X of our *Enquiry*. Presumably there were other excised anticipations also. The 'Doctor' mentioned was a Doctor of Theology, Joseph Butler, soon to be appointed Bishop of Durham; an office open in that period only to believing Christians.

1. The Aims of Our Enquiry

The first thing to be said about all this—to some—offensive material is that the findings which Hume is presenting in these passages were in his eyes the main trophies of the whole *Enquiry*. This has to be emphasized because Sections X and XI were at one time dismissed as some sort of irrelevant and intrusive interpellation. Thus, in the edition of Hume's *Essays Literary Moral and Political* in Sir John Lubbock's Hundred Books series, they are both cut out from the *Enquiry* and printed in an appendix of supplementary pieces, introduced by a remarkable note beginning: 'These essays are generally omitted in popular editions of the writings of Hume'. Again, in what after nearly a century still remains with some revisions the standard edition, the original editor maintained in his Introduction that they are 'quite superfluous'. He added nastily: 'Their insertion . . . is due doubtless rather to other considerations than to a simple desire to draw corollaries from the

[1] R. Klibansky and E. C. Mossner, *New Letters of David Hume* (Oxford: Clarendon, 1954), 2–3.

philosophical principles laid down . . .' Apparently these supposed 'other considerations' could not but have been to Hume's discredit.[2]

Such editors of former days seem never to have thought: either to ask what Hume's project was; or to refer for the answer to his own statements. His very choice of title should have been a sufficient clue. For, as all Hume's philosophically interested contemporaries would at once have recognized, it is deliberately modelled on that of John Locke's *Essay Concerning Human Understanding*. In his prefatory Epistle to the Reader Locke had explained how:

> . . .*five or six Friends meeting at my Chamber, and discoursing on a Subject very remote from this, found themselves quickly at a stand, by the Difficulties that rose on every side. After we had a while puzzled our selves, without coming any nearer a Resolution of those Doubts which perplexed us, it came into my Thoughts, that we took a wrong course; and that, before we set our selves upon Enquiries of that Nature, it was necessary to examine our own Abilities, and see, what Objects our Understandings were, or were not fitted to deal with. This I proposed to the Company, who all readily assented; and thereupon it was agreed, that this should be our first Enquiry.*[3]

It was Hume's too. In his Section I he indicates that his own findings are going to be more drastic and more this-worldly than anything in Locke. After distinguishing two kinds of philosophy he admits to pursuing 'the profound and abstract' rather than 'the easy and obvious'. The former 'is objected to, not only as painful and fatiguing, but as the inevitable source of uncertainty and error'. Here, he continues:

> lies the justest and most plausible objection against a considerable part of metaphysics, that they are not properly a science; but arise either from the fruitless efforts of human vanity, which would penetrate into subjects utterly inaccessible to the understanding, or from the craft of popular superstitions, which, being unable to defend themselves on fair ground, raise these intangling brambles to cover and protect their weakness . . .
>
> The only method of freeing learning, at once, from these abstruse

[2] These quotations come from L. A. Selby-Bigge's 1893 Introduction to D. Hume, *Enquiries Concerning Human Understanding and Concerning the Principles of Morals*, 3rd edn (Oxford: Clarendon, 1975), viii and xix. All later references to the first *Enquiry* will be given parenthetically, and will be to this publication. Fortunately the pagination has been held stable since the 1st edn of 1893.

[3] J. Locke, *An Essay Concerning Human Understanding*, P. H. Nidditch (ed.) (Oxford: Clarendon, 1975), 7.

> questions, is to enquire seriously into the nature of human understanding, and show, from an exact analysis of its powers and capacity, that it is by no means fitted for such remote and abstruse subjects (pp. 11–12).

How this emancipation is to be achieved begins to become clear in Part II of Section VIII. With disingenuous discretion Hume pretends to be embarrassed by a dilemma:

> The ultimate Author of all our volitions is the Creator of the world, who first bestowed motion on this immense machine, and placed all beings in that particular position, whence every subsequent event, by an inevitable necessity, must result. Human actions, therefore, either can have no moral turpitude at all, as proceeding from so good a cause; or, if they have any turpitude, they must involve our Creator in the same guilt, while he is acknowledged to be their ultimate cause and author (pp. 99–100).

To the first of these options Hume is delighted to respond by insisting that the distinction between virtue and vice is founded: not on 'religious fears and prejudices' (p. 11); but, much more securely, 'in the natural sentiments of the human mind: And these sentiments are not to be controuled or altered by any philosophical theory or speculation whatsoever'. About the second option Hume confesses himself embarrassed. Yet this is, of course, nothing but a prudent pretence. For he at once proceeds: first, to explain the intractable difficulties of the theologians as showing something about the limits of human understanding; and then to draw what was for him a most congenial practical moral:

> To reconcile the indifference and contingency of human actions with prescience; or to defend absolute decrees, and yet free the Deity from being the author of sin, has been found hitherto to exceed all the power of philosophy. Happy, if she be thence sensible of her temerity, when she pries into these sublime mysteries; and, leaving a scene so full of obscurities and perplexities, return, with suitable modesty, to her true and proper province, the examination of common life; where she will find difficulties enough to employ her enquiries, without launching into so boundless an ocean of doubt, uncertainty, and contradiction! (p. 103).[4]

[4] For examples of previous misunderstandings, as well as for a fuller general treatment of this Part II of Section VIII, compare my *Hume's Philosophy of Belief* (London: Routledge and Kegan Paul, 1961), 159–165. Since that was the first whole book to be devoted to this *Enquiry*, and since it seems still to be the most frequently mentioned and the most comprehensive, I am bound to

2. The Traditional, Two-stage, Rational Apologetic

Turning next to Sections X and XI, the first thing to bring out is that and how they are complementary. They are complementary in as much as each attacks one stage of the traditional two-stage rational apologetic for the Christian religion. The first consists in attempts to establish, by arguments of natural reason, and without appealing to any supposed special revelation, the bare existence of the agreeably unobtrusive God of the Deists.[5] This somewhat sketchy religion of nature (or natural religion) is in the second stage supplemented by a more detailed and abundant revelation. The authenticity of the one true candidate is established through the working of endorsing miracles. How indeed could a Creator better manifest both His existence and His approval than by thus displaying a privileged power to override the ordinary laws of nature? And what, once all this is appreciated, could be more relevant to Hume's project than to discover whether or not we are capable of completing an apologetic programme of this sort?

The form typically taken in Hume's century by that two-stage apologetic was epitomized, at the end of that century and after, in two famous works by Archdeacon William Paley: *Natural Theology* (1802) and *Evidences of Christianity* (1794). But its popularity has certainly not been confined either to a single century or to Protestants. Indeed—although, since the Second Vatican Council began to have its unintended effects of eroding the Catholic faith, this seems to have been widely forgotten—the First Vatican Council went so far as to define as essential dogma belief in the possibility of completing both stages. Thus one ruling reads: 'If anyone shall say, that the one and the true God, our Creator and Lord, cannot be [not demonstrated but] known for certain by the natural light of human reason; let him be cast out'. Again: 'If anyone shall say, that miracles can never be known for certain, or that the Divine origin of the Christian religion cannot

---

seize every opportunity to indicate the places where my treatment was, I am now persuaded, either inadequate or even downright wrong. This is one of those places. For I failed to notice or to make anything of the fact that, in talking of what 'by an inevitable necessity, must result', Hume was employing a far stronger concept of causation than that to which he was officially prepared to lend countenance. See, in particular, my 'Inconsistency Within "a Reconciling Project"', in *Hume Studies* (London, Ontario) **iv** (1978), 1–6; and, in general, my 'Another Idea of Necessary Connection,' in *Philosophy* (1982), 487–940.

[5] Here and elsewhere students are recommended to possess, and to be ever ready to consult, *A Dictionary of Philosophy*, 2nd edn (London: Macmillan and Pan Books, 1984).

properly be proved by them; let him be cast out'.[6] Let him, that is, in the traditional form of words, be anathema (anathematized).

We must, therefore, allow that Hume was sticking to the aggressive resolutions of Section I: not to 'leave superstition still in possession of her retreat'; but instead to 'perceive the necessity of carrying the war into the most secret recesses of the enemy'. Yet the tone and temper of Sections X and XI are totally different one from the other. Whereas in treating 'Of Miracles' Hume goes out of his way to give offence, in Section XI there is no coat-trailing provocation. Much of the message is put into other, imaginary mouths. It is as if Hume intended Section X to draw fire which might otherwise have been directed at Section XI; a suggestion which would explain why stage one is dealt with not before but after stage two.

To understand this difference we need to appreciate the eighteenth-century background.[7] For, whereas Hume was in Section X attacking openly and directly in an area where Deist writers had been sniping for a long time, in Section XI he was sapping to undermine a formerly unchallenged citadel. Thus Butler's *Analogy of Religion*, the classic contemporary reply to the Deists, simply assumed that the Argument to Design[8] was unthreatened and undisputed common ground: 'There is no need of abstruse reasonings and distinctions, to convince an unprejudiced understanding, that there is a God who made and governs the world, and will judge it in righteousness . . . to an unpre-

[6] The Latin texts run: *Si quis dixerit Deum unum et verum, creatorem et Dominum nostrum, per ea quae facta sunt naturali rationis humanae lumine certo cognosci non posse: anathema sit*; and *Si quis dixerit, . . . miracula certo cognosci numquam posse nec iis divinam religionis christianae originem rite probari: anathema sit*. In the second of these *certo cognosci* replaced the draft *demonstrari*. These canons are Numbers 1806 and 1813 in H. Denzinger *Encheiridion Symbolorum*, 29th rev. edn (Freiberg im Breisgau: Herder, 1953). It is often said to be a truism that everyone knows how impossible it is to prove either the existence or the non-existence of God. This 'truism' will not, however, actually become true until there are no longer any instructed and believing Catholics.

[7] The best secondary source remains Leslie Stephen, *English Thought in the Eighteenth Century*, 3rd edn (London: Murray, 1902).

[8] This is usually known as the Argument *from* Design. I prefer to call it the Argument *to* Design. For at its best and strongest it does not move: from the disputatious and question-begging premise that the Universe is an artefact; to the necessary conclusion that it must have been made by a Universe-Maker. Instead it proceeds, from the undisputatious and unprejudicial premise that the Universe manifests the regularities and the integration which it does manifest, to the conclusion that these phenomena, and indeed the very existence of the Universe, can only and must be explained by the postulation of a Designer and Maker of all things.

judiced mind ten thousand thousand instances of design cannot but prove a designer'.[9]

It is in truth the argument which Butler is citing here as sufficient and decisive which Hume sets out to destroy. For, of all the traditional arsenal of natural theology, it alone deserved and won his respect. In the exultant final paragraphs of this *Enquiry* Hume wreaks havoc already implicit in Section IV. It was all implicit in that initial fundamental dichotomy: between propositions stating, or purporting to state, the relations of ideas; and those stating, or purporting to state, matters of more than merely conceptual fact. It was also embryonic in the subsequent development of Hume's great negative thesis about causality. That is the thesis, reiterated here, that it is only by reference to the ways in which the world does actually wag—though it is always conceivable that it might have wagged differently—that we can know what things, or sorts of things, must be, or cannot be, the causes of other things, or sorts of things. In this concluding Part III of Section XII the notorious Ontological Argument is seen off in four or five short, decisive sentences:

> All other enquiries of men regard only matter of fact and existence; and these are evidently incapable of demonstration. Whatever *is* may *not be*. No negation of a fact can involve a contradiction. The non-existence of any being, without exception, is as clear and distinct an idea as its existence . . . But that Caesar, or the angel Gabriel, or any being never existed, may be a false proposition, but still is perfectly conceivable, and implies no contradiction.

All the rest of the other traditional arguments are dismissed in similarly short order:

> The existence, therefore, of any being can only be proved by arguments from its cause or its effect; and these arguments are founded entirely on experience. If we reason *a priori*, anything may appear able to produce anything (pp. 163–164).

3. The Assault upon 'the Religious Hypothesis'

The reason why Hume respected the Argument to Design is that it is of the right sort. It attempts to establish a 'matter of fact and existence' by appealing to experience, arguing from effect to cause. In Section XI Hume puts up his 'Epicurus' to define 'the religious hypothesis', thus marking out the precise nature and limits of the discussion proposed:

[9] II (ix): see, for instance, the *Works*, edited by W. E. Gladstone (Oxford: University Press, 1896). Yes, this editor was indeed the Liberal statesman.

> You then, who are my accusers, have acknowledged, that the chief or sole argument for a divine existence (which I never questioned) is derived from the order of nature; where there appear such marks of intelligence and design, that you think it extravagant to assign for its cause, either chance, or the blind and unguided force of matter. You allow, that this is an argument drawn from effects to causes. From the order of the work, you infer, that there must have been project and forethought in the workman. If you cannot make out this point, you allow, that your conclusion fails; and you pretend not to establish the conclusion in a greater latitude than the phenomena of nature will justify (pp. 135–136).

'These', the speaker continues, 'are your concessions. I desire you to mark the consequences.' The first, though important enough, is comparatively minor. It is that no one arguing in this way has any business to conclude that the hypothesized Divine Workman possesses any attributes over and above those minimally required to account for whatever is actually manifested in the Work. It will not do, therefore, notwithstanding that it is all too often done: first to postulate—in order to account for the existence of the Universe and the order and integration which we have found therein—an intelligent Super Power; and then forthwith—without any further reason given—to insist that that hypothetical Being must be, not just sufficiently powerful and sufficiently intelligent to produce the supposed creation, but in sober truth both strictly omnipotent and strictly omniscient. In fact—as has by now been remarked often—evidences of design of their very nature could not point to so extreme a conclusion. For design is essentially a matter of finding within whatever are the given limitations the best available means to whatever are the proposed ends, of exploiting the various strengths and weaknesses of inherently recalcitrant materials, and so on. But a Being which really is both omnipotent and omniscient cannot by definition be subject to any limitations; unless, of course, that Being has itself chosen to become so subject. So evidences of design can by themselves point only to a different God, and a much smaller one than the God of mainstream traditional theism.

Things are, if anything, worse with such evaluative characteristics as benevolence or perfection. For here the case is not that the evidence is insufficient to warrant, but that it appears actually to refute, the desired drastic conclusion. It is relevant to repeat the first of the two basic objections to any natural theology, as formulated by Aquinas: '. . . if of two contrary things one were to exist without limit the other would be totally eliminated. But what is meant by this word 'God' is something good without limit. So if God were to have existed no evil would have been encountered. But evil is encountered in the world. Therefore, God does not exist.'[10]

Hume, however, is here simply warming up. He has not yet so much as begun to deploy his own fresh-forged weapons. Instead he chooses first to present his opponent's argument at its strongest, and in his own person:

> If you saw, for instance, a half-finished building surrounded with heaps of brick and stone and mortar and all the instruments of masonry, could you not *infer* new additions to the effect, and conclude, that the building would soon be finished, and receive all the further improvements which art could bestow upon it? If you saw upon the sea-shore the print of one human foot, you would conclude that a man had passed that way, and that he had also left the traces of the other foot.[11] Why then do you refuse to admit the same method of reasoning with regard to the order of nature? (p. 143).

For anyone proposing to resist the Argument to Design that is indeed the sixty-four thousand dollar question. How can that parity be denied? Thanks to what he once called 'my abundant prudence' Hume's answer has to be unwrapped and pieced together before it can be appreciated to the full. In consequence many readers fail to get the message; notwithstanding that there is no wanton obscurity or obfuscation here, any more than there is anywhere else in Hume's writings.

When, however, a German translation of the first *Enquiry* eventually reached Königsberg,[12] Immanuel Kant, the other supreme philosophical talent of the Age of Enlightenment, at once recognized both the elegance and the overwhelming force of Hume's reply. It was, as Kant generously confessed, reading Hume—and above all, surely, reading Sections IV and XI—'which awoke me from my dogmatic slumbers'; stimulating Kant to develop his characteristic 'critical philosophy'.[13]

[10] *Summa Theologica*, I, Q2 A3: Aquinas, of course, believed that he had an adequate answer to this objection. For further discussion compare, for instance, my *God and Philosophy* (London: Hutchinson, 1967. Reissued in 1984 by Open Court of La Salle, Illinois, as *God: A Philosophical Critique*) or my *The Presumption of Atheism* (London: Pemberton/Elek, 1967. Reissued in 1984 as *God, Freedom and Immortality* by Prometheus of Buffalo, New York).

[11] Defoe's *Robinson Crusoe* was first published in 1719, when Hume was eight years old. So he was, presumably, a member of one of the first schoolboy generations to enjoy that splendid story book.

[12] This famous place name is not to be found on modern maps. It has been replaced by 'Kaliningrad'; in consequence of the fact that in 1945 the wholly German population was driven out, to be replaced by Great Russians.

[13] See, for instance, Kant's *Prolegomena to any Future Metaphysics*, translated and edited by P. G. Lucas (Manchester University Press, 1953).

Hume disrupts the apparent parity in the simplest and most direct way. He points out that, in the peculiar case of the Argument to Design, both the putative effect and the hypothesized cause are, essentially and inescapably, unique. Hence the implication, again, must be that the whole subject lies beyond the range of causal inference and argument from experience.

In shaping an ordinary explanatory hypothesis—such as, for instance, the Kinetic Theory of Gases—we attribute to any postulated entities, even when these are supposed not to be directly observable, some characteristics enabling us to deduce some consequences which, if our hypothesis is correct, must obtain. But in the case of the Super Entity hypothesized in the Argument to Design all such deductions are, necessarily, invalid. It is Hume's alter ego—'a friend who loves sceptical paradoxes' (p. 132)—who is scripted to make this objection.

> The Deity is known to us only by his productions, and is a single being in the universe, not comprehended under any species or genus, from whose experienced attributes or qualities, we can, by analogy, infer any attribute or quality in him. . . . The great source of our mistake in this subject . . . is that we tacitly consider ourselves as in the place of the Supreme Being. . . . But besides that the ordinary course of nature may convince us, that almost everything is regulated by principles and maxims very different from ours . . . it must evidently appear contrary to all rules of analogy to reason from the intentions and projects of men, to those of a Being so different, and so much superior (pp. 144–145).

The first half of Hume's response is thus as cool as it is crushing. It has consisted simply in drawing out—with the simplicity of genius—a necessary but previously unnoticed consequence of the accepted defining characteristics of the theist God. Had not Butler himself argued in the *Analogy*: 'Upon supposition that God exercises a moral government over the world, the analogy of this natural government suggests and makes it credible that this moral government must be a scheme quite beyond our comprehension; and this affords a general answer to all objections against the justice and goodness of it'.[14]

The second half of Hume's response is completely complementary, running perfectly parallel to the first. But it is added as an apparent afterthought, issued frankly from his own mouth:

> . . . there occurs to me . . . a difficulty, which I shall just propose to you without insisting upon it . . . It is only when two *species* of objects are found to be constantly conjoined, that we can infer the

[14] Op. cit., II (ix).

> one from the other. . . . If experience and observation and analogy be, indeed, the only guides which we can reasonably follow in inferences of this nature; both the effect and cause must bear a similarity . . . to other effects and causes, which we know, and which we have found, in many instances, to be conjoined with each other. I leave it to your own reflection to pursue the consequences of this principle. I shall just observe, that, . . . the antagonists of Epicurus always suppose the Universe, an effect quite singular and unparalleled, to be a proof of a Deity, a cause no less singular and unparalleled . . .[15]

This Parthian shot shows that Hume saw the second crucial difference, disrupting the supposed parity of reasoning. Nevertheless he preferred, for the moment, to leave it to others to insist upon it; 'lest it lead into reasonings of too nice and delicate a nature'.[16] For not only is the hypothetical cause in this case unique, by definition. The same is equally true also of its putative effect. For, although there is a regrettable sense in which the Andromeda Nebula might be spoken of as 'an island universe', the Universe whose existence and regularities 'the religious hypothesis' might be thought to explain is specified as including everything there is (with the exception of its possible Creator). But this second essential uniqueness also carries its own devastating consequence. However far back we may be able to trace the—so to speak—internal history of the Universe, there can be no question of arguing that this or that external origin is either probable or improbable. We do not have, and we necessarily could not have, experience of other Universes to tell us that Universes, or Universes with these particular features, are always, or most likely, the work of Gods, or of Gods of this or that particular sort. To improve slightly on a famous remark by C. S. Pierce: 'Universes, unlike universes, are not as plentiful as blackberries'. (Here the word 'Universe' in its first occurrence would have had an initial capital irrespective of its position in the sentence, in order to distinguish it as referring to all there is, as opposed to 'universe' referring to one of a possibly numerous class.)

It may help here to imagine some more than Methuselah in a space ship approaching some still unexplored 'island universe'. He might

[15] The initial letter of the word 'Universe' is here printed in upper case, as it was not by Hume; for reasons indicated in the following paragraph.

[16] What more Hume had to say is to be found in his posthumously published masterpiece, the *Dialogues Concerning Natural Religion*. The standard edition, by Norman Kemp Smith, was originally published in 1935 by the Clarendon Press. At the time of writing this was available only in paperback and as an item in the Library of Liberal Arts (Indianapolis: Bobbs-Merrill, no date given).

well, to the exasperated distress of his younger colleagues, refer to the wealth of his experience: 'Mark my words. Man and boy these million million years I have . . .'; and so on, and no doubt on and on and on. But the unique Universe is and must be itself all we have. How it is, is just how it is; and that's that.

The conclusion, which I myself believe that Hume drew,[17] is that we should take as our ultimates the existence of the Universe itself, with whatever fundamental characteristics our scientists discover it to posssess. This is a version of what Hume, following Pierre Bayle, called 'The Stratonician atheism'.[18]

To appreciate the strength of such a position, we need to be seized of the point that every system of explanation must include at least some fundamentals which are not themselves explained. However far you rise in an hierarchy of explanations—particular events in terms of general laws, laws in terms of theories, theories in terms of wider and more comprehensive theories, and maybe even further—still there has to be at every stage, including the last stage, some element or some elements in terms of which whatever is at that stage explained is explained. Nor is this inevitability of logic escaped by the theist. For, whatever else he may think to explain by reference to the existence and nature of his God, he cannot thereby avoid taking that existence and that nature as itself ultimate and beyond explanation.[19]

This necessity is common to all systems. It is no fault in any, and certainly not a competitive weakness. The Principle of Sufficient Reason—that there has to be a sufficient reason for anything and everything being as it is, was, and will be—is not, as has often been thought, necessarily true. It is instead demonstrably false. Granted this insight, how can we fail to see that there is no possible explanatory point in hypothesizing a First Cause, to which all and only those powers and inclinations necessary and sufficient to guarantee the production of the Universe as it is, are then gratuitously attributed? In what are always said to be the words of William of Ockham: 'Entities are not to be multiplied beyond necessity'.[20]

[17] Mainly because the *Dialogues* are a work of art, scholars disagree about what Hume's personal position was.

[18] The eponymous Strato of Lampsacus was next but one after Aristotle as Head of the Lyceum. He seems to have been an Aristotelian, but without any of Aristotle's Platonic hang-ups.

[19] See Terence Penelhum 'Divine Necessity' in *Mind* (1960). Or see, perhaps more accessibly, either my *An Introduction to Western Philosophy* (London: Thames and Hudson, 1971), 202–203, 265, and 386–387; or my *Philosophy: An Introduction* (London: Hodder and Stoughton, 1979), 107 and 135–138.

[20] The carefully situated stilted phrasing allows for the tiresome fact that this most cited sentence is not to be found in Ockham's extant works, although there are others saying much the same thing.

4. The Proof of the Miraculous

If Hume's hope in being so egregiously provocative in Section X was to draw fire away from Section XI, then his policy has to be rated a splendid success. For the single Section 'Of Miracles' must have given rise to more uproar than all the rest of his works put together. In the autobiographical note written in the year of his death Hume confessed, somewhat smugly, that—after a distressingly slow start—'Answers by Reverends and Right Reverends came out two or three in a year . . .'

So now, what was Hume arguing in this so strikingly scandalous Section X? The first point to seize is that his main aim is to show, from the very nature of the concept of the miraculous, that there must be a peculiar and extraordinary difficulty in establishing that a miracle has occurred; and that for this reason, reinforced by others of a less fundamental and less philosophical kind, 'a miracle can never be proved, so as to be the foundation of a system of religion' (p. 127). He is not concerned, or not primarily concerned, with fact but with evidence: the investigation is, for those who love to employ the big words of the syllabi, not ontological but epistemological. Once we have recognized what the aims of the first *Enquiry* actually were, all this is seen as being as it should be. For what Hume had to maintain was, only and precisely: that miracles can never be *known for certain*; or, at any rate, that the Divine origin of the Christian religion cannot thereby *properly be proved*.

Second, and consequently, there is no room for debate about the possible introduction of some alternative and perhaps more fashionable notion of what a miracle would have to be. For Hume is employing the very same concept which his chosen opponents not only did but could not but employ. Neither they nor he had any real choice. For nothing except some very strong notion of a natural order will provide sufficient purchase for a suitably Supernatural overriding. Yet that is exactly what is required if we are to have—against all competition from other pretenders—our manifest Divine endorsement of the single, approved, authentic Revelation.

A third preliminary is to underline what ought always to have been the obvious truth that Section X is contribution at the same time not only to the philosophy of religion but also to the philosophy of history, and even to that of parapsychology.[21] It is not for nothing that the author of our *Enquiry* is listed still in the catalogue of the British

[21] 'Parapsychology' is the new name for what used to be called psychical research. For the relevance of Hume's argument to this see, for instance, Antony Flew (ed.), *Philosophical Issues in Parapsychology* (Buffalo, NY: Prometheus, 1986), Part III.

Museum Library as 'Hume, David, the historian'. His interests both in 'history, sacred and profane' (p. 110) and in sound historical method are already visible here, not only in Section X but also earlier in Part I of Section VIII. It is, nevertheless, remarkable how this aspect of his treatment 'Of Miracles' has been overlooked by philosophers who should have been most alert to it. Thus F. H. Bradley in a seminal pamphlet on 'The Presuppositions of Critical History' made no mention of his main philosophical precursor;[22] while R. G. Collingwood, even in a particular discussion of Hume as an historiographer, entirely ignores this *Enquiry*.[23]

Collingwood's oversight is the more remarkable, and perhaps the more regrettable, since he could have found here gratifyingly good grist to a favourite mill. For Hume discusses only testimonial evidence for the occurrence of the miraculous. So his discussion has no direct bearing upon the question of what, if anything, might be established by a natural scientific examination of the Shroud of Turin. Such exclusive concentration upon the testimonial was something which Collingwood would have loved to denounce as 'scissors-and-paste' history; history which fails to put, and to try to force out an answer to, its own questions about what actually happened.

Hume's fundamental point, is, like all the great insights in philosophy, extremely simple. It is that 'from the very nature of the fact' (p. 114)—or, more trendily, from the very logic of the concept—there cannot but be a conflict of evidence: all the evidence we have for saying that such and such laws of nature do in fact hold must be, at the same time and necessarily, evidence against the truth of any claim that an overriding of any of these laws has in fact occurred.

By the way: if we were equipped with some trusty means of distinguishing genuinely miraculous overridings from occurrences constituting falsifications of what were previously believed to be laws of nature, then perhaps we might escape this dilemma. But this release must involve identifying miracles by reference to the Revelation, rather than validating the Revelation by reference to miracles. And this possibility, if indeed it is a possibility, is not what is at present in question.

So, returning to that, what Hume calls 'this contrariety of evidence' (p. 112) is first considered where:

> the fact, which the testimony endeavours to establish, partakes of the extraordinary and the marvellous; in that case, the evidence, resulting from the testimony, admits of a diminution, greater or less, in

[22] This nineteenth-century work is reprinted as Chapter I of Volume I of his *Collected Essays* (Oxford University Press, 1935).

[23] See his *The Idea of History* (Oxford: Clarendon, 1946).

> proportion as the fact is more or less unusual . . . when the fact attested is such a one as has seldom fallen under our observation, here is a contest of two opposite experiences; of which the one destroys the other, as far as its force goes, and the superior can only operate on the mind by the force, which remains (p. 113).

Such balancings of opposing probabilities are all very well; even though the same perhaps cannot be said of Hume's attempts to account for them in an ideally mechanical and purely quantitative way. But what they cannot provide is fulfilment of the promise of 'a decisive argument, . . . which must at least *silence* the most arrogant bigotry and superstition, and free us from their impertinent solicitations' (p. 110). In order to achieve that, Hume continues:

> let us suppose, that the fact, which they affirm, instead of being only marvellous, is really miraculous. . . .
>
> A miracle is a violation of the laws of nature; and as a firm and unalterable experience has established these laws, the proof against a miracle, from the very nature of the fact, is as entire as any argument from experience can possibly be imagined. Why is it more than probable, that all men must die; that lead cannot, of itself, remain suspended in the air; that fire consumes wood, and is extinguished by water; unless it be, that these events are found agreeable to the laws of nature, and there is required a violation of these laws, or in other words, a miracle to prevent them? (pp. 114–115).

A reader who came upon the words just quoted in innocence of arguments in the earlier sections of our *Enquiry* and in the *Treatise* would expect Hume now to develop the crucial distinction: between what is no more than immensely improbable; and what is, physically or practically, impossible. Such a development could take the hint given in that reference to 'a firm and unalterable experience'. Since nomological propositions—propositions, that is, asserting the subsistence either of (one kind of) causal connection or of a law of nature—carry entailments of physical or practical necessity and physical or practical impossibility; our evidence for asserting any nomological proposition has ultimately to be actively experimental rather than passively observational. Someone somewhere has to do or to try to do something; as opposed to merely reporting their strictly non-participant observations.

The same imaginary reader, innocent of Hume's prior commitments, might also hope to be offered at least an outline account of how the critical historian has, in examining every available relic of the past, to apply all his own knowledge, or what he must presume to be knowledge, of what is or was probable or improbable, possible or impossible. Only upon these assumptions can the historian interpret such relics as evidence,[24] and only upon those same assumptions can he justify any conclusions about what that evidence shows concerning what actually happened.

Given this understanding of the inescapable presuppositions of critical history, it becomes obvious that and why historians are by their cloth precluded from establishing that miracles did actually happen. They have to assess their evidence in the light of all that they know, or believe that they know. Now, among the propositions which they believe that they know to be true, the nomologicals are, necessarily, of vastly greater logical strength than any of the historical propositions whose truth or falsity the historians are endeavouring to determine. Thus, in any particular case, the proposition asserting that a miracle occurred will be singular and in a past tense: it is, therefore, no longer susceptible of any direct verification or falsification. But the contradicting nomological, which rules out the occurrence of the supposed miracle as physically or practically impossible, will be open and general: it has, therefore, presumably been tested and retested many times; and certainly can in principle be tested again, anywhere and at any time.

So suppose that some historians, or their successors, do become persuaded that it was a mistake to have dismissed certain stories of alleged miracles as false. There is, for instance, now good reason to believe that the reports of miracles of healing wrought by the Roman Emperor Vespasian—reports so contemptuously dismissed both by Hume himself and by all other eighteenth-century men of sense—were in fact true. But this good reason is at the same time the best of reasons for maintaining that what Vespasian did was not after all physically or practically impossible; and, hence, not miraculous.[25] Here, as everywhere, the adoption of impeccably systematic and rational methods of enquiry is no absolute guarantee against error. But where rationally justified true belief is unattainable, there can be no knowledge.

All that is what we might have hoped that Hume would be going on to say—we might have hoped this, that is, if only we had not already studied Section VII. But, once we have mastered the argument of that section, we are bound to notice that Hume has disqualified himself from making any sharp and drastic distinction: between, on the one hand, 'the extraordinary and the marvellous'—which will be, at worst,

[24] It is, for instance, only upon assumptions of this sort that documents can be identified as documents, and read as asserting what their writers intended them to assert. Compare *A Treatise of Human Nature*, 2nd edn, L. A. Selby-Bigge (ed.) (Oxford: Clarendon, 1978), 404–405.

[25] Compare *Hume's Philosophy of Belief*, Chapter VIII.

no more than vastly improbable; and, on the other hand, 'a violation of the laws of nature'—which must be, except to a Supernatural Power, blankly impossible. For in Section VII Hume has denied that there are any objective physical or practical necessities, any objective physical or practical impossibilities. There is, it appears, only logical necessity and logical impossibility. These, though he would not have put it in this way, are definable in terms of self-contradiction;[26] and, as Hume did so famously insist, they cannot serve as connections between objects and events in the Universe around us.

Given these denials, the 'reconciling project' (p. 95) of Part I of Section VIII goes through at the trot. As Hume said of himself, apropos an earlier exercise: 'Our author pretends, that this reasoning puts the whole controversy in a new light, by giving a new definition of necessity'.[27] Indeed it does. For this 'new definition' actually eliminates any idea of necessity. According to Hume's account of the matter causes regularly precede, but do not bring about, their effects: the occurrence of the cause, that is, does not make the occurrence of the effect physically or practically necessary; and its non-occurrence does not make it physically or practically impossible. Similarly a law of nature becomes a simple statement that there is, just as it happens and with no implications about any kind of connection, a one–one correlation between two variables; a very reticent assertion this, not carrying the essential entailment that this is a correlation which it is physically or practically impossible to break.[28] It is in accordance with what he is proud to call 'a new definition of necessity'—an account which in fact categorically denies that there is here any kind of necessity—that Hume aspires to effect his 'reconciling project'. The truth 'Of Liberty and Necessity', he maintains, is this:

[26] What is logically necessary is what it involves self-contradiction to deny; what is logically impossible is what it involves self-contradiction to assert. Thus $p.{\sim}p$ is logically impossible, whereas *If p then p* is logically necessary.

[27] This sentence comes from the *Abstract*, a pamphlet published anonymously by Hume in order to promote what he was later to disown as 'that juvenile work', the *Treatise*. The *Abstract* can now be found most conveniently in the edition of the *Treatise* mentioned in note 24, above. The sentence quoted is at p. 661.

[28] Selby-Bigge, at p. xviii of his Introduction, seems to have been the first to remark that and how, in what Hume calls a definition of 'a cause' at p. 76, he illicitly helps himself to an entailment which no definition on Humean lines could carry. (Since at pp. 129–130 of *Hume's Philosophy of Belief* I acknowledged Selby-Bigge's priority on this count, I should not have been faulted in *Hume Studies* (**II**, No. 2, 96–97) for failing to concede that priority to C. J. Ducasse; who was in fact writing over thirty years later.)

> If we examine the operations of body, and the production of effects from their causes, we shall find that all our faculties can never carry us farther in our knowledge of this relation than barely to observe that particular objects are *constantly conjoined* together, and that the mind is carried, by a *customary transition*, from the appearance of one to belief of the other. . . .
>
> . . . being once convinced that we know nothing farther of causation of any kind than merely the *constant conjunction* of objects, and the consequent *inference* of the mind from one to another, and finding that these two circumstances are universally allowed to have place in voluntary actions; we may be more easily led to own the same necessity common to all causes (p. 92).

Which 'necessity' is, I repeat—at the risk, long since incurred, of boring to rigidity—no kind of necessity whatsoever. Once this is recognized, then Hume is faced with a dilemma. Which is he to abandon: his reconciliation 'Of Liberty and Necessity'; or his argument 'Of Miracles'?

If there really is no such thing as practical necessity, then, surely, our choices can be physically caused without being practically necessitated?[29] In that case the 'reconciling project' will—again repeating a former phrase—go through at the trot. However, upon that same assumption, nothing whatever can be physically impossible. Hume has, therefore, failed to equip us with the promised 'everlasting check to all kinds of superstitious delusion . . . useful as long as the world endures' (p. 110).

There is, nevertheless, not an opportunity for the 'robbers of popular superstitions' to launch an offensive. These, Hume has warned us, are always lying 'in wait to break in upon every unguarded avenue of the mind, and overwhelm it with religious fears and prejudices' (p. 11). But in the annihilation of necessity they too have suffered a setback. If there are indeed no natural impossibilities to be known, then there can be no question of any Supernatural Power manifesting both His or Its existence and His or Its endorsement of some favoured, particular, putative

[29] The contrast here is between physical causes, which do necessitate, and personal or motivating or (as Hume would have said) moral causes, which do not. If someone specifies the causes of an explosion, then they tell us what brought it about; thus making that occurrence physically necessary and its non-occurrence physically impossible. But if I gave you cause to celebrate—perhaps by bringing you the news that you have earned a Grade A in A-level Philosophy—then I do not by any means ensure that you have no choice but, willy-nilly, to make whoopee. Compare, for instance, my *A Rational Animal* (Oxford: Clarendon, 1978), Ch. III.

revelation by overriding what are, on this assumption, revealed as non-existent laws of nature.

Those aspiring to validate the claims of any particular candidate revelation by showing that these have been Supernaturally endorsed become thereby committed to establishing: both that there is a strong and humanly inviolable Natural order; and that there have been some exceptional overridings. However, because all actual candidates have rivals, the sponsors of any one are committed to proving also that the putative Supernatural Authority has not vouchsafed some comparably categorical endorsement to any of the others. As Hume put it:

> in matters of religion, whatever is different is contrary; . . . it is impossible the religions of ancient Rome, of Turkey, of Siam and of China should, all of them, be established on any solid foundation (p. 121).[30]

On this present occasion it has become far too late for me to develop an argument showing that we could not have concepts either of unnecessitated choice or of natural necessity unless we had had, what in fact we do all have in abundance, experience of both. But I have elsewhere contended, and shall contend again, that this is so.[31] If indeed it is, then it is the 'reconciling project' and not the discussion 'Of Miracles', which is aborted. So let us conclude with a quotation from Lucian of Samosata, one of Hume's own favourite Classical authors:

> To defend one's mind against these follies, a man must have an adamantine faith, so that, even if he is not able to detect the precise trick by which the illusion is produced, he at any rate retains his conviction that the whole thing is a lie and an impossibility.[32]

[30] Commenting on one of the best of the early responses to Section X Hume wrote: 'If a miracle proves a doctrine to be revealed from God, and consequently true, a miracle can never be wrought for a contrary doctrine. The facts are therefore as incompatible as the doctrines.' See *The Letters of David Hume*, J. Y. T. Greig (ed.) (Oxford University Press, 1932), 350–351.

[31] See, for instance, either 'Another Idea of Necessary Connection', in *Philosophy* for 1982, or Chapter II-III of *A Rational Animal*, or my *Darwinian Evolution* (London: Granada Paladin, 1984), 80–83.

[32] This quotation is borrowed from J. Jastrow, *Wish and Wisdom* (New York: Appleton-Century, 1935), 25.

Karl Marx and Friedrich Engels

Karl Marx (1818–1883) was born in Trèves in the Rhineland. He studied law in Bonn, philosophy and history in Berlin, and received a doctorate from the University of Jena for a thesis on Epicurus (341–270 BC). (Epicurus' philosophy was a reaction against the 'other-worldliness' of Plato's theory of Forms. Whereas for Plato knowledge was of intelligible Forms, and the criterion of the truth of a hypothesis about the definition of a Form was that it should survive a Socratic testing by question and answer, for Epicurus the criterion of truth was sensation, and employment of this criterion favoured the theory with which Plato explicitly contrasted the theory of Forms (*Sophist* 246a–d), namely, the materialism of the atomists, Leucippus and Democritus.) Marx was editor of the *Rheinische Zeitung* of Cologne, 1842–1843. The paper was suppressed and he moved to Paris, becoming co-editor of the *Deutsch-französische Jahrbücher*, the one and only issue of which contained two articles by Marx and two by his friend, Friedrich Engels (1829–1895). Together they wrote *The German Ideology* (1846) and their most influential work, *The Communist Manifesto* (1848). Marx had been expelled from France in 1845, and went to Brussels, from where he was expelled during the 1848 revolutions. He went to Cologne to start, with Engels and others, a paper with a revolutionary editorial policy, the *Neue Rheinische Zeitung*. Expelled once again, Marx finally settled in London, working in the British Museum on his great historical analysis of capitalism, *Das Kapital*. The first volume was published in 1867, the remaining two volumes, completed by Engels after Marx's death, in 1885 and 1895.

The edition of *The German Ideology* prescribed by the AEB is Karl Marx and Friedrich Engels, *The German Ideology*, Part One, with selections from Parts Two and Three, together with Marx's 'Introduction to a Critique of Political Economy', edited and with Introduction by C. J. Arthur (London: Lawrence and Wishart, 2nd edn, 1974).

Supplementary reading might include the one-volume edition of Karl Marx and Friedrich Engels, *Selected Works* (London: Lawrence and Wishart, 1975) and Karl Marx, *Early Writings* (Harmondsworth: Penguin, 1975).

Of the very many books on Marx, the following may be mentioned:

A. Callinicos, *Marxism and Philosophy* (Oxford University Press, 1983)

R. Miliband, *Marxism and Politics* (Oxford University Press, 1977)

W. A. Suchting, *Marx: An Introduction* (Brighton: Harvester Press, 1983)

D. McLellan (ed.), *Marx: The First Hundred Years* (London: Fontana, 1983)
G. A. Cohen, *Karl Marx's Theory of History: A Defence* (Oxford University Press, 1978)
T. B. Bottomore (ed.), *Karl Marx* (Oxford: Blackwell, 1979)
T. B. Bottomore (ed.), *Modern Interpretations of Marx* (Oxford: Blackwell, 1981)
J. Mepham and D. H. Ruben (eds), *Issues in Marxist Philosophy*, 4 vols (Brighton: Harvester Press, 1979–81)

Marx and Engels, *The German Ideology*

C. J. ARTHUR

Introduction

The texts before us[1] are relatively *early* works. They predate the famous *Manifesto of the Communist Party* of 1848. Their importance lies in this: that here historical materialism is outlined and defended for the first time. This new philosophy is elaborated in the course of Marx and Engels' effort to settle accounts with previous German philosophy—and, perhaps, with philosophy as such. The new outlook is developed, therefore, in the context of polemic against Hegel and Feuerbach, precisely the thinkers that they most admired earlier in fact.

Marx follows Hegel in his sense of *history*. Hegel, indeed, was perhaps the *first* philosopher to take history seriously. He saw that it is within *history* that humanity develops itself, and discovers what it is, what it is capable of. History can be shown to have a pattern, an order, a direction; even if the agents whose action it is are *unconscious* of the deeper meaning of their struggles. For Hegel, this meaning lies in the emergence of our awareness of human *freedom*, and its realization in social and political institutions.

For Marx, the *problem* with Hegel's account is that the dynamic of history is understood there as the playing out of a dialectic of *ideas*. But before people can argue about ideas they must be fed and clothed. They are not disembodied spirits. They are *material* beings who must produce their means of subsistence day in, day out. For Marx, this is of enormous importance in his understanding of human nature, society, and history.

Feuerbach's *materialism* was an important point of reference for Marx in his transition from Hegelianism. Feuerbach believed that the human being must be understood primarily as a *natural* being, equip

[1] K. Marx and F. Engels, *The German Ideology*, 2nd edn, C. J. Arthur (ed.) (London: Lawrence and Wishart, 1974). This also contains Marx's *Theses on Feuerbach* and his 1857 *Introduction to a Critique of Political Economy*. Page numbers in the text below refer to this volume. Note the following *errata*: page 7 line 2, read 'dialectic'; page 7 note 1, read 'mystification'; page 7 one line from bottom, insert '2'; page 94 last line, delete last comma.

ped with a variety of senses with which to *know* the world, and with various *passions* requiring gratification. He was deeply suspicious of any philosophy that attributes autonomy, and power, to abstract ideas.

Although originally impressed with it, Marx finds Feuerbach's naturalism *wanting* precisely because it gives no account of history, of the way people in their practical activity can change their world and themselves. In a sense, Marx and Engels, in *The German Ideology*, are trying to find a middle way between Hegel and Feuerbach, by exploring the relationship between nature and history.

In the following account of their views I will first of all outline their materialistic conception of history. I will then supplement this by saying something about the relationship between the individual and society. Finally I will say something about Marx's *vision*, his vision of 'the realm of freedom'.

Historical Materialism

Before Marx's time it was common to pose the relationship of man to nature in *antithetical* terms. On the one hand there is nature, the realm of dead matter subject to immutable laws; and on the other hand there is the human realm, characterized by freedom and reason, infused with spirituality, and giving rise to a history understood as the expression of essentially free choices.

In opposition to this, Marx calls our attention to the crucial *linking* element between the natural basis of human life and the history we make. This is the practice of material production, the production and reproduction of ourselves as material beings. Because man is a *natural* being he has to interact with nature to secure his material existence. This has to be done before anything else and hence fundamentally *conditions* everything else. Through labour the material provided by nature is worked up into goods for human use. The changing ways in which this is done provides the guiding thread to history, Marx believes. The production of material life itself is a *necessary* condition of all historical development. This is, indeed, undeniable. But the undeniable is not necessarily trivial. Marx holds that changes in the mode of production are important in themselves and because of their influence on other spheres of life.

Of course, in order for production to have a history at all, man's relationship to nature must differ from that of other animals. One way of putting this is to say that other animals live in *immediate unity* with nature, but man's relationship to nature is mediated through tools. Whereas each particular species of animal has imposed on it by its naturally given constitution a certain stereotyped form of activity, man is able to *interpose* between himself and nature *means of production*. These means of production, moreover, are socially acquired, modified, and transmitted, through definite relations men enter into with each other. Production 'appears as a double relationship: on the one hand as a natural, on the other as a social relationship' (50). Marx explains that this means that a certain mode of production is always combined with a certain mode of co-operation.

The mode of production depends on the available productive forces, whether bows and arrows or modern assembly-line technology. Furthermore, co-operation 'is itself a productive force' (50). Through revolutionizing the mode of production people push back the limits originally placed on their existence by the circumstances given to them. But the *potential* for such change must *itself* be inherent in these circumstances, of course.

As I said, Feuerbach affirms the *unity* of man with nature. Marx replies that 'the celebrated "unity of man with nature" has always existed in industry . . . just like the "struggle" of man with nature' (63). Furthermore, through this activity the natural environment itself has been reshaped by industry. Nature as just 'given' exists now only on a few coral islands.

It is in such terms that Marx announces his historical materialism. History is pushed forward by changes in the mode of production. He says:

> It is quite obvious that there exists a materialistic connection of men with one another, which is determined by their needs and their mode of production, and which is as old as men themselves. This connection is ever taking on new forms, and thus presents a 'history' independently of the existence of any political or religious nonsense which in addition may hold men together (50).

He argues that at each stage of history 'a sum of productive forces, a historically created relation of individuals to nature and to one another . . . is handed down to each generation from its predecessors . . . and prescribes for it its condition of life'. The materialist conception of history shows 'that circumstances make men just as much as men make circumstances' (59).

What has now happened is that with the creation of a world market history necessarily becomes world history. In earlier times knowledge and inventions were acquired separately in each locality and were liable to be lost with some catastrophe, such as the invasion of barbarians. Only now 'is the permanence of the acquired productive forces assured' with their rapid diffusion through commerce. But there is a dark side to this development as in the first illustration Marx gives in the following passage.

> If in England a machine is invented, which deprives countless workers of bread in India and China, and overturns the whole form of existence of these empires, then this invention becomes a world-historical fact. Or again, take the case of sugar and coffee which have proved their world-historical importance in the nineteenth century by the fact that the lack of these products, occasioned by the Napoleonic Continental System, caused the Germans to rise against Napoleon, and thus became the real basis of the glorious wars of liberation of 1813 (58).

Marx, therefore, believes that history can be divided into distinct epochs, in each of which a different mode of production prevails. He presents a first crude sketch of such a history (43–46); but he acknowledges that, because each system has its own laws of motion, considerable empirical work is required to understand them. In place of the pass-key of a 'philosophy of history', we can provide ourselves only with a few abstract categories to guide such investigations and 'to facilitate the arrangement of historical material' (48) he says. He sets about this task in *The German Ideology*, but the best summary of these general considerations is provided in a later work (of 1859). It is worth quoting at length.

> The general result at which I arrived and which, once won, served as a guiding thread for my studies, can be briefly formulated as follows: in the social production of their life, men enter into definite relations that are indispensable and independent of their will, relations of production which correspond to a definite stage of development of their material productive forces. The sum total of these relations of production constitutes the economic structure of society, the real foundation, on which rises a legal and political superstructure and to which correspond definite forms of social consciousness. The mode of production of material life conditions the social, political and intellectual life process in general. It is not the consciousness of men that determines their being, but, on the contrary, their social being that determines their consciousness. At a certain stage of their development, the material productive forces of society come in conflict with the existing relations of production, or—what is but a legal expression for the same thing—with the property relations within which they have been at work hitherto. From forms of development of the productive forces these relations turn into their fetters. Then begins an epoch of social revolution. With the change of the economic foundation the entire immense superstructure is more or less rapidly transformed. In considering such transformations a distinction should always be made between the material

> transformation of the economic conditions of production, which can be determined with the precision of natural science, and the legal, political, religious, aesthetic or philosophic—in short, ideological forms in which men become conscious of this conflict and fight it out.[2]

So that was all Marx, summarizing the result of his earlier studies, in a *Preface* of 1859.

The position here outlined is that, in order to situate social and political struggles aright, one must grasp them in relation to the prevailing mode of production. This 'real foundation' underpins the 'legal and political superstructure', he says. The foundation itself comprises '*relations of production*' appropriate to a given stage in the development of the '*productive forces*'.

It is worth elucidating this latter distinction. What Marx has in mind here, I think, is that any economic system may be looked at from two points of view. In one aspect it consists in the appropriation of materials provided by nature, and their working up into goods suitable for human consumption. Anything that contributes, in some immediate and direct sense, to the production of such goods Marx terms a productive force. The most important productive force is clearly human labour itself. Nothing gets produced unless people work. Equally, various qualities of human labour, such as skills, are involved here. One must also include the type of tools that are used, and the power sources available to supplement human exertion, right up to modern robotized assembly-line factories. From another aspect, the economic system may be considered in terms of the social relations involved. These are legally endorsed in the prevailing forms of property. It is within these relations of production that the productive forces are exploited. What is of interest here is the destiny of the products, who gets what, how the ownership of the product is determined, and how it is distributed through social practices such as exchange. We are interested here also in how it is determined that some people labour and others live off that labour in various ways. So, typical relations of production include such things as slavery, serfdom and wage-labour.

There is a slightly controversial question in the interpretation of what Marx means here by relations of production. One might ask about co-operation in the labour-process, team work. In my opinion the only sensible way of interpreting Marx's distinction assigns this to the side of the productive forces, since it is clear that co-operation increases the productive power of social labour over that of the same labourers working separately. Furthermore, when one worker on a line passes the

[2] Karl Marx and Frederick Engels, *Selected Works*, 3 vols, Vol. One (Moscow: Progress Publishers, 1969), 502–504.

half-built product to the next this is not expressed as a legal transaction, obviously.

Now Marx is arguing that there must be some degree of correspondence between the productive forces and the relations of production, that certain productive forces require for their development and use suitable relations of production; otherwise they remain undeveloped, blocked off. At the same time, in the passage we are considering, the thesis is put forward that at a certain stage of the development of the productive forces the existing relations of production *will* come to fetter further advance. Let us take, for example, the capitalist mode of production. When it originated it gave a tremendous impetus to the productive forces. If one looks at the *Manifesto of the Communist Party* one finds that Marx speaks in glowing terms of the achievements of the bourgeoisie in this respect.

> The bourgeoisie, during its rule of scarce one hundred years, has created more massive and more colossal productive forces than have all preceding generations together. Subjection of Nature's forces to man, machinery, application of chemistry to industry and agriculture, steam-navigation, railways, electric telegraphs, clearing of whole continents for cultivation, canalization of rivers, whole populations conjured out of the ground—what earlier century had even a presentiment that such productive forces slumbered in the lap of social labour?[3]

Marx believes, however, that ultimately this system, great though its achievements are, must outgrow itself, must reach its limits. The relations of production cease to be capable of expanding in regular fashion the forces of production. For instance, the increasingly social character of the productive forces cannot be effectively regulated by private enterprise, and cyclical crises become more severe. In order to exploit effectively, for the benefit of society, the new productive forces, it is necessary to produce on the basis of a social plan. But only the working class can be expected to bring about such a revolution.

We see then that, for Marx, revolutions arise out of social struggles brought about through changes in the economic foundation. Of course, the protagonists, the leaders of the classes, and other social forces in motion, do not themselves typically refer to such changes, or are even aware of their role. The French Revolution, for example, was fought under the slogan 'Liberty, Equality, and Fraternity'. But the development of a market economy and the rise of the bourgeois class was the real content of the crisis, and its outcome was to clear the path for a capitalist mode of production to flourish.

[3] *Selected Works*, Vol. One, 113.

The unfortunate thing about Marx's architectural metaphor of foundation and superstructure is that it suggests forms of social consciousness are merely epiphenomenal. In truth, Marx was well aware that, even if the forms of social consciousness are conditioned by the economic structure, they are equally necessary to its continued existence. To put the point in negative terms: capitalism could not exist for a week if the medieval idea that usury is a sin were still prevalent. Furthermore, *change* is accomplished not merely through material force but through a battle of ideas. It is in ideological terms that people 'fight it out', Marx says. The point is that the *source* of their ideas is to be traced to the underlying changes in the sub-structure. For various reasons, ideological thought generally disguises its source from itself, however. Marx illustrates this point by reference to an analogy with the individual. Directly after the passage I gave above about the ideological forms in which the struggle is fought out, he continues:

> Just as our opinion of an individual is not based on what he thinks of himself, so can we not judge such a period of transformation by its own consciousness—on the contrary, this consciousness must be explained rather from the contradictions of material life, from the existing conflict between the social productive forces and the relations of production.[4]

We may be entitled to say of an individual that, although he believes himself to be actuated by honourable motives, in truth he is moved by jealousy, pride, or vengeance, and that he has repressed knowledge of his true motives. So, Marx holds, in the case of social ideologies we must not take them at face value. It is not enough to refer the French Revolution to slogans about liberty and equality. We must look behind the ideological debates to the real social forces in motion, and the class interests making themselves felt in noble ideals.

Thus Marx is against explaining historical change solely in terms of agent's self-ascribed intentions. He is telling us to look in another place. He is not *denying* the reality of ideas, or even their *effectivity* in moving masses of people to act. He holds only that reference to such ideas is not a 'rock bottom' explanation, so to speak. It is always in order to ask *why* certain ideas became popular at a certain time, and to refer in this explanation to structural changes unintended by individuals and going on beneath their feet, so to speak.

It is in these terms that Marx is able to deal with possible objections to the materialist conception of history. Thus in a footnote to *Capital* he replies to those who concede that in the modern world material interests predominate but claim that in the Middle Ages it was religious matters

[4] *Selected Works*, Vol. One, 504.

that were the moving issues and that in the ancient world it was political alternatives that dominated people's minds. Marx responds that, whatever conception they had of themselves, 'the Middle Ages could not live on Catholicism, nor could the ancient world on politics'. He adds, further, that it might be possible to show, on the basis of the specific modes of production concerned, 'why in one case politics, in the other Catholicism, played the chief part'.[5]

Marx's sense of history leads him to a new view on socialism itself. It is not an eternal truth but a *result* of premises created in the movement of history. He says: 'Communism is for us not a *state of affairs* which is to be established, an *ideal* to which reality will have to adjust itself. We call communism the *real* movement which abolishes the present state of things. The conditions of this movement result from the premises now in existence' (56–57).

Both material and social preconditions must be established for revolution to be on the historical agenda, and for socialism to be possible as a successful system of production. Human liberation depends more on the production of such material premises than on any philosophy of freedom. Thus scientific socialism studies the really existing circumstances, and bases its claim to validity on tendencies immanent in history, not on a supposed natural goodness of man. Still less is it an ideal preached to people in abstraction from their present circumstances and interests. The material conditions for communist revolution include the development of adequate productive forces to sustain a society free from want, and also the emergence of a social class that can solve its problems only through overthrowing the existing order. Marx concludes: 'If these material elements of a complete revolution are not present (namely, on the one hand the existing productive forces, on the other the formation of a revolutionary mass . . .) then, as far as practical development is concerned, it is absolutely immaterial whether the *idea* of this revolution has been expressed a hundred times already, as the history of communism proves' (59).

If Marx is right in his account of the dynamics of social evolution, then most writing on history is *wrong* in so far as it attributes great importance to the ideas men have and the struggles between adherents of different ideas, whether about politics or religion, or what. But why *would* people write history as if it were solely a question of ideological struggles? According to Marx, this tendency *itself* has material roots.

Originally, he argues, the production of ideas was 'directly interwoven with the material activity and the material intercourse of men, the language of real life' (47). This remains true even where people

[5] Karl Marx, *Capital*, Vol. One (London: Penguin Books, 1976), 175–176.

believe the opposite, believe in the rule of ideas. 'If in all ideology men and their circumstances appear upside-down as in a *camera obscura*', he says, 'this phenomenon arises just as much from their historical life process as the inversion of objects on the retina does from their physical life-process' (47).

There are various reasons why the ideas in people's heads begin to appear as having a certain autonomy with respect to the material conditions of life. Marx draws attention to the emergence of the division between mental and manual labour. 'From this moment onwards', he says, 'consciousness *can* really flatter itself that it is something other than consciousness of existing practice, that it *really* represents something without representing something real; from now on consciousness is in a position to emancipate itself from the world and to proceed to the formation of "pure" theory, theology, philosophy, ethics etc.' (51–52). Intellectuals, who work with thought material are thus particularly liable to absolutize the role of ideas in history. They neglect, Marx says, 'the real basis of history' in 'the relation of man to nature' (59). They see in history only 'the political actions of princes and states, religious and all sorts of theoretical struggles, and in particular in each historical epoch have had to *share the illusion of that epoch*. For instance, if an epoch imagines itself to be actuated by purely "political" or "religious" motives . . . the historian accepts this opinion' (60).

It is perhaps worth stressing that Marx is not supposing that the 'true motives' of *individuals* are their selfish economic interests. It is perfectly possible for a Prime Minister, without any property of her own to speak of, to act on behalf of private property under the illusion that this is the only alternative, that good government requires such encouragement of the property owners. As Marx puts it: 'the ideas of the ruling class are in every epoch the ruling ideas . . . the class which is the ruling material force in society is at the same time its ruling *intellectual* force' (64). The ruling ideas simply reflect the existing material relationships as they present themselves. The naturalness and reasonableness of these relationships is taken for granted by everyone. Even the *lower* classes will accept these ruling ideas until a time of crisis shakes their confidence in the existing order. So Marx argues that the way in which idealist philosophy comes to be produced is that it accepts the prevailing ideas, ignoring the fact that they are the ideas of the ruling class, and that the rule of this class is rooted in certain material conditions. Taking these ideas in abstraction from their social basis, they attribute to them independent existence. They content themselves with saying that at one time honour and loyalty were the predominant values but that later people were seized with ideas about liberty and equality—hence the French Revolution. For Marx, by contrast, progress at the level of the spirit presupposes progress at the level of the production of material life itself, transformations of productive activity.

It is worth pointing out that the stress in Marx's theory on production, and on activity generally, sets him apart from the materialist tradition as he found it. He articulates this difference in the jottings known as the *Theses on Feuerbach* (1845), which may be regarded as preliminary notes towards *The German Ideology*. Let us examine the first of these theses in order to grasp the specificity of Marx's position. He says there the following:

> The chief defect of all hitherto existing materialism . . . is that . . . reality . . . is conceived only in the form of the object or of contemplation, but not as sensuous human activity, practice, not subjectively. Hence, in contradistinction to materialism, the *active* side was developed abstractly by idealism—which, of course, does not know real, sensuous activity as such (121).

Now this first sentence gives notice that Marx, while acknowledging himself a materialist, considers all materialism hitherto defective. This is because it construes the relationship between subject and object in a one-sided manner whereby the latter, the object, contributes everything in the experience of the former, the subject. The subject merely *receives* into itself the impression of the object. It merely contemplates this object entirely passively. It is worth noting that the term here translated as 'contemplation', namely '*Anschauung*', has a history in German philosophy, notably in that of Kant. Philosophy translators normally render it as 'intuition'. Translators of Marx, however, reject this, because of its unwanted popular connotations of extra-sensory acquaintance. The term is used here, nevertheless, in exactly the sense as in Kant, namely to indicate a direct unmediated acquaintance with a thing, a mirror-like 'view' of it just as given.

In Marx's second sentence, the reference to idealism reminds us precisely that Kant and others insisted that such an account of experience is objectionable. They argued that the activity of the *subject* is important in organizing the forms of intuition, and in contributing conceptual categories that give some *sense* to experience. Thus our acquaintance with reality is the outcome of *work* by the subject on it. What is noticeable is that Marx gives *credit* to idealism for its stress on the *activity* of the subject in knowing. For idealism this activity is mental or spiritual in character. Marx condemns this as 'abstract'. Instead he appeals to the subject's practical objective activity.

In this condensed thesis, Marx argues that we learn about our world primarily through interacting with it, and transforming it through material practice.

In the remainder of the thesis Marx says that, though Feuerbach insists that the objects of the senses are distinct from thought objects, he does not conceive human activity as out there in the world. Paradoxically, therefore, this 'materialist' takes 'the theoretical attitude as the only genuinely human attitude'. He does not grasp 'the significance of "revolutionary", of "practical-critical", activity'. The point here is that if one has already been *given* acquaintance with objects, through the senses, then all that is left to *do* is to *theorize* about the given data. Practice is set aside as a sordid question of merely utilitarian interest. Marx believes there is more to it than this, as we have seen. Feuerbach appeals to the certainty of sense experience. But Marx replies (in *The German Ideology*) that he should remember that the cherry-tree he admires outside his window was brought into our zone by world trade. Only thus has it become a 'sensuous certainty' for Feuerbach. As for Feuerbach's theoreticism: a typical example of the kind of thing Marx has in mind is the following remark from Feuerbach's *Essence of Christianity*.

> The first philosophers were astronomers. It is the heavens that admonish man of his destination, and remind him that he is destined not merely to action, but also to contemplation[6]

Clearly astronomy is a good paradigm for anyone wishing to establish the independence of theoretical knowledge from material practice. One does not engage with the stars physically; nor can one experiment upon them. One observes their course and speculates about their trajectories and configurations. However, in truth the history of astronomy was always motivated by *practical* interests; for example astrological guidance, or predicting the flow of the Nile, or constructing navigation tables. Even where observation itself is concerned the activity of the scientist enters into the matter; for example, in the construction of instruments. Galileo claimed to have discovered moons of Jupiter, but his opponents said the observations were illusory artefacts of his telescope.

To turn to the main point: Marx's *historical* materialism is a materalism that prioritizes *practice*, material practice. It is through this that we reproduce ourselves, learn about our world, and develop our social and human potentials.

The Individual and Society

I now turn to Marx's views on the individual and society. Here a useful starting point is the statement about human nature found in the sixth of

[6] *The Essence of Christianity* [1841], trans. Marian Evans (George Eliot) (reissued New York, 1957), 5. 'Contemplation' here='*Beschauung*'.

the *Theses on Feuerbach*: 'The human essence is no abstraction inherent in each single individual. In its reality it is the *ensemble* of the social relations' (122).

This is meant as a criticism of Feuerbach, who is accused by Marx of taking this essence as 'an internal, dumb generality which *naturally* unites the many individuals'.

So Marx is claiming that separate individuals do not contain within themselves an identical human nature. A brick, by contrast, has the nature of brickiness as a single brick. And even if a pile of bricks is organized into definite relationships, for example, one is on top of another, this hardly affects the character of the individual bricks. The case of human nature is different, Marx is arguing. Hardly anything of interest can be said to inhere in human beings as isolated organisms. Human nature is inherently *social* in the sense that it is constituted and developed through interactions within organized social relationships. As society changes so does the nature of the human beings making it up.

Marx's thesis may be misleading about Feuerbach if it gives the impression that he was unaware of the specific differences between individuals or of the importance of relationships between them. Feuerbach characterized humanity as a 'species being', by which he indicates how each not only recognizes that the others, however different, belong to the same species, but also that each is aware of the *necessity* of these differences and their *complementarity*. The point is to grasp the human essence as a unity in difference. He quotes with approval a letter from Goethe to Schiller: 'Only all men taken together cognize nature, and only all men taken together live human nature'.[7] Feuerbach thinks this statement expresses very well both the universality of human beings and their need for one another. None of us can incarnate all human perfections, and none of us can partake in all human activities. But *together* we can aspire to such divine plenitude.

Feuerbach's paradigm of a truly human relationship is that of love between the sexes. This demonstrates perfectly the complementary character of difference. At the same time this gives us some sense that Marx's criticism is ultimately correct, when he says that in Feuerbach the unity of the species is given *naturally*. In Marx the whole picture is historicized. Revolutions in the mode of social production bring forth new kinds of difference and new kinds of unity—and within these, new struggles also, of course. Human beings are not naturally 'made for each other' but they continually *make each other* through their social relationships.

[7] *The Fiery Brook*, selected writings of Ludwig Feuerbach, trans. Zawar Hanfi (Garden City, NY: Anchor Books, 1972), 56.

Marx believes that human beings are essentially social; that is to say, that the very concept of what a human being is cannot be divorced from its formation in society. A contemporary of Marx's, John Stuart Mill, writes (a couple of years before Marx's theses) that 'men are not, when brought together, converted into another kind of substance'.[8] Marx believes strongly that they are. Or rather, that the very notion of 'bringing them together' makes no sense because they are always 'together' from the outset. Society is an ever pre-given condition of human existence. If someone becomes separated, a Robinson Crusoe, he carries that society with him in his head and the activities he undertakes when he is alone are conditioned by it. A wolf-child could never become properly human.

Against metaphysicians like Hegel who try to interpret history in terms of supra-human principles such as the self-development of the 'world-spirit', Marx insists that history is made by men; but just as real as the individuals are the relations they have to each other, the ones they are born into, reproduce, and transform. Here Marx also disagrees with the implications for social science of Mill's individualism. Mill says that 'human beings in society have no properties but those which are derived from, and may be resolved into, the laws of nature of individual man'.[9] Marx, by contrast, argues that the laws of individual nature are shaped by the properties of the social formation. The evidence of history, and that of comparative anthropology, shows us great variations in human behaviour in all fields of human experience. With regard to Marx's pet subject, economics, we find that he insists that the laws governing economic activity are quite different in a capitalist economy from those of previous modes of production, or, indeed, of the socialist future.

Marx is able to carry the argument into the enemy camp by pointing out that the very individualism of modern society is *itself* a social product. Hobbes, Locke, and Mill take the individual to be the elementary unit of social life because in *this* society, based on private property and market exchange, individuals really are separated and opposed to one another. But in no *other* society would individuals take themselves to be autonomous centres of value and choice. They would identify themselves in terms of their membership of the community. Modern individualism is itself the product of a long historical development whereby society allowed this differentiation *within* itself. A Stock Exchange speculator may be a model of selfishness, but the Stock Exchange is an institution evolved within society. Thus individuation

[8] J. S. Mill, *A System of Logic* [1843] (London: Longmans, 1965), Book 6, 'On the Logic of the Moral Sciences', Ch. VII, 573.

[9] Ibid.

is itself possible only with the support of the social network and within avenues prescribed by it (124–125).

Let us remember again that the most important social relations are those of material production. Hence, from the point of view of historical materialism, Marx opposes any account of human nature that tries to specify its peculiarity in terms of *spiritual* features: consciousness, religion, morality, or whatever. Such accounts speak as if our material needs dragged us down to the level of the beasts. At the outset of his *Essence of Christianity*, Feuerbach gives such a traditional reply to the question of the essential difference between man and animals. Marx and Engels respond to this, in *The German Ideology*, as follows:

> Men can be distinguished from animals by consciousness, by religion, or anything else you like. They themselves begin to distinguish themselves from animals as soon as they begin to *produce* their means of subsistence . . . (42).

The mode of production must not be considered simply as a means of reproducing their physical existence; it makes them what they are. It is a definite mode of life on their part. 'The nature of individuals thus depends on the material conditions determining their production' (42).

Because of Marx's historical and social understanding of human nature he is able to reply to those apologists of present conditions who insist that they accord with human nature. For Marx, on the contrary, it is the existing conditions that have shaped the people we know. Thus if someone says that people are innately competitive, aggressive, greedy, and selfish, and that social institutions must allow for this, Marx replies that these characteristics are not innate, but acquired, and that human nature can change with changes in the structure of social relationships.

This is not to say, as some do, that for Marx there is no such thing as human nature; there is. Besides those features it has in common with other animals, the specifically human comes out in its *historical* character. History continually generates new structures of social being.

Thus, if someone says that socialism is 'against human nature' or refers historically specific modes of production, or superstructural phenomena, to an assumed eternal human nature as their ground, then one may reply, in a *purely popular but strictly unscientific manner*, that 'there is no such thing as human nature'. But it is quite *reasonable* to say that human nature is essentially social, or that human activity is distinguished from that of other organisms by work of a productive and teleological character,[10] or that human nature is material in the first

[10] 'We presuppose labour in a form in which it is an exclusively human characteristic . . . what distinguishes the worst architect from the best of bees

instance, that is, it depends on a material metabolism and hence requires means of subsistence provided through material production.

It should be noted that these determinations are just as much the ground of their opposites. 'Anti-social behaviour' is a *social product*; and the complete incapacity of the eighteenth-century aristocrat to produce so much as a boiled egg is by no means a disproof of work as a universal character of the human species; parasitism in this case is not biologically given but a function of a historically determinate mode of production.

The Realm of Freedom

Marx is loathe to go into detail on the organization of socialist society for methodological reasons, namely that the task is not to build up an ideal but to look at the implications of existing tendencies. None the less he does throw in some striking generalities. Before concluding with some remarks on his vision of liberation I want to look first at just one, rather puzzling, aspect—the future of labour.

To begin with, let us look at what he says about the *division* of labour in *The German Ideology*. The discussion there is not helped by the fact that Marx runs together two separate issues. Let us first explain these. In his *Capital* Marx *distinguishes* clearly between two kinds of division of labour: first, what he calls the *social* division of labour; second, the technical division of labour, or the division of labour *within manufacture*. By 'social division of labour' is intended the kind of thing Marx is talking about when he says in *The German Ideology* that 'division of labour and private property are . . . identical expressions'. He explains that 'in the one the same thing is affirmed with reference to activity as is affirmed in the other with reference to the product of the activity' (53). What we are dealing with here are independent producers whose labours become socially useful only in so far as their products are accepted in the market place. In such a system the remote consequences of individual decisions are unpredictable because the social synthesis is not planned but grows up spontaneously. Marx says of it:

> The social power . . . which arises through the co-operation of different individuals as it is determined by the division of labour, appears to those individuals . . . not as their own united power, but as an alien force existing outside them, of the origin and goal of which they are ignorant, which they thus cannot control, which on the

---

is that the architect builds the cell in his mind before he constructs it in wax. . . . Man not only effects a change of form on the material of nature; he also realizes his own purpose in those materials' (*Capital*, Vol. One, 283–284).

> contrary passes through a peculiar series of phases and stages independent of the will and the action of man, nay even being the prime governor of these (54).

Marx refers in this connection to 'an English economist' as the author of the view that the power of the world market is like an 'invisible hand' deciding the fates of men. This English economist was Adam Smith, whose book *The Wealth of Nations* Marx was studying closely at this time. In contrast to this system, Marx claims that with the abolition of private property 'the communist regulation of production' would put men back in control of their destiny (55).

Now let us turn to the question of the nature of the division of labour *within* the enterprise and see what principles are involved. As I have said, Marx does not clearly distinguish this problem from the first in *The German Ideology*. In this he follows his mentor Adam Smith. I therefore introduce the point at issue through analysis of Smith's presentation. In the first chapter of *The Wealth of Nations* Smith argues that increase in the wealth of the nation depends upon increasing the productivity of labour. He argues further that the greatest single impetus to the increase in productivity has been the benefits derived from the division of labour. He illustrates his point by a pin factory in which the work is divided among eighteen different operatives, thereby increasing output hundreds of times over. The peculiar thing is that Smith appears to think that this example differs only in scale from the division of labour 'in the general business of society'. However, his argument in the second chapter on the *origins* of the division does not cohere at all with the pin factory example. For he finds its origin in 'the propensity to truck, barter, and exchange one thing for another'. Now it is perfectly clear that the operatives in the pin factory do *not* exchange one thing for another. What we find is that the labours of the pin makers are divided and controlled within a *plan* of production laid down in advance by the management of the factory. Clearly, therefore, the distinction between the social division of labour mediated by markets and the division of labour within a particular manufacture is not simply one of *scale* but of *kind*.

In *The German Ideology*, however, it seems that Marx, like Smith, does not properly make this distinction, because, when he talks of the communist regulation of production, he not only supposes that it abolishes the power of the market but that it abolishes the technical division of labour also. For he says that in communist society no one has a particular exclusive sphere of activity thrust upon them.

There are clearly two different problems mixed up here because it is not obvious that the regime of the pin factory necessarily changes if it produces not for the market but for the socialist plan.

Marx notices in *Capital* that the bourgeoisie have no greater argument against socialism than that it would turn society into one immense factory.[11] Thereby, of course, they implicitly acknowledge the brutality of life in their factories. Certainly Marx wants to do something about the technical division of labour too. But the illustration of a communist working day in *The German Ideology* is strangely bucolic. He says there that in a communist society

> each can become accomplished in any branch he wishes, society regulates the general production and thus makes it possible for me to do one thing today and another tomorrow, to hunt in the morning, fish in the afternoon, rear cattle in the evening, criticize after dinner, just as I have a mind, without ever becoming hunter, fisherman, herdsman, or critic (54).

The influence on Marx's thought here is undoubtedly that of Charles Fourier, the French Utopian socialist. Marx was familiar with his work. What he liked about it was that it shifted the attention of socialists away from *distribution* ('fair shares' and so on) to the question of the reorganization of *production* itself.

In Fourier's works we find the following illustration of life in socialist society. It is a description of a typical summer day in the life of a man called Mondor.[12]

Mondor's Day in Summer

Gets up at 3.30 and breakfasts
At 5.30 he goes out with the hunting group
At 7 he works with the fishing group
At 8 he has lunch and reads the newspapers
At 9 he has a session with the horticulture group under a tent
At 10 a.m. he goes to mass
At 10.30 he joins the pheasant breeders group
At 11.30 he is in the Library and studies there until dinner at 1 p.m.
At 2.30 he works in the greenhouses, followed by a session with the fish breeders
At 6 he has a snack in the fields and tends the sheep until 8 when he goes to the work-exchange (to set up his programme for the next day)
9 p.m. is time for supper
and from 9.30 'til bed at 10.30 he attends artistic events.

[11] *Capital*, Vol. One, 477.
[12] C. Fourier, *Oeuvres complètes Tome VI* (Paris, 1966–68), 68.

You will notice that he has not been left much time to sleep. You will also notice the predominance of agricultural work. This is because Fourier held that industrial labour is only one quarter as attractive as agricultural. He designs his Utopia accordingly.

Now Marx already in 1844 had criticized Fourier for taking agricultural work as exemplary, so we might suppose that the working day in *The German Ideology* is half an ironical echo of Fourier. Nevertheless it seems that Marx thinks that the idea of abolishing the division of labour makes sense. (He is especially opposed to the division between manual and mental labour.) The difficulties in the way of such a project are too complex to enter into here.

Another odd feature of *The German Ideology* is that Marx and Engels go on to speak of the abolition of *labour itself* (92–94).

Although Marx became interested later in the possibility of total automation[13] that is not envisaged here. Rather, Marx contrasts 'labour' with 'self-activity'. People will still be productively active in socialism, even manual labour will still exist, but when it is under their own direction their activity is thereby freed from its determination by alien powers such as private property and the market. Later Marx recognized that there would still remain 'a realm of necessity' in so far as certain jobs just have to be done even though they are not fulfilling in themselves. All that can be done is to shorten the working day.[14]

Conclusion

In conclusion let us stress that Marx is above all a revolutionary. In 1845 he proclaims that 'the philosophers have only *interpreted* the world, in various ways; the point is to *change* it' (123). It is in this light that the three sections of my presentation can be drawn together.

Firstly, historical materialism recognizes that *men* make history, albeit not under conditions of their own choosing. Marx inserts a marginal note in *The German Ideology* to the effect that 'so-called *objective* historiography just consists in treating the historical conditions independent of activity' and that it has a 'reactionary character'. If we want to understand this remark it is useful to look at Marx's book *The Eighteenth Brumaire of Louis Bonaparte*. He compares *his* account of the 1851 *coup d'état* with that of Victor Hugo and of Proudhon. Victor Hugo ascribes everything to the machinations of the future Napoleon III. Proudhon, in contrast, represents the event as the

[13] *Marx's Grundrisse*, trans. M. Nicolaus (London: Penguin Books, 1973), 704–706.

[14] See *Capital*, Vol. Three (London: Penguin Books, 1981), 958–959.

product of its historical conditions. But Marx complains that this apparently *objective* account 'becomes an historical *apologia* for its hero'. He continues: 'I, on the contrary, demonstrate how the *class struggle* in France created circumstances and relationships that made it possible for a grotesque mediocrity to play a hero's part'.[15]

In the same way, historical conditions are making possible—even in some sense necessary—communist revolution; but the *activity* of the revolutionary party will bring it about.

As far as human nature is concerned, we have shown that Marx thought it conditioned by prevailing relationships, but—just on that account—open to transformation. Again, nevertheless, human activity is essential. 'Revolution is necessary', he says, 'not only because the *ruling* class cannot be overthrown in any other way, but also because the class *overthrowing* it can only in a revolution succeed in ridding itself of all the muck of ages and become fitted to found society anew' (95).

As far as economic conditions are concerned, Marx is above all the theorist of 'the natural laws of capitalist production' which work themselves out 'with iron necessity' as he puts it in *Capital*[16]. The point is, however, to overturn this system. 'Communism differs from all previous movements', he says, in that it strips economic relations of their natural character 'and subjugates them to the power of the united individuals' (86). This is the meaning of socialism.

In sum, anyone reading *The German Ideology* cannot but be impressed by two things: that it is a call for a scientific study of the material foundations of human existence and, at the same time, a philosophy of revolution.

[15] *Selected Works*, Vol. One, 395.

[16] *Capital*, Vol. One, 91. The necessity inheres in 'the economic law of motion of *modern* society' (92). This is *misquoted*, in a very significant way, by Karl Popper, in his *Poverty of Historicism* (London: Routledge, 1961) as 'the economic law of motion of *human* society' (p. 49). (My emphases.)

John Stuart Mill

John Stuart Mill (1806–1873) was born in London, son of the Scottish historian of India and philosopher, James Mill, by whom he was educated in, among other things, the principles of British empiricism and Benthamite utilitarianism. Like his father, he worked for the East India Company, being in charge of the Company's relations with the native states 1836–1856, and head of the examiner's office from 1856 until the powers of the Company were transferred in 1858. The book which established Mill as a philosopher was his *System of Logic* (1843), described in its full title as 'a connected view of the principles of evidence and the methods of scientific investigation'. Book 6 of the *System of Logic* was 'On the logic of the moral sciences', and at the end of it Mill declared, without trying to justify it, his opinion that there is a 'general principle to which all rules of practice ought to conform'; namely that of 'conduciveness to the happiness of mankind, or rather, of all sentient beings'. For example, we should keep our promises not because we can see intuitively the truth of the precept, but because it passes the utilitarian test. Mill's justification for this opinion was in his *Utilitarianism* (1863). Mill's version of utilitarianism differed from Bentham's in that he recognized not only quantitative but also qualitative differences between pleasures.

In 1830 Mill met Mrs Harriet Taylor, to whom, he says in his *Autobiography* (1873), he owed none of his technical doctrines but many of his liberal ideals for the individual and society. He married her, after her husband died, in 1851. She died in 1858. In *On Liberty* (1859), he defended liberal views they had shared, such as that 'the sole end for which mankind are warranted, individually or collectively, in interfering with the liberty of action of any of their number, is self-protection'. He served as an independent Member of Parliament for Westminster 1865-1868, and proposed votes for women as an amendment to Disraeli's Franchise bill. He died where he and Harriet had spent much of their time together, in Avignon, France, in 1873.

The edition of Mill, *On Liberty*, prescribed by the AEB is Mill, *On Liberty*, edited with an introduction by Gertrude Himmelfarb (Harmondsworth: Penguin, 1982).

Further reading might include:

Fred R. Berger, *Happiness, Justice and Freedom* (California: University of California Press, 1984)

Maurice Cowling, *Mill and Liberalism* (Cambridge University Press, 1963)

John Gray, *Mill on Liberty: A Defence* (London: Routledge and Kegan Paul, 1983)

John C. Rees, *John Stuart Mill's Liberty* (Oxford University Press, 1985)

Alan Ryan, *J. S. Mill* (London: Routledge and Kegan Paul, 1975)

C. L. Ten, *Mill on Liberty* (Oxford University Press, 1980)

Mill's Essay *On Liberty*

ALAN RYAN

John Stuart Mill is—surprisingly—a difficult writer. He writes clearly, non-technically, and in a very plain prose which Bertrand Russell once described as a model for philosophers. It is never hard to see what the general drift of the argument is, and never hard to see which side he is on. He is, none the less, a difficult writer because his clarity hides complicated arguments and assumptions which often take a good deal of unpicking. And when we have done that unpicking, the task of analysing the merits and deficiencies of the arguments is still only half completed. This is true of all his work and particularly true of *Liberty*. It is an essay whose clarity and energy have made it the most popular of all Mill's work. Yet it conceals philosophical, sociological and historical assumptions of a very debatable kind. In his introduction, Mill says

> the object of this essay is to defend one very simple principle, as entitled to govern absolutely the dealings of society with the individual in the way of compulsion and control, whether the means used be legal penalties, or the moral coercion of public opinion (*Liberty*, 68).

One hundred and twenty-seven years after the essay first appeared, Mill's commentators still do not agree about just what that principle was, nor about just how it governs the dealings of society with its members.

It is easier to see what Mill was trying to argue, if we have some sense of the context in which Mill was writing—both the biographical and intellectual context so far as Mill himself was concerned, and the social and political context for which *Liberty* was intended. It is worth remembering that Mill himself thought of his essay as aimed almost wholly at an English audience; it was the intellectual and social oppressiveness of Victorian England which was his target, and the lesson he preached was, he thought, one which most of Europe did not need to be taught. Mill thought that Britain was *politically* much freer than most of Europe—where, indeed, parliamentary government and a free press were in 1858 almost unknown. Conversely, he thought that *socially* most of Europe was freer than Britain—the British were intellectually timid and conformist, where Europeans were much more willing to question traditional moral and religious beliefs. Although

Liberty is by a long way the best remembered, most admired (and most criticized) of all his works, it was, and is best understood as, a product of its own time and place.

Mill painted his own picture of his times and gave his own account of what he thought his intellectual duty to his contemporaries amounted to in the most immediately readable of all his work—his *Autobiography*. It is, as Mill intended it to be, interesting as the record of an extraordinary education. He was brought up by his father, with the advice and assistance of Jeremy Bentham and Francis Place, to be something like a one-man Open University, a storehouse of advanced thinking on all matters, who would enlighten the politically influential middle-class audience who read the political quarterlies. Readers of his *Autobiography* will not need reminding of the strenuous educational programme this required. He was taught Greek at three (with the aid of 'flash cards' of the kind still used by educational psychologists), read enormous amounts of Roman history, Greek drama, and European poetry before he was in his teens, and rounded off the diet with logic, utilitarian moral philosophy and the latest ideas in economic theory. Most of us feel exhausted merely reading the titles of the books which Mill got through before he was sixteen; and few of us are surprised that Mill had a nervous breakdown in his early twenties.

A strange feature of this nervous collapse is that although none of Mill's friends or contemporaries appear to have noticed that anything was amiss, it mattered so much to Mill that he made his account of it the centrepiece of the *Autobiography*. It seemed to him that the collapse had been brought on when he had asked himself a fatal question—'if everything he had campaigned for was suddenly achieved, would that make him happy?' The answer seemed to him to be an unequivocal 'no'. And the sense that the social and political good works to which he was devoted really had a feeble hold on his heart and his imagination plunged him into profound depression. He had assumed, as a convinced utilitarian, that the projects to which Bentham and James Mill and the other Philosophical Radicals had devoted themselves would make people happy, and would make their benevolent promoters happy, too. The experience of disillusionment and his struggle out of it had a profound impact on Mill's thinking. He came to believe that the event was a symbol of the tensions of the age, and that his recovery from it was an exemplary case—to put it dramatically, he thought that the lesson he had learned for himself was one which the age at large needed to learn. But what was that lesson?

For himself in particular, Mill thought that he had been trained too hard in the use of his analytical abilities and too little in the development of his emotions; his imagination had not been sufficiently stretched, and he had never been taught to understand the variety and flexibility of human nature. And this failure to appreciate imagination and variety was a failure of old-fashioned utilitarian radicalism itself. This implied that his main task was to re-educate the radicals and reformers. He did not think that his teachers had been wrong to try to make him a social scientist and a utilitarian; all his life he was absolutely clear that if there was to be any hope of social reform, or of introducing an acceptable socialism into economic life, or acceptable democracy into political life, or equality between the sexes, this would require the best knowledge of social cause and effect we could achieve. Such knowledge was not to be left to 'intuition' or tradition; it had to be a matter of social science. The difficulty was that all previous accounts of that science had been far too narrow. The economic theories of his father and Ricardo had rightly been complained of as contributions to the 'dismal science'; they were dismal because they made it look as if working men were everywhere and always doomed by necessity to live and work as they did in early Victorian England. His father's politics, as spelled out in his *Essay on Government*, were founded on the view that mankind were inevitably self-interested. But this was plausible neither as description nor prescription. So Mill was left to argue that before we offered recipes for social reconstruction based on the new social sciences, we had to widen our understanding of human nature—social science was useless otherwise.

Similarly, Mill never renounced his early allegiance to utilitarianism. He always defended what he believed to be the fundamental idea of utilitarian ethics—its commitment to rationality. He never wavered in the belief that rationality meant that we must have some ultimate standard by which to justify all the rules of conduct society requires, and that that standard can only be the general happiness. But, once again, he thought that his teachers had had a terribly narrow idea of what people were like and what human happiness consisted of. From Goethe he borrowed the slogan 'many-sidedness', and argued whenever he had the chance that what made man different from the beasts was a spirit of divine discontent which made individuals strive after their own self-perfection. In *Utilitarianism* he argues 'better Socrates dissatisfied than the fool satisfied'; and there, too, he argues that 'self-perfection', the search for one's own better self, is not only a means to the general happiness, but is, properly speaking, part of happiness itself. This allowed him to clear utilitarianism of the charge levelled against it by Carlyle, that it was it was 'pig philosophy', passing off the contentment of the swinish multitude as the highest goal of ethics. Mill's utilitarianism had—he claimed—plenty of room for the highest aspirations of mankind.

Lastly we have to bear in mind Mill's reaction to the rise of democracy. Mill was a democrat; or, to be more accurate, he was a committed defender of representative government. But he was a frightened democrat. He read Alexis de Tocqueville's *Democracy in America*, and was alarmed at the picture the book painted of a society where equality led to conformism and uniformity. Equality was an admirable ideal; Mill always defended equality of opportunity, always attacked snobbery, always condemned aristocracies which insisted on their privileges but refused to accept their obligations. None the less, he thought that the point of equality was as an aid to justice and merit. Only if everyone started equal would success fall to the most meritorious; only if success was proportioned to merit would justice be achieved. Mill was what one might call a 'moral aristocrat'; he thought that some men were simply the moral superiors of others, just as some men were the intellectual superiors of others. Moreover he believed that all social progress depended on the efforts of those few superior characters and intellects. So equality of opportunity is, paradoxically, defended by Mill as a means to finding and liberating the intellectual and moral vanguard on whom progress depends. And what Mill feared was that a general social equality would result in a grey uniformity of opinion and attitude which would stifle vitality and progress.

We should pause for a moment, as I promised we would, to see what sort of oppression Mill had learned from de Tocqueville to fear above all else, and how that was related to his fears about democracy. The oppression Mill expected was what de Tocqueville had described as the coming of a society of 'industrious sheep'. Neither Mill nor de Tocqueville anticipated the police terror of modern totalitarian states such as Nazi Germany and Stalinist Russia. What they expected was a 'soft despotism'. They thought that a society in which uniformity and conformism had got the upper hand would be one in which everyone would try to think like his or her neighbour, would regard public opinion as the final court of appeal on all subjects, and would be frightened to strike out on an independent tack in anything. This would not be a conformism enforced by brute force or the terrors of the Inquisition. It would be enforced by a silent ganging up of the majority against the minority. The pressure of public opinion would be felt in the form of judgments that non-conformists were 'odd', 'not normal', not quite nice. It would be the sort of pressure which sustains clubs, school common-rooms, suburban housing estates—those declared 'odd' would be shunned, their views would not be taken seriously, they would find themselves unobtrusively shut out from friendship and success. Because Mill and de Tocqueville thought that an egalitarian society would be anxious for a *comfortable* life above all else, they did not think that such a society would become passionately attached to political or religious causes which would lead to the persecution of the Inquisition or the Cheka or the Ayatollahs. They thought it would be the uniformity of the flock of sheep which they had to fear, not the ferocity of the pack of wolves.

But it was, for all that, a form of social oppression which was almost more dangerous than that of the persecutor with the sword in his hand. For it was a pressure which worked continuously, silently, unobtrusively. Violent persecution arouses its own opposition; its victims may not be able to protect themselves but they are likely to want to resist. The pressure of public opinion is not like that. It is much less likely to arouse opposition except in the hearts of those who have strongly independent characters already. Certainly Mill was anxious about the political consequences of such a social conformism. In the nineteenth century, government was increasingly under the sway of public opinion, even if it was not formally a parliamentary democracy. Public opinion would therefore dictate the shape of legislation, and a conformist public opinion which did not recognize the right of individuals to do as they pleased wherever the vital interests of others were not at stake would not hestitate to pass oppressive laws. Temperance legislation, to take an obvious example from *Liberty* itself (156–158), could be expected from a society which insisted on minding everyone else's business. Censorship of books, state regulation of school syllabuses, an insistence on subscription to some formal religious organization or other—all of these might well be enshrined in law as the result of the pressure of opinion. But law not backed up by public opinion provokes resistance. What does not provoke resistance in anything like the same way is public opinion. It is opinion, therefore, which is the underlying danger. Most of us are likely to succumb to the pressure to conform; worse yet, many of us are likely to avoid any disagreeable conflict between our own views and those of the public at large by adjusting our own views in advance, even before argument breaks out. When society

> issues wrong mandates instead of right, or any mandates at all in things with which it ought not to meddle, it practises a social tyranny more formidable than many kinds of political oppression, since, though not usually upheld by such extreme penalties, it leaves fewer means of escape, penetrating much more deeply into the details of life, and enslaving the soul itself (*Liberty*, 63).

By no means *all* social pressure is a disaster. Society only exists because we are amenable to social pressure; children begin, if not by being simply selfish, at any rate by being pretty unbothered about the welfare of everyone else. They are, as Hobbes had remarked two centuries earlier, 'born inapt for society', and have to be trained for it. That training consists in part of being forced into good habits, and in part of being got to believe things which we *could* certainly argue about, but simply don't. But it was important that society should confine this sort of coercive and non-rational pressure to children and the incapable; people 'in the maturity of their faculties' had to be dealt with in other ways.

Like de Tocqueville, Mill thought that the great need of democracy was to preserve 'the antagonism of opinions'; so much of *Liberty* is about the social requirements of that antagonism. What makes *Liberty* something quite other than a commentary on de Tocqueville is that Mill had complicated philosophical views which went beyond de Tocqueville's sociological and political insights. Mill defended his insistence that society should coerce individuals only in order 'to prevent harm to others' with an account of the nature and scope of morality and more particularly of the area of morality covered by the idea of 'rights' which was a philosophical *tour de force*. Since our interest lies primarily in Mill the philosopher, it is time we turned to these details.

Mill begins *Liberty* by sketching the rise of democracy; as a defence against mismanagement and ill-will by monarchs and aristocrats, the people at large had to build up their own power. But this process has now gone so far that what men are discovering is that 'self-government' turns out not to be the government of each man or woman by himself or herself, but the government of each of us by all the rest (*Liberty*, 60–62). Moreover, says Mill, matters are made much worse by the lack of any agreed principle by which to decide when government ought or ought not to act. It is, he says, only the 'likings and mislikings' of mankind which have determined the issue—a phrase to which we shall have to pay careful attention in due course. Some people have thought that wherever anything was amiss society and government should act and correct it; other people have so feared government that they would tolerate any amount of mischief rather than give more powers to government. What has been lacking is any coherent theory of what does and what does not justify coercive measures against individuals. It is important to understand that Mill's aim was not simply to *diminish* the role of government; indeed, he advanced a much enlarged role for government and public opinion alike in making parents meet their obligation to educate their children and in making couples meet their obligation to avoid bringing into the world children who would be a burden to the rest of society. These 'private' matters, which many people even now would think were too sensitive and too private for outside pressure, were not so described by Mill. Mill intended to produce a principle which, though it would certainly reduce *many* of the present pressures of government and public opinion, would equally certainly add to those pressures in other areas.

So, we must recur to the crucial question Mill asks himself: on what general principle is the coercive interference of society with its members to be organized? Mill is careful to confine his question to the *coercive* interferences of society with its members; many people—including Professor Himmelfarb throughout her introduction to the Penguin edition of *Liberty* and her longer book on *Liberty and Liberalism*—ignore this vital point. They think that Mill's view is that society should be 'neutral' about the private , or 'self-regarding' behaviour of its members. But Mill expressly disavows this interpretation of *Liberty*. He is, on the contrary, eager to assert just the opposite; our usual notions of good manners make most of us reluctant to tell other people just what we think of them. We are reluctant to tell them that we think they have low tastes, or that they lead lives which are fundamentally lacking in the concern for self-perfection which alone makes our lives better than those of the beasts. But this is a great mistake, says Mill. We owe it to each other to try to keep each other up to the mark; what we don't have is the right to force other people to live according to our standards. It is coercion which Mill is concerned to circumscribe.

'Exhortation and entreaty' are not coercive, says Mill, and where we may not coerce others, we certainly ought to exhort and entreat them to make the best of themselves. Not to do that is not to practise a virtuous neutrality about their conduct, it is to display a selfish unconcern for their higher welfare. Mill's critics' failure to take this point is not entirely blameworthy; many of us would feel that being exhorted and entreated to live up to our better natures would, if it went on for long, or went on very often, be just as bad as the coercion of public opinion, and might wonder about the point of Mill's distinction between the coercion of opinion on the one hand and 'entreaty' on the other. But it is to such doubts that Mill thought he had an answer.

Mill commits himself to the view that we may force others to act in ways they do not wish only for the sake of 'self-protection'. This causes Mill a problem. He was a utilitarian, and on the face of it a utilitarian is committed to one principle only—that we should do whatever maximizes happiness. Suppose that paternalism made people happier—the paternalistic legislator is moved by the sufferings of his ignorant and incompetent fellows, and is happy when they have been protected from themselves; his ignorant and incompetent fellows do not much mind the laws and other pressures which restrict their freedom, and are manifestly better off when not doing themselves a mischief through their own folly. Mill denies that this gives anyone the right to act in a paternalist fashion. Having enunciated his 'one very simple principle' he glosses it by saying,

> His own good, either physical or moral, is not a sufficient warrant. He cannot rightfully be compelled to do or forbear because it will be better for him to do so, because it will make him happier, because in

> the opinions of others, to do so would be wise or even right. These are good reasons for remonstrating with him, or reasoning with him, or persuading him, or entreating him, but not for compelling him or visiting him with any evil in case he do otherwise. To justify that, the conduct from which it is desired to deter him must be calculated to produce evil to someone else (*Liberty*, 68).

Many people have thought that in asserting this Mill was simply renouncing utilitarianism. Writers such as Immanuel Kant did denounce paternalism as an outrageous despotism; but they did so as part of an attack on utilitarian arguments. For Kant, the sovereignty of the individual was the starting point of moral argument; it was a metaphysical presupposition of ethics that each individual was an end in himself, a member of a kingdom of ends, someone whose highest achievement as a human being was to lay down the moral law to himself. But this is not the language of utilitarianism. The utilitarian considers individuals as sentient creatures, experiencing pains and pleasures, with an interest in having as few pains and as many pleasures as possible; from where is Mill to derive the prohibition on paternalism, and the insistence that coercion is only appropriate in order to defend others from harm? Before we answer that question, we must notice that Mill himself sharpens the problem for himself. He says, almost at once,

> It is proper to state that I forgo any advantage which could be derived to my argument from the idea of abstract right as a thing independent of utility. I regard utility as the ultimate appeal on all ethical questions; but it must be utility in the largest sense, grounded on the permanent interests of a man as a progressive being. Those interests, I contend, authorize the subjection of individual spontaneity to external control only in respect of those actions of each which concern the interest of other people (*Liberty*, 69–70).

So we have to answer the question of how Mill comes to think that utility implies the principle that the only basis of a right to dictate how others behave is self-defence. Some part of the answer will have to be spelled out shortly, when we follow Mill's defence of freedom of thought and discussion, and when we follow his argument about individuality and the need for experiments in living—for it is in the course of these arguments that Mill relies on his picture of 'man as a progressive being', to whom freedom is a prerequisite of happiness. But the interesting semi-technical question we must answer at once is that of how Mill derives concepts like that of *a right* from utility.

There is no agreed answer to this; indeed, disagreements on the issue are the staple of discussions of both *Utilitarianism* and *Liberty*. But the elements of an answer are as follows. The principle of utility is not itself a principle which anyone does or should follow; it is a principle for assessing the goodness or badness of *anything* whose goodness or badness we might wish to assess. It is not itself and straightforwardly a moral principle. It cannot be that, because absurdities would result. Suppose I go to the cinema and see a film I enjoy much less than I had expected. This is a bad outcome, and I made a mistake. I did not, however, commit a *wrong* in going to it; even if I did not bother to check up on the film, made no effort to make sure I would enjoy it, and even after the event did not care much that I hadn't enjoyed it, I should not have acted *wrongly*. A person who doesn't take care to choose sensibly will no doubt waste his or her money and be imprudent; but folly and imprudence are not the same thing as wickedness or wrongdoing. Mill's aim is to draw the line between folly on the one hand and the violation of other people's rights on the other in the place where reflective common sense and utilitarianism would coincide in placing it. It is this principled drawing of the line between legitimate and illegitimate intervention and non-intervention which is meant to replace the 'likings and mislikings of society' as the guide to coercive interference.

How does utilitarianism draw the line? Mill thinks of *morality* as essentially concerned with enforcement and punishment; to call an action wrong is, by definition, to say that it is the sort of thing which other people are, in principle, entitled to stop. This is not to say that everyone ought in fact to try to stop every wrong action; there are innumerable actions which are indeed wrong, but which we must simply let past on the grounds that their prevention would be a greater evil than they. This also is a matter of degree. Every promise creates a right in the beneficiary; if I promise to provide you with a house, sign, seal and deliver a contract, and then go back on it, the law is right to intervene and give you damages in the first place, and if I have committed a fraud to punish me too; but if I promise to make you a cup of coffee and then decide I can't be bothered, you will be justified in reproaching me, but not in trying to haul me into court. Mill's view, in outline, is that society is to be understood as a device whereby we are protected against the ill-will and aggression of others, and enabled to rely on them in co-operative activities, by means of social pressure on individuals. Society is not based on a contract, but our relationships with each other can usefully be visualised as if it was. Mill explains what he means in chapter IV, 'Of the Limits to the Authority of Society over the Individual'.

> Though society is not founded on a contract, and though no good purpose is answered by inventing a contract in order to deduce social obligations from it, everyone who receives the protection of society owes a return for the benefit, and the fact of living in society renders

> it indispensable that each should be bound to observe a certain line of conduct towards the rest. This conduct consists, first, in not injuring the interests of one another; or rather certain interests, which, either by express legal provision or by tacit understanding, ought to be considered as rights; and secondly, in each person's bearing his share (to be fixed on some equitable principle) of the labours and sacrifices incurred for defending the society or its members from injury and molestation (*Liberty*, 141).

One difficulty in Mill's account is that it is not entirely clear how to draw the line between the area of morality which is concerned with rights and the wider area of morality generally. Mill seems to draw it along two lines. The first is by asking whether it would be good to protect the 'interest' in question by coercive measures—which is why Mill refers to 'certain interests . . . which ought to be considered as rights'; the other is to ask whether it is essential to security to protect an interest. So, for instance, the right to life plainly succeeds on both counts—it is for the greatest good to protect our interest in continued existence, and but for such protection we should feel exceedingly insecure. My right to the fulfilment of small promises succeeds rather better on the first count than the second; I might not be much *harmed* by many non-fulfilments, but the whole business of promising and co-operating on the strength of promises to each other would be frustrated if we did not enforce promises.

Except where the obligation rests on agreements and promises, most 'rights' will impose duties of a negative kind. Your right to life primarily imposes on me the duty not to kill you. Your right not to be assaulted primarily imposes on me the duty not to attack you. However, this is only the general rule; there are, says Mill,

> many positive acts which he may rightfully be compelled to perform, such as to give evidence in a court of justice . . . and to perform certain acts of individual beneficence, such as saving a fellow creature's life or interposing to protect the defenceless against ill-usage . . . (*Liberty*, 70).

So Mill's crucial test for a 'right' is not attached by definition to the idea that other people's rights can only impose duties of abstention on us. That would be the doctrine of 'abstract' right which he rejects.

One further point which is worth noticing is that when Mill discusses rights in the body of *Liberty* he explains them in terms of interests. In essence, he holds that there are some interests which utilitarianism requires us to treat as rights. If we set great store by this explanation, as I think we should, we can then see that Mill asks himself the question—'what interests would it promote in the long run happiness of humanity to treat as rights?' If society is, as he often says, impossible except on the understanding that it exists in the first place to afford security to its members, it is evident that rights as immunities must be the most basic and the best protected rights we possess. It is also evident, however, that such rights as the right to a fair trial, which impose on others duties of giving evidence in a court of law, are readily defensible as protecting the sort of interests whose protection utility would demand. This position reflects the flexibility of a utilitarian, interest-based theory of rights. This flexibility is equally apparent when Mill qualifies the opening statement of his case by pointing out that he intends it to apply only to 'human beings in the maturity of their faculties' (*Liberty*, 69). He has two exceptions in mind; children and young people on the one hand, and 'those backward states of society in which the race itself may be considered as in its nonage' (*Liberty*, 69). Until they are of an age to be improved by argument and discussion both require paternalistic government. Mill's twentieth-century readers tend to flinch at the cheerfulness with which Mill (as befitted the senior permanent official of the East India Company) accepted the virtues of colonialism and despotism. There are also twentieth-century critics who would think Mill entirely underestimated the capacity of young people. Two other points are perhaps more likely to be overlooked. The first is that Mill's argument is in no way a criticism of the growth of democracy in Britain; the British working class—he thought—had long since passed beyond the stage at which arguments directed at children or the population of India applied to them. The other is that this is one of the places where Mill's utilitarian account of rights diverges sharply from an account such as Kant's. For Kant, despotic government was simply wrong. It was no use the East India Company, Akbar, or Charlemagne pointing to their benevolence and superior wisdom, for the point was that they simply had no right to govern without consent. Mill was entirely serious in saying that he appealed to utility.

All the same, the utility in question was that of a progressive being, and the interests which were at stake were the interests of progressive beings. We now need to follow Mill through the central chapters of *Liberty* to see how this makes a difference. In these chapters Mill first defends an absolute freedom of thought and discussion, then gives an account of the virtues of individuality, before recurring to a general discussion of the line between the individual's sphere and society's and some awkward examples. Mill's claim for the absolute inviolability of thought and discussion is one of the most famous parts of the entire essay. It is dragged into all sorts of twentieth-century discussions where it is rather dubiously at home, but even if we are fastidious about avoiding that, we are in controversial terrain enough.

The first thing to notice is that Mill does not employ his principle about not coercing others save in self-defence in the argument. He does not try to do anything very elaborate to show, for instance, that we are not 'harmed' by hearing opinions we very much dislike. In this area, Mill seems ready to admit that we may be shocked by, or very much dislike, a professed opinion, but he insists that this does not give us grounds for repressing it. What he rests on is an argument about fallibility and an argument about the worthlessness of merely conventional belief. To put it simply, the argument is, first, that suppressing opinions deprives humanity of the opportunity of discovering whatever truth they may contain, and, second, that it is important that our ideas should genuinely be *our own*, a condition which can only be fulfilled if we have some experience of hearing arguments against them and learning how to fend off those arguments. It is plain that a utilitarian argument for this case is going to have to rely quite heavily on the idea that mankind is in some sense progressive. A utilitarian who thought that mankind was, and should be, content to stagnate would happily argue that utility demanded that conventional opinion should always be upheld so far as possible. If people were only happy when they were undisturbed, the utilitarian argument against intellectual, moral, artistic and any other sort of innovation would be conclusive. So, we must dig into Mill's view of progress a little.

Mill was unlike his father and Bentham in being obsessed with history. They knew perfectly well that 'time and place' made a difference to whether laws would work, and to what sort of government it would be wise to install. Mill, however, held that the central discovery of the social sciences was that history progressed in a certain direction, and did so under the impact of changes in ideas. As I have said, it is this conviction which justifies Mill's entire life work. Mill's abiding hostility was to forms of philosophy which suggested that the ultimate test of truth was 'intuition'. In his *System of Logic* he attacked the philosophy of science put forward by William Whewell, because Whewell claimed that the truths of mathematics and geometry were known intuitively, and that the fundamental laws of nature were also known by intuition, even though it might take a lot of experiment and observation to make those laws as intuitively obvious as they ought to be. Mill detested this way of thinking, because he saw that what made intuitionism in mathematics and the philosophy of science attractive to its defenders was ultimately that it provided support for intuitionism in ethics.

Intuitionism in ethics seemed to him to sanctify custom and tradition and to encourage people in what they are anyway all too ready to do, that is in believing that their own strong feelings on ethical matters are enough of an argument and render further debate superfluous.

Mill was an empiricist. He thought that knowledge grew only by observation and experiment and reflection upon their results; increased knowledge in ethics could only come through deepening our understanding of human nature and its needs, and for this absolute freedom of enquiry was essential. Intuitionists cut short this process by claiming that we already know all the most important moral truths and cannot need further argument for them; Mill claimed two things in reply, the first that this amounted to an unwarranted boast of infallibility, the second that even where truths were in the end unchallengeable, they lost their life and their power over the imagination if men were not allowed to challenge them. Indeed, says Mill at one point,

> So essential is this discipline to a real understanding of moral and human subjects that, if opponents of all-important truths do not exist, it is indispensable to imagine them and supply them with the strongest arguments which the most skilful devil's advocate can conjure up (*Liberty*, 99).

Mill's argument is intended to be extreme and absolute. He explicitly repudiates any suggestion that his arguments for free speech must not be taken to extremes. It is, he thinks, necessary that they should be taken to extremes. So, we have to ask what sort of doctrines are included in the scope of Mill's case. In the United States, for instance, the sellers of pornography have, with varying degrees of success, argued that the constitutional prohibition on abridging free speech implies that they can sell their magazines and show their films, subject only to the usual restrictions on how anyone carries on any commercial activity. Needless to say, Mill does not address exactly this case—he does address the issues of the sale of narcotics and the carrying on of prostitution, but not as a question of free speech, of course. Mill's position is, however, clear enough. As to speech, narrowly construed, it must be lawful for anyone to express any opinion whatever. So, for instance, if the Pedophile Information Exchange confined itself to ventilating the question whether sexual relations between adults and children did either party any harm, it could not, in Mill's world, be touched by law, and even more importantly, it ought not to be touched by unofficial 'ganging up' of polite society against its members. Even if it advocated the abolition of most of the present laws against sexual relations between adults and children, it should not be touched. But, between this absolute licence and *incitement*, a sharp line had to be drawn. The same argument runs right the way through Mill's case. It would be impossible in a society run as Mill intended to forbid anyone from publishing the view that white Anglo-Saxon Protestants were chronically stupider and more idle than Jews, Indians, or whoever, and impossible to forbid anyone from publishing the reverse view. But, the line would always be held between that, and incitement to attacks of one sort and another. Unlike most of us, who tend to attach a high value to free speech, and a high value to public order, and then to worry about how to square the National Front's desire to march through Brixton with the local inhabitants' desire not to be insulted by their enemies, Mill thought his utilitarian account of rights could be relied on to yield an answer—not necessarily a simple answer, but an answer.

This answer is, in effect, that we should have no protection against the discomfort of knowing that other people had a low opinion of us—they might be right to have such an opinion, it would not be for the long-term good of humanity to protect us against such discomfort, and the desire for emotional security carries no weight against long-run utilitarian factors. But, society would be intolerable unless everyone had complete protection against the sudden and uncontrolled worsening of his or her position, and against actual attack by others. Applied to a case such as that of pornography, Mill's arguments fall awkwardly. One reason for this is that Mill himself expressly ruled out questions of decency and indecency from his discussion; there are many innocent actions which it would be indecent to perform in public—urination and defecation are in themselves innocent, but it is indecent to engage in them in a crowded street; sexual relations between married people are paradigmatically innocent, but if performed in the middle of Oxford Street are every bit as indecent as sexual intercourse between unmarried persons. Mill simply pushes such questions to one side, and it is impossible to guess how he thought utilitarianism could handle them. The shock of merely knowing that others have strange sexual tastes is not one which Mill would wish to protect us from, any more than from the shock of any other form of knowledge. (Equally, Mill would not wish to prevent Jews and Muslims knowing that their neighbours eat pork.) What there is no discussion of in Mill's account is the principles on which social space is to be shared by people with very different sexual or religious taboos. This is a genuine loss to the theory, for Mill envisages a plural society, and therefore ought to offer some solution to the question of how we are to cohabit peacefully while pursuing different intimations of the good life. The obvious answer would seem to involve an extrapolation of the principle of non-aggression—I may eat pork, but I may not so to speak eat it *at* my Jewish neighbours; I may pursue my tastes as a rubber fetishist but I may not *obtrude* them on the old lady next door. Mill thought that utilitarianism dictated our ordinary intuitions of what constituted 'fair shares' and he may have thought it obvious that the only solution in cases like this is fair shares too, allowing everyone space to pursue their own way of life, but preventing them from encroaching on the deep-seated feelings of others. On the other hand, he may have taken a more directly utilitarian line, and have thought that the only rights and immunities which people really had were those which they would have asked for if they had been fully informed utilitarians themselves. What division of social space we have to have now is then not a matter of principle in the allocation of fair shares, but a matter of the tactics which will bring about the enlightened utilitarian society in which these prejudiced, instinctive reactions do not occur. But what the inconclusiveness of any such attempt to extrapolate from Mill's discussion of opinion to twentieth-century concerns with sexual issues shows most plainly is how different Mill's own concerns were.

What they were, in addition to his concern to defend his account of progress and strike another blow against intuitionism, included an anxiety to stop respectability and Christianity ganging up against eccentricity and agnosticism. He was outraged by the way in which people had been denied justice in English courts because they would not swear on the Bible, but wished to affirm instead. He was outraged by the way working men were boycotted by employers for holding unorthodox religious views or none. He insisted that such unofficial pressure was as bad as outright persecution, seeing that a man might just as well be put in jail as denied the chance of earning a living. His hostility to Christianity in particular—not as a creed, but as manifested in the oppressive habits of his contemporaries—was increased by his sense that Christians had better reason than most to beware of persecution. He observed that there was nothing which a Victorian Christian could say in favour of suppressing dissent which had not been said before and better by Marcus Aurelius in favour of suppressing Christianity. He rejected the cant view that persecution never really destroys a doctrine; on the contrary, says Mill, wherever persecution is persisted in it succeeds in its objects. Catholicism survives wherever sixteenth-century governments persecuted their Protestant subjects with any determination; Lollards, Hussites, Anabaptists were all wiped out without any hope of revival. The only thing to be said on the other side is that where a suppressed belief is literally true, there is the prospect that it will be rediscovered over and over again until eventually its discovery coincides with a period of toleration. Although it is not true that *Liberty* is primarily concerned with Christian intolerance, it must be said that it bulks large in Mill's concerns—much larger than sexual intolerance.

Chapters III and IV of *Liberty* belong together; they belong together because in Chapter III Mill unveils his account of individuality, and in Chapter IV draws the implications for where the line is to be drawn between individual freedom and social control. Mill begins the discussion of individuality by agreeing that actions are not as free as opinions. It is here that he employs his famous example of the opinion that corn dealers are robbers of the poor, which 'ought to be unmolested when simply circulated through the press, but may justly incur punishment when delivered orally to an excited mob assembled before the house of a corn dealer, or when handed about among the same mob in the form of a placard' (*Liberty*, 119). But, says Mill, this restriction is comprehended under the requirement that a man must not make himself a nuisance to others. The purpose of the chapter is to defend the proposition that where others are not primarily concerned, individuals must be allowed, at their own risk and expense, to live according to their own opinions.

The elaboration of this case, considered as a philosophical defence of Mill's proposed line between the coercible and the non-coercible, comes in Chapter IV, and has to some extent been anticipated in our discussion of Mill's utilitarianism. What precedes it is Mill's defence of individuality as a good in itself. This is not *philosophically* very elaborate; it contains, rather, what one might call an extended picture of what individuality consists in, why Mill thinks it matters, and what about the present age threatens it. Mill's argument is two edged. One edge amounts to a claim about what the individual gets out of individuality, the other a claim about what the rest of mankind gets out of it. And, again, part of the argument is negative—showing what we lose by taking any other view—and part positive, celebrating the pleasures of active individuality.

Mill's hero is Wilhelm von Humboldt, whose book on *The Sphere and Duties of Government* provided Mill with the epigraph of *Liberty*:

> The grand, leading principle, towards which every argument unfolded in these pages directly converges, is the absolute and essential importance of human development in its richest diversity (*Liberty*, 57).

Where this concern for diversity, originality and individuality is lacking, 'there is wanting one of the principal ingredients of human happiness, and quite the chief ingredient of individual and social progress' (*Liberty*, 120). Individuality consists in our having a strong sense that whatever the views we hold and whatever way of life we adopt should be truly *ours*. In effect, it amounts to holding the view which justifies Mill's argument in favour of freedom of opinion—the view that it is not just a matter of what we believe and do but a matter of the liveliness with which we believe and act.

Negatively, Mill observes that a person who is prepared to take the opinions of others as a complete guide to life needs no other talents than 'the ape-like one of imitation' (*Liberty*, 123). Positively Mill claims that using all our faculties is itself a contribution to happiness. The man who feels himself to be fully stretched feels a happiness not available to anyone less vigorous. This is Mill's argument in *Liberty* which corresponds to his claim in *Utilitarianism* that Socrates' discontent is better than the fool's contentment, that Socrates would be unhappier if he were less moved by his discontent. It is an argument with which many philosophers have quarrelled, but which others have frequently tried to resurrect. For there is an obvious difficulty in asserting that a man who is, say, clinging with his finger-nails to a cliff is at that very moment 'happy'—he may not be enjoying the experience in the least and may be longing to get down or get up. But, we are also moved by the thought that he would not himself want to have avoided his predicament; he has chosen to be there. His being there is, we must admit, in some sense *a good for him*; and it is this that Mill relies on. The psychological fact which makes Mill's case impressive is, of course, that it is such 'stretching' activities which those who practise them are most reluctant to give up. If the natural test of whether somebody finds happiness in an activity is the enthusiasm with which he pursues it, Mill's case is a plausible one. In essence, Mill is relying on an asymmetry in the attitudes of his fully active characters and their more custom-minded fellows. Once fully awoken, people do not wish to go back to sleep; when the sleepers wake, they are glad. It is not an elaborate argument, but it strikes many people on reflection as about the best that this sort of discussion admits of.

Mill's attack on other conceptions of life proceeds along a path which is by this stage in the essay a familiar one. That is, he assails the Calvinist view that the proper attitude to ourselves is one of self-abnegation. Certainly, the ability to subordinate our own interests to those of others is essential to social life; extreme self-abnegation may sometimes be essential, too. There are good utilitarian reasons for agreeing to these claims; some ability to act unselfishly is needed if society is not to dissolve into civil war, occasional emergencies demand heroic self-sacrifice. None the less repression is a false ideal. What we want is strong characters, capable of standing up for themselves. Even if they sometimes act wrongly, it is better to take that risk than to have a society of enfeebled creatures such as the repressed ideal aims at. At this point, Mill begins to sound a little like Nietzsche, and his attack on the Christian ethic begins to sound a little like Nietzsche's attack on 'slave morality'. But, as many people have pointed out, it is more than a little unfair of Mill to saddle Calvinism with such a self-destructive view of the world. Calvinism is notorious for producing decidedly strong-minded, self-reliant and independent-minded individuals—they may be rigid, one-track, intolerant and tough, but they aren't exactly given to slavish imitation of their fellows. Mill might have done better to have gone down the same track as Matthew Arnold and said outright that he wanted somehow to combine the Protestant conscience and the Greek ideal of the good life.

As for why the rest of mankind should allow us to pursue our individual excellence in this fashion, the answer is simple enough. Just as we ought to be glad to see others think differently from ourselves, since their doing so is an exploration of ideas from which we may possibly benefit, so we ought to be happy to see others explore the possibilities of other ways of life even if we have no inclination to pursue them. We are the gainers by their experiments—if they discover new sources of happiness and new ways of life, we benefit, and if they discover dead ends, we benefit by learning which roads not to travel. Something which is less visible is an assumption which may underlie a lot of Mill's argument. This is that if people become more convinced of the truth of a generally utilitarian picture of morality, they will cease to feel threatened by their differences with their fellows. Mill's arguments are, so to speak, better arguments for utilitarians than for anyone else. Since Mill supposes that rational people will become utilitarians, he must suppose that he can argue with them on two fronts—persuading them to see the world in utilitarian terms, and persuading them to interpret utilitarianism in the way he does.

That this process of argument is more necessary now than ever before follows from Mill's perspective on history generally. Once, it was essential that society should try to get the upper hand over individuals; violence and self-assertion were the order of the day, heroic individuals were two a penny and a menace to their neighbours. Progress demanded order. It was important, too, that this order was more than skin deep. It would not have been enough for law and order to be established without an underlying moral commitment to the idea that the well-being of society at large was a legitimate reason for restricting the freedom of individuals. But, Mill thought, as he so often said, that in the contest between socialibility and anti-social individuality, sociability had got the upper hand to such a degree that further progress demanded a redressing of the balance. Mill was reading a lesson to his friends in saying this, as well as fighting a holy war against social conformity. For it was reformers like Auguste Comte and administrators like Mill's friend Edwin Chadwick who risked sacrificing individual liberty for the sake of the general welfare. Comte was 'liberticide' by temperament as well as by theory; Chadwick had none of the wildly dictatorial ambitions of Comte (who saw himself as the creator of a new religion and a new Church as well as a new society), but his benevolence made him unperceptive about the threats to freedom which his tidying up involved. The explicit, centralized desire for order which came from politicians and administrators worked with the other pressures of the age. The development of the economy meant that organization, communications, education, marketing—all were on the side of uniformity and the predominance of the large scale over the individual. Mill did not quite anticipate the twentieth-century idea that the manager and the bureaucrat were the central figures of our age, but he came very close.

> What, then, is the rightful limit to the sovereignty of the individual over himself? Where does the authority of society begin? How much of human life should be assigned to individuality, and how much to society? (*Liberty*, 141).

With these large questions, Mill begins Chapter IV of *Liberty*, and in the pages that follow he spells out the implications of the answer he gave at the beginning of the essay. That is, he spells out the implications of his claim that individuals may be coerced out of attacking others, and coerced into bearing their fair share of 'common defence'—and otherwise may only be exhorted, entreated and persuaded. As we saw, Mill is sometimes thought to be arguing for a 'let-alone' policy; but he denies it.

> It would be a great misunderstanding of this doctrine to suppose that it is one of selfish indifference which pretends that human beings have no business with each other's conduct in life, and that they should not concern themselves about the well-doing or well-being of one another, unless their interest is involved (*Liberty*, 142).

Moreover, Mill is also eager to point out that he does not suppose that how people act in 'self-regarding' matters can be a matter of indifference to others. If we ourselves have any sort of standards, we are bound to have strong views about the behaviour of others. We cannot think that our own tastes and interests are ones which serious people would share and not think the worse of people who don't share them. The man who spends all his time watching video nasties or drinking too much does not harm us, violates no positive duty towards us; but we are unlikely to think he is the sort of man we want as a friend, and we shall hardly be able to help thinking that he is a pretty poor specimen of humanity. Mill does not wish us to think anything else. What he wishes is that we should not think we may punish him for his self-regarding vices. This requires us to draw a careful line between what we may and may not do. Mill's thought is that punishment is essentially social; where we think someone is punishable, we think that we ought to gang up with others in inflicting punishment. But where we think only that in the exercise of our own freedom of action we may avoid the company of another, this is not a matter of encouraging everyone to gang up against him, only a matter of claiming for ourselves the freedom we do not deny him. Certainly, it is true that if someone is such a low specimen of the human race that none of us can bring himself or herself to make friends with him, the effect is the same as if we were to organize a boycott. None the less, it makes all the difference which way we think of it.

To enforce this line of argument, Mill insists on some familiar distinctions, and fights off some obvious objections. The familiar distinction between wickedness and imprudence is one which Mill has to rely on in the same way as the rest of us. If we ask what the logic is of describing behaviour as 'imprudent', it is plain that it is all to do with the agent's own welfare; if, when we point out that an action is imprudent, he says either that he does not care or that he can avoid the ill consequences, our objections on the score of imprudence must be much reduced. A wicked action, on the other hand, is much more plausibly one which does damage to others. Were the agent whose actions are complained of to reply that he does not much mind, or that he can bear the results, our response would be to try to *make* him mind, where it seems rather odd to try to back up claims about imprudent behaviour by making a man mind.

Similarly, Mill relies on a commonsense view of the distinction between direct and remote consequences. It may well be that a man does self-regarding actions which eventually and remotely make him behave in a way which is genuinely culpable; Mill's view is that this gives us no licence to repress the self-regarding behaviour, but only the other-regarding behaviour which directly violates rights. It may, say, be the case that I rarely read anything carefully; unpredictably, I fail to read the manual of the coach I am driving, crash and injure my passengers. Mill insists that we cannot force people to read carefully just in case; what we do is hold people responsible if they cause accidents, and punish them particularly severely if they cause accidents by carelessness. Analogously, merely getting drunk is no offence; a man who loses his temper because he is drunk and then assaults another is punishable for the assault. If he does it again, he is then punishable more severely. The same doctrine applies to the effects of circumstances. It is obviously a matter of my free choice when I go to bed—but if I am on sentry duty or driving a train. Mill's consequentialism resists any suggestion that we somehow try to see whether an action is *essentially* self-regarding or other-regarding. Many actions which would be self-regarding under some conditions become other-regarding under others. But since society is not always under the same conditions as an armed camp, no good purpose is served by abolishing the distinction in usual conditions.

We then have to step back once more and ask why Mill resists the suggestion that since he is a utilitarian, he ought to accept that *any* methods are legitimate if they achieve the appropiate goal. However, the answer is simple enough. Mill maintains the nature of the goal is such that coercive measures simply aren't in place. That is, once we have decided in virtue of the arguments in Chapter III that a major part of the utilitarian goal is itself the creation of a certain sort of character—fearless, tolerant, many-sided and so on—the means we can use to promote that goal are also fixed. We cannot create heroes by compulsion, we cannot make people spontaneous by fiat, we cannot really even make people prudent by compulsion—we can at best prevent the worst consequences of their imprudence.

What Mill has to attack is the thought that we are entitled to have others either live up to our standard of personal excellence or to do for the public at large everything they are capable of doing. This, of course, he has done throughout the essay. Here he argues it again in the context of laws against drink. Temperance campaigners claim that their 'social rights' are invaded if they have to live in a society in which people drink too much; Mill in effect asks what degree of tyranny such a principle would *not* licence. None of us would be safe from the moral preconceptions of other people, and there would be an end to all forms of liberty.

> So monstrous a principle is far more dangerous than any single interference with liberty; there is no violation of liberty which it would not justify . . . The doctrine ascribes to all mankind a vested interest in each other's moral, intellectual, and even physical perfection, to be defined by each claimant according to his own standard (*Liberty*, 158).

It is obvious to Mill that nobody can seriously propose a theory of rights which has such a result. Once again, we see the strength of Mill's belief that his brand of utilitarianism supports an account of rights which favours libertarianism.

Mill's 'applications' of the argument in his final chapter are interesting less for what they rule in and out than for the subtlety with which the argument develops. Mill, that is, is eager to argue not only that various legal restraints which presently exist ought not to do so, and that various social pressures which apply at present ought not to do so, but to argue for the imposition of social and even legal pressure at points where it is not presently applied. Basically, Mill's approach is simply to take particular issues and show what are the consequences of his case. Thus, he insists that the sale of poisons is an area where governments may not stop people buying poisons, but may insist on their signing a register, so that if there is misuse, it is simple to trace whether suspects have purchased the means of crime. Recurring to the question of laws against drink, he conceded that a man who cannot get drunk without becoming violent may properly be penalized for getting drunk—because *in his case* the connection is direct enough to warrant it. More interestingly, he argues for the prohibition of people selling themselves into slavery on the peculiar ground that 'it is not freedom to be allowed to alienate his freedom' (*Liberty*, 173). It was not slavery which he had in mind, but marriage, for the principle he wants to defend is the principle that people should not be allowed to bind themselves to personal ties which are legally irrevocable. Slavery is an acute example, but marriage was a more pressing one.

Mill's claim that selling oneself into slavery is not freedom is awkwardly made. On the face of it, if we have the right to dispose of ourselves as we please, and we please to be a slave, then it is in the exercise of our freedom that we renounce it. No doubt it is the last free choice we make, but so too is the free choice of suicide as a better alternative to a painful and lingering death by some fatal illness. Mill might have done better to employ another argument which surfaces in his *Principles of Political Economy*. That is, he might have pointed out that buying and selling—entering into marriage too for that matter—all require social conventions which back up the arrangements we make. Property is essentially conventional, as is marriage; the grounds for creating and sustaining such conventions must be utilitarian and libertarian, namely that they extend people's choices. Slavery and irrevocable marriage both frustrate that goal; They ought therefore not to be recognized. If someone wishes to behave in a slavish fashion, that's his business; but that is infinitely far from suggesting that the rest of us ought to support institutions which force him to go on behaving in a slavish fashion when he has changed his mind.

In general, Mill does rest on the thought that trade is a conventionally assisted activity. The regulation of trade may often be an error—which is why *laissez-faire* is a sound principle—but it is not in principle illicit. However, there is a difficulty in this, which is that some sorts of trade look as if they are no more than an application of Mill's principle that whatever a man is free to do he ought to be free to do in common with others (subject to the usual restriction that the effects of their so doing ought not to be damaging to others). If applied to prostitution and gambling, this seems to imply that brothels and gaming houses ought not to be prohibited. Gambling itself cannot—save where, as in the case of the drunk who gets aggressive, the gambler is out of control—and fornication cannot be—though it may provide grounds for divorce. What of those who provide the service? Mill says that these are cases which are exactly on the borders of two distinct principles, and evades giving a decisive answer. The general principle is not too hard to work out, however; the dangers of gaming houses and brothels are what Mill himself had earlier called 'contingent'—that is, there is always a risk that the owners and managers will cheat, rob and defraud their clientele, will blackmail them, or will themselves be preyed upon by other criminals. So some sort of regulation is needed where prohibition is not.

Mill, however, was most interested in cases where dependent individuals needed to be protected from those to whom they are closest. This interest comes out clearly when he discusses the state's role in education. Parents owe their children a duty of education; indeed, they owe that duty not just to their children but to society at large. Not merely are their children dependent on them for the intellectual and psychological resources they will need in later life, but the whole society is dependent on their not sending out into the world young people who are a drain on everyone else's resources. Society is entirely within its rights in insisting that parents see to the education of their children. Mill was, of course, eager that the state should not monopolize the provision of education; the whole of *Liberty* implies that educational provision should be as diverse as possible. But it would obviously be intolerable if parents were compelled to provide education in spite of their poverty, so the general principle has to be that they should be compelled to see that their children get an education, the education itself be provided by a diversity of bodies which can be supervised for their factual efficiency, but not for any sort of doctrinal orthodoxy, and the parents given grants if they need them, or some schools provided free as an alternative. Mill's general stance is to shy away from the state providing either all education or a free back-up service.

> An education established and controlled by the state should only exist, if it exist at all, as one among many competing experiments, carried on for the purpose of example and stimulus to keep the others up to a certain standard or excellence . . . if the country contains a sufficient number of persons qualified to provide education under government auspices, the same persons would be able and willing to give an equally good education on the voluntary principle, under the assurance of remuneration afforded by a law rendering education compulsory, combined with State aid to those unable to defray the expense (*Liberty*, 177).

The hope is rather that the state will provide experimental education to balance any lack of variety in the market place. Only in under-developed societies must the state take the lead.

Mill's insistence on intervention in this area goes along with an insistence that it is within the state's proper sphere to regulate marriage. People who marry without the resources to provide for the children they will certainly have are in effect imposing burdens on others—they are violating the rule that they must not make themselves nuisances. So Mill was perfectly happy that there should be 'laws which, in many countries on the Continent, forbid marriage unless the parties can show that they have the means of supporting a family . . . (*Liberty*, 179). These did not exceed the legitimate province of government; those who objected to such laws showed the odd state of thinking on the subject in Britain.

> When we compare the strange respect of mankind for liberty with their strange want of respect for it we might imagine that a man had an indispensable right to harm others, and no right at all to please himself without giving pain to others (*Liberty*, 180).

Mill ends *Liberty* with what is strictly a digression from its main theme, namely the consideration of those cases where government action is legitimate in terms of his 'very simple principle', but where there are other objections to it. Though it is a digression, it is a topic which reappears in his *Considerations on Representative Government* and in the famous fifth book of his *Principles of Political Economy*, and it is the centrepiece of his theory of government. Moreover, it might be said that it fits in perfectly with the rest of *Liberty* simply because it is a restatement of the creed of 'self-dependence' to which the essay is devoted. Mill claims, first, that generally speaking people manage their own affairs better than a government manages for them—this is not true of colonial dependencies, but they are, as we have seen, precisely the sort of exception he is concerned with. Secondly, and more to the point, when individuals look after their own affairs, it does them good. They learn new skills, acquire more energy, take a wider interest in the world. So, where there is a choice between government activity and voluntary organization we should always choose the latter. Finally, the growth of bureaucratic government is itself a bad thing. It deadens the energies, it drains talent out of the rest of society and sends it to sleep in the government service. A good bureaucracy must be a small bureaucracy. Russia, China and to a large extent France among European nations, show the evils of allowing the government machine to absorb too large a share of the life of society. And this is a lesson which reformers ought to bear in mind. Better to cure evils slower than to create a state which dwarfs its members. For that is the self-defeating conclusion of such reform—such a state

> will find that with small men no great thing can really be accomplished; and that the perfection of machinery to which it has sacrificed everything will avail it nothing, for want of the vital power which, in order that the machine might work more smoothly, it has preferred to banish (*Liberty*, 187).

It is a proposition which every reformer appalled by the slowness and disorder of the process of improvement ought to have engraved on his heart.

Friedrich Nietzsche

Friedrich Nietzsche (1844–1900) was born in the village of Röcken, in Prussian Saxony, the son and grandson of Lutheran ministers. He studied theology and classical philosophy at the University of Bonn, but in 1865 he gave up theology and went to Leipzig. Then he discovered the composer Richard Wagner and the philosophers Schopenhauer and F. A. Lange (author of *History of Materialism and Critique of its Present Significance*, 1866). He won a prize for an essay on Diogenes Laertius, the biographer of ancient Greek philosophers, and was appointed associate professor of classical philology at Basel, when he was only twenty-four. He became a full professor the following year. His principle writings between then and 1879, when illness made him resign from the university, were *The Birth of Tragedy* (1872) and *Human, All Too Human* (1878). After his resignation his principal writings were *Daybreak* (1881), *The Gay Science* (1882), *Thus Spoke Zarathustra* (Parts 1 and 2 published 1883, Part 3 published 1884, Part 4 issued privately 1885, published 1892), *Beyond Good and Evil* (1886), *On the Genealogy of Morals* (1887), *The Wagner Case* (1888) and *Twilight of the Idols* (1888). Nietzsche became insane in January 1889, and vegetated until his death in 1900. His madness was probably tertiary syphilis, which he may have contracted while ministering to sick soldiers in 1870 as a medical orderly in the Franco-Prussian war.

The edition of *Beyond Good and Evil*, prescribed by the JMB, is Friedrich Nietzsche, *Beyond Good and Evil*, translated, with an introduction and commentary by R. J. Hollingdale (Harmondsworth: Penguin, 1973).

Three commentaries are:

R. J. Hollingdale, *Nietzsche* (London: Routledge and Kegan Paul, 1973)

F. A. Lea, *The Tragic Philosopher* (London: Methuen, new edn, 1973)

E. Heller, *The Disinherited Mind* (London: Bowes and Bowes, 1975).

Nietzsche, *Beyond Good and Evil*

MICHAEL TANNER

Although Nietzsche's greatness is recognized more universally now than ever before, the nature of that greatness is still widely misunderstood, and that unfortunately means that before I discuss any of *Beyond Good and Evil* (henceforth *BGE*) in any detail, I must make some general remarks about his work, his development and the kind of way in which I think that it is best to read him. Unlike any of the other philosophers that this series includes, except Marx and Engels, Nietzsche is very much concerned to address his contemporaries, because he was aware of a specific historical predicament, one which he would only see as having worsened in ways which he predicted with astonishing precision in the century since he wrote his great series of works. For he was above all a philosopher of culture, which is to say that his primary concern was always with the forces that determine the nature of a particular civilization, and with the possibilities of achievement which that civilization consequently had open to it. One of the reasons that *The Birth of Tragedy*, his first book, published when he was twenty-eight, created such a surge of hostility in the world of classical scholarship was that in it, whilst undertaking an investigation of what made possible the achievements of fifth century BC Greece in tragic drama, he felt it necessary to elicit the whole set of fundamental beliefs which the Greeks shared, and also to draw metaphysical conclusions from the fact that they were able to experience life in such a way that they needed great tragedies in order to endure it.

Although nearly all of Nietzsche's later work is sharply unlike *The Birth of Tragedy*, it is entirely characteristic of him that, having embarked on a study in aesthetics, he should move into a consideration of historical circumstances, of the nature of tragic enjoyment, of the rise and decline of Greek tragedy, of the forces at work in Greek culture, of the metaphysics which underlay that culture, of the relationship between Greek art and Greek philosophy, and finally of the possibilities of resuscitating tragedy in his own age and in Germany. Yet *The Birth of Tragedy*, like nearly all his books, is short—about one hundred and fifty pages. This means that his method cannot be one that recommends itself to the characteristic academic temperament, which counsels rigour, caution, imposing standards of evidence and proof, minute investigation of particular phenomena, and above all a compartmentalizing of studies. The combination of abusive hostility and contemptuous indifference with which *Birth* was received in the academic community alerted Nietzsche to the hopelessness of gaining respect from his colleagues while remaining true to what he felt to be his essential task, and that, combined with increasing and incessant ill-health throughout the 1870s, led him to abandon academic life completely before the end of the decade, and to spend what turned out to be the remaining nine years of sanity as a solitary, writing what he pleased for a public that turned out not to exist.

Nietzsche never lost the sense of the urgency of his mission—on the contrary. And the fact that his books sold fewer and fewer copies, until his masterpieces sold, to all intents and purposes, none at all, only made him the more determined to say things his way. It was some time before he hit on the form that was both most suited to his own temperament and to the kind of message that he had to convey. As early as his superb essay *On the Uses and Disadvantages of History for Life*, the second of the *Untimely Meditations*, he had concluded that each of us

> must organize the chaos within him by thinking back to his real needs. His honesty, the strength and truthfulness of his character, must at some time or other rebel against a state of things in which he only repeats what he has heard, learns what is already known, imitates what already exists; he will then begin to grasp that culture can be something other than a *decoration of life*, that is to say at bottom no more than dissimulation and disguise; for all adornment conceals that which is adorned. Thus the Greek conception of culture will be unveiled to him—in antithesis to the Roman—the concept of culture as a new and improved physis [nature], without inner and outer, without dissimulation and convention, culture as a unanimity of life, thought, appearance and will.[1]

Although what this vision of culture came to in detail and in practice was something that changed dramatically between the time he wrote that (1873) and when he wrote *BGE* (1885), every word he wrote there applies to his later works. What he found, in pursuing his investigations and 'experiments', as he often called them, was that the form in which he could best express—and expression and experience, outer and inner, were always inseparable for him—his insights was not a linear, consecutive mode, but rather collections of short essays, often a paragraph long, rarely more than a couple of pages, interspersed with what are recognizably aphorisms. Though he was a brilliant aphorist, as Part Four, 'Maxims and Interludes', of *BGE* conclusively shows, it was not

[1] *Untimely Meditations*, trans. R. J. Hollingdale (Cambridge University Press, 1983), 123.

his most characteristic or most impressive form of writing. But the mode that he did most often adopt, and above all in the series of books from *Human, All Too Human* through to *BGE* (with the exception of *Thus Spoke Zarathustra*, which is an exception to everything) is one that is best approached in the spirit that aphorisms typically require.

What is that spirit? Aphorisms are the most risky form of writing. If they succeed they strike one as being brilliant and memorable, but a failed aphorism is, considering its brevity, especially depressing. Successful ones, such as a high proportion of La Rochefoucauld's, tend to come into the 'What oft was thought but ne'er so well expressed' category. But the profoundest aphorisms, and the adequately profound response to them, make and draw forth rather different claims and efforts. The best account I know of what the aphoristic mode of discourse comes to and hence of how to read Nietzsche (and the same applies to a great deal of Wittgenstein) is given by Tracy Strong in his uneven book *Friedrich Nietzsche and the Politics of Transfiguration*. Indeed, it is so impressive that it amounts to a set of aphorisms about aphorisms, and is therefore scarcely paraphrasable. But short of quoting a lengthy passage *in toto*, I'll try to convey what Strong says, while urging that the whole passage be read and pondered.[2] A deep aphorism forces us to find out what it is an answer to, always something one should have in mind when reading Nietzsche. It disturbs us, and in doing so makes us see what it is in it and in us that carries this disturbing force. Unlike discursive argumentation, which can be impressive and convincing while leaving us in a sense outside, it insists that we construct ourselves, or a part of ourselves, round it. It demands, that is, an effort of self-creation or re-creation. That presents problems for the expounder of aphorisms. He has to get his listeners to share rather than to observe and consider. A series of aphorisms of this kind is thus an injunction, implicit, or often in Nietzsche's case explicit, to change one's life. As in all invitations to be creative, it disrupts and upsets us as much as it illuminates. 'Dionysos [the presiding deity of aphoristic thought]', says Strong, 'calls not for argumentation, as might a dialectician, nor for inner light, as does an evangelist, but for creation, the building of a world in which the aphorism will not present itself as a problem.'[3] One consequence of this, if it's accepted, is that an attempt to read aphorisms through at the speed one might read an argument, even a very subtle one, is futile. Nietzsche says that to appreciate them 'one has to be almost a cow, and certainly not a modern man'.

[2] Tracy Strong, *Friedrich Nietzsche and the Politics of Transfiguration*, (Berkeley: University of California Press, 1975), 132–134.

[3] Strong, ibid., 134

Actually, although Strong is extremely helpful on the subject, and although almost all of what he says is a commentary on various remarks from *BGE*, the work in which Nietzsche is most self-conscious about his methods of conveying insights, the situation is in one way more tricky, in another less so. If *BGE* were as completely aphoristic as Strong suggests, and in a deep sense, it would be an even more taxing book than it is. But in fact it combines aphorism and argumentation in a way unique to Nietzsche. Much of the time, as we shall see, what Nietzsche writes is discussable in a way that one is familiar with from other philosophers. Indeed, much of it consists in attacking them, and while some of the attacks are upon the terms that they argue in, some are on their own terms. Not surprisingly, it turns out to be these latter passages that commentators seize on to deal with Nietzsche. But if one concentrates only on them, the crucially, inherently aphoristic nature of his thinking, as I've tried to sketch it, is lost, and hence what makes him truly disturbing, as opposed to exciting, infuriating or 'stimulating', goes by the board. For how can one argue with an aphorism? And if one can't, what does one do with it? The answer is usually very simple: one forgets it. For it is one of the most striking features of reading Nietzsche, even when he is at his best—an amazingly high proportion of the time—that he is both very striking and strangely unmemorable. If one goes through the text of *BGE* using a high-lighter, one's likely to find that one has marked more than half the book. It comes as a shock when one re-reads it a month later, say, and finds not only that one is reading many of the high-lighted passages as if for the first time, but that one is scandalized by one's non-high-lighting of other wonderful passages, and occasionally bewildered at what one *did* mark. Since aphorisms are related non-linearly, one can't retrace them, as one can an argument, by recalling the steps in it. And if the effect is, as so often, one of dazzlement, that's all the more likely to lead to forgetfulness.

Nietzsche himself says, in *Thus Spoke Zarathustra*, 'Whoever writes in blood and aphorisms wants not to be read but to be learned by heart'. But is one to learn most of his writings by heart? Apart from deficiencies of memory, even if one did it might still get one nowhere. They need, in a metaphor that Nietzsche is very fond of, to be digested. But how does that metaphor work out in detail, especially if one's not intending to devote most of one's life to thinking about Nietzsche?

Instead of answering that question directly and immediately, I want to say a little about the place of *BGE* in Nietzsche's work; then I shall deal with a very few of its salient passages and hope to show how I find it most helpful to cope with him. It is always important to locate anything of his one is reading in the progression of his thought. For it developed at an extraordinary rate and he can easily be made to seem absurd, self-contradictory, or sometimes more remarkable than he is if excerpts from separate periods of his sixteen-year writing career are juxtaposed as if they were contemporaneous. There is a widely held view about his development, one which he himself was not averse to, and which seems to me to be fundamentally wrong. It isn't at all difficult to see why he was inclined to impose a pattern on his works, as he also does on his life—they are hardly distinguishable. That is what he does in *Ecce Home*, his bizarre but still marvellous autobiography. The accepted account goes like this: Nietzsche began as a disciple of Schopenhauer, with whom he shared the connection of the world as essentially Will, and his pessimistic valuation of existence. Also, and more importantly, he was a disciple of Richard Wagner, who at that stage—the stage of *The Birth of Tragedy* and *Untimely Meditations*—he saw as the person who could do for contemporary Germany what the Greek tragedians had done for Athens. Then, beginning in 1874 he became disillusioned both with Wagner's works, which he later devoted two books to attacking, and at least as significantly, with the personality of Wagner himself, though Wagner remained the most important single influence in his life, as he freely admitted time after time, even when attacking him. And his distaste for Schopenhauer's superficial pessimism evaporated painlessly at the same time. Nietzsche, naturally a believer in great men and a hero-worshipper (however much he disapproved in theory of the latter trait), spent the next few years in a philosophical wilderness, writing a series of aphoristic works which culminated in *The Gay Science*, and reaching, so the commentators say, such an impasse of scepticism that the alternatives were to cease altogether or to create something wholly new. Thanks to the great idea which he had in the Swiss Engadine in 1881, 'six thousand feet above man and time', the idea of the Eternal Recurrence of all things, he was able to write his central work (this is still the authorized version), *Thus Spoke Zarathustra*, and after that unrepeatable masterpiece he wrote a further series of books, all of them to be seen more or less in the light of commentaries on *Zarathustra*. Indeed, when he sent a copy of *BGE* to Jacob Burckhardt in 1886, he included a letter saying 'Please read this book (although it says the same things as my *Zarathustra*, but differently, very differently)'. To a large extent that is false. Of the doctrines for which *Zarathustra* is famous, the Will to Power, the *Übermensch* and the Eternal Recurrence, he mentions the last only once, and not by name, in *BGE*, and the second, which is perhaps the single term most closely associated with his name, not once. The Will to Power is certainly ubiquitous as a motif in *BGE*, but that doesn't go far to constituting Nietzsche's claimed identity between the two works. Furthermore, in a writer as literary as Nietzsche, that is to say one in whom the substance of what he says is so intimately bound up with his way of saying it, it scarcely makes sense to talk about saying the same things in a very different way. What the remark in the letter shows is rather that Nietzsche was intent on self-mythologizing as he went along, and not only in retrospect; that he wanted his works to have a unity or continuity with one another, or to represent tellingly sharp oppositions, when often they do none of these things. It is, after all, Zarathustra's supreme task to herald the arrival of the *Übermensch*, since he is so nauseated by man and what he has made of his possibilities that he is convinced that man must be overcome—that the whole concept *man* must be overcome. Readers of *Zarathustra*, perhaps including its author, and certainly very patient and sympathetic ones, have tended to find not only that the *Übermensch* is underdescribed, but that the means whereby he might arrive on earth are left entirely unclear. In so far as ideals that have never yet been realized—and Zarathustra says 'there has never yet been a superman'—are problematic in their specification, and necessarily so if they involve any radically new departure, the criticism may be an unfair one. It is one of the problems with ideals that if we use our already existing concepts to delineate them, they tend to come too close to what already occurs; while if they don't, it's hard to see in what way they can be elucidated. A tell-tale sign of this is Nietzsche's use of such oxymoronic phrases as 'Caesar with the heart of Christ'. A celebrated case of the same kind is the Christian heaven, which is either represented in a tawdry and vulgar way, or else said to be ineffable. As for the *Übermensch*, though we've certainly had plenty of tawdry and vulgar caricatures of him in the twentieth century, no one has appeared who can be seen as a significant advance on humanity, and therefore deserving of the title.

It isn't always realized that Nietzsche has two separate concepts, that of the *higher man* and that of the *Übermensch*. Higher men are simply very remarkable examples of mankind, and among them Nietzsche numbers Goethe, Napoleon and, notoriously, Cesare Borgia. Though he devotes quite a lot of space to celebrating them, they still aren't good *enough* for him to rest content with. Nietzsche failed to develop the concept of the *Übermensch* sufficiently for it to occupy the central position in his thought that is strongly suggested in *Zarathustra*; and in *BGE* and the books that follow it he confines himself to a more modest task—that of working out the conditions under which higher men might flourish, our civilization being inimical to them to a degree which makes their occurrence less likely than it would anyway be. That does mean that *Zarathustra* can't occupy the key place in his work that he and many of his readers have taken it to. And although it is a masterpiece, though a seriously flawed one, it could be omitted from Nietzsche's works without there being, in one way, any noticeable effect on the others. The works that succeeded it were designed as commentaries on it, but that isn't at all the impression they give.

If that proposition, which the majority of Nietzsche scholars would find questionable, is rejected, my reply is this: move straight on from reading *The Gay Science* to *BGE* and see how much of a gap you feel compared with moving on from *Daybreak* to *The Gay Science*. I can't believe that anyone who was ignorant of the existence of *Zarathustra* would feel that anything strange was going on, or would feel that he had lost his bearings any more than he probably will anyway. *The Gay Science* is said to mark the climax of his 'positivist', 'sceptical', etc., phase, but I find it impossible to use such terms as a basis for making a contrast with *BGE*, whose scepticism, especially in relation to morality and to the very concept of truth is more drastic by far than anything to be found in the earlier book. Furthermore, there is a human warmth, a belief in the possibilities of fruitful contact between people, in *The Gay Science* which is both moving in itself and not something that re-appears, at least in Nietzsche's published works.

To quote two passages from *The Gay Science*: first, very early in the book:

> There was a time in our lives when we were so close that nothing seemed to obstruct our friendship and brotherhood, and only a small footbridge separated us. Just as you were about to step on it, I asked you: 'Do you want to cross the footbridge to me?'—Immediately, you did not want to any more; and when I asked you again, you remained silent. Since then mountains and torrents and whatever separates and alienates have been cast between us, and even if we wanted to get together we couldn't. But now when you think of that little footbridge, words fail you and you sob and marvel.[4]

The second passage opens Book Four, and was written on 1 January 1882:

> Today everyone permits himself the expression of his wish and his dearest thought; hence I, too, shall say what it is that I wish from myself today, and what was the first thought to run across my heart this year—what thought shall be for me the reason, warranty and sweetness of my life henceforth. I want to learn more and more to see as beautiful what is necessary in things; then I shall be one of those who make things beautiful. *Amor fati*: let that be my love henceforth! I do not want to wage war against what is ugly, I do not want to accuse; I do not even want to accuse those who accuse. *Looking away*

[4] *The Gay Science*, transl. Walter Kaufmann, (New York: Vintage Books), 90.

> shall be my only negation. And all in all and on the whole: some day I wish to be only a Yes-sayer.[5]

Not only is this an affecting and lovely passage—though it went the way, of course, of almost all New Year resolutions. It also prefigures the basic attitude of Zarathustra towards life and announces that love of one's destiny which is a leading motif in all of Nietzsche's later writing.

What is true of *The Gay Science* is that it is unsystematic to an extreme degree, and that it isn't compartmentalized into subject-organized groups of numbered sections, in the way that *BGE* is, albeit slightly artificially. *The Gay Science* may be thought of as what Nietzsche said that *Daybreak* is: a book for dipping into while going for long walks, though that suggests a teasing underestimate of its profundity. But, so far as its content is concerned, I can't see that Nietzsche has reached any kind of limit, except one of psychological penetration, in it.

If *BGE* does signal a new departure in Nietzsche's thought, heralded by the prolonged fanfares of *Zarathustra*, it is by virtue of a more insistent querying of basic themes, attitudes and concepts in Western civilization. He subtitles it 'Prelude to a Philosophy of the Future', but it would be more accurate to describe it as 'Meditations on the Culture of the Present'. It is much more a work of diagnosis than of anticipation, except in the sense that all diagnoses that are helpful indicate that something is wrong in a specific enough way to enable us to deduce what is required for cure, if the disease isn't terminal. Some of Nietzsche's diagnoses do lead him to suggestions as to how the complaint he describes with inimitable acuteness might be remedied, though his remedies are always so drastic that one flinches from taking them. But many of his accounts indicate that the patient's condition is hopeless, and that we had better turn our thoughts to future generations, or to a development of man which, even if not superhuman, is sufficiently different from us as we have resigned ourselves to being; for, Nietzsche says, 'Man is the animal whose nature has not yet been fixed' (*BGE* §62). A great deal of *BGE* is devoted to cataloguing and examining ways in which man's nature has been taken to be fixed; all of the book, one might say with only slight exaggeration, up to the end of the penultimate Part. The last Part, 'What is Noble?', is the one in which Nietzsche adumbrates his own view—and it is also notably the vaguest area of the work.

BGE doesn't begin *ex nihilo*; Nietzsche by now takes for granted that God is dead, the celebrated proclamation of the Madman in §125 of *The Gay Science*. What he does in *BGE* is explore the implications of that for our view of ourselves. As Erich Heller puts it:

[5] Ibid. 223.

> It is like a cry mingled of despair and triumph, reducing, by comparison, the whole story of atheism and agnosticism before and after him to the level of respectable mediocrity and making it sound like a collection of announcements by bankers who regret that they are unable to invest in an unsafe proposition.[6]

There is no area of our lives, not even the most theoretical, that will remain untouched once we have allowed to sink in, if we ever do, the fact that the world can no longer be seen as the creation of God. That may seem obvious—as obvious as anything could be. But Nietzsche shows how even the allegedly most theologically liberated spirits tend to proceed as if very little had happened except the removal of a vast ontological postulate. So his first endeavour in *BGE* is to show how the removal of this basic dichotomy, God and the world, necessitates, if we are to practice the virtue of truthfulness—something whose virtuous status itself is not left unquestioned by him—the removal of many other dichotomies which order and simplify existence, and thereby make it more comfortable for us. That is a central task of the first Part of the book, 'On the Prejudices of Philosophers'. It shouldn't be thought that he is concerned only with professional philosophers—a tribe that has existed for only two centuries, and when Nietzsche wrote only for one. For philosophers, in his view, which can hardly be disputed, are only purveyors of tendencies that are to be found in very many people in an unthought-out way. Everyone is a philosopher; it's just that most people don't realize it, and, one might add, despise those who pursue the subject for a living. But very obviously all Christians, at least in any traditional sense, are philosophers, since to be a Christian is to take on board a great deal of counter-commonsensical metaphysics. But Nietzsche would argue that philosophers are, in a crucial respect, worse than other people. For philosophers claim to dedicate themselves to the pursuit of truth at whatever cost. But in §5 of *BGE*, Nietzsche says:

> They pose as having discovered and attained their real opinions through the self-evolution of a cold, pure, divinely unperturbed dialectic . . . while what happens at bottom is that a prejudice, a notion, an 'inspiration', generally a desire of the heart sifted and made abstract, is defended by them with reasons sought after the event—they are one and all advocates who do not want to be regarded as such, and for the most part no better than cunning pleaders for their prejudices, which they baptize 'truths'.

[6] Erich Heller, *The Artist's Journey into the Interior*, (London: Secker and Warburg, 1966), 176.

That this is true in the history of philosophy from Socrates onwards is embarrassingly evident: the arguments by which all the great philosophers have claimed to establish their positions are so appalling, when they are intelligible, that beginners in the subject have to be persuaded that the philosophers *are* great—but by virtue of the views they held, which are imaginative feats, rather than by the production of grounds on which they are self-allegedly driven to them. In the case of Plato, the greatest of philosophers, this is so clear that there is a whole industry of commentators devoted to explaining why he used such bad arguments. I am not saying this to denigrate the role of argumentation in philosophy, a position some contemporary philosophers find congenial. It is one thing to claim that great philosophers *are* great in spite of their level of argument, another to claim that good arguments are not of great importance in the subject. The second claim seems to me to be false.

Nietzsche's own position on this subject is one of unease. He is sufficiently impressed by the failure rate of arguments intended to establish metaphysical conclusions to be inclined, often, to dismiss them as entirely factitious. Yet when he thinks of a good argument for countering a position, he is happy to use it, as for instance in §17 of *BGE*, where he attacks logical inferences that are based purely on grammatical habits, as in the case of Descartes' *Cogito*, or in §15, where he produces a *reductio ad absurdum* of phenomenalism, which he calls sensualism. But it is characteristic of, and consistent with, his aphoristic mode of thinking to seek not so much to refute as to replace, and not so much to argue for as to allure. And his arguments, when he uses them, as he does to a considerable extent in *BGE*, largely serve the negative purpose of exposing the fallacies and presuppositions of philosophers in general.

The first bomb he drops in *BGE* is one that calls the whole philosophical enterprise into question: 'Granted that we want truth: *why not rather* untruth? And uncertainty? Even ignorance?' In the light of the aspersions that he is very soon casting on philosophers' honesty, the question is not only radical but also less clear in import than it at first seems. For he is quickly saying that philosophers don't really want truth, but only their hearts' desire. So his complaint against them, if he is doubtful about the value of pursuing truth, is that that is what they claim to be doing, so their dishonesty turns out to be about the nature of their quest, not about their methods of reaching it. This might seem to be a quibble, of a kind peculiarly inappropriate in dealing with anything as grand as *BGE*. But since Nietzsche is clearly trying to induce a feeling of walking on quicksand, one is entitled to grasp at anything that might help to avert one's being sucked in. On the other hand, it may be part of Nietzsche's strategy to leave us unsure of what counts as an objection to his procedures, a particularly lethal, if unfair, weapon to employ. When, at the beginning of §3 he writes 'the greater part of conscious thinking must still be counted amongst the instinctive activities, and this is so even in the case of philosophical thinking', he is making one point and leading his readers, perhaps, to make another. The point that he is making is that philosophers, with their 'fundamental *faith in antithetical values*' (2) are at pains to distinguish sharply between instinctive behaviour on the one hand, and conscious thought, which philosophers think reaches its apogee in metaphysics, on the other. I'll come back to that. The point he leads me to make is that he is a philosopher too, and that what he says about philosophical thinking is either necessarily the case, and so applies to him as well; or else is only very likely to be the case, so that one needs to be more patient than he is and to examine any given piece of philosophy on its merits to see whether it betrays signs of being no more than instinctive activity—not that he has anything against instinctive activity, but that he has, as always, a great deal against people who delude themselves and others about what they are up to.

In taking the line that 'Philosophers do *x*, but I'm going to do *y*', where *y* implies a degree of sophistication and self-awareness not available to pedlars of *x*, Nietzsche is actually, while attempting to place himself outside a tradition, placing himself securely within one—for the whole enterprise of philosophy has been characterized by a recurrent questioning about how it should proceed, what its goals can or should be, and the need to make a fresh start. To that extent Nietzsche is a further manifestation of a familiar trend. On the other hand, no philosopher before him had gone so far as to question the value of the will to truth, or had done what he does throughout his last years—replace objective properties by psychological drives. In this Part of *BGE*, it is the will to truth, or truthfulness, that he is more interested in than truth itself. And that can easily make him seem not so much a philosopher as a psychologist of philosophers, and one who proceeds, moreover, in a hazy, slapdash, abusive way that lowers further any dignity his enterprise as such may have.

The difficulty in coping with this part of *BGE* is that Nietzsche is doing two things at least, more or less simultaneously, and just as one is preparing to see what he says about one of them he moves on to the other, and then back again. He *has* got views on truth, for instance, very pronounced but not very clear; and views on the search for truth, both strong and clear. The reason, I think, why instead of working out one issue and then moving on to the other, he oscillates between them is that he wants to connect both investigations to a third and still more basic one: the Will to Power in all its manifestations. He has put himself in a very difficult position because he has decided that the Will to Power is all that there is; in that sense he is an archmetaphysician, a monist as extreme as any in the history of the subject. But waiving for the moment any doubts about validating such an extravagant claim as he is making, we can see that, with an odd kind of consistency, he is intent on relating everything to that Will, since everything must be a manifestation of it. There can be, for him, no concept which isn't ultimately to be grasped in terms of it, and that includes the concept of truth. That means trouble, though it's not clear that Nietzsche realized how much. For as soon as a philosopher commits himself to a general claim about truth or meaning which is of a drastically revisionary or restrictive kind, he is liable to have his own claims turned against him. If he says, for example, that no single statement is wholly true, but only a set of statements taken together, he will be asked about the status of *that* statement. If he says that only statements which are verifiable by sense-experience have meaning, he will be asked whether that statement is verifiable by sense-experience. The history of philosophy from Plato through Descartes to Logical Positivism is full of unresolved conundra or paradoxes of that sort, and it seems that Nietzsche is no exception. Strategies of self-exemption are common but likely to seem comic to opponents. 'Every statement except this one . . .' is bound to elicit sniggers. Moves such as Russell's Theory of Types give too strong an impression of being constructed for the occasion. Suicidal claims that what one is saying *is* nonsense, because all philosophical statements are, are liable to be buried in unconsecrated ground. But although these and other devices have failed, at least their originators have recognized the awkwardness of their position. What about Nietzsche? In the first place, it must be said that it is not the sort of problem he is disposed to recognize, or to cope well with if he had recognized it. He had no professional philosophical training, and the kind of recurring vexation in the history of philosophy that haunts its latter-day practitioners wasn't something that he bore in mind. He knew about vicious circles, of course, and delights in spotting them. But the general question of the status of his own philosophy is something that he either ignores, or else deals with by sheer bravado.

But in the second place, and more interesting, the hypothesis of the Will to Power as all that there is leads him into a perspective on truth and its seekers which, even if it still leaves logical embarrassments for him to cope with, is fascinating and profound. His implicit thought can thus be put in this way: look at the world as I claim it to be, and see if that way doesn't make more sense than any alternative on offer. But he doesn't just rest on that; he is, as I've said, more concerned to replace than to refute, but he has principles of replacement, one of which is evidently the time-honoured one of the economy of explanation. Where he scores over other philosophers and sceptical observers of the philosophical scene is not merely in seeing the metaphysical constructions of others as redundant and pernicious, but in his extraordinary perspicacity in tracing their motives. He is aware, of course, as a whole section of *The Genealogy of Morals* shows, of the danger of lapsing into 'the fallacy of origins', that is, of thinking that one has refuted a view by showing what gave rise to it, however discreditable that might be. However, he is also aware of the damage that is done to a view, especially one for which the evidence is anyway none too impressive, if it can be shown to take its origins from the ardent desire of its proponent that the world should be a certain way. Here he is on strong ground. In the first place, the systems of philosophers, at least in the West, have been usually optimistic at least in that they have involved the construction of other worlds, somehow more real than this one, and preferable in various ways—e.g. one doesn't die in them or suffer pain; or one can't commit error or crime; or everything is extremely beautiful. Most Western metaphysical systems involve believing such things, in other words come very close to being religions. In the Preface to *BGE*, Nietzsche calls Christianity 'Platonism for the people'—which is characteristic of him in being somewhat unfair and only vaguely accurate, but also in having a very shrewd sense of essentials. For Platonism itself, has its metaphysical fairy-tale land of unchanging ideal objects, the trinity of which, Truth, Beauty and Goodness, involves some obscure kind of identity (Goodness is knowledge; to err is to be ignorant) and presides over the other Ideas in a way that has striking similarities to the Holy Trinity of Christianity, which is none the less mysterious enough not to be graspable by us while we remain on the earth (the equivalent of Plato's cave). Christianity, for all its evident differences from Platonism, is still a vulgar version of it. One can't imagine a Billy Graham of Platonism, which is an altogether more élitist affair. But the adjustments that have to be made to get from Plato to Christ aren't all that drastic, as sophisticated Christian philosophers have often noted.

Platonism is only an obvious case of wish-fulfilment, with an added touch of poignancy. Spinoza, far more difficult to understand and believe, is a much subtler one, whom Nietzsche in §198 of *BGE* diagnoses as stupidity mingled with prudence; 'that no-more-laughing and no-more-weeping of Spinoza', he says, 'that destruction of the emotions through analysis and vivisection which he advocated so naively'. And Kant, whom Nietzsche admired enormously in some respects, shocks him even more in the end for bringing back, at the behest of the moral law, the metaphysical conceptions of the soul, immortality and God, which he had conclusively shown in the Trascendental Dialectic of the first *Critique* to be senseless. Kant indeed becomes the philosopher *par excellence* for Nietzsche in his later writings, and justly so. It is Kant who helps Nietzsche to effect the link between Part One of *BGE*, 'On the Prejudices of Philosophers', and Part Five, 'On the Natural History of Morals'. §6 begins

> It has gradually become clear to me what every great philosophy has hitherto been: a confession on the part of its author and a kind of involuntary and unconscious memoir; moreover, that the moral (or immoral) intentions in every philosophy have every time constituted the real germ of life out of which the entire plant has grown. To explain how a philosopher's most remote and metaphysical assertions have actually been arrived at, it is always well (and wise) to ask oneself first: what morality does this (does he) aim at?

This might seem irrelevant to at least the contemporary Anglo-American philosophical scene, which is full of articles on areas which no degree of ingenuity could link to their author's morality; and I think this point must be granted. Philosophers have to a large extent become 'scholars' as Nietzsche, for once bending over backwards to be fair, describes them in the same section:

> In the case of scholars, to be sure, in the case of really scientific men, things may be different—'better' if you will—there may really exist a drive to knowledge there, some little independent clockwork which, when wound up, works bravely on *without* any of the scholar's other drives playing any essential part. The scholar's real 'interests' therefore lie in quite a different direction, perhaps in his family or in making money or in politics; it is indeed, almost a matter of indifference whether his little machine is set up in this region of science or that [or, we can add, in this or that area of contemporary philosophy] whether the 'promising' young worker makes himself into a good philologist or a specialist in fungus or a chemist—he is not *characterized* by becoming this or that.

The fact that Nietzsche could now add 'philosopher' to the list marks the development of the subject over the past century. He continues:

> In the philosopher, on the contrary, there is nothing whatever impersonal; and above all, his morality bears decided and decisive testimony to *who he is*—that is to say, to the order of rank the innermost drives of his nature stand in relative to one another.

It is this identification in philosophy of the work and drives of the personality that produced it that leads Nietzsche to his apparently impertinent enquiry into the characteristic vices of philosophers, their calculated *naïveté*, for instance, in alleging that something cannot originate in its opposite—truth in error, the unselfish in self-interest.

In aiming to establish the quite separate sources of *apparent* opposites, they have to postulate the transcendental, the unknown, or whatever, since what often stares them in the face is what they least want. Thus they fail to establish connections between things that are only superficially disparate, and the rapid result, in one philosophy after another, is the supreme metaphysical distinction, that between appearance and reality, a distinction which Nietzsche resolutely refuses to recognize.

Once more, it isn't my claim that Nietzsche *establishes* this but that he shows how readily metaphysics can be understood in these terms. Once that is demonstrated, though not proved, he is able to make convincing his central charge: that whereas philosophers have most often tried to show that the moral system they produce is the result of the way they see the world, and specifically the human world, as being constituted, in fact the reverse is true. The drives of which their personalities consist lead them to a set of valuations, and they deduce from them what the world has to be like in order for the valuations to be applicable, and then assert that the world *is* like that. That the history of philosophy is the history of a particular kind of mendacity seems to me so clear as to verge on the banal, but I'm no longer sure how much it is my reading of Nietzsche that makes me feel that.

Having set up his investigation into the will to truth, and accused philosophers of being deficient in it, at the same time as they express their devotion to truth itself, Nietzsche then makes things confusing by announcing that

> The falseness of a judgment is not necessarily an objection to the judgment: it is here that our new language perhaps sounds strangest. The question is to what extent it is life-advancing, life-preserving, species-preserving, perhaps even species-breeding; and our fundamental tendency is to assert that the falsest judgments (to which synthetic judgments *a priori* belong) are the most indispensable to us, that without granting as true the fictions of logic, without measuring reality against the purely invented world of the unconditional and the self-identical, without a continual falsification of the world by means of numbers, mankind could not live—that to renounce false judgments would be to renounce life, would be to deny life (*BGE* 4).

Once again several things are going on: in the first place an attack on Kant, who held that synthetic judgments *a priori* were, when true, necessarily so, and claimed to demonstrate how such judgments are possible—how it is possible to make a statement which applies to all experience yet is not derived from it; whereas, Nietzsche says, 'it is high time to replace the Kantian question: "how are synthetic judgments *a priori* possible?" with another question: "why is belief in such judgments necessary?"' (*BGE* 11). He thinks that such judgments aren't possible, but that it is a condition of our survival that we should believe them. And he says that Kant's answer to *his* question 'belongs in comedy', specifically in Molière's *Le Malade imaginaire*, where opium is famously explained as putting people to sleep because it has a dormitive faculty. Nietzsche's attacks on Kant, the 'catastrophic spider' as he calls him in *The Antichrist*, take their point of departure from his ridiculing of this view. But that isn't his central point, which is the much more sensational one that we can't live without falsehoods, and that what we believe most instinctively, or unquestioningly, is false. The reason he gives for this, as we have seen, is that the world of the unconditional and the self-identical is 'purely invented'. In fact this claim is very similar to some things that the ironist Hume suggests, and if Nietzsche had known Hume's writings better he might have been somewhat taken aback by the extent to which at least two great minds think alike. His only reference to Hume in *BGE* is a piece of ignorant abuse in §252. And anyway, by now, when we have widely accepted the influence of our turbulent unconscious lives, and the consequent compelling fantasies, on what we believe, we won't be as shocked by Nietzsche's claim as he would have liked us to be. Even so, it's true that we go on, by and large, paying lip-service to the view that it is better, in several senses, to believe the true rather than the false, and a vigorous querying of why we should think this does no harm, though I shan't undertake it here. What makes Nietzsche's trumpeting of it slightly odd is that he brings it forward in close juxtaposition to his attack on metaphysicians for their cavalier attitude towards the truth. For mightn't we say, in F. H. Bradley's too famous phrase, that at least some 'metaphysics is the finding of bad reasons for what we believe upon instinct'?

Nietzsche's answer couldn't be a simple one. He'd need to say that what we believe upon instinct is nothing like the concoctions of metaphysicians, certainly not, if they'd been available to him, those of Bradley, who disbelieved in time, space and matter. Nietzsche is concerned with what we can't avoid or help believing if we are to survive, what in his words is 'life-advancing, life-preserving', etc. But like other people who use 'life' as a criterion, Albert Schweitzer, say, or D. H. Lawrence, Nietzsche distinguishes sharply if not clearly between life that is worth advancing and preserving and life that isn't. In §9, attacking Stoics, he makes this very clear. 'You want to *live* "according to nature"?' he asks.

> Oh, you noble Stoics, what fraudulent words! Think of a being such as nature is, prodigal beyond measure, without aims or intentions, without mercy or justice, at once fruitful and barren and uncertain

> . . . To live—is that not precisely wanting to be other than this nature? Is living not valuing, preferring, being unjust, being limited, wanting to be different? And if your imperative 'live according to nature' meant at bottom the same thing as 'live according to life'—how could you *not* do that?

And from attacking the Stoics for giving a false picture of nature, he moves on to any philosophy that 'begins to believe in itself. It always creates the world in its own image, it cannot do otherwise.' So, on the one hand one can't not 'live according to life', and on the other, that is very far from, as it were, letting things take their course. Valuing, preferring, being unjust, being limited, are the essence of life and living. Therefore, anyone who appeals to life actually has up his sleeve a set of valuations, such as, in Schweitzer's case, preferring the life of human beings to that of many species of bacteria. Or in general, as Nietzsche might have put it—probably did, somewhere—life is against life, and therefore one has always to take sides. Blake's celebrated line 'Everything that lives is holy, life delights in life', is thus incoherent. And certainly it is very far removed from any position that Nietzsche ever held. To live is to choose, and to choose one thing is to deny all the other possibilities, in whatever sense that they might have been open to one.

It is on the extremely elusive concept *life* that the whole of Nietzsche's philosophy turns, though it is through talking of the Will to Power as opposed to the Will to Live that he actually works it out, and thereby adds to the confusion which reading him generates. His immediate reason for substituting 'power' for 'life' is that he wants to put the maximum distance between himself and Schopenhauer, who did see the Will to Live as the animating principle of the world, but thought that it was evil, and therefore advocated its extirpation. Nietzsche makes no bones, from the outset of *BGE*, of his opposition to all such pessimisms, especially when, as in Schopenhauer's case, they are held so superficially that he still advocates good behaviour and enjoys music; hence the quip at the end of §186: 'A pessimist, a world-denier and God-denier who *comes to a halt* before morality and plays the flute, affirms the *injure no one* morality: what?—is that actually a pessimist?' But beyond the immediate polemical intent, Nietzsche has other reasons, which are spelt out at length, for stressing the Will to Power. In §13 he writes 'A living thing desires above all to *vent* its strength—life itself is will to power: self-preservation is only one of the inherent and most frequent *consequences* of it'. In other words, if the will to live means the will to survival, Nietzsche considers that it is simply untrue that that is what living things desire or strive for above all else. They are only interested in survival in so far as, in surviving, they can enhance their power.

Nietzsche is careful to explain that he doesn't take the concept of will, even though it is basic in his thinking, as unproblematic. 'Willing seems to me to be above all something *complicated*', he says in §19, and continues 'something that is a unity only as a word—and it is precisely on this *one* word that the popular prejudice resides which has overborne the always inadequate caution of philosophers.' He goes on to list the component elements in willing, and then crucially relates the 'freedom of the will' to the sense of command, and subtly stresses how the apparently unitary 'I' covers both what commands and what obeys. The section ends:

> In all willing it is absolutely a matter of commanding and obeying, on the basis . . . of a social structure composed of many 'souls', on which account a philosopher should claim the right to include willing as such within the field of morality: that is, of morality understood as the theory of the relations of dominance under which the phenomenon 'life' arises.

It is on the basis of that claim, which can be understood as his own affirmed version of the view that morality enters into philosophy from the outset, that it does and must, and is not something that one comes to after one has provided a 'factual', 'value-free' account of the world, from which one moves on to one's moral position, that he works out some of his own moral views, mainly negatively in Part 5 and more positively in Part 9. None the less, Part 5 seems to me one of the greatest of all contributions to moral philosophy, though Nietzsche is constantly claiming that he wants to undermine morality as such. I shall end this paper by making a few comments on this exhilarating and liberating piece of writing.

First, Nietzsche is opposed not to morality as such but to how we more or less inevitably conceive of it; that is, either as a matter of obedience or of imitation, or a mixture of the two. He is devastating and unanswerable about the first of these. In §199 he writes that 'the herd instinct of obedience is inherited best, and at the expense of the art of commanding', and draws attention to those who

> would suffer from a bad conscience and in order to be able to command would have to practise a deceit upon themselves: the deceit that they too were only obeying. This state of things actually exists in Europe today: I call it the moral hypocrisy of the commanders. They know of no way of defending themselves against their bad conscience other than to pose as executors of more ancient or higher

commands (commands of ancestors, of the constitution, of justice, of the law or even of God).

This is one of the passages about which I can only exclaim: how true! The model of issuing moral laws on the basis of *receiving* them from somewhere is pervasive, and contemporary philosophers working from widely different directions, such as G. E. M. Anscombe[7] and Bernard Williams[8] have reiterated Nietzsche's point, even if they have not been directly influenced by him. The other model, that of imitation, is one that Nietzsche deals with more fully elsewhere. He has, as usual, at least two grounds for objecting to it. One is that the objects of imitation that we are offered are in one way or another repulsive, e.g. Christ, for all the sympathy with which Nietzsche surprisingly delineates him in *The Antichrist*. The other, and more profound, is that a crucial element in anyone who may be deemed worth imitating is that he is inimitable—what makes people models, in one sense, is that they are so completely themselves, and therefore that to imitate them is to violate their basic nature. As Pope put it in the context of poetry, 'He who imitates Homer does not do what Homer does'. Hence the distastefulness of all disciples, and Zarathustra's frequently expressed desire not to have any, except those who disagree with everything he says.

Nietzsche has a further grudge against moral laws, and thus, as he puts it with pardonable ellipsis, against morality. They are only to be thought of as moral if they apply to all men as such, which already assumes that all men can be seen as equal, at least in their capacity to obey the moral law. And yet, as Nietzsche points out time and time again but never too often, everything that we value in the way of human achievement is exceptional. We thus tend to lead double lives, with all the hypocrisy and self-deception that that implies. In the first place, we demand of people that they behave decently, that they cultivate the 'herd virtues' of modesty, humility, fairness, pity, etc. But in the second place, if everyone *did* behave always and only in that way, as the moral law seems to require, everything that makes life interesting and valuable would disappear. For Nietzsche, art and its glories are always at the forefront of his mind—the paradigm of human achievement; and in art there is an absolute lack of democracy, a ruthless élitism. Nietzsche often says that he wants people to be 'artists of life', to make their lives into works of art. But if one applied the moral law to art, everything we care for would be an offence.

[7] In her paper 'Modern Moral Philosophy', *Philosophy* (1958), reprinted in many places.

[8] In his recent book *Ethics and the Limits of Philosophy*, (London: Fontana Books, 1985).

A salient example of our hopeless division of mind on this matter is one that, by the time he wrote *BGE*, Nietzsche couldn't, for many reasons, cite directly: that of Richard Wagner. His wholly exceptional art is not only the product of probably the most indomitable will to power that the history of art has ever seen; but his life too, an astounding and improbable success story if ever there was one, consisted extensively in violations of herd-morality (Nietzsche uses that expression for the first time in *BGE*), of a kind which has kept biographers frenetically active for well over a century. He is a paradigm of the ruthless and triumphant achiever—and yet many passionate admirers of his art shake their heads sadly over his defective character, as if the former would have been possible without the latter. Wrong-headed as I think Nietzsche, in his later years, was about Wagner, he was surely right in his own terms when he wrote, in the last section of Part 5, 'There are few more grievous pains than once to have beheld, divined, sensed, how an extraordinary man missed his way and degenerated', a remark surely intended to apply to Wagner. For Nietzsche, Wagner had missed his way, and since he was by far the greatest personality and creator that Nietzsche had encountered, his decline, as Nietzsche saw it, was more painful to him than anything else he experienced. And Nietzsche also felt, as he contemplated Bismarck's Reich, that boring and depressing as his fellow Germans were, they would get far worse. He concludes Part 5 by saying

> The *collective degeneration of man* down to that which the socialist dolts and blockheads today see as their 'man of the future'—as their ideal!—this degeneration and diminution of man to the perfect herd animal (or as they say, to the man of the 'free society'), this animalization of man to the pygmy animal of equal rights and equal pretensions is *possible*, there is no doubt about that! He who has once thought this possibility through to the end knows one more kind of disgust than other men do—and perhaps also a new task! . . .

Appalled by what he saw then, even Nietzsche might be rendered speechless by what he would see now, the triumph of civilization without culture.

BGE raises in the sharpest terms the question of what point life can have if the cardinal virtues are equality and democracy, and hence hostility to the exceptional. If everyone's life is worth living, it seems, then no one's is worth much. The conditions of significance in living are harsh, competitive and even brutal. That is something which anyone brought up in contemporary Western civilization and with a reasonably warm heart, is desperately keen to overlook. At the very least, Nietzsche spells out for us what this systematic and deliberate oversight is bound to cost.

Bertrand Arthur William Russell

Bertrand Russell (1872–1970), born in Trelleck, Wales, was the grandson of the first Earl Russell, who introduced the Reform Bill of 1832 and served as prime minister under Queen Victoria. He studied mathematics and philosophy at Trinity College, Cambridge, 1890–1894, was a Fellow of Trinity College, 1895–1901, a Fellow of the Royal Society in 1908, and was a lecturer in philosophy, 1910–1916. Among his publications in philosophy in this period were *An Essay on the Foundations of Geometry* (1897), *A Critical Exposition of the Philosophy of Leibniz* (1900), *The Principles of Mathematics* (1903), *Principia Mathematica* (with A. N. Whitehead, 1910–1913), *The Problems of Philosophy* (1912) and *Our Knowledge of the External World* (1914).

In 1916 he was prosecuted and fined for a leaflet on conscientious objection, and in 1918 jailed for six months for a second article. Between then and 1936 he wrote and lectured mainly on social questions, putting his views on education into practice at a school at Beacon Hill near Petersfield, which he had started in 1927 with his second wife, Dora. He became the third Earl Russell in 1931 on the death of his brother. In 1934 he left the school and in 1938 went to America where he taught in Chicago, Los Angeles and Philadelphia. The Lectures at the Barnes Foundation in Philadelphia were the basis for his *History of Western Philosophy* (1945).

In 1944 he returned to Cambridge. *Human Knowledge: Its Scope and Limits* was published in 1948, and *Logic and Knowledge* (ed. R. C. Marsh) in 1956. In 1949 he became an honorary fellow of the British Academy and was awarded the Order of Merit. In 1950 he received the Nobel Prize for Literature, being described as 'one of our times' most brilliant spokesmen of rationality and humanity, and a fearless champion of free speech and free thought in the West'.

From 1954 until his death in 1970 he was preoccupied with the danger of nuclear war, being imprisoned with his fourth wife for a short period in 1961 for taking part in a sit-down demonstration in Whitehall. In his *Autobiography 1872–1914* (1967) he wrote:

> Three passions, simple but overwhelmingly strong, have governed my life: the longing for love, the search for knowledge, and unbearable pity for the suffering of mankind.

Bertrand Russell, *The Problems of Philosophy* (Oxford University Press, 1967) is prescribed by the AEB.

There are a great many commentaries on Russell's philosophy. Four that may be mentioned are:

D. Pears, *Bertrand Russell and the British Tradition in Philosophy* (London: Fontana, 1967)
A. J. Ayer, *Russell* (London: Fontana, 1972)
R. Jager, *The Development of Bertrand Russell's Philosophy* (London: Longman, 1972)
R. M. Sainsbury, *Russell* (London: Routledge and Kegan Paul, 1979)

Russell on Acquaintance

R. M. SAINSBURY

In Russell's *Problems of Philosophy (PP)*, acquaintance is the basis of thought and also the basis of empirical knowledge. Thought is based on acquaintance, in that a thinker has to be acquainted with the basic constituents of his thoughts. Empirical knowledge is based on acquaintance, in that acquaintance is involved in perception, and perception is the ultimate source of all empirical knowledge.

Russell's theses about acquaintance can be divided into three groups: (1) those which delimit the possible objects of acquaintance; (2) those which use acquaintance as a constraint on thought; and (3) those which connect acquaintance with the acquisition of knowledge of truths. I shall confine myself to the first two.

1. The Objects of Acquaintance

Russell said that acquaintance is a 'direct cognitive relation' between a mind and an object (*Knowledge by Acquaintance and Knowledge by Description—KAKD*—p. 152). A subject is acquainted with an object when he is aware of it in a direct fashion, not involving inference; when the object is 'presented' to him (*KAKD*, p. 152); when he *knows* the object (*PP*, pp. 23, 25). Russell argues that the only particulars with which we are acquainted are sense data, memories and, possibly, ourselves. We are also acquainted with universals or properties, but only with those which pertain to sense data with which we are acquainted. Finally, we are acquainted with facts, though the particular and universal constituents of facts with which we are acquainted must be particulars and universals with which we at least could be acquainted (*KAKD*, p. 155: a fact is a complex). We are not acquainted with any physical objects. It is possible to accept Russell's concept of acquaintance, yet reject his views about what the objects of acquaintance are. In arguing for this rejection in this section, I aim to explain how Russell came to his incorrect view.

Consider the arguments he gives in *PP* for the view that we are not acquainted with tables. He says that a table 'appears to be of different colours from different points of view' (p. 2), and that, because it looks flat to the naked eye but rough through a microscope, we 'cannot trust what we see with the naked eye' (p. 3). He concludes that 'the real table. . . is not *immediately* known to us' (p. 3), and sense data are introduced as 'the things that are immediately known in sensation' (p. 4). Hence tables are not sense data. As acquaintance is later said to be immediate knowledge of things (pp. 23, 25), this means that tables are not objects of acquaintance.

The argument is this: acquaintance is a form of knowledge, but it 'does not give us the truth about the table itself' (p. 3); it does not give us the truth about the real colour of the table, because the colour appears to change though it doesn't really, and it does not give us the truth about the real texture of the table because it appears smooth when it is not. Knowledge entails truth. What doesn't yield *truth about* the table cannot be *knowledge of* the table.

There are at least three lines of criticism of this argument. First, it runs together disparate considerations. The case of colour is supposed to lead to the conclusion that 'we are compelled to deny that, in itself, the table has any one particular colour' (p. 3), whereas the case of smoothness is said to lead not to the conclusion that the table lacks any one particular degree of smoothness, but simply to the conclusion that it is not smooth, and so sense is untrustworthy.

Secondly, the argument has dubious premises. There is a clear sense in which a table's colour does not appear to change when we walk round it, despite the fact that we are successively having qualitatively different experiences. In this sense, words like 'looks' and 'appears' are used to report dispositions to make judgments about how things are, and typically we are not in the least disposed to judge that tables change colour as we walk round them. The only correct point that Russell can be making here is that there can be a change in the nature of our experiences even if there is no intrinsic change in the table. We can also use idioms involving 'looks' and 'appears', not in the way previously mentioned, but to report on the nature of our experience, and this explains their occurrence in Russell's argument. Holding to this understanding of the premises, however, will make the third criticism the more telling.

This is that, however we understand the premises, they do not entail the conclusion. Suppose that we understand the premises in a way that makes them uncontroversially true. Russell offers not the slightest suggestion concerning how we might bridge the gap between the fact that we have experiences of different kinds as we look at the table from different points of view, or with and without the aid of the microscope, and the claim that the table has no real colour, or the claim that our senses are unreliable. Now suppose that we understand the premises as saying that we are disposed to make different judgments about the colour of the table, viewed from different points of view, or about its smoothness, viewed with or without a microscope. Russell suggests that this would show that we are left helpless when it comes to choosing between the dispositions: we cannot tell the real colour of the table or its real degree of smoothness. But this does not follow. Stronger dispositions can override weaker ones: perhaps we have some disposition to judge that the table is rough when we look at it under a microscope, but this is overridden by the reflection that the table is really smooth, judged by the standards of smoothness appropriate to tables, which are consistent with microscopic roughnesses. The most fundamental criticism of the validity of Russell's argument is this: let us grant that we sometimes arrive at false beliefs about tables on the basis of perception. Why does this show that we are not acquainted with them? It is Russell himself who so emphatically distinguishes between knowledge of things—acquaintance—and knowledge of truths. (The distinction is marked grammatically by the contrast between the direct object construction, e.g. 'John knows London', and the that-clause construction, e.g. 'John knows that London is larger than Paris'.) The most important gap between premises and conclusion arises because the argument under discussion gives us no reason to suppose that we cannot be acquainted with a thing unless *every* belief we form as a result is a case of knowledge.

The gap is so conspicuous that we require an explanation of how Russell could have sailed so calmly across it. His confidence that he *had* to get to the other side is part of the story. What was the source of this confidence? An obvious suggestion is that he believed that for any object of acquaintance its existence is indubitable. He certainly says that this holds for sense data (*PP*, p. 26).[1] But the problem then is: why did he not simply use a Cartesian argument to establish that we are not acquainted with tables?

One suggestion is that he did not believe that indubitability is constitutive of the nature of acquaintance. The indubitability of sense data are due to special features of these objects, rather than to the mere fact that we are acquainted with them. Hence he could not accept the soundness of the argument from the doubtfulness of tables to their not being objects of acquaintance.

There is something in this response. In particular, it accords well with the fact that Russell holds in *PP* that some objects of acquaintance are *not* indubitable: he says that there is room for doubt concerning propositions arising from acquaintance with facts, because of the

[1] He says the same for universals (p. 59). We cannot take this very seriously, if we take seriously his earlier claim that 'we cannot strictly prove that there are such entities as *qualities*' (p. 54). Presumably, if the existence of something is indubitable, the question of proving its existence does not arise.

fallibility of the process of analysis (*PP*, p. 80): we have to separate out the constituents 'the sun' and 'shining' from the complex fact that the sun is shining, and in this process error may be introduced.[2] Although he is not absolutely explicit, it is clear from this discussion that he would say that our knowledge of the existence of a fact with which we are acquainted is not indubitable. This strongly suggests that he does not think that indubitability is a feature of acquaintance *per se*.

On the other hand, he does almost certainly think that objects of acquaintance *ipso facto* have a feature that we could call *demon-proofness*. Demon-proof objects are those which Descartes' evil demon cannot remove from the universe without our noticing. It is not the same notion as indubitability, since a fact with which we are acquainted could be demon-proof, even though the fallibility of analysis means that there is room to doubt the proposition that it exists. It is clear that tables are not demon-proof, so we would have some understanding of why Russell felt so sure that we are not acquainted with them.

The explanation, attributing to Russell, quite plausibly in my view, the implicit conviction that objects of acquaintance are *ipso facto* demon-proof, is not perfect, for we would still have to account for why he did not use a simple Cartesian argument to establish that we are not acquainted with tables. I do not know the answer to this question, but I want to consider another. The explanation would require supplementation by some account of the source of Russell's conviction that objects of acquaintance are demon-proof. Here is a suggestion. Russell, in *PP*, has not fully come to terms with the implications of the distinction he himself makes in his discussion of idealism: the distinction between the act of acquaintance and its object. I shall make this distinction in terms of two different ways in which one could characterize sense data.

On one approach, sense data are thought of as intrinsic to the occurrence of perceptual experience.[3] Apparently unary predicates like '. . . is having an experience of kind K' turn out to be binary, and

[2] This example of a fact with which we are acquainted does not accord with the official doctrine that the universals and particulars which constitute such facts must be possible objects of acquaintance. The sun and shiningness do not meet this condition. The possibility of error, however, is not related to these features of the fact in the example.

[3] An example of this approach is found in Jackson (1977, esp. Ch. 3). Russell's subsequent acceptance of neutral monism (see *Mind* p. 141ff.) commits him to the view that sense data constitute the whole of perceptual experience and are physical. Within neutral monism there is no room for the distinction between sense datum as component of experience and sense datum as object of experience. A corollary of the new view is that the notion of acquaintance is rejected on the grounds that it presupposes the *self* as genuine entity rather than logical construction.

involve an argument place to be filled by a term for an essentially *mental* object. The term 'sense data' would be introduced as a generic term for such objects. This approach, which I shall call the 'component approach', is marked by two features: first, the *esse* of sense data is their *percipi*: there is no question of their existing unexperienced, since they are essentially nothing but components in acts of experience; secondly, it could consistently be held that one had a sense datum while being aware of nothing, for example in a dream.

On the other approach, the basic notion is that of an object of acquaintance, and the term 'sense data' is introduced to apply to those objects of acquaintance that are made available by the senses. On this approach, which I shall call the 'object approach', there is no immediate inference to the conclusion that sense data are mental; but it would be inconsistent to suppose that a sense datum could be experienced without there being anything of which the subject was aware.

Confusing the two approaches is likely to lead to idealism: components of acts of awareness are mental; if these are taken to be also the objects of awareness, one will conclude that one can be aware only of mental things.

Very soon after writing *PP*, Russell adopted a view of sense data which clearly belongs to the object approach. In 'On the Relation of Sense Data to Physics' (*RSP*), he says that sense data are not mental, but rather are mind-independent. Necessarily, if something is a sense datum, then someone is aware of it, so nothing could be a sense datum unless there were minds. But things which are in fact sense data do not have to be: they might have remained unsensed sensibilia. So each sense datum could have existed even if no minds had existed. Since sense data are things capable of existing unperceived, it is clear that Russell is here adopting the object approach.

In *PP*, Russell's position is not quite so clear. Certainly there are some emphatic commitments to the object approach.

> The faculty of being acquainted with things other than itself is the main characteristic of a mind. Acquaintance with objects essentially consists in a relation between the mind and something other than the mind (*PP*, p. 22).

He cites universals as examples of non-mental objects of acquaintance. And in pointing out the confusion between *acts* of apprehension and *objects* apprehended, of which he accuses Berkeley (*PP*, pp. 21–22), he shows awareness of the distinction between the component approach and the object approach. But there is also evidence that he was capable of relapsing into the component approach.

First, he says that sense data are 'subjective, in the sense that they depend upon us' (p. 21). Yet, as we have seen, if we take him to be adopting the object approach, he gives no even faintly plausible argument for this. On the component approach, however, it requires no argument.

Secondly, it is natural to read his account in the chapter on idealism as modifying Berkeley's position only to the extent of allowing merely descriptive knowledge of non-mental particulars, and hence as refusing to allow acquaintance with such particulars. Though there is a clear argument for the positive part of this claim (that one can know that something exists with which one is not acquainted), there is no argument for the negative part. Indeed, it is hard not to read Russell's endorsement of Berkeley's conclusion that sense data are in the mind (p. 20) as other than a manifestation of the component approach.

Thirdly, he construes Descartes' possibility—that only he and his experiences exist—so as to include the existence of his sense data. This would be a quite correct move on a component account, on which the existence of the experiences guarantees the existence of their components, but would cry out for justification on an object account.

PP is a work of a mind in transition. In particular, the account of physical objects as inferred from sense data was replaced, very soon afterwards, by an account according to which they are constructions out of sense data (see, e.g., *RSP*). *PP* contains vestiges of a component account of sense data, which have been purged by the time of the article. These vestiges in part account for the presence of, and the lack of argumentation for, his view that we are not acquainted with tables.[4]

Russell's arguments concerning the objects of acquaintance seem to me to be beyond repair. A correct account, in my view, would show that tables and other physical objects are objects of acquaintance, and would do so by analysing acquaintance in terms of causation and information[5].

[4] The account is incomplete. When Russell extricates himself from the component approach, he still holds that we are not acquainted with tables, only with their parts (e.g. in *RSP*). This feature, however, can be traced to his conception of *presence*, according to which the fact that what is past cannot be present supposedly establishes that an enduring thing could not *in toto* be present to us.

[5] A classic recent account of the role of causation in perception is by Grice (1961). For the role of information, see Dretske (1981, Ch. 6). It has to be said that as soon as Russell's view that physical objects are not objects of acquaintance is abandoned, certain problems that are absent from his scheme become pressing. If acquaintance is going to be enough to guarantee that a true belief that arises from it counts as knowledge, as Russell seems to have hoped (e.g. *PP*, pp. 79–80), then we shall have to explain why the pattern of light six inches from our eyes, or the invisible torch which illuminates the door handle, are not things of which we are aware (the problem of the right location on the causal chain); and we will

It would not be appropriate to consider such an account here, for it would be too far removed from Russell's philosophy. However, we can follow Russell's own example: in introducing his important theses about acquaintance he typically abstracts from his views about what its objects are. We have a grasp of the nature of acquaintance in the claim that it is a form of non-inferential awareness which can yield knowledge; a grasp, therefore, which is prior to and independent of the theses about what its objects are. In talking about the relation between acquaintance and thought, for example, we can try to remain neutral about what objects we are aquainted with, and see if this permits the stating of a substantial and important thesis. This is the project of the next section.

2. Acquaintance and Thought

2.1. The Principle of Acquaintance

Only objects of acquaintance are objects of thought. This is how I interpret Russell's famous Principle of Acquaintance:

> Every proposition which we can understand must be composed wholly of constituents with which we are acquainted (*PP*, p. 32).

Could 'proposition' mean sentence in this context? Surely not, for the constituents of sentences are words, whereas Russell plainly means the constituents mentioned in the Principle to be non-linguistic. The only correct interpretation, I think, is that 'proposition' means thought, and that to understand a thought is just to have it. What the 'constituents' of thoughts are is a more difficult question, to which I shall return later.

On this interpretation the Principle is not essentially about language. But it will have consequences for language. Sentences express thoughts, and understanding a sentence involves knowing what thought it expresses. It follows that the only sentences we can understand will be ones expressing thoughts with all of whose constituents we are acquainted.

The interpretation is confirmed by a passage in *KAKD*, published just a year before *PP*, some of which is reproduced verbatim as part of *PP*'s Ch. 5. He says that the Principle of Acquaintance

> can be re-stated as follows: *Whenever a relation of supposing or judging occurs, the terms to which the supposing or judging mind is*

---

also have to explain why the redwood trees are not something of which we are visually aware if our visual experience as of redwoods is in fact caused by their smell (the problem of the right kind of causal chain—the 'non-deviant' kind). On the former, see Pars (1976); on the latter, see Peacocke (1979, Ch. 2).

> *related by the relation of supposing or judging must be terms with which the mind in question is acquainted* (p. 160; cf. also the concluding reformulation on p. 167).

We cannot regard the Principle as speaking of propositions, since later in *PP* he denies that there are such things:

> The necessity of allowing for falsehood makes it impossible to regard belief as a relation of the mind to a single object, which could be said to be what is believed (*PP*, p. 72).[6]

A proposition could be defined as *what* is believed, supposed, asserted, or whatever; as what is specified in the that-clause in such a sentence as 'Othello believes/supposes/asserts that Desdemona loves Cassio'; in short, as the object of so-called 'propositional attitudes'. Russell's claim is that this account of propositions does not make proper allowance for falsehood. But why not? Propositions are typically held to be abstract objects, and it may be conceded that there is some difficulty about all such objects, propositions included. But it is not to any such nominalistic scruple that Russell appeals. He differentiates sharply: *true* propositions may be acceptable, but *false* ones are not. Nominalism has no room for this differentiation.

Understanding Russell on this point is essential to a grasp of his philosophy, but it will involve a somewhat lengthy detour. Before embarking, I shall make three preliminary observations about the Principle of Acquaintaince.

First, we must remember that Russell said that there is a good sense in which we can think 'about' things with which we are not acquainted:

> All thinking has to start from acquaintance: but it succeeds in thinking *about* many things with which we have no acquaintance ('On Denoting', p. 104).

The contrast between something being an object of acquaintance and something being a thing we can think *about* is retained in *PP* (e.g. p. 30). So we should not criticize the Principle on the grounds that it entails that we cannot think about things with which we are not acquainted.

Secondly, however, it is integral to Russell's account that thought 'about' something with which we are not acquainted, that is, thought (e.g. knowledge) *by description*, cannot reach to just any object in an

[6] He makes a more emphatic attack on propositions in *PLA*, also in connection with the analysis of belief: 'obviously propositions are nothing' (p. 223). However, even here the situation is not clear, for he also uses 'proposition' to mean sentence, and on this usage there *are* such things are propositions: 'A proposition is just a symbol' (*PLA*, p. 185).

unconstrained manner. One can know a particular by description only if one knows that exactly one thing has a certain property or complex of properties, and one is acquainted with the property, or with each property in the complex. The unique possessor of this property or complex of properties is what one's thought is 'about'. This means that in Russell's system one can think about particulars with which one is not acquainted only if they are somehow analyzable in terms of sense data and properties thereof; and a similar point holds for universals. But it would be wrong to base a criticism of the Principle of Acquaintance just on doubts about the availability of such analyses. The restriction on what objects can be thought 'about' to just those analyzable in terms of sense data is achieved by the combination of two separable theses: the Principle of Acquaintance together with the doctrine, examined earlier, about the objects of aquaintance. Confinement to sense data can be placed at the door of the account of the objects of acquaintance, rather than at the door of the Principle. Russell gives examples of beliefs in which the actual constituents, as opposed to things thought 'about', do not conform to the thesis about the objects of acquaintance. This shows that he is willing to consider the theses separately, and we should do the same.

Thirdly, it has to be admitted that in *PP* Russell gives no argument of any value for the Principle, confining himself to saying:

> . . . it must be possible to meet these [unspecified] objections [to the Principle], for it is scarcely conceivable that we can make a judgment or entertain a supposition without knowing what it is that we are judging or supposing about (*PP*, p. 32).

Given that he allows that we *can* think 'about' objects with which we are not acquainted, this remark does not help.

2.2. *The 'No Concept' Theory of Judgment*

Understanding Russell's views about propositions and the Principle of Acquaintance involves appreciating their setting within an account of the mind upon which there are no representations or ideas or concepts: I shall call this the non-conceptualist theory. On this theory, there are no propositions, for propositions represent the world as being thus-and-so, and there are no concepts, if concepts are understood as what compose propositions.[7] The theory is much more explicit in *KAKD* than in *PP*:

[7] Russell uses 'concepts' for universals of which we are aware. These, however, do not have any representational function (far from representing reality, they partially constitute it), and do not compose propositions (as understood on the proposition theory I am discussing).

> I therefore see no reason to believe that, when we are acquainted with an object, there is in us something that can be called the 'idea' of the object. On the contrary, I hold that acquaintance is wholly a relation, not demanding any such constituent of the mind as is supposed by advocates of 'ideas' (*KAKD*, p. 161).

True propositions might be reinterpreted by the non-conceptualist as facts (since every true proposition, on the proposition theory, corresponds to a fact); but there is no hope for false propositions. So for the non-conceptualist there will be a genuine difference between the claim that there are true propositions, which might be interpreted as the truth that there are facts, and the claim that there are false propositions. Facts are innocent of concepts; but there is nothing thus innocent which false propositions could be.[8]

How could the non-conceptualist theory work? There appear to be two places at which an account of the mind would need representations or concepts: one is in perception, for does not perceptual experience represent the world as being thus-and-so? The other is in thought, for we certainly believe, suppose, assert that things are thus-and-so, and what could this involve, unless holding before our minds a representation of things as thus-and-so, and then adopting some attitude (belief, supposition, assertion) towards this representation?

In both *PP* and *KAKD*, Russell links the Principle of Acquaintance with a non-conceptualist theory of belief (which could be extended to any other 'propositional attitude').[9] This theory is designed to allow for beliefs being true or false, without allowing for anything representational or conceptual.

The theory is that, for example, Othello's believing that Desdemona loves Cassio is a relation holding between Othello and three actual objects: Cassio, Desdemona and the universal *love*. (To understand Russell's doctrine, we have to pretend that Shakespeare's story is history rather than fiction.) The logical form is first order:

(1) Believes (Othello, Cassio, love, Desdemona).

So judging or believing no more involves concepts, ideas or representations than does a fact like: Oxford is nearer to Cambridge than London is to Durban. Both could be formalized by the formula: $R(a, b, c, d)$.

[8] I put this thought in Russell's mouth, without myself wishing to prejudge the question whether one might not distinguish between fact-types and fact-tokens in such a way that every sentence corresponds to a fact-type, and all and only true sentences correspond to fact-types of which there are tokens.

[9] For Russell's earlier advocacy of a conceptualist (proposition) theory of belief, it is well worth looking at his 'Meinong's Theory of Complexes and Assumptions', esp. pp. 71–76.

Before assessing this theory I shall consider two consequences. First, whether he realized it or not, Russell's non-conceptualism, involving his repudiation of propositions, solves the problem he had once called that of the 'unity of the proposition' (see *Principles of Mathematics*, pp. 49–50). The problem for the advocate of propositions is that, according to Russell, the constituents of a proposition like 'Desdemona loves Cassio' are just Desdemona, Cassio and love. But the three constituents do not reconstitute the proposition: they do not capture the idea that a proposition *says* something. So there is no room for an explanation in terms of constituents of the difference between 'Desdemona loves Cassio' and 'Cassio loves Desdemona'. The constituents are exactly the same in both cases. We want to say: in the first, the relation relates Desdemona to Cassio, whereas in the second it relates Cassio to Desdemona. But this seems wrongly to require the propositions to be true: if Desdemona is related to Cassio by the love-relation, then she loves Cassio. On Russell's theory, which dispenses with propositions, the roles they would otherwise have played fall to beliefs or other such mental acts. But there is no corresponding problem of the unity of beliefs or other thoughts. The difference between Believes (Othello, Desdemona, love, Cassio) and Believes (Othello, Cassio, love, Desdemona) no more requires explanation than does the difference between Greater-than (four, seven) and Greater-than (seven, four).

The other consequence of the non-conceptualism to which I wish to draw attention is that it transforms what would otherwise be an inexplicable *non sequitur* into a valid inference. Russell has been accused of a quite unwarranted inference in his theory of logically proper names.[10] A logically proper name is defined as one such that if it had no bearer it would have no meaning.[11] Russell takes a consequence to be that two logically proper names for the same thing must mean the same. How could he have made such an extraordinary move? His non-conceptualism provides the explanation. The conceptualist can suppose that two names, even if they refer to the same thing, can be associated with different *ways of thinking* about the object: different 'modes of presentation', as Frege (1892) said. The distinct names can be associated with different concepts, which makes it possible for the names to differ in meaning, as manifested by someone's understanding a truth of the form $\alpha=\beta$ yet not being in a position to realize that it is a truth. This option is not available to the non-conceptualist, for on his view there are no such things as concepts or modes of presentation or representation. The

[10] The accusation is made by Evans (1982, pp. 42–43).

[11] Cf. *PM*, Vol 1, p. 66. There is a clear statement of the alleged consequence in *PLA*, p. 245. The conclusion and the premise are both quoted by Evans (1982, p. 43).

mind comes directly into contact with the world. So there is no way in which the mind can register an other than notational difference between two co-referential names. What strikes the conceptualist as a *non sequitur* is a valid reference in the non-conceptualist framework.

Russell himself later criticized the *PP* theory of belief. In his lectures on 'The Philosophy of Logical Atomism' (*PLA*), he says that the early theory was 'a little unduly simple' (p. 226), and takes it to task for having treated 'loves' as a term whereas, in 'Othello believes that Desdemona loves Cassio', it really occurs as a verb. He also observes that it is a consequence of his theory that there are an endless number of different belief relations. For example, consider Othello's belief that Desdemona is beautiful. Applying the previous pattern of analysis, this amounts to:

(2) Believes (Othello, Desdemona, beauty).

Here 'believes' is a three-term relation, whereas in the other case it was a four-term relation. On standard assumptions, this means that the relations are different, which in turn means that the word 'believes' is ambiguous. Russell found nothing objectionable about this. He was at the time promoting the theory of types advanced in *Principia Mathematica*, and this theory allows for a kind of systematic ambiguity that, arguably, is harmless. Is the ambiguity Russell attributes to 'believes' harmless? One might say: it is no harder to see the connection between (1) and (2) than between (3) and (4):

(3) Loves (John, Mary)
(4) Loves (John, Mary, Jane).

But there is a contrast. If we understand (4) at all, it is through an envisaged reduction of the superficially three-term occurrence of 'loves' to a two-term one. For example, we treat (4) as equivalent to 'John loves Mary and John loves Jane'. No such reduction is available in the case of (1) and (2). Just as one who understands (3) is not thereby enabled to understand (4), if (4) is treated as an irreducibly three-term relation, so someone who understands (1) ought not to be able thereby to understand (2), even if he understands 'beauty'. Yet the fact is that it is enough to learn 'believe' in an English sentence corresponding to (1) to understand it in the English sentence corresponding to (2) (assuming that one understands 'beautiful'). Russell's position appears to be inconsistent with this fact.[12]

There is a deeper objection to the non-conceptualist theory of belief: it obliterates the non-extensionality of belief with respect to both

[12] The argument here is guided by what Evans (1982) calls the Generality Constraint (pp. 100–105).

singular and general terms, just as it obliterates the possibility of co-referential names differing in meaning. For consider some other name for Cassio, *n*, and suppose Othello understands it. Though he believes that Desdemona loves Cassio, the possibility remains open that he does not believe that Desdemona loves *n*. Yet the argument

Believes (Othello, Desdemona, love, Cassio)
Cassio=*n*
Believes (Othello, Desdemona, love, *n*)

is plainly valid.

Russell is, of course, aware of this issue, but in his enthusiasm to show that all thought is expressible in the syntax of *Principia Mathematica* he takes the extensionality of his account of belief to bc a merit. Rather than adjust it to the sort of data to which I have alluded, he reinterprets the data. The objects of thought must, as representationalists would put it, admit of no more than one representation. This gives Russell a motivation for identifying them with sense data and universals holding of sense data. There is no plausibility at all in the suggestion that there is only one way in which a mind can come into contact with a material object; but there is some initial plausibility in the suggestion that this holds for sense data and their properties (universals).[13]

2.3. *The 'No Concept' Theory of Acquaintance*

Does the present criticism strike not just at Russell's account of belief, but also at his very conception of acquaintance? Must his view that, in acquaintance, the mind comes 'directly', i.e. non-conceptually, into contact with objects, fall with the fall of his non-conceptual theory of belief?[14]

What is wrong with the non-conceptual theory of belief is that it makes no room for different ways of thinking about the same thing. Othello thinks of Cassio in one way rather than another; he might also think of the same man in a different way, and be in no position to know

[13] However, it is incorrect. For example, a shape property of sense data could be thought of in more than one way, e.g. the determinate shape property shared by the figures □ and ◇.

[14] In *PP*, Russell speaks of sense data 'representing' physical objects (see e.g. p. 27). In *Theory of Knowledge*, he says that belief in a conceptual component in acquaintance (he is here considering Meinong's 'contents') is encouraged by the 'belief that visual data are "subjective modifications"' (p. 43). There is perhaps a connection in *PP* between the vestiges of a component approach to sense data, and the traces of a view of them as representations.

that both ways of thinking relate to the same man. If objects can come before the mind only under some concept or mode of presentation, then Russell's notion of acquaintance as a non-conceptual form of awareness is wrong.

The criticism shows that, if acquaintance is non-conceptual, whatever mental modification is required for a subject to become acquainted with an object does not add up to the mental modification required for a subject to come to have a thought of which that object is a constituent.[15] In other words, to salvage Russell's position on acquaintance, once his non-conceptual account of judgment has been rejected, will require the admission of two ways in which an object can 'come before the mind'. The conceptual way, as when an object is a constituent of a thought; and a non-conceptual way, exemplified by acquaintance. The Principle of Acquaintance will be the doctrine that the non-conceptual species of contact is a necessary condition for the conceptual species.

I shall take it that there is no question about the need to recognize the former, conceptual, species of contact (*pace* Russell), so a defence of this two species account of the mind's contact with the world should address itself to the question of whether there really is a non-conceptual species of contact. If there is, presumably it takes place in perception. So the view that most endangers the non-conceptual account of acquaintance is the view that perceptual experience is essentially conceptual. I shall briefly sketch this view and some considerations allegedly in its favour; and then I shall defend the Russellian non-conceptual account.

The essence of the contrary account is that (a) our perceptual experiences have a conceptual content and (b) this content is *intrinsic* to the experiences in the following sense: difference in content ensures difference in the phenomenal type of the experience.[16] When we want to focus on the nature of our experiences, in abstraction from whether we are perceiving anything, and if so what, we use idioms like 'I had a visual experience *as of* a tomato'. We typically use material object expressions in specifying the *as of* content, but we do not thereby commit ourselves to the experience involving contact with material objects. This much can be agreed by all parties. The conceptualist about perceptual experience must now show that this *as of* content is genuinely *conceptual* and that it is really *intrinsic*.

[15] This is consistent with acquaintance with an object being causally sufficient for it to be a thought-constituent. A fuller development of the position I offer Russell confronts the problem of making acquaintance with an object genuinely a *cognitive* relation, given that the object does not thereby become a thought-constituent.

[16] Cf. Peacocke (1984, p. 9). For a discussion, see Millar (1985).

To show the first it is enough to point out that a subject cannot have perceptual experience with *as of* content requiring specification by means of a concept, ϕ, unless he possesses ϕ. Your visual experience cannot be said to be *as of* a tomato unless you have the concept of a tomato. This restriction would be inexplicable unless the content is conceptual.

Various arguments might be used to show the second. One might appeal to cases of 'gestalt switch'. Looking at a Necker cube, or a duck/

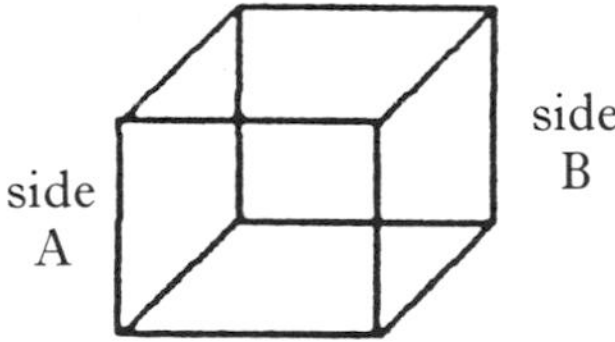

The Necker cube

The duck/rabbit

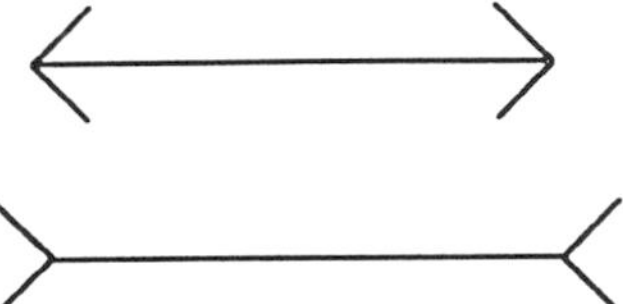

The Müller-Lyer figure

rabbit diagram, we may be inclined to say that when the switch occurs (a) the nature of one's perceptual experience changes and (b) the only change is in *as of* content. If this is correct, it establishes the intrinsicality of content at least for these cases; and then it is hard to see how one could resist the generalization of the claim.

Another argument is that in practice we seem to have no effective way of specifying the nature of our perceptual experiences except via their *as of* content, and this may be held to suggest that the content is intrinsic.

A third argument for intrinsicality is that it is needed in order to explain the possibility of *mis*perception. How can perceptual error be explained except in terms of some perceptual experience having a content which does not match the world? And how could this be, unless the content were intrinsic to the experience?

Taking these arguments in reverse order: the non-conceptualist will explain all cases of perceptual error as inferential error. It is not that our senses misrepresent the way things are to us, for they do not represent at all. Rather, on the basis of awareness, we reach falsehoods. If, for example, confrontation with the Müller–Lyer diagram leads us to conclude that the lines are of unequal length, this is not because our senses have delivered a defective representation, but because we have made a faulty inference.

Though this is Russell's view in *PP*, he is aware that it requires some refinement.

> A circular coin . . ., though we should always *judge* it to be circular, will *look* oval unless we are straight in front of it (*PP*, p. 14).

The problem for Russell is this. The coin's looking oval appears to be a case of misperception. Yet here there is no false judgment. Indeed, he might have said, there is not even a disposition to make a false judgment. So it would seem that he cannot account for this kind of case of misperception.

There is no problem on the conceptualist view of acquaintance: this is simply a case in which our vision misrepresents the way the coin is.

There are two responses open to Russell. They cannot be made together for the same case, but for each case of purported misperception, one or other will be appropriate. The first involves admitting that the alleged case is one of error, but denying that this need be understood in terms other than that of false judgment. The second involves denying that the case is one of error.

We have already seen (in the case of the normal and microscopic viewings of the table) that a given experience can give rise to dispositions to make different, and even inconsistent, judgments. A less controversial example is the following: you see something which normally you would have taken for a snake. Knowing that you are in snake-free Ireland, the disposition to judge that there is a snake before you is overcome, and you judge that there is just a tangle of roots. You might express this by saying that it looked like a snake but wasn't. Adopting this strategy involves admitting that error is in the air: there is a disposition to make a judgment which is false. But it denies that this error need be located in the intrinsic nature of the experience.

The second response denies that there is error at all. This is the right response, and indeed I think the one which Russell makes, for the case of the coin which looks oval. In normal circumstances of seeing a penny obliquely there would be no disposition, not even an overridden one, to judge that it is oval. However, we need not regard the use of 'looks' here as indicating the presence of error, a delusive appearance contrasting with the reality of the roundness. We can use such expressions to characterize the intrinsic nature of our experiences. For example, we could analyze 'the penny looks oval', understood in the only way in which it is true under normal circumstances, along the lines: to exactly obscure the penny, as I am now seeing it, by placing an opaque object between it and my eyes, perpendicular to the line of sight, the obscuring object would need to be oval. In the passage which follows the one recently quoted, Russell puts what I believe to be essentially this point in terms of objects in private space.

The second argument for intrinsicality is that in practice we seem to have no effective way of specifying the nature of our perceptual experiences except via their *as of* content. The premise is somewhat overstated, since the method of specification just mentioned is not by *as of* content. Perhaps the premise holds for *some* experiences.[17] Even so, the argument remains quite unpersuasive, since there is nothing problematic about the idea of specifying something by features that are extrinsic to it. The *as of* content of a perceptual experience, I suggest, is determined by the dispositions to judge which the experience produces in us. In different circumstances, it would have produced different dispositions. None the less, we can say something informative about the nature of a perceptual experience by specifying the judgments it inclines us to make in the actual circumstances in question. Consider the following analogy. We take a medicine which has certain effects on us. We report to our doctor. We might be quite unable to identify the medicine by its intrinsic properties (its chemical composition, say); we might only be able to say anything useful about it in terms of the effects it has had on us.

The remaining argument for the intrinsicality of content was drawn from cases of gestalt shift. However, it is not obvious that the only change, in such cases, is in the *as of* content. For example, in the case of the Necker Cube, it is not obvious that the difference between side A appearing to be in front of side B, and side B appearing to be in front of side A, is not a *sensational* difference, a difference not requiring

[17] A putative example would be the perceptual experiences of chicken-sexers: they apparently can offer no other characterization of the differences between the experiences which cause them to make the sexual discrimination than that some birds look male and some female. The 'look' can be understood only in terms of dispositions to make the corresponding judgments.

explanation in terms of *as of* content. One would need a quite lengthy discussion to have any hope of settling this issue. These phenomena do not provide a knock-down argument against non-conceptualism about acquaintance.

So much for arguments against Russell's position. An important concession will serve to disarm another line of attack, and also to make his view more plausible. It should be conceded that there is a 'low-level', non-conceptual, notion of content, and that perceptual experiences must be allowed to have content of this kind. Examples are: that the sand contains information about what has passed over it since it was last washed by the tide;[18] that the rings on a tree contain information about the rainfall in the various years of its life in the area in which it has grown. Any kind of instrument or detector carries information in this low-level sense: thermometers, cameras, voltmeters. Sense-organs are kinds of detectors. It cannot be doubted but that they carry information in this low-level sense. Yet, as the examples make plain, though we have to use concepts in order to say what this information is, the possessor of the informational state (the tree, the thermometer) need not possess any concepts at all, let alone the concepts (rainfall, temperature) which we must use to specify the contained information. Conceding that acquaintace involves low-level content makes no dent in Russell's view of it.

I now offer two considerations which favour Russell's position. The first is that treating acquaintance as not essentially conceptual makes it a relation into which non-conceptual beings, birds, for example, can enter. There is no doubt that in some sense birds perceive: they are sentient, they have some sort of awareness. On the intrinsicalist view, their awareness can without equivocation be called *awareness* only if they are concept-possessors. But is controversial whether they are. Russell's view is well adapted to this fact. In *us*, awareness leads to something conceptual: judgment. In birds, it is controversial whether it does so, for it is controversial whether they are concept-possessors, and so controversial whether they can judge. Since there is at most an *a posteriori* and contingent link between acquaintance and judgment, there is no *a priori* problem with the view that acquaintance occurs in creatures who cannot judge.

The second consideration is that I think that the nature of an experience can be entirely determinate even when its *as of* content is not. If correct, this shows that the *as of* content is not intrinsic to the experience. Suppose you are looking at a country scene on a bright, clear day. There are some creatures in the distance. You have some inclination to judge that they are sheep or goats; but you wouldn't be surprised to

[18] Cf. Peacocke (1984, p. 6).

learn that they are something else, pigs perhaps. In fact, you wouldn't be totally horrified by the suggestion that they are not creatures but cardboard cut-outs or even shadows. So far as dispositions to judgment go, there is no one judgment you would be willing to commit yourself to. There are a series of potential judgments, no doubt associated with different probabilities. What, then, is the *as of* content of your experience? I suggest that there is no determinate answer. In particular, the answer is not: *as of* its being probable to such-and-such a degree that there are sheep or goats over there; for you might not possess the concept of probability.

Now that I have defended Russell's non-conceptualism about acquaintance it is time to see whether he can use the notion to state a valuable condition upon thought.

2.4. Objects of Acquaintance and Thought-constituents

There is a danger that the Principle of Acquaintance will be trivial, unless we have some distinct access to the notion of an *object* or *constituent* of thought, as opposed merely to something the thought is 'about'. For how do we make this distinction? If we distinguish an object of thought, as opposed to something a thought is 'about', as something which can enter into our thought only if we are acquainted with it, we would make the Principle a truism. Russell himself at one point appears to do just this.

> One way of discovering what a proposition deals with is to ask ourselves what words we must understand—in other words, what objects we must be acquainted with—in order to see what the proposition means. . . . By applying this test, it appears that many propositions which might seem to be concerned with particulars are really concerned only with universals (*PP*, p. 60).

If acquaintance is the only test for whether something is a thought-constituent, the Principle of Acquaintance says that in order for something to stand in a relation to a thought constituted by our being acquainted with it, we must be acquainted with it.

Russell's immediate answer to the question of what thought-constituents are is not helpful: 'the constituents of the judgment are simply the constituents of the complex which is the judgment' (*KAKD*, p. 159). It would be reasonable to ask *why*

> if we make a judgment about (say) Julius Caesar, it is plain that the actual person who was Julius Caesar is not a constituent of the judgment (*KAKD*, p. 159).

This question cannot be answered by appeal to doctrines about sense data, unless the Principle of Acquaintance is already assumed to determine what objects can be thought-constituents.

There are two types of approach: a negative type, specifying thought-constituents in terms of what they are not, and a positive type.

For the negative approach, we need to admit a notion of what a thought *concerns*. For example, the thought that the founder of Mantua was wise will concern both the founder of Mantua and wisdom. Among the things a thought concerns, some will be genuine constituents and some will be what I shall call pseudo-constituents: things that the thought is 'about', in Russell's sense, but which are not genuine constituents of it. If we could provide necessary and sufficient conditions for an object to be a pseudo-constituent, then we could define a constituent as anything a thought concerns but which is not a pseudo-constituent.

It is reasonably clear how Russell would supply these necessary and sufficient conditions, but it is doubtful whether they provide a notion of *constituent* according to which the Principle of Acquaintance is true.

The account of pseudo-constituents takes a different form, depending as we are concerned with particulars or with universals. For particulars, a pseudo-constituent, with respect to some part of a thought, is something which that part of the thought concerns by having a content expressible by a definite description, a phrase of the form 'the so-and-so'. This involves what Russell calls merely descriptive knowledge of the pseudo-constituent.

> We have *descriptive* knowledge of an object when we know that it is *the* object having some property or properties with which we are acquainted; that is to say, when we know that the property or properties in question belong to one object and no more, we are said to have knowledge of that one object by description (*KAKD*, p. 166).

We could adapt this idea to our purposes along the following lines:

> an object, *o*, is a pseudo-constituent of a thought *T* if and only if *T* contains the thought that exactly one thing is F, and *o* is uniquely F.

The same object can be both a genuine and a pseudo-constituent of a thought, as in the thought, supposing it to be true, that *this is the F*.

For universals, while Russell says that there is a distinction between those known by acquaintance and those known by description (*PP*, p. 58), he gives no examples of what it is for a universal to be known merely in the second way. Descriptive knowledge of it would need to be 'based on' acquaintance, and the only connection between base and superstructure that could be attributed with any plausibility to Russell is definition. For example, given that Russell says that the only universals with which we can be acquainted are those belonging to particulars with which we are acquainted, and given that most people would agree that we are not acquainted with electrons, it follows that we are not acquainted with the universal *electronhood*. It seems that Russell is forced to say that this universal is definable in terms of universals with which we are acquainted, and this view has had a deservedly bad press.[19]

One objection to the negative approach, then, is that it can allow the intelligibility of a thought such as: electricity involves the flow of electrons, only at the price of a positivistic reduction of all properties to observable properties. Another objection concerns particulars. What is it for a thought to contain the thought that exactly one thing is F? Does the thought that Kissinger is bald do so? On the face of it, it does not. Yet according to Russell's theory that 'proper names . . . are usually really descriptions' (*PP*, p. 29), it does. How would such a controversy be resolved *without* appealing to the Principle of Acquaintance together with an account of what the objects of acquaintance are?

It is now customary to characterize Russell's notion of a thought-constituent in terms of a thought's truth conditions. A positive approach of this kind provides an answer to the question at the end of the last paragraph. We can extract from Russell's theory of belief the following metaphor: thought-constituents *enter into* belief. Bearing in mind that beliefs are, for Russell at this time, the bearers of truth and falsehood, it is reasonable to interpret this, less metaphorically, as saying that thought-constituents enter into the truth conditions of beliefs: they are such that, whether or not the belief is true turns on how things are with them.[20] This suggests the following account of what it is to be a thought-constituent:

> *o* is a constituent of *T* if and only if the truth of *T* with respect to any possible situation turns on how things are with *o*.

The same does not hold for pseudo-constituents. A man is giving a lecture. With him in mind, you think:

> *This person* is bald.

The truth or falsity of this thought turns on how things are with *this person*: whatever the circumstances relative to which we are assessing

[19] See, e.g. Nagel (1961, Ch. 6, Sc. 2). It may be that a weaker relation than definition could be devised.

[20] This is an application to thought of the notion of rigid designation: see, e.g. Kripke (1972, esp. p. 269ff.); Peacocke (1975, p. 110ff.).

the thought for truth, it is true if and only if he is, in those circumstances, bald. Now consider the following thought:

The inventor of the jet engine is bald.

As things are, this is true just on condition that whoever in fact invented the jet, say α, is bald. But consider a circumstance in which someone else, say β, invented the jet. The very same thought would then be true if and only if β is bald. Which object matters varies from circumstance to circumstance. Unlike the previous case, there is no single object which with respect to every circumstance is the one that matters.[21]

On this account of a thought-constituent, the truth of the Principle of Acquaintance requires a broad interpretation of the notion of acquaintance. There is no difficulty about people long dead, or places we have never visited, being thought-constituents in the sense just given. Aristotle has the property that my current thought that Aristotle might not have taught Plato depends just on how things are with him. Not only are these not objects of acquaintance in the sense of being sense data, they are not objects of aquaintance in the sense of being things with which we are 'presented', or things of which we have direct awareness. It would seem, then, that if our access to the nature of thought-constituents is through truth conditions, the Principle of Acquaintance will be simply false.

However, there would still be something to salvage. It is plausible to suggest that a person cannot think a thought containing a constituent (in the truth conditions sense) which is completely beyond his ken, having impinged on him in no way whatsoever. This goes as much for universals as particulars, and suggests that an object can be a thought-constituent for a subject only if a relation which permits a flow of information, or even knowledge, obtains between object and subject: let us call this the 'information relation'. It would be valuable to elaborate just what this relation is. But for our exegetical purposes, we must simply note two things: first, that while this suggestion constitutes something structurally analogous to the Principle of Acquaintance, it involves a large departure from Russell's conception of acquaintance: the information relation can hold of a subject and an unperceived or even imperceptible object; secondly, the suggestion does not constitute a total abandonment of Russell's position, for the information relation is certainly *cognitive*.

It is far from obvious, however, that it is this relation which supports our intuition that a man blind from birth could not have an idea of scarlet. Such a person might be related to scarlet as we are to Aristotle: there might be a channel of information from the property to the

[21] It is unclear that this test could happily be extended to universals.

subject, even though the subject did not have the kind of perceptual awareness of it required for him genuinely to have an 'idea' of it. For example, it would seem to be enough for the information relation to obtain between him and scarlet that he be linked to a machine which systematically delivers an auditory signal reliably indicating the predominant colour of the light falling on the unseeing eyes. The information is retained, even if it is 'transduced'. However, this situation is still one in which, intuitively, he has no 'idea' of scarlet: he cannot really have thoughts concerning it.[22] The wider conception of acquaintance that would be needed to make the Principle of Acquaintance true, if a thought-constituent is defined in terms of truth conditions, looks to be too wide to effect all the constraints we intuitively require.

What this suggests is that there should be available an alternative notion of thought-constituent, not given wholly (perhaps not at all) in terms of truth conditions, a notion according to which a blind man's thoughts cannot contain scarlet as a constituent, and relative to which the Principle of Acquaintance will be a substantive principle. We need to be able to ground the view that scarlet is not a thought-constituent without appeal to the principle, and then use the principle to explain why this is so.

If we ask what grounds our intuition that the man blind from birth, even if equipped with the auditory colour-signalling device, has no 'idea' of scarlet, one answer would be that he has no immediate sensitivity to this property: the property to which he is directly sensitive, and in terms of which we can provide a sufficient explanation of the mental state he is in when he sincerely affirms, e.g., 'This is scarlet', is an auditory one. If we ask him to pick out the scarlet objects from among a presented collection, and he does so, we must attribute to him a sequence of thoughts: 'This makes my device emit such-and-such a sound' and 'This sound is emitted if and only if there is a scarlet object before me'. By contrast, a sighted man's belief, 'This is scarlet', is normally to be explained just in terms of the visual property, and an explanation of his acting upon scarlet objects need require no thought correlating scarlet with some other property, of the kind we had to attribute to the blind man.

How would this apply to particulars? If we are to have a more restrictive relation than the information relation, we can focus on an

[22] It is another question whether we say that the blind man can understand the word 'scarlet'. There is a notion of thought and thought-constituent upon which we can allow that he does understand the word, yet scarlet is not a constituent of his thought. If you find my assumption that the blind man *can* understand the word unacceptable, you could replace occurrences of 'is scarlet' in sentences which I suppose the blind man can understand by 'has the property called "scarlet"'.

analogue of the second aspect just considered. To explain the action of a man who is asked to point to the tallest man in the room, we have to attribute to him a thought like 'That is the tallest man'. By contrast, under appropriate circumstances no such identifying thought need be invoked in order to explain his action in response to the request: point to *that man*. Understanding the latter request requires that he identify the man in question in a way adequate to explain the subsequent pointing. Understanding the request 'Point to the tallest man' imposes no such requirement. Using this idea, we could characterize particular constituents of thoughts as ones which occur in such a way that they can be used, without the intermediary of further thoughts like 'This is the tallest man', to explain actions on particular objects. The contrast holds *within* the category of objects entering into the truth conditions of a thought. Suppose some subject, S, has a thought whose truth conditions contain Kissinger. Even so, we may be able to explain S's success in acting upon Kissinger only by ascribing to him some thought like 'This is Kissinger'. Here, both singular thoughts-parts (the one corresponding to 'this' and the one corresponding to 'Kissinger') introduce an object which enters into truth conditions, and both introduce an object with respect to which S must stand in the information relation. But only the thought-part corresponding to 'this' introduces an object in the way needed to account for S's action upon Kissinger. We could use this way to explicate a narrower notion of thought-constituent, and then the Principle of Acquaintance would be a substantive and plausible thesis.

This is a rapid sketch of a project, essentially that developed by Peacocke (1984, Ch. 7). It is too rough to admit serious evaluation here, but good enough to enable me to bring out a feature which will throw light on Russell's position. To identify it, notice how close the previous paragraph came to a contradiction. It would be potentially contradictory to say that the object introduced by 'this' is related to the subject in the narrower way, whereas the object introduced by 'Kissinger' is not, for these are the same object if the judgment is true. Thought-constituents will not be merely objects, but objects together with ways in which they occur in thought. The contrast will be between the way such that no further thought is required to explain action on the object, and the way such that some further thought is required (e.g. the further thoughts 'This is Kissinger', 'This sound is emitted if and only if there is a scarlet object before me'). Correlatively, the Principle of Acquaintance will have to address not objects simply, but ways in which objects can occur in thought. This *way* will be held to affect the identity of thoughts, but it will not be in *any* sense something the thought is about. The projected view makes it absolutely clear how essential to the identity of thoughts are modes of presentation. Rehabilitating Russell's Principle of Acquaintance essentially involves abandoning the no-concept theory of judgment with which, in Russell's mind, it was intimately connected.

In conclusion, when Russell said that he could scarcely conceive that the Principle of Acquaintance could be false, this might have been because he was surreptitiously using acquaintance as a prime factor in his explanation of what it is to be a thought-constituent. Once we look for an independent account of this notion, the Principle of Acquaintance becomes indeed a non-trivial principle, but one which, if it is to be true, will require some modification of Russell's view. If we use a truth conditions method of saying what a thought-constituent is, acquaintance loses its special connection with perception, and becomes the relation which holds between a subject and an object if and only if there is a flow of information from the latter to the former, in a way that can give the subject knowledge of the object. If we explain a thought-constituent in terms of thoughts capable of explaining actions of a certain kind, the Principle of Acquaintance is indeed plausible, but we are involved in a more radical departure from Russell's views: on this approach, the notion of a thought-constituent essentially involves modes of presentation, whereas Russell's Principle of Acquaintance is linked with a non-conceptual theory of judgment.

References

F. I. Dretske, *Knowledge and the Flow of Information*, (Blackwell, 1981).

Gareth Evans, *The Varieties of Reference* (Oxford University Press, 1982).

Gottlob Frege [1892], 'On Sense and Reference', in *Translations From the Philosophical Writings of Gottlob Frege*, P. Geach and M. Black (eds) (Blackwell, 1960).

H. P. Grice, 'The Causal Theory of Perception', *Proceedings of the Aristotelian Society, Supplementary Volume* **35** (1961).

Frank Jackson, *Perception* (Cambridge University Press, 1977).

Saul Kripke, 'Naming and Necessity', in *Semantics of Natural Language*, D. Davidson and G. Harman (eds) (Reidel, 1972).

Allan Millar, 'What's in a Look', *Proceedings of the Aristotelian Society* **86** (1985/6).

E. Nagel, *The Structure of Science* (RKP, 1961).

Christopher Peacocke, 'Proper Names, Reference and Rigid Designation', in *Meaning, Reference and Necessity*, S. Blackburn (ed.) (Cambridge University Press, 1975).

Christopher Peacocke, *Holistic Explanation* (Oxford University Press, 1979).

Christopher Peacocke, *Sense and Content* (Oxford University Press, 1984).

David Pears, 'The Causal Conditions of Perception', *Synthese* **33** (1975).

David Pears, 'The Function of Acquaintance in Russell's Philosophy', *Synthese* **46** (1981).

Bertrand Russell, *Principles of Mathematics* (Allen and Unwin, 1903).

Bertrand Russell, 'Meinong's Theory of Complexes and Assumptions' [1904], reprinted in *Essays in Analysis by Bertrand Russell*, Douglas Lackey (ed.) (Allen and Unwin, 1973).

Bertrand Russell, 'On Denoting' [1905] reprinted in *Essays in Analysis by Bertrand Russell*, Douglas Lackey (ed.) (Allen and Unwin, 1973).

Bertrand Russell [*KAKD*], 'Knowledge by Acquaintance and Knowledge by Description' [1910], reprinted in his *Mysticism and Logic* (Allen and Unwin, 1963 reprint).

Bertrand Russell [*PP*], *Problems of Philosophy* [1912] (Oxford University Press, 1969 reprint).

Bertrand Russell, *Theory of Knowledge* [1913], in *Collected Papers of Bertrand Russell*, E. R. Eames and K. Blackwell (eds) Vol. 7. (London: Allen & Unwin, 1984).

Bertrand Russell [*RSP*], 'The Relation of Sense-Data to Physics' [1914], reprinted in his *Mysticism and Logic* (Allen and Unwin, 1963 reprint).

Bertrand Russell [*PLA*], 'The Philosophy of Logical Atomism' [1918], in *Logic and Knowledge*, R. C. Marsh (ed.) (Allen and Unwin, 1956). (This collection also contains a reprint of 'On Denoting'.)

Bertrand Russell [*Mind*], *The Analysis of Mind* (Allen and Unwin, 1921).

Bertrand Russell and Alfred North Whitehead, *Principia Mathematica* (Cambridge: C.U.P. 1910–13).

Russell on Universals

J. O. URMSON

It might seem that there are two separate questions about universals, the question of what they are and the question why we should believe that there are such things, and that the former question should be taken first; it might seem that until you know what they are it cannot be sensible to ask whether one should believe in them. How, for example, could one know whether it was sensible or even possible to believe in Father Christmas until one knew who or what he was supposed to be? But appearances could be deceptive. In the case of universals the position is different. What happened was that philosophers found themselves faced with certain problems of which they were inclined to say: this problem is insoluble unless there are some entities which have certain characteristics, the characteristics which would enable the problem to be solved. The things which, if they existed, would solve their problems they called forms or universals. So universals are things which have whatever properties they need to have to solve certain problems. This being so, it is clearly sensible to approach the theory of universals from the problems which led to philosophers postulating their existence.

If I say 'That is my brother' or 'Elizabeth is Queen of England', in each case there is just one person whom I refer to first as 'That' or 'Elizabeth' and then as 'my brother' or 'Queen of England'; here 'is' means much the same as 'is the same thing as'. I have just two ways of talking about one unproblematic thing. But I might say 'Mary is beautiful and Jane is beautiful'. How is that to be explained? Clearly neither Mary nor Jane is the same thing as beautiful or beauty—if one is they both are and so must be the same thing as each other. All this is absurd. So 'Mary is beautiful' has to be explained in a way different from the simple way in which we explained 'That is my brother'. One way of explaining it is to say that there must be such a thing as beauty which is something different from either Mary or Jane but which Mary and Jane both exemplify, or instantiate, or of which both of them partake, or which is present in both of them. Philosophers have used all these expressions indifferently. So to explain 'Mary is beautiful' we have to posit, it seems, that there are two ultimately different kinds of things in the world; particular things like my brother, the Queen, Mary and Jane, chairs and tables on the one hand; on the other hand there must be things like beauty which particulars exemplify or instantiate. Moreover, since Mary is a girl and to be a girl is to be young and female, Mary must also exemplify femaleness and youth. There must be many universals and any particular will exhibit lots of them.

But what are these universals like youth, beauty, redness and roundness like? Clearly, unlike the particulars that instantiate them, they are nowhere in particular. Perhaps we should say that they are in no place at all, or, if we want to say that beauty is present in Mary, we must also allow that it is also present in Jane and therefore in two places at once or potentially everywhere. But particulars cannot be in two places at once.

Moreover, universals must be timeless. We can use tensed verbs of Mary; she was a baby, is a girl and, with luck will be an old woman; but beauty does not come into existence, grow old or die. So universals are changeless. Mary may come to instantiate senility and ugliness, but beauty and ugliness, youth and old age, just are what they are and cannot change into each other.

Further, it seems that these timeless and placeless entities cannot be seen, heard, tasted, smelt or touched; they are not objects of sense. How, indeed could they be since everything we sense certainly has to be in some place or other? Instances of youth and beauty we may certainly see or otherwise sense, but they themselves are objects of thought, intelligible objects whose existence we know not through observation but through the arguments that we are now considering. The arguments for the existence of such intelligible entities as forms or universals are the basis of Plato's distinction, so influential ever since, between a perfect, unchanging and eternal world of intelligible forms and a derivative, changing, and imperfect world of sense.

But, even if we put aside Platonic metaphysics, these intelligible universals appear to be of fundamental importance for thought, language, and all communication. We can refer to things by proper names—Mary, Jane, London, Liverpool, Mars, Venus, or demonstratives—this, that, but more often as men, women, oranges, triangles, etc. But it seems that what enables us to sort things out as men, women, oranges and triangles just is the presence of one or more of these universals, maleness, femaleness, triangularity, and whatever set of properties distinguishes oranges from other things. And, when we want to say something about any of these particulars that we refer to, surely it must involve asserting or denying their instantiation of some further universal. Thus, 'This triangle is equilateral', seems to say that this instance of the universal triangularity is also an instance of the universal equilateralness. Unless these universals existed to be instantiated how could we come to recognize or classify things at all; how could any thought be possible?

Moreover it can appear, and did appear to Plato, that these timeless universals exist quite independently of their instances and may indeed have no instances. For example, we all know what we mean when we speak of perfect justice, but quite likely there are no instances of perfect justice. Plato thought there were none, and I am not sure that I have come across any. If that example is not convincing, consider dragonhood, magic, and all the apparatus of fairyland. We can think of these things, but cannot observe them because they do not exist to observe.

So considerations such as these have led Plato and other philosophers to believe that there are two fundamentally different kinds of things, on the one hand intelligible, timeless, placeless, unchanging entities, on the other temporal, spatially located, changing and sensible things. The former of these two classes philosophers have called Platonic ideas, or forms or universals. The latter have been called particulars. Particulars are what they are in virtue of instantiating or exemplifying universals. Each particular will exemplify indefinitely many universals. Thus an apple may exemplify roundness, redness, juiciness, sweetness, etc.

Philosophers have introduced a number of technical terms to label the various views that have been held about universals. Giving technical names to theories does not advance our understanding of the problems, but it is useful to know them and it sometimes saves verbiage. All those who believe that there are universals existing independently of minds and thoughts and words are called realists (in one of the many senses of 'realist'). It is confusing that Plato, who introduced the doctrine of eternal ideas, should be called a realist, but he is. Those who, like Plato, believe in the existence of ideas, forms, universals, or whatever other term is preferred, as quite independent of particulars were said by the medievals to believe in *universalia ante rem*, literally, universals before the thing. Those who, like Aristotle, believed in objective universals but only as one aspect of particular things and not as independent of them were said to believe in *universalia in re*, universals in the thing.

Aristotle found the notion of universals like redness and triangularity just existing on their own, without anything that was red or triangular, unacceptable. The line he adopted went something like this: consider a round ball made of wood; the shape, roundness, is really there and the matter, the wood, is really there; but there cannot be a shape without something that instantiates that shape and there cannot be matter, wood, brass, or what you will, that does not instantiate some shape or other. There can no more be form without matter, or matter without form than there can be something on top and nothing underneath. They are complementary facets of a unity. Platonic examples like perfect justice were clearly a problem for the Aristotelian.

But not all philosophers have been willing to accept realism about universals even in the less bold Aristotelian version. Timeless, placeless, changeless, imperceptible entities known to but independent of human minds have seemed to some to be grossly implausible. We, they say, divide the world up into kinds for convenience. The notion that from all eternity there have been entities that could be called 'chairhood' and 'sofahood' waiting for men to make chairs and sofas to instantiate them is more than these empiricists can stomach. Thus there come to be those who traditionally are called conceptualists and nominalists. The conceptualists say that beauty, youth, redness and all universals are merely concepts or ideas (in a non-Platonic, subjective sense of 'idea') which human beings construct or invent for convenience of thought and discourse. The nominalist is even more economical; for him the only things that are universal are words. Thus, having been told that something we observe is called a telephone box we find it convenient to call anything like it a telephone box. Philosophers nowadays do not always distinguish carefully between conceptualism and nominalism, but they used to. Thus Locke's account of abstract ideas in Book II of his *Essay on the Human Understanding* is a classical example of conceptualism which was violently attacked by the nominalist Berkeley in the Introduction to his *Principles of Human Knowledge*. The medievals called both conceptualism and nominalism theories of *universalia post rem*, universals after the thing, which term is self-explanatory.

It should be becoming clear why I said right at the start that the questions of what universals are and why we should believe in them are inseparable. Consider a typical archaeological argument. As the result of a dig the archaeologist may say: 'There must have been people here who had such and such tools, who had such and such techniques with metals, who lived in such and such kind of dwellings, etc.'. The argument starts from certain facts, the results of the dig, and then offers the account of the people as being the best possible explanation of the facts. There is no question of describing a certain sort of people and then looking for arguments for and against their existence.

The realist argument for universals is of the same kind. It starts from such facts as that you can call both Mary and Jane beautiful and, generally, that we can classify things and then says that the existence of things having the features they ascribe to universals is the best or only possible explanation of these facts. To refute the realist one must either show that his alleged facts are not facts, which would be difficult, or else find a better explanation of them.

After these introductory remarks let us now turn to Russell's two chapters on universals in *The Problems of Philosophy*. What importance, if any, have they? I think that they are important in two ways.

First, we have here the best, the clearest and most powerful short defence of a realism of the Platonic type that can be found anywhere. We have no such account from Plato himself—he assumes the position in his written works and his arguments have to be reconstructed laboriously from oblique references and the critical comments of other ancient philosophers such as his younger contemporary Aristotle. Later statements of Platonic realism tend to be long, full of technical jargon and of references to other philosophers of which most of us will be ignorant. So Russell is the best philosopher to start with if one wants to understand the theory of universals. The other way in which these chapters are important is the stress Russell lays on universals of relation; this is an important and original feature of Russell's position which in other ways is not original. We shall turn to this matter a little later in this discussion.

In Chapter 8, headed 'How is *a priori* knowledge possible?', Russell has raised two points which lead to the chapters on universals. In the first place he has claimed that *a priori* knowledge is about neither particular existing items in the physical world about us nor about our thoughts, a point which leads to the problem what such knowledge is about. In the second place he has pointed out that every sentence we utter, whatever its subject-matter, contains words which have meaning, but do not seem to denote any particular objects, mental or physical; in particular, these words, such as 'in', seem to refer to qualities and relations, whose nature we must explore.

At this place in our discussion it would be as well to raise a matter which is perhaps mainly terminological but has some significance in the philosophy of language. Towards the end of Chapter 8 Russell says: 'These entities are such as can be named by parts of speech which are not substantives; they are such entities as qualities and relations'. Early in Chapter 9, headed 'The World of Universals' he says: 'When we examine common words, we find that, broadly speaking, proper names stand for particulars, while other substantives, adjectives, prepositions, and verbs, stand for universals'. There are two points arising from these and similar remarks. In the first place it seems odd to say that words other than substantives are names at all; the very first example Russell uses in Chapter 9 is justice; it seems proper to say that the word 'justice' names a quality, but if I say 'Socrates was just' it seems odd to say that the word 'just' is the name of a quality. 'Socrates was justice' would seem very odd. In the second place it may seem odd to say that only proper names name particulars, for obviously I may refer to particulars by such expressions as 'an apple'. If I say that I have just eaten 'an apple' I surely claim to have eaten something particular and not at all abstract.

I think that it is queer to say that both the word 'justice' and the word 'just' are names of a quality. But what I think Russell had in mind was the view that to say 'Socrates was just' is a way of saying 'Socrates (the particular) instantiated justice (the quality)'. Similarly it is odd to say that the word 'in' is a name of a relation. But we may perhaps hold that 'The dog is in the kennel' is a way of saying that the kennel and the dog are related by the relation of containment. Perhaps it would be better to say that adjectives and prepositions and the like implicitly refer to qualities and relations and agree that qualities and relations are named by abstract nouns such as 'justice', 'redness', 'juxtaposition' and 'marriage'.

It would also be odd to say that such words as 'apple' and 'horse' are names of qualities or relations. But it is easy to see why Russell will only count proper names as names of particulars. For if I say: 'Dobbin is a horse', I surely name the horse when I say 'Dobbin' and the rest of the sentence says something about Dobbin, it does not just name him again. Perhaps, parallel with reading 'Socrates was just' to be a way of saying that Socrates instantiated or exemplifies justice, we may say that 'Dobbin is a horse' is a way of saying that Dobbin instantiates or exemplifies horsiness or equinity, or whatever we wish to call the group of qualities which make something a horse. So perhaps we should not call 'horse' the name of a quality but rather say some such thing as that it implicitly refers to a quality.

Russell starts his chapter on the world of universals by distinguishing the questions of 'the nature of this kind of being' (what universals are like) and 'what objects there are that have this kind of being' (what things are universals). He claims to separate as well as distinguish the questions, saying that he will discuss the second first. As we saw, this separation is not so easy, for in the very first two paragraphs of his solution of the problem we hear that universals are real essences, supra-sensible, unchanging. As he himself says, his view is very like that of Plato and his argument starts from the question how it is possible to classify things. The answer given is precisely that we classify together just those things that share a common nature. But you cannot see or smell common natures themselves, so they are supra-sensible; a particular may change and so cease to instantiate a common nature but the common nature itself is unchangeable, and while horses may become extinct someday, their common nature is not alive and cannot therefore die—it is eternal. This is the basic argument on which all champions or universals have relied throughout the ages.

It would not be profitable for us now to go sentence by sentence through Russell's discussion of universals and our knowledge of them. Instead I want to concentrate on one theme, Russell's insistence on the importance of the recognition of universals of relation. I shall try to amplify some of the points he actually makes on this topic and also to mention some considerations which Russell quite certainly was aware of but did not emphasize in this book.

I. The Relation of Resemblance

Russell mentions Berkeley and Hume as having claimed that all ideas are particular and everything in the world is particular. Thus in paragraph 12 of the Introduction to his *Principles of Human Knowledge* Berkeley holds that a word is used generally not by referring to anything universal or abstract but by standing indifferently for all particulars *of the same sort*. Hume in Section VII of the First Part of Book I of *A Treatise of Human Nature* says 'When we have found a resemblance among several objects, that often occur to us, we apply the same name to all of them'. Russell's objection is that they use the expressions 'of the same sort' (Berkeley) and 'resemblance' (Hume) without seeing that these are the very notions that need explaining and which, in Russell's view, can be explained only by a theory of universals. It is sometimes thought that Russell's argument can be countered by pointing out that classification is arbitrary. Thus we classify dining room chairs and armchairs as chairs but treat the sofa as being of a different kind. But, it is correctly pointed out, we might easily have recognized a class of loungers, what we now call armchairs being called loungers for one, sofas being loungers for more than one person; upright chairs might have been regarded as a separate class. So, it is asked, how can we claim that chairhood and sofahood are immutable eternal essences. But while these contentions are undoubtedly correct, it is not the case that they weakened Russell's argument. What he can say in reply is that all this argument shows is that while it is logically an arbitrary decision which universals we shall take into account in classification, still chairs, sofas and the rest do really instantiate those complex universals which we arbitrarily select.

II. Relations and Monism

If one ignores or denies the existence of universals of relation, holding that every meaningful statement applies some quality to some object, then no doubt one must accept either monism or monadism. If there are many things but it is impossible to say anything about their relationships, then each must be a microcosm, a monad, having no relationship to any other. In Leibniz's aphorism, 'monads are windowless'. Again it is clear that any monist, who holds that all differentiation and separation are but appearance, and that reality or the absolute is one and unchanging, will have no room for relational statements. What is not clear is why Russell claims to explain these metaphysical positions by the denial of or blindness to universals of relation. They seem to be the same thing as the denial of relations, rather than being based on it. Parmenides, the first known Western monist, based his monism on a logical point, but one which asserted the impossibility of negation, not the impossibility of relations. Bradley's argument for monism, as found, for example, in his *Principles of Logic*, claims equally that applying predicates of quality and applying predicates of relation to anything less than the whole of reality involves falsification. Russell's claim that Leibniz's monadism is based on a rejection of relations is developed at length in his book on Leibniz; the merits of this claim are disputed.

III. Relations and *a priori* Knowledge

Russell presents some sort of a dilemma with regard to the nature and even the possibility of *a priori* knowledge. On the one hand, he holds that we cannot know of the existence or nature of any particular thing except on the basis of experience. Either we must directly observe or be sensibly acquainted with a particular, on the one hand, or else we can infer its existence, on the other; but if we infer its existence, as we may infer the existence of people in a room with closed doors, it must be on the basis of evidence itself based on observation, such as the sound of voices. But, on the other hand, it seems to be impossile to deny that we do have knowledge that is *a priori*, that is, not based on experience. No doubt, as Kant said, our *a priori* knowledge arises out of experience. We all, except for great innovative geniuses, gained our knowledge of mathematics by being taught by our instructors. But a schoolboy who offered 'My maths teacher says so' as a proof of his geometrical theorem would not get very high marks in his examinations. But mathematics, as Russell argues in *Problems*, is clearly *a priori*; we found that some swans were black when we discovered Australia, and it is just possible that there are green swans in some unexplored corner of the world; but we are never going to find some unusual spot where two plus two is not equal to four—what would it be to make such a discovery? Just how far *a priori* knowledge extends beyond logic and mathematics is a hotly disputed question, but that there is some such knowledge can be denied only with absurdity.

Now, if we confine ourselves to what Russell calls the world of particulars, we have an insoluble problem; we can have no *a priori* knowledge of particulars, but we do have *a priori* knowledge. Russell solves this problem, as we know, by making a double appeal to the world of universals: the entities about which we have *a priori* knowledge are universals, and what we know about them is their relationship to one another. Let us explain this view a little more fully than Russell has space for. Suppose that we take the proposition that every Euclidian triangle has its interior angles equal to two right angles, which seems to make a statement about an infinite class of particulars, for a triangle is not a universal. We must say that this appearance is misleading and might try to show this by recasting the proposition to read 'The universal property of being a Euclidian triangle entails the universal property of having interior angles equal to two right angles'; this can be true even if there are no Euclidian triangles. The universal relation that we rely on here is that of logical entailment. Perhaps it is an *a priori* truth, in virtue of the meaning of the words, that every chair has legs. If it is, we can say that 'All chairs weighing a million tons have legs' is true *a priori*, even if we are sure that there are no chairs of that weight; for we can construe it as saying that the universal quality of being a million-ton chair entails the quality of having legs, whether these universals can be instantiated or not. On this basis we might go further than Russell and claim that we can know that if Brown and Jones are two, and Robinson and Smith are two, then Brown and Jones and Robinson and Smith are four, which Russell denies (*Problems*, p.60), claiming that to know this we should need to know that there were such people, which we could know only through experience. Might we not claim that we know that if Cheiron was a centaur he had a man's head and a horse's body, even though we do not believe in centaurs, construing the proposition to mean that the instantiation of the compound property of being a centaur and being called Cheiron entails the instantiation of that odd anatomical constitution.

IV. Relations and Logic

I should like now to say something about another way in which relations are important for the *a priori* truths of logic, a way of which Russell was certainly well aware but which he does not discuss in *The Problems of Philosophy*. If we consider that area of logic known as predicate logic, the area where the validity of inferences depends on the internal character of the premises and conclusion, the syllogistic logic discovered (or invented) by Aristotle was all we had for about fifteen hundred years. This logic was discussed and refined with great subtlety in the Middle Ages, but was not supplemented by the recognition of other forms of inference. Syllogistic inference proceeds by inferring the relation of two terms from premises relating each to the same third term. Thus the syllogism in Barbara says that if all M is P and all S is M then all S is P and the syllogism in Celarent that if no M is P and all S is M then no S is P. Clearly it is necessary that the same M, the middle term, should be the same in both premises; from 'All M is P and all S is N' nothing follows. Here all the premises and conclusions are taken as ascribing a predicate to a subject—that is why the letters S and P are traditionally used in the formal schemata.

But now let us consider the *a priori* truth that if A is greater than B and B is greater than C then A is greater than C. What will happen if we construe it on the syllogistic model? Well, the first clause will have as its subject A and its predicate will be 'greater than B'; similarly the second clause will have B as its subject and 'greater than C' as its predicate, while the conclusion will have A as its subject and 'greater than C' as its predicate. So we have four terms *A*, *greater than B*, *B* and *greater than C*, and the argument must be symbolized as 'If M is P and S is N then S is P' which is invalid. But suppose that we introduce a formalism that uses relation, and see what happens. Let us formalize 'All M is P' as 'M is included in P' and other propositions similarly and we now have:

If M is included in P	If B is greater than C
and S is included in M	and A is greater than B
then S is included in P	then A is greater than C

It now appears that the syllogistic and mathematical arguments are very similar in form, depending for their validity on the similar logical properties of the relations of *inclusion* and *being greater than*. If we symbolized both these relations, very plausibly, by the symbol $>$ the arguments would be seen to be of the same form. Russell and others transformed logic by making a systematic use of relations in a way which I have tried to illustrate by a simple example.

So much for our supplementary and explanatory comments on Russell's treatment of universals which, except on a few matters of detail, has been completely uncritical. We ought to make sure that we understand Russell before we criticize him. But now the time has come to ask whether we should accept the general position advocated by Russell, in particular the claim for the existence or subsistence of this world of universals of which philosophers may become aware but which is ignored by all others. When we approach this large question we seem to find ourselves, as so often happens in philosophy, torn between arguments for two incompatible theses, each set of arguments being equally convincing when we attend to it.

If one were to come upon the sentence: 'Roses, though very varied, have none the less many common characteristics' in a horticultural book, one would think it a quite appropriate remark and certainly not a wildly irrelevant excursion into metaphysics. But if it is true then there must be common characteristics for roses to share. But common characteristics are not particulars—one could not, for example, arrange them in a vase. But if what we mean by a universal is something which is not a particular it follows that there must be universals. To deny it is to say either such outrageous things as that roses have no common characteristics or that common characteristics are the sort of thing which might be put into a vase or bumped into. Moreover it seems clear that roses would continue to have common characteristics even if all rational beings were exterminated, so that we could not construe the statement that roses have common characteristics as meaning that they are thought of or spoken about in a certain way; roses would have had common characteristics if there never were any rational beings. This argument of mine might remind us of Russell's example of Edinburgh being north of London. So, looked at this way, the existence of universals seems more like a very stale platitude, a glimpse of the obvious, than a great metaphysical theory, for the development of which Plato is regarded as one of the world's great philosophers. Diogenes Laertius tells us that when Diogenes the Cynic raised the childish objection that universals were not perceptible particulars, saying 'I see a table and a cup, but certainly not tableness and cupness', Plato told him that that was because he had eyes but no intelligence. In the way we have been looking at the matter it seems that we need very little intelligence to recognize them.

Yet people have strenuously rejected the Platonic theory of forms. Partly this is because of the mystical developments of the theory, referred to by Russell, in which it goes far beyond anything we have considered. One well-known illustration of this is Plato's view in the *Republic* that it would take about thirty years of higher education before anyone had any hope of becoming acquainted with the form of the good. Yet the way we have been looking at the matter, anyone who remarks of two apples that they are both good must *ipso facto* be acquainted with the common characteristic, or universal, or form of goodness. Nothing, however, in Plato approaches the wild excesses of the later neo-Platonics, such as one may find in, for example, Proclus' *Elements of Theology*.

But these mystical developments of, or excrescences on, the theory of universals are not a complete explanation of the resistence to the doctrine of universals, for the non-mystical statement of the theory in Russell is by no means generally accepted. We are told that battles were fought, and blood was shed, by nominalists and conceptualists in the Middle Ages in their fight against the supporters of a fairly non-mystical variety of universals; nominalists and conceptualists are today unlikely to appeal to the sword, but there are still many of them whose objections we must try to understand.

Some who object do so on the basis of some very general metaphysical position rather than on the basis of finding some specific weakness in the type of argument used by Russell in favour of universals. We cannot consider all such possible positions, but may consider materialism as one example. The materialist denies reality to everything except material objects. Talk about anything else has to be rejected by him as either illegitimate or else reinterpreted to be a disguised way of talking about material objects. Thus he rejects mental events as well as universals interpreted in any save a nominalistic way. Ontology, the discussion of what is ultimately real, always seems to me to be a rather odd subject. Plato, it seems, rejected everything, including material objects, as being less than real, save his forms, because all save forms was changeable, perishable and not ultimately intelligible; in other words, the physical world is unreal because it is unlike the world of forms. Materialists reject the mental, universals, and everything not within the domain of the physical sciences, because it is not empirically observable by scientific procedures; universals are rejected because they are not like material objects. But why Plato thought there was something unreal involved in not being a form, and why materialists think that there is something unreal involved in not being a material object is something I do not understand. Ultimately, such ontological positions seem to me to be without real intellectual content.

But, all the same, many people do have an uneasy feeling when they read Russell, or Platonists, talking about a world of universals on the one hand and a world of particulars on the other, and I share this uneasy feeling with them; so I shall devote the rest of this discussion to an attempt to turn this inarticulate unease into an explicit statement.

It is generally held that, with the possible exception of some very queer elementary particles, nothing can be in two different places at the same time. But let me now claim to be in two different places at this very moment, for I am simultaneously in London and in Gordon Square and nobody can claim that London and Gordon Square are one and the same place. This is, no doubt, absurd, but in explaining its absurdity we must not fall into the opposite absurdity of suggesting that London and Gordon Square are identical with each other, for they certainly are not. What we have to make clear is that while Gordon Square is not the same as London it is not an extra place in addition to London, so that, in listing places, I will have left some territory unaccounted for if I do not mention Gordon Square in addition to London. So Gordon Square is a perfectly genuine place, and London is a perfectly genuine place, and Gordon Square is not the same place as London, but Gordon Square is not an extra place in addition to London. We are not at present inhabiting two different worlds or two different places, but one world specifiable in different ways. What is the relevance of this to universals?

Well, let me try a parallel argument: I draw two rectangles and ask you how many things you are aware of as you contemplate the board. 'Two' might be the answer of the unsophisticated common man, but we philosophers will say 'three' since we are aware of two particular rectangles and also a universal—the common characteristic rectangularity which they share. Now I think that we should neither accept this claim as correct, for it seems to me very like the claim that Gordon Square is a place additional to London; but neither should we on the opposite extreme reject it by denying that there is a common characteristic which we call rectangularity, which seems to me very like denying that there is such a place as Gordon Square.

Now it seems to me that Russell at least appears to exemplify the one extreme by talking about a world of forms, additional to the world of particulars, a world known to philosophers but not to unreflective people. Why cannot we add the populations of two worlds together, just as we can add the populations of two cities together? If we can, then it would seem that we should accept my claim that two rectangles plus one rectangularity add up to three things. On the other extreme, the nominalists and conceptualists seem to be in danger of denying the obvious; for I take it as obvious that all rectangles do have a common characteristic which we may call rectangularity.

When we contemplate objects we seem to be able to distinguish various qualities which they possess and various relations in which they stand to other objects; we can also distinguish the thing from its qualities, the tomato from its colour and the figure from its shape. If we want to call the qualities and relations universals and the bearers of these qualities particulars, no harm need be done. But surely we should not now talk of the qualities and relations as though they were themselves objects in a world of their own instead of something distinguishable when we contemplate objects. The bearer of qualities and the qualities are distinguishable, but neither without the other is a countable object in the one world in which we live.

Aristotle made use of the concepts of matter and form. If we consider a particular cube of wax we can distinguish its form, or shape, from that which has the shape, the matter, the wax. But the object which we consider, the cube of wax, is matter with a form; the wax without a shape or the shape without the wax would be nothing. Aristotle generalized this, using the word *form* to stand for all qualities and not just shape and *matter* to refer to all bearers of qualities and not just physical objects, so that if I were to say 'Go away' we could state the fact that my utterance was an imperative by calling the utterance the matter and saying it was imperative in form. Every significant utterance must have a form, imperative, indicative or interrogative, and there could be no utterance without the form and no form without the utterance.

When I say 'Go away' you do not hear two things, an utterance and an imperative, though it is true that you heard an utterance and true that you heard an imperative.

This no-nonsense and unspectacular way of looking at the matter, very typical of Aristotle, seems to me to be good. I tend to sympathize with his rather impatiently and contemptuously expressed view that to talk of a separate world of universals is 'empty verbiage and poetic metaphor'. So I should wish to revise those parts of Russell's writings when he talks in the 'two-world' idiom. But this view certainly need not lead to a rejection of Russell's discussion as worthless. Very much of what he has to say in the chapters we have been considering is independent of the two-world position. This, I believe is true of his claim for the importance of relations and of his account of the nature of *a priori* truth in terms of the relation between universals. How fully we can accept Russell's views on these and other topics must be discussed from other standpoints as well, but my criticism, if correct, does not vitiate them, though it might require us to reformulate some of them.

Alfred Jules Ayer

Alfred Jules Ayer (1910–) was born in London and educated at Eton and Christ Church, Oxford. He attended sessions of the logical positivist 'Vienna Circle' in 1932, and taught at Oxford from 1933 until joining the Army in 1940. His *Language, Truth and Logic* was published in 1936, and *The Foundations of Empirical Knowledge* in 1940. After war service he returned to Oxford in 1945, and became Grote Professor of the Philosophy of Mind and Logic at University College, London, the following year. *The Problem of Knowledge* was published in 1956. In 1959 he returned to Oxord as Wykeham Professor of Logic, a post he held until his retirement in 1977. He had been made a Fellow of the British Academy in 1952, and was knighted in 1970. Among his publications after he returned to Oxford are *The Concept of a Person* (1963), *Philosophical Essays* (1965), *The Origins of Pragmatism* (1968), *Metaphysics and Common Sense* (1969), *Russell and Moore: the Analytical Heritage* (1971), *Probability and Evidence* (1972), *The Central Questions of Philosophy* (1973), and *Philosophy in the Twentieth Century* (1982).

A. J. Ayer, *Language, Truth and Logic* (Harmondsworth: Penguin, 1971) is prescribed by the AEB.

The following may prove useful:

- F. Waismann, *The Principles of Linguistic Philosophy* (London: Macmillan, 1965)
- J. O. Urmson, *Philosophical Analysis* (Oxford: Clarendon Press, 1967)
- F. Waismann, *Wittgenstein and the Vienna Circle* (Oxford: Blackwell, 1979)
- G. F. Macdonald (ed.), *Perception and Identity*, Essays presented to A. J. Ayer with his replies to them (London: Macmillan, 1979)
- O. Hanfling, *Logical Positivism* (Oxford: Blackwell, 1981)
- O. Hanfling (ed.), *Essential Readings in Logical Positivism* (Oxford: Blackwell, 1981)
- J. Foster, *A. J. Ayer* (London: Routledge and Kegan Paul, 1985).

Ayer, *Language, Truth and Logic*

OSWALD HANFLING

When, in 1979, A. J. Ayer was asked for an evaluation of his youthful *Language, Truth and Logic (LTL)*, he replied: 'I suppose the most important of the defects was that nearly all of it was false'.[1] Like many of the claims in the book itself, this verdict is open to question. What was wrong with *LTL* was not so much that what it said was false, but that it presented philosophical issues in an excessively simple and aggressive way. Yet it was just this quality that put the book and its author on the philosophical map, ensuring for them an important place in the history of twentieth-century philosophy. *LTL* presented a challenge to traditional ways of doing philosophy, the reverberations of which are still evident today.

The book was first published in 1936, when the author was only twenty-five years old; but in the second edition of 1946 he conceded, in his new Introduction, that 'the questions with which it deals are not in all respects so simple as it makes them appear' (7). He went on to make a number of modifications and concessions to critics, but made it clear that he still adhered to the same general point of view—one that is also to be found in his subsequent writings.

This point of view, or various strands of it, are also evident in the works of many other philosophers, both since that time, and in earlier periods, as was pointed out in the book. Thus the analysis of empirical facts into simple, homogenous elements (whether 'sense-data' or 'simple objects') had its ancestry in the systems of Locke, Berkeley and Hume, and more recently, Wittgenstein's *Tractatus*. The subjectivist treatment of ethics was anticipated by Hume, and so was the 'elimination of metaphysics' as meaningless. The 'criterion of verifiability', one of the most prominent features of the book, stems from the Logical Positivists of the 'Vienna Circle', whose meetings Ayer had attended. And in treating philosophical questions as essentially questions about language, Ayer was an important exponent of the 'linguistic turn'—probably the most important general feature of philosophy in our century. These affinities (to which Ayer drew attention) with long-standing and perhaps perennial trends in philosophical thought give the book a historical depth without destroying its originality.

[1] B. Magee, *Men of Ideas* (London, 1978), 131. He went on to say, however, that he still believed in the same 'general approach'.

The main themes of the book may be put under three headings. Its most striking feature, and the one that attracted most critical attention, was the criterion of verifiability—a criterion for distinguishing between meaningful and meaningless statements—with the resulting 'elimination of metaphysics'. A second main theme is the *analysis* of meaningful statements of various kinds, which takes up most of the book. Finally, there is the underlying conception of philosophy—that it consists in the analysis of statements, and that its problems are to be solved—and can easily be solved—by this method.

The Criterion of Verifiability

(a) The Criterion and its Status

'We say', proposed Ayer in the opening pages of *LTL*, that a proposition is meaningful 'to any given person, if, and only if, he knows how to verify [it]—that is, if he knows what observations would lead him, under certain conditions, to accept the proposition as being true, or reject it as being false' (48).[2] Here is a principle which gives a simple and plausible answer to an important question. How are we to distinguish sense from nonsense, a meaningful statement from a meaningless one? If someone assures us that 'The slithy toves did gyre and gimble' is *not* nonsense, what should we say? A suitable question here would be: How would one verify this statement? How should I recognize a slithy tove, and what observations would enable me to verify that they gyre and gimble? If these questions cannot be answered, then we may well conclude that the statement is meaningless, contrary to what we had been told.

However, this simplicity is deceptive. As we shall see, various difficulties emerged in Ayer's attempts to define his criterion, and redefine it in response to critics. Moreover, it may be doubted, as we shall see, whether that criterion is really about verification. But an initial difficulty is simply that of acceptance. Of course no one has put forward 'The slithy toves . . .' as a meaningful claim. But what of the claims of philosophers and religious believers which Ayer's criterion

[2] This is a simplified quotation. In the original Ayer spoke of sentences which 'purport to express' propositions. 'Proposition' had been defined by philosophers to be necessarily true or false—and hence meaningful. Some of Ayer's critics objected that his criterion was incoherent because sentences, but not propositions, could be meaningless; whereas propositions, but not sentences, were capable of verification. Ayer replied in his new Introduction. However, I believe the difficulty can be avoided by using the term 'statement' (or perhaps, 'alleged' or 'putative statement') in a suitable sense. For discussion see my *Logical Positivism*, section 2.1.

was designed to eliminate? Why should they give up their beliefs, rather than reject that criterion? This difficulty was brought out in a broadcast debate between Ayer and Father F. C. Copleston, who held certain religious beliefs which were not verifiable. To illustrate his objection to these, Ayer invented the word 'drogulus'. A drogulus was to be 'not the sort of thing you can see or touch, it has no physical effects of any kind, but it's a disembodied thing'.[3] He then supposed that he had said to Copleston: 'A drogulus is standing just behind you'. Ayer was unwise enough to end on a rhetorical question: 'Does that make sense?' But Copleston replied that it did make sense. He did not see that the issue depended on verifiability. He could, he said, form the idea of a disembodied thing from his ideas of body and mind, and this was enough to give it sense.

This example was, in any case, more favourable to Ayer than an example from actual religious discourse would be. For whereas 'drogulus' was an *ad hoc* introduction, having no connection with any existing discourse or practices, this could not be said about religious statements, which are intertwined with various practices and attitudes to the world.

A similar point may be made about metaphysical claims made by philosophers. On the first page of his book Ayer declared:

> If a putative proposition fails to satisfy this principle [of verifiability], and is not a tautology, then I hold that it is metaphysical, and [hence] literally senseless (2nd edn, 41).

But this would mean that any piece of nonsense, such as 'The slithy toves did gyre and gimble', must be described as metaphysics! It is obvious, however, that even if metaphysics is nonsense, not every kind of nonsense can be metaphysics. The propositions of metaphysics are put forward in a context of argument which differs from that of the nonsense verses of Lewis Carroll; and this context must be considered when enquiring into the meaning of these propositions. As an example of metaphysical nonsense, Ayer quoted the statement 'The Absolute enters into, but is itself incapable of, evolution and progress'. This statement, he said, had been 'taken at random' from F. H. Bradley's *Appearance and Reality*. Now when such a statement is taken out of its setting, it may indeed strike the reader as nonsensical, and he may think that there is little to choose between it and the nonsense of Lewis Carroll. But when the context is supplied, it will be found that Bradley's statement, unlike the nonsense verse, is surrounded by argu-

[3] 'Logical Positivism—A Debate'. See Paul Edwards and A. Pap (eds), *A Modern Introduction to Philosophy* (New York: Free Press, 1965), 747.

ments, without which the purport of the statement cannot be understood. These arguments, moreover, may be designed to show that, contrary to the empiricism represented by Ayer, it is both possible and necessary to describe the world in ways that are not accommodated by his criterion. Now it may turn out that these arguments are faulty, and that Bradley's statement is, after all, meaningless. But to come to this conclusion, we shall have to examine the arguments.

In the second edition, Ayer showed himself more sensitive to this point. The 'effective elimination of metaphysics', he now conceded, 'needs to be supported by detailed analysis of particular metaphysical arguments' (21). Here is a considerable dilution of the value of Ayer's criterion of meaning. Moreover, in another passage he admitted that, in some senses of 'meaning', 'a statement may properly be said to be meaningful' even if it did not pass his test (20). He claimed, however, that 'there was at least one proper use of the word "meaning" in which it would be incorrect to say that a statement was meaningful' if that were the case. But this claim (that there is such a sense of 'meaning') is open to challenge no less than the original claim.

Did Ayer mean that this sense of 'meaning' was an existing one? Or was he proposing a new use for the word? His criterion, he said, should be regarded as 'a definition, [but] it is not supposed to be entirely arbitrary' (21). Conceding that it was 'open to anyone to adopt a different criterion of meaning', he claimed that a statement which satisfied that criterion but not his would not be understood 'in the sense in which either scientific or common-sense statements' are understood. But this would neither surprise nor embarrass the metaphysician or theologian, for he had never intended his statements to be understood in those ways. Finally, conceding that it now seemed to him 'unlikely that any metaphysician would yield' to his claims, Ayer said he would 'still defend the use of the criterion as a methodological principle' (21).

In the writings of Ayer and other Logical Positivists there was a good deal of fudging about the meaning and status of the criterion. Ayer, helping himself to the word 'literal', claimed that it was 'literal meaning' which the statements in question lacked (7, 20). Others spoke of 'cognitive' meaning in this connection. Carnap, in describing metaphysics as nonsense, offered a special definition of the word 'nonsense'. Unconsciously paraphrasing *Pickwick Papers*, he placed the following 'Advice to the Reader' at the front of his 1934 monograph *The Unity of Science*:

> *Nonsense* (or *pseudo*-expression) is intended to carry none of its usual abusive connotations. Technical use—whatever cannot be verifed in experience (p. 30).[4]

[4] Rudolf Carnap, *The Unity of Science* (London, 1934). In Charles

Carnap also described his version of the principle of verifiability as 'a proposal or requirement', which is similar to Ayer's description of it as 'a methodological principle'.[5]

In describing the criterion or principle thus, Ayer and Carnap can avoid questions as to its truth, since a proposal or methodological principle cannot be described as true or false. (They also avoid the objection, made by some critics, that the principle was self-eliminating, since no way of verifying it had been produced.) However, the question of truth cannot be set aside in this way. For what, after all, would it mean to adopt such a proposal or methodological principle? We cannot *choose* to describe a given utterance as meaningless—any more than we can *choose* to describe grass as green. Of course, we can choose to utter the word 'meaningless', but if we did, would we mean it? This depends on whether we believe the utterance in question to *be* meaningless. Without this, the epithet 'meaningless' will itself be meaningless.

There is a place, in philosophy, for proposals to introduce a new terminology. Thus it might be proposed to use the words 'empirical', '*a priori*' and 'analytic' to characterize and distinguish certain kinds of propositions. There was, indeed, a time when these expressions were not in use, and it can be argued that their introduction made it more convenient to discuss such topics as truth and knowledge. But what advantage is gained by the proposal to describe unverifiable statements as meaningless?

'Empirical' and the others are, to some extent at least, technical terms; it was thought that the resources of ordinary language could be improved on by introducing them. They mark certain distinctions for which there are, perhaps, no convenient or equally suitable expressions in the ordinary vocabulary. But 'meaningless' is not a technical term (except in its Pickwickian sense); nor does it help us to mark the distinction between empirical and metaphysical. For we already have a convenient way of marking this—by using the words 'empirical' and 'metaphysical'.

Another difference is that 'meaningless', unlike 'empirical' and the others, is a derogatory term. This aspect was taken up by C. L. Stevenson in his 'Persuasive Definitions' (*Mind*, 1938). Stevenson compared the description of metaphysical statements as meaningless with the claim made by certain nineteenth-century critics, that Alexander Pope was not a poet. This, he said, followed from their definition

---

Dickens's novel, Mr Blotton is persuaded to agree that when he called Mr Pickwick a humbug, he had meant this word in a special sense and not with its usual connotations.

[5] R. Carnap, 'Testability and Meaning', in *Readings in the Philosophy of Science,* H. Feigl and M. Brodbeck (eds) (Appleton, 1953), 84.

of 'poet'; but the definition was itself motivated by an unfavourable attitude towards writings of that kind. Turning to the verificationists' claim about meaning, he claimed that they were

> stating an unquestionable fact in their sense of meaning, just as the nineteenth-century critics were, in their sense of poet. The truth of such statements, however, is utterly beside the point. Controversy hinges in the emotive words that are used. . . . Shall our terminology show science in a fine light, and metaphysics in a poor one?[6]

He went on to speak of ways of justifying a new definition. The critics of whom he spoke were not, he said, 'condemning Pope with sheer bombast'.

> Their narrow sense of 'poet' had the function of stressing, in the reader's attention, certain features common to most poetry, but lacking in Pope's. Perhaps they meant to say this: 'We have long been blind to fundamental differences between Pope's work and that of a Shakespeare or Milton. It is because of this difference alone that we have been content to give Pope a laudatory title. Let us note the difference, then, and deprive him of the title.'

Here is an important point about the development of concepts in the course of time, and the way in which this is affected by important judgments of value. (Hence it is sometimes inappropriate to dismiss a dispute as 'merely a matter of words'. Some matters of words are of the greatest importance.) But are the cases of 'meaning' and 'poet' similar? Stevenson claimed that they were. The verificationist, he suggested, could also be taken as saying that we had 'long been blind to fundamental differences'—in this case, the difference between science and metaphysics.

But who is or was blind to this difference? Those who make metaphysical claims have not usually been blind to it. Sometimes, indeed, they make a point of drawing attention to it, seeing in this the special interest and importance of what they are saying. The same is true of those who speak of God as a transcendent being, beyond the reach of empirical science.

Again, the denial of meaning is derogatory in a stronger sense than the denial of poetry. To describe Pope's works as 'not poetry' is not, after all, to deny them a place, perhaps an honourable one, in literature. By contrast, the epithet 'meaningless' implies that the statements in question ought never to have been made; that those who made them were the victims, and perhaps perpetrators, of an illusion. Thus the

[6] Reprinted in Stevenson's *Facts and Values* (Yale, 1963).

claim about meaning is both bolder and less well supported than that about poetry.

(b) The Meaning of 'Verification'

So far, the term 'verification' has been understood in the ordinary sense, in which we speak of verifying some everyday empirical statement. For example, 'There is a book on the table' can be verified by looking in the appropriate direction and finding these objects in the relevant position. But when Ayer spoke of verification, he meant something rather different. According to his use of the term, such ordinary statements as these could never be verified. 'All empirical propositions', he held, 'are hypotheses which are continually subject to the test of further experience.' From this it followed that their truth 'never was conclusively established [and] never could be. For however strong the evidence in its favour, there could never be a point at which it was impossible for further experience to go against [such a proposition]' (13).[7]

In common with many empiricists and sceptics, Ayer is here drawing a conclusion that is not warranted by the premise. It is true that some future experience might go against the statement that there is (or was) a book on the table; and the statement might be false in spite of the original 'verification'. But it does not follow from this that the truth of the statement—assuming it *is* true—cannot be conclusively verified or established, according to the normal meaning of these terms. Someone who claims to have verified a statement is not thereby committed to the (impossible) requirement that no future experience could possibly go against it.

Having ruled out conclusive verification, Ayer qualified his criterion of meaning accordingly. 'If we adopt conclusive verifiability as our criterion . . ., our argument will prove too much' (50), since ordinary empirical statements would turn out to be meaningless. He therefore introduced a '"weak" sense of the term "verifiable"' (50). A statement would be verifiable in the weak sense, he said, 'if it is possible for experience to render it probable' (50).

These proposals were criticized by Morris Lazerowitz, who pointed out that since the 'strong' sense of 'verifiable' had, apparently, no conceivable application, there was no sense in the qualification of this term as 'weak'.[8] In the second edition, Ayer replied that he now thought

[7] See also Ayer's *The Foundations of Empirical Knowledge* (London, 1940), 239–240.

[8] 'Strong and Weak Verification', *Mind* (1939). Reprinted in *The Structure of Metaphysics* (London, 1955).

that certain empirical statements could be verified in the strong, conclusive sense. These were not 'hypotheses'; they 'referred solely to the content of a single experience, and what may be said to verify them conclusively is the occurrence of [that] experience' (13). Examples of these were 'I am in pain' and 'This is green' when used 'merely to designate a sense-datum' being experienced at the time of speaking.[9]

The term 'sense-datum' will be examined below, but it is clear from the quotation that Ayer meant by this (in common with others) a kind of occurrence, of the same type as a sensation of pain. Is the term 'verify' applicable to such statement as 'I am in pain'? In its most usual sense, to verify means to find out whether, or check that, p is true. Thus someone who needs to verify that (or whether) the book is on the table, can do so by going to the table and having a look. But such verification has no place in the case of 'I am in pain'. Verification implies uncertainty; but there is no place for uncertainty in the case of this statement. To speak of verifying that (or whether) one is in pain makes no sense. (This is not to deny that someone—a foreigner, say—might be in doubt about the *word* 'pain'.)

However, there is another sense in which 'verify' might be understood. It might be taken to mean *what makes* a statement true, as opposed to the act of verification whereby its truth is ascertained. We might speak of this as an 'impersonal' sense of 'verify'. In this sense, the statement that p is 'verified' (made true) by *the fact* that p, or some other facts suitably related to p. Thus we might say that 'I am in pain' is made true ('verified') by the corresponding fact. This is very different from the (more normal) 'personal' sense, in which verification is an act performed by some person, who has a suitable reason for doing so. It is, however, in the impersonal sense that we would have to understand Ayer when he says that 'what may be said to verify them conclusively is the occurrence of the experience to which they uniquely refer' (13).

If we understand 'verify' in this impersonal sense, then the criterion of verifiability will be affected accordingly. We must take it to be, not about the ordinary kind of verification, which is carried out by a person, but about the occurrence of 'experiences'—or, to use Ayer's preferred term, 'sense-contents'. And this, indeed, was what Ayer meant by 'verification', in both the strong and the weak case.

(c) Problems of Application

The initial formulation of Ayer's criterion was, as we saw (p. 262) in terms of observations which would lead someone to regard a given

[9] 'Verification and Experience', *Proceedings of the Aristotelian Society* **XXXVII**.

statement as true or as false. Having made the point about strong and weak verification, he formulated the criterion in terms of 'experiential propositions' (such as 'this is green' as described above).

> It is the mark of a genuine factual proposition, not that it should be equivalent to an experiential proposition, or any finite number of experiential propositions, but simply that some experiential propositions can be deduced from it in conjunction with certain other premises without being deducible from those other premises alone (52).

Here we find two changes, one acknowledged, the other not. The first is the explicit disclaimer of 'strong' verification ('not that it should be equivalent . . .'). The second is the change to the 'linguistic mode'. In place of 'observations which would lead him, under certain conditions', we now have experiential *propositions*, conjoined with other *premises*, these being *deducible* from the proposition under test. Both of these changes lead to difficulties.

The linguistic mode, with its talk of 'deduction', gives an impression of logical rigour, and may seem an improvement on the empiricism of Locke and Hume, which was expressed largely in psychological terms. But this advantage is an illusion. Consider the statements: 'It is snowing', or 'It snowed last night'. If these are true, then, if I look out of the window, I should be able to see something white. But how is the proposition 'this is white' supposed to be *deducible*? There is no deduction which runs: 'It is snowing; I am looking out of the window; therefore, this is white'. This is so whether we take 'this is white' in the (alleged) experiential sense ('to designate a sense-datum') or in the ordinary descriptive sense. Nor could the statement 'I observe something white' be deduced, strictly speaking. Firstly, conditions about normal vision, presence of light, etc., would need to be added. But even then, the statement would not follow. Whether we perceive an object depends on its context: a book surrounded by other objects may not be perceived; and a colour may be perceived differently. It also depends on one's interest and attention. If my mind is on other things, I may fail to make the observation, or make it correctly.

This is not to deny that there is a connection, and a logical one, between an empirical statement and suitable observations. If the statement is true, then one *should be able* to make these observations, given suitable circumstances, such as are taken for granted in ordinary conversation. This, after all, is what is meant by 'empirical'. But it is a mistake to think that this concept can be defined by a deductive schema such as that proposed by Ayer (to say nothing of the equation of 'empirical' with 'genuinely factual').

The other feature of Ayer's criterion was, as we saw, the resort to 'weak' verification. We have already noticed that Ayer used 'verification' in a rather peculiar sense. With the introduction of the 'weak' formula, the connection with verification, as normally understood, is lost altogether. This can be seen most easily with general statements, such as 'All cows are brown'. According to Ayer's criterion, this will be 'genuinely factual' if 'some experiential propositions' (at least one) can be deduced. Suppose now that I look at a cow and say 'this is brown'. This would be enough to satisfy the criterion. Yet it is obvious that this one observation (or occurrence of the relevant 'experience', 'sense-datum' or whatever) cannot be regarded as *verifying* the statement. This is not weak verification; it is no verification at all. In short, what Ayer's criterion is about is not verifiability, but the deducibility of 'experiential propositions'.

Another difficulty of the 'weak' formula was that it could be made to accommodate statements which were metaphysical or even obvious nonsense. An example was given by Ayer himself in the second edition, following an objection from Isaiah Berlin.

> Thus, the statements 'the Absolute is lazy' and 'if the Absolute is lazy, this is white' jointly entail the observation-statement 'this is white', and since 'this is white' does not follow from either of these premises, taken by itself, both of them satisfy my criterion of meaning (15).

To meet the difficulty Ayer put forward a modified version of his criterion, the main purport of which was that the 'other premises' must themselves consist of observation-statements (i.e. 'experiential propositions'). This was intended to prevent statements like 'the Absolute is lazy' from appearing among the premises. But Carl Hempel argued that such measures could not prevent the criterion from producing absurd results. The new criterion, he said, 'allows empirical significance to any conjunction S & N, where S satisfies Ayer's criterion while N is a sentence such as "the absolute is perfect", which, taken alone, would not'.[10] The point was that if S had the right entailments, then S & N must have them too, for whatever is entailed by S is also entailed by S conjoined with any other statement.

It may be thought that the obvious comment about 'S & N' would be that part of it (S) is admissible while another part (N) is not. However, the separation of S from N may not be so easy. As we saw, Ayer's

[10] 'Problems and Changes in the Empiricist Criterion of Meaning', *Revue Internationale de Philosophie* (1950). A revised version appears in section 4 of Hempel's *Aspects of Scientific Explanation*.

criterion would be satisfied if at least one observation-statement (O) could be deduced from the statement (P) under test. But O would not be the whole of the meaning of P. What happens, then, about the rest? May not P contain a metaphysical component?

What Ayer needs is analysis and not merely deduction. He needs to say *what* the meaning of a statement consists in, and not merely that it has meaning if certain statements are deducible from it. Such a version of verificationism was expressed in the 'Verification Principle' of the Vienna Circle: 'The meaning of a statement is the method of its verification'. This principle *entails* a criterion of verifiability (no method of verification = no meaning), but it also tells us what meaning consists in.[11]

Surprisingly, Ayer made no mention of the Verification Principle; but, as we shall see, most of his treatment (and 'elimination') of philosophical problems consisted of analysis rather than mere deduction. An example is his treatment of the statement that God exists. If this was intended in a purely metaphysical sense, then he would, obviously, reject it as meaningless. But what if it were linked with observable facts, such as the existence of order in the world? In that case he would not simply admit the statement as meaningful (even though observation-statements could be deduced from it); he would *limit* its meaning to those observations: 'then to assert the existence of a god will be simply equivalent to asserting that there is the requisite regularity in nature' (152).

Analysis

(a) Physical Objects

In the case of the existence of God, there would at least be agreement about the distinction between empirical and metaphysical. As Ayer pointed out, the religious believer would not *wish* his meaning to be taken in a merely empirical sense; 'he would say that in talking about God he was talking about a transcendent being' (152). But when we turn to Ayer's analyses of other kinds of statements, this agreement is no longer evident. For according to him, all empirical statements are reducible to observation-statements (or statements about the occurrence of 'sense-data').

Consider the statement that there is a book on the table. This would seem to be an empirical statement if anything is. Yet someone who makes this statement may not agree that its meaning is reducible to

[11] For discussion of the Principle, and its relation to the criterion, see my *Logical Positivism,* 15–37.

statements about observations (or sense-data). He may say that this fact is distinct from the relevant acts of observation; the latter being evidence (perhaps conclusive evidence) for the fact, but not identical with it. The same is true of statements about the past, and about the thoughts and feelings of others. As we shall see, Ayer claimed that these and other empirical statements were, one and all, reducible to statements about sense-data, anything else being metaphysics. But this claim cannot be construed as an attack on metaphysics, if we mean by this a kind of statement that had been put forward by metaphysicians and religious persons. In the latter case, Ayer's adversary will readily agree that his statements are non-empirical and not verifiable in that sense (and there was no need for Ayer to point this out to him). However, the person who states that there is a book on the table, but rejects Ayer's analysis, may be astonished to hear that he is, therefore, engaged in metaphysical claims or speculations. The issue now is not about the elimination of metaphysics, but about the correctness of Ayer's analysis of statements which would normally be regarded as straightforwardly empirical.[12]

'Material things', wrote Ayer, 'are logical constructions out of sense-contents'; they are 'reducible to sense-contents' (86, 92). This claim, he explained, should be understood in a linguistic sense. It is, he said,

> a linguistic proposition, which states that to say anything about [a material thing] is always equivalent to saying something about [sense-contents] (185).

What did Ayer mean by 'sense-contents'? The difference between 'sense-contents' and 'sense-data' is unimportant. Ayer introduced his term to refer to 'what is immediately given in sensation' (71). Sense-contents, he explained, are neither mental nor physical, 'or rather . . ., the distinction between what is mental and what is physical does not apply to sense-contents. It applies only to objects which are logical constructions out of them' (162). Moreover, we are to think of sense-contents as 'occurring' rather than 'existing', so as 'to avoid the danger of treating [them] as if they were material things' (162).

Without going into the details of Ayer's theory, it is clear that he belongs to those many philosophers (including Locke, whom he mentions), who hold that perception consists in the existence or occurrence, within the perceiver, of suitable items of 'sensation'. This assimilation of perception to sensation has been a source of much confusion. As we saw (p. 268), Ayer spoke both of 'I am in pain' and 'This is green' as

[12] One of the best expositions of this type of analysis is Schlick's 'Positivism and Realism' of 1932, reprinted in *Philosophical Papers,* Vol. II (Reidel, 1979) and in my *Essential Readings in Logical Positivism* (Oxford, 1981).

being used to 'designate a sense-datum' which was supposed to occur at the time of speaking. These statements are, however, of different logical types. To say 'I am in pain' is to say how one feels; but pain is not an object of perception. I do not find out by means of the senses (or anything else) that I am in pain. To say 'This is green', on the other hand, is to describe an object of perception, and not to say how one feels; nor is it to say that certain occurrences (sense-contents or whatever) are taking place within the perceiver. It is true that certain physical processes are necessary in order to perceive; but they are not what we mean when we describe something as green.

The assimilation of perception to sensation leads easily to the view that statements about the physical world are essentially inferential (and hence not verifiable in the 'strong' sense). Suppose I am someone who suffers from rheumatism in the left leg whenever it is raining. Here we have a case of inference from sensation to the physical world—an inference that may be more or less secure. Suppose now that I go outside to *see* whether it is raining. According to the sensational analysis, this makes no difference to the logic of the situation; it merely means that I now have another sensation (sense-content, etc.)—this time a visual one—from which to make my inference. But these visual sensations are a myth, and perception is not inferential.

The assimilation of perception to sensation is part of the reductionist outlook which characterizes *Language, Truth and Logic* (as well as many other philosophical works). We are not to think that there is a variety of types of statement (which would perhaps make it plausible to include metaphysics as one more type). No, all *bona fide* statements are essentially of the same type, and made of components of the same type (i.e. sense-contents); and anything else must be rejected.

> Our remarks apply to all empirical propositions without exception, whether they are singular, or particular, or universal. Every synthetic proposition is a rule for the anticipation of future experience [of sense-contents] (134).

> Propositions referring to the past have the same hypothetical character as those which refer to the present and those which refer to the future (134).

> Just as I must define material things and my own self in terms of their empirical manifestations, so I must define other people in terms of their empirical manifestations—that is, in terms of the behaviour of their bodies, and ultimately in terms of sense-contents (171).

Some of these definitions will now be examined.

(b) The Past

Statements about the past, claimed Ayer, 'are rules for the prediction of those "historical" experiences which are commonly said to verify them' (135). Presumably he meant those sense-contents which are supposed to take place when one looks, say, at the pavement to see whether it has been snowing, or into a history-book to verify some historical fact. Now it is true that, by making such observations, *we verify* the statements in question; but it is not true—nor would it be 'commonly said'—that *they are verified* (= made true) by these observations (or by sensations taking place within ourselves). There is more to the meaning of such statements than their power to predict verificatory observations.

'For my own part', declared Ayer, 'I do not find anything paradoxical [in this reduction].' He suspected that those who objected to it were misled by the assumption that 'the past is somehow "objectively there"', 'that it is "real" in the metaphysical sense' (135). But Ayer's view is paradoxical without this assumption. There is, of course, a logical relation between past events and subsequent evidence; but there is more to the meaning of such a statement than its predictive powers. Moreover, this common-sense distinction between truth and evidence does not imply that the past is 'somehow there', or any other strange metaphysical doctrine.

Here it is useful to consider speech-acts other than statements. Our concern about the past may take the form of *wondering whether* something happened (or *what* happened). And it would be absurd to claim that someone who wonders, say, who killed the Princes in the Tower, is really wondering whether such and such verificatory experiences will take place in the future.

In the second edition, Ayer gave a less paradoxical analysis. Statements about the past, he now maintained, 'can be taken as implying that certain observations would have occurred if certain conditions had been fulfilled'—i.e. if someone *had been* present. This showed, he claimed, that such statements can still be 'analysed in phenomenal terms' (25). But 'imply' is different from 'analyse'. Of course the statement 'Caesar was killed by Brutus' *implies* that certain observations would have occurred if, etc.; but it does not follow that the statement can be *analysed* in these terms.

Even so, the emendation of the second edition is an improvement, since it comes nearer to doing justice to the *difference* between past and future. But, by the same token, it spoils the uniformity of the original thesis. We must now analyse some statements in terms of subjunctive conditionals (what might have happened, though it did not), as opposed to predictions. In a later essay, Ayer tried to restore uniformity by claiming that the tense of a statement was not part of its 'factual content'. There was, he said, 'no difference in meaning' between the statements that George VI was, is being, or will be, crowned in 1937. This being so, it would not matter if the pastness of a statement prevented its verification by the speaker (*Phil. Essays* 186, 188–189). But, apart from the desire for uniformity, there is no need for such drastic surgery in speaking about the meaning and verification of statements in the past tense. Resisting this desire, we may say, with common sense, that 'George VI was crowned' does mean something different from 'George VI is being crowned'. This difference, moreover, is reflected in the different methods of verification appropriate to each. The method of direct observation is—or rather, may be—available for the present tense, but not for the past tense.

There are also differences *among* these classes of statements. One such difference, concerning the past tense, is that between statements which we verify by consulting evidence, and statements which we know to be true from memory. This difference would also disappear under Ayer's analysis; for according to him, to say of a person A that he remembers

> is to say merely that some of [his] sense-experiences . . . contain memory images which correspond to the sense-contents which have previously occurred in the sense-history of A (166).

A problem that arises here is how one would be able to tell the difference between a sense-content and the 'corresponding' memory-image—a problem that was raised, but not solved, by Hume in the eighteenth century. In any case, such treatments conceal the radical difference between memory-knowledge and knowledge obtained by means of evidence—including, perhaps, the having of sensations. To say 'I remember that p' is already to claim knowledge that p; it is not to cite *evidence* in favour of the truth of p. Contrary to a familiar metaphor, we do not 'consult' our memories, as we might consult a history-book. From an entry in my diary, I may infer (or verify) that I went to Austria last October. But if I *remember* doing so, then there is (on my part) no inference and no verification. There is not, in my mind or anywhere else, something *distinct* from my knowledge, from which I infer the truth of the statement. (This is not, of course, to deny that there may be images of the visit in my mind.) (There are also various 'mixed' cases, for example, remembering that the Battle of Hastings was in 1066, which call for further distinctions to be made.)

(c) Myself and Others

As we saw (p. 15), Ayer thought he could 'define other people' in terms of the behaviour of their bodies, this in turn being reducible to the perceiver's sense-contents. The second stage of this reduction is part of his general treatment of physical objects, already discussed. But the first stage—known as 'behaviourism'—raises special difficulties. According to Ayer, 'the distinction between a conscious man and an unconscious machine resolves itself into a distinction between different types of perceptible behaviour' (172).

Am I to believe, then, that another person's toothache is nothing other than the behaviour which I perceive? If so, must I say the same of my own toothache? If not, does the word 'toothache' have two different meanings? The example of toothache was used by Wittgenstein in his Cambridge lectures of 1930–1933.[13] Here we can see him drawing away from the 'verification principle' (quoted on p. 269), largely because of these difficulties. He pointed out that whereas one could speak of verifying that another person is in pain, it made no sense to do so in the first person.

In *Language, Truth and Logic* there was hardly any attempt to face up to these difficulties, and the matter cannot be taken further here. It is enough to point out that a behaviourist analysis of thoughts and feelings is implied by Ayer's overall programme, and that this raises a fresh set of difficulties for that programme.[14]

(d) Mathematics and Logic

So far we have dealt with Ayer's analysis of empirical statements of various kinds. We must now turn to his account of certain statements, which, though not empirical, could not be treated as 'metaphysical nonsense' either. A common objection against empiricism was, he said, that it made it 'impossible . . . to account for our knowledge of necessary truths' (96). As we have seen, Ayer held that ordinary empirical statements are 'hypotheses' which can never be verified conclusively, since their meaning went beyond any given set of sense-contents. Thus 'no proposition which has factual content can be necessary or certain' (97). Yet 'the truths of mathematics and logic appear to everyone to be necessary and certain' (97). How are these claims to be reconciled?

The answer, according to Ayer, was that these propositions are 'devoid of factual content' (105–106); 'they tell us only what we may be said to know already' (106). However, these propositions are not 'senseless in the way that metaphysical utterances are senseless' (106). Their function is to 'call attention to linguistic usages' and 'conventions'. Thus

[13] Notes of Wittgenstein's lectures are published in G. E. Moore, *Philosophical Papers* (London, 1959).

[14] For further discussion by Ayer, see *The Problem of Knowledge,* 214ff.

> in saying that if all Bretons are Frenchmen, and all Frenchmen Europeans, then all Bretons are Europeans . . ., I am . . . indicating the convention which governs our usage of the words 'if' and 'all' (106).

Mathematical equations, he held, are nothing more than statements of synonymity. Thus the expression '7 + 5' is 'synonymous with "12", just as "eye-doctor" is synonymous with "oculist"' (113). This was true even of such equations as '91 × 79 = 7189', where we have to 'resort to calculation . . . to assure ourselves that [these expressions] are synonymous' (114).

Now the statement that an oculist is an eye-doctor may fairly be described as devoid of factual content, since these expressions are, indeed, synonymous. But is this so in the case of mathematics? To say that '7 + 5' is synonymous with '12' is a misuse of the word 'synonymous'. It is one thing to say that two expressions are mathematically (or logically) equivalent, and another to say that they are synonymous. 'Douze' is synonymous with 'twelve'; '7 + 5' is not.

It is because mathematical equations are not (merely) expressions of synonymity that their truth is a matter of discovery, sometimes requiring considerable effort. Again, our knowledge that an oculist is an eye-doctor does not have any practical application; it does not help us, for example, with the treatment of eye-diseases. By contrast, mathematical knowledge has a wide practical application.

Ayer was not unaware of these points. He would need, he said, to 'explain how a proposition which is empty of all factual content can be true and useful and surprising' (97). The explanation, he thought, was 'very simple'. Our powers of reasoning being limited, we are not able 'to detect at a glance' the consequences of a mathematical expression (114). This is true enough. But it also goes against the assimilation of mathematical statements to statements of synonymous terms. The former do *not* 'tell us what we know already', and are not 'empty of all factual content'.

The emptiness of statements of synonymous terms is connected with the fact that the meanings of words are, in a certain sense, conventional. Thus the use of 'oculist' to mean an eye-doctor is something that may be adopted, rejected or altered. For example, we might decide that only eye-doctors having a certain qualification are to be called 'oculists'. But this is not so in the mathematical case. It is not up to us to choose whether eight sevens are fifty-six. It is true that whether, say, we use the word 'eight' to mean eight is a matter of convention. We might decide to use some other word—say 'acht' or even 'nine'. But this would not alter the fact that eight sevens are fifty-six—whatever words may be chosen to express this fact.

Why did Ayer want to deny factual status to the propositions of mathematics? The reason he gave (as we saw) was that they have certain characteristics (being 'necessary and certain') which are not shared by empirical propositions. But this is no reason for denying that they have factual content—unless it is assumed that there is only *one* kind of factual content. But no argument has been given for this assumption.

(e) Moral Statements

In another chapter Ayer turned his attention to 'statements of value'. These statements, he pointed out, were not empirical hypotheses, and yet they might be regarded as having factual content. They might seem, therefore, to present 'an insuperable objection to our radical empirical thesis' (136). His reply was to deny factual content to statements of value. They were, he held, expressions of feeling and not statements of fact.

> Thus if I say to someone, 'You acted wrongly in stealing that money', I am not stating anything more than if I had simply said, 'You stole that money' . . . I am simply evincing my moral disapproval. . . . It is as if I had said 'You stole that money' in a peculiar tone of horror (142).

He responded to an objection made by G. E. Moore, that, on this view, 'it would be impossible to argue about questions of value' (146).

> If a man said that thrift was a virtue, and another replied that it was a vice, they would not . . . be disputing with one another. One would be saying that he approved of thrift, and other that *he* didn't; and there is no reason why both these statements should not be true (146).

Ayer's response was to accept the conclusion, maintaining that it was indeed 'impossible to dispute about questions of value' (146). Since these sentences 'do not express propositions at all, we clearly cannot hold that they express incompatible propositions' (146).

He did not deny that people appear to dispute about questions of value; but, he said, 'in all such cases we find, if we examine the matter closely, that the dispute is not really about a question of value, but about a question of fact' (146). In support of this claim, he pointed out that even when the (non-moral) facts of a case have been agreed, the disagreement about value may remain, and it may be impossible to resolve it.

> if our opponent . . ., even when he acknowledges all the facts . . ., still disagrees with us about the moral value of the actions under

> discussion, then we abandon the attempt to convince him by argument. We say that it is impossible to argue with him . . . (147).

This is true enough, but a similar point may be made about non-moral disputes. What if someone refuses to accept that eight sevens are fifty-six, that there is a book on the table, or that this paper is white? All our arguments can only serve to bring the horse to the water (or the water to the horse), but he cannot be forced to drink. And if he will not, then 'we abandon the attempt to convince him by argument. We say that it is impossible to argue with him'. But it does not follow that these are not facts—whether in the moral or the non-moral case.[15]

The view that there are no moral facts, that morality is not a matter of knowledge and truth, but of personal feeling, is not peculiar to Ayer, but is widely held. In ordinary conversation, the remark 'That's a value-judgement' is often held to put an end to rational dispute. Yet it is not easy to produce an argument for this view. On the other hand, such words as 'know' and 'true' are commonly applied to moral statements. This is especially so when *contrasting* morality with personal preference, as when we say 'I know (or it's true) that I ought to do X, but I don't want to'.

Some of these points were recognized by Ayer in an essay published in 1949. He now admitted that the view that 'ethical statements are not really statements at all . . ., that they cannot be either true or false, is in an obvious sense incorrect' (*Philosophical Essays*, 231–233). In ordinary English, he conceded, it is 'by no means improper' to refer to such statements as statements, or to use the words 'true' and 'fact' in this context. Nevertheless, he continued,

> when one considers how these ethical statements are actually used, it may be found that they function so very differently from other types of statements that it may be advisable to put them into a separate category altogether; either to say that they are not to be counted as statements at all, or . . . that there are no ethical facts.

Yet, after all, 'if someone still wishes to say that ethical statements are statements of fact, only it is a queer sort of fact, he is welcome to do so'.

Here is a beautiful illustration of the reductionist dogma lying behind Ayer's claims and arguments. We knew, or course, that ethical statements are *different* from others, but why should that make them 'queer'? And for what reason is it 'advisable' to put them into the category of non-statements and non-facts? The assumption here is that

[15] The limits of argument were beautifully illustrated by Lewis Carroll in 'What the Tortoise said to Achilles', *Mind* (1985).

empirical facts and statements, and only they, are 'the real thing'; and that the credentials of other kinds of statements and facts must be established by reference to them. But no reason has been given for rejecting the alternative view—that there are many different kinds of statements and facts, which are not reducible to a common pattern or basis.

The Nature of Philosophy

'The function of philosophy', wrote Ayer,

> is not to devise speculative theories . . ., but to elicit the consequences of our linguistic usages. That is to say, the questions with which philosophy are concerned are purely logical questions (176).

Thus, instead of asking 'What is a number?', we ought to ask 'some such question as whether it is possible to translate propositions about the natural numbers into propositions about classes'.

> And the same thing applies to all the philosophical questions of the form 'What is X?' They are all requests for definitions . . . (78).

Having endorsed Hume's 'phenomenalist account of the nature of the self', he pointed out the difference between that approach and his own. Whereas Hume held that 'the self is an aggregate of sense-experiences', his own account was put in linguistic terms. Thus '*to say* anything about the self is always *to say* something about sense-experiences' (168, italics added).

Ayer was one of the pioneers of what has been called 'the linguistic turn', which is perhaps the most important feature of twentieth-century philosophy. This is the belief—it might be called insight—that philosophical problems are essentially linguistic and must be dealt with accordingly.

But if Ayer can take credit for pioneering the linguistic approach, he can also be blamed for bringing this approach into disrepute. This is because of his repeated insistence that, once the linguistic nature of the problems had been recognized, their solution must be an easy matter, requiring only a certain analytical skill. People may dispute about logical questions, including those which comprise philosophy, but, he declared, 'such disputes are always unwarranted' (176). In Chapter 1, as we saw, he claimed to have achieved 'the elimination of metaphysics'; various other problems are disposed of in the following chapters; and in the final chapter we have 'Solutions of Outstanding Philosophical Disputes' (176).

How are these quick-fire solutions achieved? 'Ethical philosophy', he tells us, 'consists simply in saying that ethical concepts are pseudo-concepts and therefore unanalysable' (148). Having raised the problem of induction—of 'finding a way to prove that certain empirical generalizations which are derived from past experience will hold good also in the future' (66), he immediately concludes that 'since there is no possible way of solving the problem . . ., this means that it is a fictitious problem' (67). Again, the problem of other people's thoughts and feelings is not 'the insoluble, and, indeed, fictitious problem' which has puzzled many thinkers; it is only a matter of 'indicating the way' in which the relevant statements are to be analysed. Finally, 'there is no problem of truth as it is ordinarily conceived' (119). This apparent problem 'is due, like most philosophical mistakes, to a failure to analyse sentences correctly' (119). The correct analysis showed that 'in all sentences of the form "p is true", the phrase "is true" is logically superfluous', since to say that p is true is logically equivalent to saying that p.

But if it is true that philosophical problems are essentially linguistic, it does not follow that they are not genuine, and indeed difficult, problems. To transfer these problems into the linguistic mode is by no means to diminish their depth and importance. The problem of other people, for instance, retains its importance even when approached in the linguistic way. What Ayer has done is not to show that these problems are fictitious, but to offer his own *solutions* to them. But, as we have seen, these solutions are far from convincing. This also applies to the problem of truth. It may be correct that 'p is true' and 'p' are logically equivalent (each entails the other), but does it follow that 'is true' is superfluous? What is this expression doing in our language? Again, someone who agrees that the expressions are equivalent may still ask what the truth of p *consists* in, whether truth is a relation, and so on.

As we have seen, Ayer saw the function of philosophy as being 'to elicit the consequences of our linguistic usages'. What did he mean by this phrase? A fundamental issue in philosophy, especially since the appearance of Wittgenstein's later works, has been whether philosophical questions are, not merely about language, but about *ordinary* language—that which we use, and need to use, in everyday life. Wittgenstein believed that what was required was 'to bring words back from their metaphysical to their everyday use' (*Phil. Investigations* 116). He also stressed the variety of this use, denying that it could be captured by a single definition or analysis. Others, however, have rejected the ordinary language approach. In discussions of scepticism, for example, it is sometimes claimed that there is a philosophical or 'strict' sense of 'knowledge', whereby ordinary knowledge-claims (ordinary uses of the word 'know') are not justified. Sometimes it is said explicitly that a philosopher can and should go beyond the ordinary uses of words, providing strict definitions in place of the flexibility and vagueness of ordinary usage. An objection to this view is that if this is done, one is no longer speaking about the original question. A question about *knowledge*, for example, is answered in terms of 'knowledge'—an artificial concept of the philosopher's creation. Moreover, if the standard of ordinary usage is abandoned, it is not clear why any other standard or definition should be accepted by the critical reader.

Where did Ayer stand on this issue? In his reference to 'our linguistic usages' he may seem to be invoking the authority of ordinary usage. But when we examine his claims (for example, that empirical statements are about 'sense-contents') it is clear that ordinary usage is left behind, and some other justification must be sought. That Ayer was not one of those who simply rejected ordinary usage, is apparent from his later treatment of moral statements. Here, as we saw, he conceded that his view was 'in an obvious sense incorrect', since it was contrary to ordinary usage. But this recognition was opposed by his desire for reduction and uniformity; and the tension remains. A philosopher may either follow the standard of ordinary usage, and then he must make sure that his claims conform to it; or he may reject that standard, and then he must justify his rejection, explain what other standard is being used, and why.

Conclusion

This review of *Language, Truth and Logic*, like many that have gone before, has been largely critical. Ayer himself, as we saw, has been among its critics; though it may be doubted whether his subsequent qualifications went far enough. But the book remains an important and forceful expression of certain trends in philosophical thought, which, rightly or wrongly, remain influential. Among these are the desire for, and belief in, the reduction of language and experience into homogenous elements; the views that philosophy consists essentially of analysis, that statements of necessary truths, and statements of value, have no factual content; and that ordinary empirical statements cannot, strictly speaking, be verified or known to be true. Someone who wants to get to grips with these issues would still be well advised to turn to Ayer's book.

Another merit of the book (which it shares with other Logical Positivist writings) is that it brought into prominence a fundamental question that arises both inside and outside philosophy—namely, whether a given question is meaningful. The question of meaningfulness is, only too often, overlooked—as if finding an answer to the original question were a more urgent and interesting task than to ask what, if anything, the question means.[16] As we have seen, the criterion proposed by Ayer for deciding whether a question is meaningful is open to various objections. But the idea of looking for such a criterion remains important.

[16] An example is the flourishing literature, in the philosophy of mind, about materialism, which began largely with J. J. C. Smart's 'Sensations and Brain Processes' of 1959. In 1964 Norman Malcolm objected to Smart's thesis: 'I do not know what it *means* to say that a . . . thought is a brain-process. In saying this I imply, of course, that the proponents of this view also do not know what it means. This implication is risky for it might turn out, to my surprise and gratification, that Smart will explain his view . . .' (in *The Mind-Body Problem,* C. V. Boost (ed.), 171–172). It is safe to say that Malcolm never had his surprise and gratification.

Jean-Paul Sartre

Jean-Paul Sartre (1905–1980), nephew of the Alsatian theologian, Albert Schweitzer, was born in Paris, passed his agrégation at the École Normale Superieure in 1929, and was a lycée teacher between 1931 and 1945. He was called up to the French Army in 1939, captured by the Germans in 1940 and released after the armistice. In 1938 he published a novel, *La Nausée*, translated by Robert Baldick as *Nausea* (Harmondsworth: Penguin, 1965), and in 1940, *L'Imaginaire: Psychologie phénoménologique de l'imagination*, translated by Bernard Frechtman as *The Psychology of Imagination* (London: Methuen, 1972). His major philosophical work, *L'Etre et le Neant*, was published in 1943, and translated by Hazel E. Barnes as *Being and Nothingness* (London: Methuen, 1957). As a novelist he is best known for a trilogy, *Chemins de la Liberté* (*Roads to Freedom*), comprising *L'Age de raison* (1945) translated by E. Sutton as *The Age of Reason* (Harmondsworth: Penguin, 1961), *Le Sursis* (1945), translated by E. Sutton as *The Reprieve* (Harmondsworth: Penguin, 1963) and *La Mort dans l'âme* (1949), translated by G. Hopkins as *Iron in the Soul* (Harmondsworth: Penguin, 1965). His main work of literary criticism is *Qu'est-ce que la littérature?* (1947), translated by B. Frechtman as *What is Literature?* (London: Methuen, 1950). Plays include *Les Mouches* (1943) and *Huis Clos* (1944), both translated by S. Gilbert and published in one volume, as *The Flies* and *In Camera* (London: Hamish Hamilton, 1965).

Sartre refused all official honours, including the Nobel prize for literature.

The work by Sartre prescribed by the AEB is Jean-Paul Sartre, *Existentialism and Humanism*, translation and introduction by Philip Mairet (London: Methuen, 1973). It is the translation of a lecture originally published in 1946. Help with it can be got from reading *What is Literature?*, *Being and Nothingness*, Part IV, and the two plays mentioned above.

Works on Sartre include:

A. Danto, *Sartre* (London: Fontana, 1975)
A. Aronson, *Jean-Paul Sartre—Philosophy in the World* (London: Verso, 1980)
P. Caws, *Sartre* (London: Routledge and Kegan Paul, 1979)
F. Olafson, *Principles and Persons* (Baltimore: Johns Hopkins Press, 1970).

Sartre, *Existentialism and Humanism*

THOMAS BALDWIN

Sartre presented 'Existentialism and Humanism'[1] to a popular audience in Paris late in 1945.[2] As he implies in the discussion which is appended to the text of the lecture (pp. 57–58), he was here simplifying his views so as to make them intelligible to a wide audience.[3] In this he succeeded only too well; the lecture has become exceedingly well known and has been regarded as a definitive presentation not only of Sartre's philosophy at the time, but also of 'existentialism'. One thing I hope to show in this essay is that this is not a sensible view to take; Sartre's text requires a good deal of interpretation and qualification in the light of his other writings of the period, and what emerges is a position which is uniquely his own. One way in which this can be seen is by considering Heidegger's 'Letter on Humanism' of 1947[4] which is a response to Sartre's lecture and is, indeed, Heidegger's only direct response to Sartre's work. In the lecture Sartre had associated Heidegger with himself as an 'existential atheist' (p. 26), but in his letter Heidegger emphatically dissociates himself both from atheism and from existentialism as characterized by Sartre, and goes on to criticize the position advanced by Sartre in the lecture. Yet despite the popular exaggeration of the significance of Sartre's lecture, it is certainly worth studying; for not only is it short and accessible, though in some respects misleading, it is also one of Sartre's few indications of the positive ethical theory which so many of his writings require but do not supply.

Very briefly, Sartre's aim in his lecture is to exhibit existentialism as an optimistic account of the human condition (pp. 44, 56), in the sense that each of us has the possibility of living a life worth living. This conclusion is not far from the theological thesis that each of us has the

[1] Sartre's title is 'L'Existentialisme est un humanisme', whose meaning is distorted in Mairet's translation of it. Despite this error, Mairet's translation is largely reliable, although his introduction is not. My references are to the 1948 edition (Methuen: London).

[2] The occasion is described by S. de Beauvoir in *The Force of Circumstances* (Penguin: London, 1968), 46.

[3] According to Sartre's friend Francois Jeanson, Sartre even came to regret the publication of the lecture. Cf. F. Jeanson, *La problème Morale et la pensée de Sartre* (Paris: Seuil, 1965), 36.

[4] In M. Heidegger, *Basic Writings*, D. M. Krell (ed.) (London: Routledge, 1978).

possibility of salvation; but Sartre is emphatic that God does not exist (p. 28), so the possibility of salvation has to be understood in secular terms. This is, indeed, one reason why existentialism is a 'humanism', by which Sartre means here that the values in terms of which human life is worth living are imposed by us upon ourselves (this is another point Heidegger rejects). 'Humanism' is, however, a dangerous word for Sartre to use, for it is also associated with the thesis that we should be guided in the conduct of our lives by a simple love of humanity. This is a thesis Sartre had ridiculed in his earlier book *Nausea*[5] (pp. 168ff.), and in *E&H* Sartre seeks to maintain his distance from a humanism of this kind (pp. 54–55). Yet other aspects of Sartre's position in *E&H* bring him rather closer to it than he admits: for does he not here proclaim respect for human freedom as a fundamental value whose recognition by us is an essential element of that self-realization 'as truly human' (p. 56) which he presents as within our reach? A few years later Sartre would have responded to this challenge by insisting that there is no question of achieving his ideal respect for others without a radical egalitarian transformation of society that goes beyond anything conceived within the simple humanism he rejects; only within such a transformed society can we attain the 'true and positive humanism' which in the *Critique of Dialectical Reason*[6] (p. 800) he contrasts with the 'bourgeois humanism' he had ridiculed in *Nausea*. An important question concerning *E&H* to which I shall return is how far this response is actually implicit in the position there advocated. Although attributing it to Sartre at this time helps to make sense of what he says, it also threatens the optimism of the work: for if attainment of the ideal requires a new kind of society, then that ideal may be, for all practical purposes, unattainable.

The optimism of *E&H* also comes under threat from a different source: it stands in very sharp contrast to the position advanced in Sartre's earlier, and most directly philosophical, book *Being and Nothingness,*[7] where he had written that 'man is a useless passion' (p. 615) and that 'we discover that all human activities are equivalent, and all are in principle doomed to failure' (p. 627). Passages such as these would very naturally seem to invite the criticisms to which, as Sartre says at the start (p.23), the lecture is intended to respond. Yet since in

[5] First published in 1938; my references are to the translation by R. Baldick (Penguin: London, 1965).

[6] First published in 1960; my references to it as *CDR* are to the translation edited by J. Ree (London: New Left Books, 1976).

[7] First published in 1943. My references will be to the 1958 edition of the translation by H. Barnes (Methuen: London), which is now the standard edition of this translation. There are other editions, however, with different page numbers.

this earlier work Sartre seems to be articulating in detail precisely the existentialist position which, in *E&H*, he claims to imply the contradictory conclusion, we face an immediate difficulty in interpreting Sartre's response. Is he now rejecting the position of *B&N*, or are the premises from which he draws contradictory conclusions different in the two cases? There is no way of resolving the issue without looking further at the arguments, so let us now turn to examine Sartre's 'existentialism'.

The term 'existentialism' was, I think, introduced in 1943 by the French philosopher Gabriel Marcel, and applied by him to Sartre. Sartre initially tried to dissociate himself from it. But by 1945 he had come to embrace it, and in *E&H* he states what he takes to be the common doctrine of existentialists as follows (p. 26): 'What they have in common is simply the fact that they believe that *existence* comes before *essence*—or, if you will, that we must begin from the subjective' (as I have already said, Sartre should be here taken to be speaking for himself alone). What does Sartre mean by the famous phrase 'existence precedes essence', which is intended to be understood as a distinctive characterization of men (and women)? He gives us some help by describing some kinds of things for which 'essence precedes existence', and some conceptions of man according to which the same would be true for men. Cases of the former are 'paper-knives and books' (examples expressive of Sartre's primary interests!), which are produced to fulfil a purpose; and one case of the latter is the conception of man as a creature of God. But Sartre goes on to add, as further cases of the latter, secular conceptions of man as possessed of an essential human nature which is prior to any individual's actual historical experience of life. Hence it looks as though, under the slogan 'existence precedes essence', Sartre wants to repudiate all conceptions of human nature according to which there are certain universal features constitutive of humanity. Indeed he seems to say just this (pp. 45–46): 'it is impossible to find in each and every man a universal essence that can be called human nature'. Yet one wants to protest, surely 'existence precedes essence' is itself intended to provide a universal account of human nature? And does not Sartre himself write (p. 52) of 'freedom as the definition of man'? I think that this protest is justified. But for the moment I want to reflect on the significance of his apparent position, that there is no universal human nature.

In the case of things for which 'essence precedes existence', it seems clear that the 'essence' of the thing (its purpose or function) not only explains significant features of it, but typically also provides criteria for its evaluation as such—for determining whether it is good of its kind. Hence if men were things of this general sort, their essence or nature should provide criteria for their evaluation and thus a foundation for moral reflection. Such, indeed, was the line of thought pursued by

Aristotle and it is no surprise to find Sartre explicitly rejecting Aristotle's approach to ethics. If, therefore, we take Sartre's repudiation of all conceptions of human nature at face value, we can link this with the rejection of that very influential tradition of ethical thought which seeks to ground moral values in human nature. And once moral values are not grounded in that way, and are also denied any supernatural foundation in a divine plan, it seems reasonable to infer that Sartre's view is that judgements of moral value have no objective content at all, and are instead to be interpreted simply as expressions of choices or preferences. There are several passages in *E&H* which suggest that this is the correct way to interpret his position: one has only to put together the anti-naturalism apparent in the following passage (p. 34)—'Thus we have neither behind us [i.e. in human nature], nor before us in a luminous realm of values [i.e. in God's will], any means of justification or excuse'—and the emphasis on the role of choice apparent in the following passage (p. 29)—'to choose between this or that is at the same time to affirm the value of that which is chosen; for we are unable ever to choose the evil. What we choose is always the good.' Once passages like these are judged to be central to Sartre's position, it seems appropriate to set it alongside the influential position propounded by Hare in *The Language of Morals* (1952), and to treat Sartre's existentialist ethics as a rhetorical version of the position familiar in the more sober context of British philosophy as 'emotivism' or 'prescriptivism', according to which judgments of value are essentially expressive or prescriptive, and not descriptive (it is notable that Hare connects his prescriptivism with the denial that the concept *man* is a 'functional' concept—cf. *LOM* p. 145—which again seems just a sober restatement of Sartre's repudiation of a morally significant concept of human nature). This interpretation of Sartre's ethical theory is certainly the standard one current amongst British and American discussions of it.[8] Yet despite its pre-eminence, and the apparent basis for it in *E&H*, I want to argue that it needs to be substantially qualified.

The most obvious reason for this is that in *E&H* Sartre states that a correct understanding of human life imposes certain values upon one—honesty to oneself in one's own life, and sufficient respect for the freedom of others that they are able to live their lives as they choose, subject to the constraint on their part of similar respect for others. For

[8] Cf. A. MacIntyre, both in his early article 'Existentialism' (which occurs in *Sartre*, M. Warnock (ed.) (New York: Anchor, 1971), esp. pp. 54–55 and in *After Virtue* (London: Duckworth, 1981), esp. Ch. 3; M. Warnock, *Existentialism* (London: Oxford University Press 1970), 123; A. Danto, *Sartre* (London: Fontana, 1975), 141; F. Olafson, *Principles and Persons* (Baltimore: Johns Hopkins, 1967), 65–66.

whatever one thinks of this claim, which I shall discuss in detail, it implies that these values have a privileged status, are in a sense rationally founded, in a way which is inconsistent with a straightforward emotivism that denies a rational basis to any judgment of value. This privileged status is indeed apparent in the optimism of *E&H*, for this implies that a life which embodies these values is a life worth living, and this is a thought which has no obvious place within an emotivist ethical theory.

I shall not immediately specify, and argue for, my alternative interpretation of Sartre's position. Instead I want to return to Sartre's slogan 'existence precedes essence', for it does not simply have the negative significance I have so far discussed. For as far as that goes, at least if 'essence' is understood to imply facts of any evaluative significance, it would seem legitimate to classify together men with such things as islands and chemical elements which lack any intrinsic moral significance. But it is clear that Sartre would reject any such classification, on the grounds that human life has a subjective aspect which makes it quite different in kind from that of anything else; he writes (p. 28) 'we mean to say that man primarily exists—that man is, before all else, something which propels itself towards a future and is aware that it is doing so. Man is, indeed, a project which possesses a subjective life, instead of being a kind of moss, or a fungus, or a cauliflower.' Sartre's discussion here is not, I think, as precise as one might wish, but his position can be elucidated with some help from Heidegger's *Being and Time*,[9] from which Sartre took the phrase 'existence precedes essence' (*B&T* p. 68). Heidegger is very careful to separate the ordinary concept of existence, which applies to any actual object, from a special concept which he takes to apply distinctively to man and which he often expresses by the use of a hyphen, as in 'ex-istence', or, sometimes, with an idiosyncratic spelling as well, as 'ek-sistence' (cf. *Letter on Humanism* pp. 204ff.). The point of this idiosyncratic spelling is not just to mark a distinction, for, relying in a far-fetched but characteristic way on etymology, Heidegger hopes also to suggest something of the content of the latter concept—that it is a mark of man to 'stand out' from himself, in particular by forming intentions concerning his future by reference to which his present actions have to be understood. Returning now to Sartre, my view is that when, explaining the sense of 'existence precedes essence' he says that 'man primarily exists' (*E&H* p. 28) he has switched from the ordinary concept of existence which he was employing in his discussions of paper-knives and such-like to something like Heidegger's concept of ex-istence, in which paper-knives do not ex-ist

[9] First published in 1927. My references to it as *B&T* are to the translation by Macquarrie and Robinson (Oxford: Blackwell, 1973).

at all, and neither do islands and chemical elements. So although these things lack any intrinsic purpose and might therefore be said to be things for which 'existence precedes essence', since they do not ex-ist at all they do not fall within the intended scope of Sartre's slogan.

My present concern is not with the question as to the extent to which Sartre faithfully reproduced Heidegger's account of human ex-istence (Heidegger certainly felt that Sartre had not done so—cf. *Letter on Humanism* p. 207). Rather I want to elucidate some aspects of the account of human life that Sartre himself propounds. Some parts of this are easy: first, determinism is false of us—'since we have defined the situation of man as one of free choice, without excuse and without help, any man who takes refuge behind the excuse of his passions, or by inventing some deterministic doctrine, is a self-deceiver' (*E&H* pp. 50–51). In *Being and Nothingness* Sartre several times (pp. 35, 120, 439; cf. *CDR* p. 235) interprets 'essence' as 'past', and though there is no hint of this in *E&H* it is easy to see how, on this interpretation of 'essence', combined with a Heideggarian interpretation of 'existence', 'existence precedes essence' entails the absence of any determination by the past. This is probably the most famous doctrine of Sartre's early philosophy. It is obviously highly contentious,[10] but I will say little about it beyond observing that Sartre's thesis is not a simple-minded affirmation of a contra-causal power of the human will. One aspect of Sartre's more radical position emerges from the passage I have just quoted: according to Sartre we choose our passions, or emotions, as much as any other feature of our lives (*B&N* pp. 443ff.). In propounding this thesis Sartre realizes that he is departing from our familiar concept of choice: for he is seeking to exhibit both our familiar choices and those aspects of our lives which we usually regard as involuntary, such as some of our emotions, as rooted in a deeper choice, which in *Being and Nothingness* he calls the 'original choice of fundamental project'. This doctrine is alluded to in *E&H* when Sartre writes (pp. 28–29)—'what we usually understand by willing (vouloir) is a conscious decision taken—much more often than not—after we have made ourselves what we are. I may will to join a party, to write a book or to marry—but in such a case what is usually called my will is a manifestation of a prior and more spontaneous decision.' The theory of this deep choice is developed at length in part IV of *Being and Nothingness* and applied in Sartre's studies in 'existential psychoanalysis', e.g. those of Baudelaire, Genet, Flaubert, and of course himself in *Words*. In the earlier among these works, and in *E&H* itself (p. 43), Sartre links this theory with the thought that at any point in our lives each of us can

[10] In so far as Sartre argues for it, the arguments occur at *B&N* pp. 23–24, 433–438, and in other earlier writings.

radically transform our characters. But as his detailed biographical studies developed, Sartre came to place great emphasis upon the reactions of young children to their early environment, and to acknowledge that although these reactions are in some sense voluntary, once they have occurred they fix the pattern of life in ways that cannot in practice be significantly modified later; he writes (*Search for a Method*[11] p. 65 fn. 5)—'Of course, our prejudices, our ideas, our beliefs, are for the majority for us unsurpassable because they have been experienced first in childhood; it is our childish blindness, our prolonged panic which accounts—in part—for our irrational reactions, for our resistance to reason'. This is clearly a substantial change of view. I shall return later to assess its significance for the 'optimism' of *E&H*.

In sketching Sartre's conception of human life as rooted in the sovereignty of the deep will, I have been trying to present the psychological significance he attaches to the thesis that in man existence precedes essence. The resulting psychology is deeply problematic, especially in respect of our cognitive capacities since the inherent commitment of these capacities to truth, and their dependence upon causality, conflicts with the description of them as voluntary. At the time of *E&H* Sartre sought to elude these problems by inviting us to conceive of man in the image of God the omnipotent creator,[12] but there is good reason to doubt whether this is a satisfactory resolution of the issue, since most truths are not subject to our will. For our purposes, these problems do not matter crucially, but what is relevant is Sartre's use of the term 'humanism' to present this conception: 'It took two centuries of crisis . . . for man to regain the creative freedom that Descartes placed in God, and for anyone finally to suspect the following truth, which is an essential basis of humanism: man is the being as a result of whose appearance a world exists'.[13]

Since in *E&H* Sartre is primarily concerned with questions of value, the 'humanism' that he here presents might be expressed by saying 'man is the being as a result of whose appearance values exist'. However there is an important difference between Sartre's views about values and those about the world: in the latter case, Sartre is emphatic that he is not an idealist, for although the conception of 'brute existents' independent of us is, for some reason, not the conception of a world, it is none the less essential to any conception of a world (*B&N* p. 482; cf.

[11] First published in 1957. My references are to the translation by H. Barnes (New York: Vintage, 1968). Cf. also Sartre's comments in 'Itinerary of a Thought' in *New Left Review* **58**, (Nov.–Dec. 1969), 44–45.

[12] Cf. 'Cartesian Freedom' in Sartre's *Literary and Philosophical Essays* (London: Hutchinson, 1955).

[13] Op. cit., note 12, p. 184.

the role of 'matter' in *CDR* p. 180). By contrast in his account of values there is no analogue of 'brute existents': he explicitly commits himself to the 'ideality'[14] of values, which he associates with the thought, which we have already encountered, that by our choices we express, or even create, values, and it is in this context that he introduces his concept of anguish—'it is anguish before values which is the recognition of the ideality of values' (*B&N* p. 38; cf. *E&H* pp. 30–32).

This doctrine of the ideality of values seems to imply the emotivist account of values which the standard interpretation ascribes to Sartre. As I have already indicated I do not believe that this interpretation does justice to Sartre, but in the light of this doctrine of the ideality of values it would be obviously incorrect to ascribe to Sartre a straightforward realist conception of values as facts within the world. In *B&N* that conception is rejected as belonging to the 'bourgeois' misapprehension of life—it is from within that misapprehension that 'values are sown on my path as thousands of little real demands, like the signs which order us to keep off the grass' (*B&N* p. 38). In coming to a more satisfactory interpretation of Sartre's views, it helps first to introduce a conception of values as someone's deepest preferences; this is a thoroughly subjectivist conception of value in which values are always someone's values, and there is a fact of the matter as to what someone's values are: his values are determined by his deepest preferences. I introduce this primarily in order to set it aside, for it is a completely uncritical concept of value, within whose terms conflicts of value are reduced to differences of preference. But it does have some relevance to Sartre in that some of what he says in *B&N* about value is surely to be understood in terms of this concept of value; e.g. when he says (p. 92) 'Now we can ascertain more exactly what is the being of the self; it is value' he is employing this concept of value, and the remark just expresses his psychological doctrine of the sovereignty of the deep will.

The concept of value employed in *E&H*, however, is not simply descriptive of preferences. On the standard interpretation of Sartre, his position none the less remains close to that which identifies values with deep preferences; for on the emotivist view, although judgments of value do not describe one's preferences, they express them. But, as I observed before, this does not yield the result that Sartre commits himself to in *E&H*, that some judgments of value are rationally founded. To understand how this is possible, I think we have to recognize that in *E&H* Sartre employs a critical concept of value such that these values are defined in terms of the choices made by ideally

[14] By 'ideality' here Sartre of course means, not that values are ideals (as, say, justice or mercy might be) but that they are 'ideal' in the sense which contrasts with 'real'.

reflexive Sartrean subjects, that is, people who understand correctly both themselves and the nature of values. Those who fail to understand themselves, or the nature of value, certainly have values in the psychological sense of deep preferences, and their choices will express and realise these values. But their choices will not define the content of the critical concept of value, or, as Sartre puts it (*E&H* p. 51), will not define *moral* values. Morality is to be understood in terms of the choices of ideally reflexive Sartrean subjects.

Obviously it still has to be shown that any choices are required of these ideally reflexive subjects, but to get a better grasp of Sartre's intentions, one needs first to introduce the concept of freedom to which that of value is linked in his thought. Three kinds of freedom are present in Sartre's work. One is the freedom of will, undersood in a full-blooded libertarian sense to exclude any compatibilist compromises with determinism. But in *E&H* Sartre is more interested in a freedom which is defined in relation to values as the condition of being the 'foundation of values' (p. 51). I think one can best understand this freedom by thinking of it in quasi-political terms, as a 'negative' freedom from any authoritative source of moral guidance, either supernatural (e.g. divine) or natural. This freedom is not epistemological: Sartre's view is not that we lack knowledge about how we should live, although there is a fact, perhaps supernatural, of the matter about it. Rather his thought is that as far as natural and supernatural facts go, nothing is determined about moral value. It is when he expresses this thought that Sartre seems to have just an emotivist conception of value—as in the following passage from *Being and Nothingness* (p. 38): 'It [value] can be revealed only to an active freedom which makes it exist as value by the sole fact of recognizing it as such. It follows that my freedom is the unique foundation of values and that *nothing*, absolutely nothing, justifies me in adopting this or that value.' This passage certainly seems to conflict with the thesis about the content of the concept of moral value advanced in *E&H*. There are two ways of responding to this apparent conflict. One is to invoke the fact that there are good reasons, which I shall discuss later, for supposing that some of *Being and Nothingness* should not be taken as an unqualified expression of Sartre's views. Alternatively, and I think preferably, one can take Sartre to be saying here only that nothing external to my freedom, and my grasp of it, justifies me in adopting this or that value; which leaves space for the view of *E&H* that certain values are required of one who has a grasp of his freedom. On this view, then, our negative freedom from moral authority does not extend to all considerations: for some questions as to value are determined by facts about human consciousness and its relation to others, where these facts are not regarded as natural facts. Behind this last proviso lies the ontological distinction in *Being and Nothingness* between the Being-in-itself of natural facts and the Being-for-itself of facts about consciousness; but it would not be sensible to pursue that matter here, so let us just assume the coherence of this proviso.

What are the facts about human consciousness that are relevant to questions of moral value? Sartre's view, I think, is that the facts are basically those embodied in the assertion of the two freedoms we have already encountered, the metaphysical freedom of an uncaused will and the negative freedom from moral authority. Hence the content of the critical concept of moral value can be defined by reference to the deliberative perspective of someone who understands his freedom in these two respects. Furthermore, we can introduce a third 'positive' freedom, that of someone who has attained this ideal deliberative perspective.[15] The first two freedoms are unavoidable, and in respect of them 'man is condemned to be free'; but the third, moral, freedom has to be achieved through the self-conscious orientation of one's life in accordance with the principles of the other freedoms. And it is in relation to the possibility of achieving this freedom that the optimism of *E&H* is to be understood (p. 56)—'we show that it is . . . by seeking an aim which is one of liberation or of some particular realization, that man can realize himself as truly human'. The fact that Sartre does thus conceive of morality as a kind of 'liberation' shows clearly, I think, that despite his initial protestations to the contrary, there is for him a deep connection between his conception of human nature and that of morality. Indeed this works at two levels: first, the content of morality is defined in terms of the will of an ideally reflexive Sartrean subject, one who grasps himself as that whose 'existence precedes its essence', although it remains to be seen whether Sartre can here obtain what he hopes for. Secondly, the fact that such a subject achieves a kind of freedom through his ability to determine himself as a moral subject implies that through morality one comes to be in harmony with oneself, with one's own nature as a being whose 'existence precedes its essence'.

Anyone familiar with Kant's ethical theory will have recognized many similarities between that theory and that which I am ascribing to Sartre. This is neither a novel comparison (it was central to G. Lukacs' brilliant critique of Sartre[16]) nor unacknowledged by Sartre himself who in *E&H* describes his attitude to Kant as follows (p. 52)—'Thus

[15] The description of Sartre's views in terms of a contrast between negative and positive freedoms also occurs in Jeanson's book op. cit., note 3, pp. 27, 249ff.

[16] In *Existentialisme ou Marxisme* (Paris: Nagel, 1948), esp. pp. 128ff. I consider Lukacs' to be still the most helpful critical study of Sartre's early ethical theory.

although the content of morality is variable, a certain form of this morality is universal. Kant declared that freedom is a will both to itself and to the freedom of others. Agreed: but he thinks that the formal and the universal suffice for the constitution of a morality. We think on the contrary that principles that are too abstract break down when we come to defining action.' So Sartre agrees with Kant that there is a 'universal form' of morality, which can be specified by reference to a will, or choices made in accordance with freedom. His disagreement with Kant consists in denying that a specification of this universal form of morality generates, in the abstract, a specification of the content of morality. The significance of this disagreement obviously depends upon the form/content distinction Sartre is employing, and he is unhelpful in specifying it. But it is in this context that he tells his well-known story about a young Frenchman during the last war who had to choose between looking after his mother in Occupied France and leaving her there alone in order to join the Resistance in England. Sartre rightly observes that the Kantian principle that one should never regard another as a means, but always as an end, will not enable the young man to resolve this dilemma, since whichever choice he makes will leave him open to the accusation that he has not fulfilled his duty, and therefore failed to respect as an end the person to whom the duty is owed. So Sartre concludes that one cannot determine in advance how a dilemma of this kind should be resolved; the right thing to do can only be defined by the choice made by an ideally self-conscious agent whose will is (somehow) determined by the Sartrean ideal of moral freedom—he writes (pp. 52–53): 'The content is always concrete, and therefore unpredictable; it is always to be invented. The one thing that counts, is to know whether the invention is made in the name of freedom.'

The implication of this story would seem to be that Sartre's form/content distinction is just a distinction between general moral rules and particular moral decisions. Thus the disagreement with Kant would amount only to the thought that the application of general rules to particular cases, especially where there is a conflict of rules, is not determined *a priori*, but requires reference to the situation of the particular moral agent. This is scarcely a contentious thought. However, I do not think that Sartre's disagreement with Kant, and his criticisms of 'abstract' systems of morality, concerns only the distinction between general rules and particular cases. For this would leave all general moral principles to be determined without reference to the situations in which they are to be upheld, and Sartre frequently inveighs against any such abstract conception of morality; for example in his *Notebooks* he writes (p. 522). 'The project pursued by the man of authentic action is not directed to "the good of humanity", but, in certain particular circumstances with certain particular means at a particular historical occasion to the liberation or development of a particular concrete group' (cf. *E&H* p. 47, *What is Literature?* p. 57). Thus for Sartre the moral values appropriate to a situation are to some degree relative to that situation, and somehow defined by the agents in that situation. Sartre, I think, never spells out how these values are defined, and this is a major omission from his ethical theory. One line of thought consistent with his general approach would be the 'contractualist' view developed by John Rawls and others,[17] according to which the content of the concept of justice is defined, in particular historical situations, by reference to the principles which free and equal agents in those situations would choose to impose on themselves. There is here a 'form/content' distinction which roughly matches Sartre's intentions; and it fits well that those who follow this line of thought regard themselves as in some measure of agreement with Kant.

I should emphasize that I am not proposing the 'contractualist' conception of justice as an interpretation of Sartre's views; I am only suggesting that it provides an acceptable way of filling the large gap which is manifest in his theory when one tries to determine how the moral values appropriate to a particular situation are supposed to be determined. It may still be objected that since, on the contractualist view, moral values are defined by communal decisions, it cannot be right to employ it to fill out Sartre's existentialism, since this embodies a radically individualist perspective. I have some sympathy with this objection, which focuses on a source of genuine tension within Sartre's philosophy; but I will discuss it in more detail later when I consider whether Sartre can legitimately build his Kantian framework—that 'in willing our own freedom we will that of all others' (*E&H* p. 52)—upon the conception of the determination of moral values by a free will that he has offered.

Before attempting this task, however, I want briefly to indicate how the characteristic pessimism of *B&N* is to be fitted into this picture. For, as I mentioned, that pessimism stands in sharp contrast to the optimism of *E&H*. The key to resolving this conflict is the recognition that the form of human life generally described in *B&N* is conceived as misapprehending itself radically and, as a result, leading a life that is largely futile. This misapprehension is supposed to consist basically of a self-deceiving flight from the freedoms that are unavoidably our own: finding our responsibility for ourselves too distressing, we lapse into deterministic beliefs which offer us the illusory comfort of causal excuses. Likewise, finding the fact that we lack authoritative guidance concerning moral issues too much to bear, we fall back into a belief in the reality of values. Obviously, Sartre's descriptions of these beliefs as

[17] Cf. *A Theory of Justice* (Oxford University Press, 1972).

misapprehensions is dependent on the truth of his claims about our two unavoidable freedoms, and in *B&N* he strains plausibility by holding that these misapprehensions are always self-deceiving, since, in his view, we are all aware of these two freedoms. But what matters in the present context is that because much of the gloom that pervades *B&N* is supposed to arise, not from Sartre's existentialism itself, but from a failure to make explicit to oneself the truth of that existentialism, and thus to attain Sartre's third freedom, moral freedom, there is no essential conflict with *E&H* which is explicitly addressed, on the contrary, to those who have a correct awareness of themselves, as in the following passage (p. 52): 'Consequently, when on the level of total authenticity I recognize that man is a being whose existence precedes his essence, and that he is a free being who cannot, in any circumstances, but will his freedom, at the same time I realize that I cannot not will the freedom of others'.

Yet there are two respects in which this reconciliation of *B&N* and *E&H* is too quick. First, it may be said, is it not a thesis of *B&N* that the characteristic misapprehensions of oneself there described are essential features of human life? Yet if they are, then there is no possibility of the enlightened position which *E&H* presents. Secondly, it may be felt that the account which Sartre gives in *B&N* of our relations with other people, according to which we are always 'de trop' in relation to others (p. 410), does not take as a premise the characteristic misapprehension of oneself. But if so, then there is a conflict between the commitment to willing the freedom of others which is emphasized in *E&H* and the position of *B&N*, that 'respect for the Other's freedom is an empty word; even if we could assume the project of respecting this freedom, each attitude which we adopted with respect to the Other would be a violation of that freedom which we claimed to respect' (p. 409).

Both of these points raise important issues. In relation to the first, I think it has to be accepted that in *B&N* Sartre vacillates, without clearly indicating that he is doing so, between an absolutely general point of view from which the misapprehensions characteristic of the flight from freedom appear as contingent and a more restricted point of view within the perspective of a life informed by these misapprehensions. This makes the text, already formidably difficult, even harder to interpret, and explains Sartre's notorious footnotes (pp. 70, 410) in which he shifts from the restricted point of view of the main text to a more general point of view within which he withdraws from the position laid out in the main text. Yet even in the main text there are some unequivocal statements about the possibility of living a life informed by a correct understanding of oneself (pp. 159–160, 580–581, 626–628). In *E&H* such a life is described as one embodying 'authenticity' (p. 52), a term which comes from Heidegger (though he characteristically felt that his use of it had been misunderstood—*Letter* p. 212). More frequently, Sartre uses the terms 'impure' and 'pure' reflection to describe the two points of view, and I shall follow this practice. He initially associates these terms with the distinction to be found in the work of the philosopher Edmund Husserl between our ordinary introspective consciousness of ourselves, which is held to be 'impure' because we conceive ourselves as things within the world, and a special form of 'pure' self-consciousness in which we somehow apprehend ourselves as that through whose activity there is a world.[18] I doubt whether 'pure reflection' as thus conceived describes anything coherent, but this doubt does not matter much now. For Husserl this distinction, although of great philosophical significance, has no immediate ethical implications.[19] But in Sartre's writings it is these implications which are crucial. *Being and Nothingness* is primarily an exploration of impure reflection (p. 581); but he closed the book with the promise of a further work devoted to ethics (*La Morale*) in which he would explore for the first time a life of pure reflection. Unfortunately, Sartre never produced this work, and much of the difficulty in interpreting his ethical theory is a consequence of his failure to do so.

Not surprisingly, *Existentialism and Humanism* has often been used as a guide to this hypothetical work.[20] But Sartre's recently published notebooks *Cahiers pour une Morale*[21] (written 1947–48, published 1983) reveal for the first time his intentions for this work. Since there are two notebooks which are together 600 pages long, there is no question of summarizing here their content. But one theme in particular is very marked: that to attain pure reflection is to overcome alienation—from nature, oneself, others, and history. For Sartre these forms of alienation all embody misunderstandings of ourselves—essentially we conceive ourselves as just another thing within the world. It might seem therefore that pure reflection requires only a proper understanding of oneself, and its attainment is only a theoretical transformation, as it is for Husserl; but Sartre makes it clear that since, in his view, pure reflection includes a recognition of our responsibility for ourselves and of our role as creator of values, it constitutes also a moral transformation. Its significance for him is well expressed in a lecture he gave in

[18] Cf. Sartre's essay *Transcendence of the Ego* (New York: Noonday, 1957), 64–65.

[19] A point rightly stressed by J. Habermas in the appendix to *Knowledge and Human Interests* (Boston: Beacon, 1971).

[20] Likewise Sartre's *What is Literature?* (originally published in 1948; my references will be to the English translation published by Methuen in 1967).

[21] I would recommend anyone interested to start by reading the second notebook (pp. 429ff.) which includes (pp. 484–487) something like a prospective table of contents for the projected book.

1947 in which the intended connections between pure reflection, Kant's ethics, and—a new theme—Marxism, are very straightforwardly set out:[22]

> It may be that one can imagine a society of men living out their lives, from infancy, so that reflection would never appear . . . We can also conceive a society in which reflection would always be a world of lies. We can do so the more readily since it is our own society. There is also a third type of society, realizable though perhaps utopian, a society in which one would practice pure reflection; this would be a city of Kantian ends . . If the city of ends were realized by some miracle, this city would endure by itself because we would have obtained the beginning of a new era, as Marx says.

Although passages such as this make very clear Sartre's intentions concerning pure reflection, it is still proper to ask whether his ethical theory, and his account of human life, suffice to substantiate these intentions. In particular, in *Existentialism and Humanism* Sartre claims that the pure reflector must avoid self-deception (p. 51) and respect the freedom of others (p. 52). The issue we face is whether Sartre is entitled to attach these implications to his conception of pure reflection.

In the case of self-deception, it may seem entirely straightforward, since self-deception is inconsistent with pure reflection. But, as Sartre explicitly allows (*E&H* p. 51), a question can still be raised as to why the pure reflector has to choose to avoid self-deception and preserve his conditions of pure reflection. Illusions about oneself can after all be comforting. One response is simply to observe that since belief aims at the truth, self-deception, the inculcation of beliefs which one takes to be false, is inherently irrational. But this is too brief; for although the general point can be conceded, we can also envisage cases in which, it would seem, the inherent irrationality of self-deception is more than compensated for by other advantages (self-esteem, peace of mind, freedom from distractions), and thus in which, all things considered, a modest degree of self-deception is the rational choice. For the pure reflector, however, this outcome is excluded. Sartre aims to exclude it by insisting that 'when once a man has seen that values depend upon himself, in that state of forsakenness he can will only one thing, and that is freedom as the foundation of all values' (*E&H* p. 51). In so far as this offers us any help, it surely requires us to assign to the pure reflector a pre-eminent desire to avoid self-deception, grounded in a recognition by him of the great value of the condition of pure reflection. Yet this

[22] 'Consciousness of Self and Knowledge of Self', pp. 136–137 in *Readings in Existential Phenomenology*, N. Lawrence and D. J. O'Connor (eds).

gets things the wrong way round for Sartre, since here the choice is grounded on a recognition of value, and not vice versa, as Sartre's Kantian theory requires. None the less, it is only by tacitly appealing to some such consideration that Sartre can make plausible the thought that the pure reflector is committed to rejecting self-deception in all circumstances.

This is a point of considerable strategic significance in relation to Sartre's ethical theory. For at this point the theory looks as if it is grounded in a conception of human nature more substantive than that presented under the formula 'existence precedes essence'. That formula, I suggested, is at work in Sartre's appeal to the perspective of choices made by an ideally self-conscious subject, the pure reflector. What I have now argued is that this perspective does not by itself yield the result Sartre wants concerning self-deception. But we can get what we want here if we introduce a feature which in *Being and Nothingness* is presented as the essential characteristic of human consciousness, namely that it is always attended and informed by a mode of self-consciousness; this is why the being of consciousness is said to be being-for-itself (*B&N* pp. xxxiff.). Typically this mode of self-consciousness is only inchoate ('non-thetic' in Sartre's terminology), but the pure reflector differs from the rest of us precisely in having a lucid grasp of that which is inchoate for us (*B&N* pp. 155ff.). Thus the pure reflector's judgment of the great value of a condition which excludes self-deception can be seen as grounded in his recognition that this condition is the explicit articulation of what, for Sartre, just is the essential strucure of human life.

This, I repeat, is not how Sartre himself presents the matter. My claim is only that Sartre's discussion invites a completion of this kind. For his theory, like Kant's, suffers from the defect that the formal structure provided by the will of an ideal subject, in this case that of the pure reflector, does not suffice by itself to determine the intended moral values. We have to add a specification of the judgments of value which the ideal subject brings to his choice, and these judgments cannot themselves be the outcome of choices. Instead it is plausible to represent them as grounded in an understanding of human nature, and my claim is just that Sartre's acount of human consciousness in *Being and Nothingness* provides the basis for the judgment of value which is presupposed by his pure reflector's condemnation of self-deception.

It is now time to turn to Sartre's argument for the other substantial ethical feature of the pure reflector's life: that he wills the freedom of others. As I indicated some time back, there is an obvious difficulty in combining this view with the position presented in *Being and Nothingness*. The strategy I have been pursuing implies that the resolution of this difficulty lies in the switch of perspective from that of impure to pure reflection. But, again, it is one thing to say that pure reflection requires respect for the freedom of others; it is another thing to substantiate this implication. In *Existentialism and Humanism* Sartre attempts to do so by introducing a thesis about our mutual interdependence—'in thus willing freedom, we discover that it depends entirely upon the freedom of others and that the freedom of others depends upon our own' (p. 51). When we recall that Sartre's three freedoms are, respectively, the metaphysical freedom of the free will, a negative freedom from external moral authority, and the moral freedom of the pure reflector, this must strike us as an unwarranted thesis. Clearly, the first two freedoms are, for Sartre, unavoidable, and thus in no way dependent upon others; and so far nothing has been said about the transition from impure to pure reflection to imply that the attainment of moral freedom is dependent upon others. Sartre acknowledges the first of these points, when he goes on to say (p. 52): 'Obviously, freedom as the definition of man does not depend upon others'; but he then just repeats the conclusion he needs to argue for—'I cannot make liberty my aim unless I make that of others equally my aim'. This is a manifestly unsatisfactory argument. If anything the stress on the role of the will in Sartre's early philosophy lends support, not to an ideal which requires respect for others, but to the single-minded pursuit of self-fulfilment irrespective of others.[23] Something like this ideal does find expression in Sartre's work; for example, in writing in 1947 of Baudelaire, who is held by Sartre to have stopped just short of the moral freedom of pure reflection, he writes.[24] 'the man who is damned enters into a solitude which is like a feeble image of the great solitude of the man who is really free'. I think that Sartre here touches on an authentic feature of existentialism (if one can so speak), for the stress on the perspective of the solitary individual is very prominent in the writings of Kierkegaard (who is an existentialist if anyone is). This perspective is part of the legacy of Protestant Christianity, with its stress on the unmediated relationship between God and the individual Christian, and the implication that salvation is to be found by pursuing that essentially solitary relationship.[25]

Part of the interest of Sartre's philosophy derives from his developing appreciation of the inadequacy of this existentialist individualism. In

[23] For a clear expression of this tendency cf. the Air Vice-Marshall's speech in Ch. 12 of Rex Warner's novel *The Aerodrome*. The similarities with some Sartrean theses is almost uncanny, but the moral implications are developed in a direction Sartre would not have liked.

[24] *Baudelaire* (London: H. Hamilton, 1949), 70.

[25] Despite his stress on 'being-with' the perspective of the individual is still primary in Heidegger's *Being and Time*; cf. the significance of death (p. 284) and the 'sober anxiety' described on p. 358.

his early philosophy this individualist perspective is grounded in a Cartesian epistemology, which is emphatically proclaimed in *Existentialism and Humanism* (p. 44): 'Our point of departure is, indeed, the subjectivity of the individual . . . And at the point of departure there cannot be any other truth than this, *I think, therefore I am*, which is the absolute truth of consciousness as it attains to itself'. If this is the 'absolute truth' which we grasp in self-consciousness, then there seems no inherent reference to others in the pure reflector's explicit articulation of his consciousness. In *Existentialism and Humanism* Sartre attempts to mitigate this result by saying that in self-consciousness we also grasp ourselves as apprehended by others in one way or another (p. 45), and thus that self-consciousness does, after all, involve our relations with others. But apart from the fact that there is here still no reason why pure reflection should require respect for others, rather than any of the other attitudes to others which self-consciousness reveals to us as ours, it still seems that others are conceived to concern me only in so far as their attitudes to me infect my own self-consciousnes, and thus that I need have no conception of them as subjects of consciousness in their own right, irrespective of their attitudes to me. But some such conception is a prerequisite of any genuine respect for others.

Yet Sartre's theoretical commitment to this ideal is unquestionable. His remarks in *Existentialism and Humanism* are not idiosyncratic, but can be matched in almost all his writings of the period.[26] He usually expresses it in the terms I have already cited by linking pure reflection to the achievement of the 'city of ends', i.e. a community in which the actions of each are guided by an equal concern for all. The phrase comes, of course, from Kant and confirms the essentially Kantian slant of his ethical theory. But the question which remains is how this theoretical commitment is to be justified. Sartre's answer to this question must lie in the account of impure reflection and what the attainment of pure reflection requires. Yet in *Being and Nothingness* the predominant theme is that impure reflection is motivated by fear of freedom, and there are no inherent social implications to this account which belongs within the tradition of existentialist individualism. However, there is also in *Being and Nothingness* a subordinate line of thought, to the effect that in impure reflection we think of ourselves as we are for others (p. 161), a thought which has to be understood in the context of Sartre's general account of our relations with others in *Being and Nothingness*, which is that these are relations of conflict which lead us to have an improper, alienated conception of ourselves in so far as we

[26] Cf. *What is Literature?*, pp. 44, 203–204, 216–217, *Cahiers*, pp. 487, 516.

are led to think of ourselves only as we are for others (p. 285). What we have to consider, therefore, is whether there is here a basis for an argument to the conclusion Sartre maintains.

This question is given added significance by the fact that in the 1947–48 notebooks I have mentioned it is this line of thought which is now given prominence. Sartre here suggests that impure reflection arises within social relationships which lead us to conceive ourselves wrongly as things within a world structured by deterministic causes and objective values. Just what kinds of social relationship are thus alienating is answered in several ways in the notebooks: at different points Sartre mentions oppression, social stratification, and the dehumanization of workers by the machines at which they work. But he suggests a more general approach in the following passage, from the start of the second notebook (p. 429):

> All history is to be understood in terms of this primitive alienation from which man cannot escape. The alienation is not simply oppression. It is the predominance of the other in the couple of Other and Self, the priority of the objective and, as a result, the necessity for all conduct and all ideology to be projected in the element of the Other and to return alienated and alienating upon their promoters.

A question which this passage raises is what Sartre here means by 'this primitive alienation from which man cannot escape'. Since the focus of the notebooks is precisely upon the radical conversion through which alienation is overcome and pure reflection attained, Sartre cannot here mean that it is not possible to transcend this 'primitive alienation'. Rather his thought must be that each of us has to pass through the experience of primitive alienation. And when the point is understood in this way it is very natural to interpret it in the light of Sartre's accounts of the experience of childhood, of the inescapable experience of growing up in a world dominated by others—especially parents and siblings. If Sartre's thought is interpreted in this way, it connects directly with a central thesis of his later writings, that alienation is unavoidable as long as people meet each other under conditions of scarcity, which he takes to be inevitable as things now stand (*CDR* pp. 120ff.). For he also advances the view, as we saw before, that our childhood prejudices are insurpassable and if , as I am suggesting, these prejudices are a mark of our primitive alienation, then their unsurpassability is of a piece with the thesis of the general impossibility of escaping from alienation which informs his later work. This thesis conflicts with the optimistic tone of *Existentialism and Humanism* and the notebooks; what makes the difference is the introduction in the later work of the thesis about the presence of scarcity and its consequences.

We need not concern ourselves with these later writings, and I want to return to the question of the significance of conceiving of impure reflection as essentially motivated through the 'primitive alienation' of growing up in a world dominated by others. For once it is understood in this way it does follow that pure reflection requires relations of mutual respect in which free agents meet each other in circumstances in which they do not seek to subordinate one another. In the notebooks Sartre attempts to specify in detail what such relations involve, and he alludes critically to the account of social relationships which he had presented in *Being and Nothingness*. But he draws the conclusion he wants in an emphatic form early on (p. 16): 'One cannot achieve the conversion *alone*. In other words, morality is only possible if everyone is moral.'

This now looks as though it provides a grounding for the thesis of *Existentialism and Humanism*, not there grounded, that in willing our own (moral) freedom, we are bound to will that of all others. Yet there remains here an issue comparable to that encountered in connection with self-deception. In that case it was easy to see that pure reflection excluded self-deception, but less easy to see just why the pure reflector should choose to remain a pure reflector by refraining from self-deception. In the present case, the new account of impure reflection has the consequence that pure reflection requires respect for others. But it still remains to be explained why the pure reflector should regard this aspect of his situation as one to be preserved. I think, however, that one can in this case simply exploit the earlier line of argument to provide an instrumental justification. For the earlier argument, which invoked the pure reflector's recognition of his condition as the explicit development of the essential structure of all human consciousness, led to the conclusion that the pure reflector had a pre-eminent interest in his condition. What has now been argued by Sartre is that this condition requires relations of mutual respect and it therefore follows that the pure reflector has an interest in the maintenance of these relations. It is no objection to this reconstruction of Sartre's position that this interest is only derivative; for that is how Sartre presents the matter in *Existentialism and Humanism*. But what is true is that on this view pure reflection is a good deal harder to attain than appeared within the perspective of existentialist individualism. The moral content of pure reflection is in this respect purchased at the cost of severely qualifying the optimistic view that it is readily attainable by us. For even without the bleak pessimism of Sartre's later writings, with their associated thesis of the ineliminability of scarcity, the transformation of the concept of pure reflection, or authenticity, into a condition with social implications takes away from any individual the possibility of attaining that condition alone. And there is a further problem inherent in this approach: how can Sartre, a member of a less than ideal society, regard himself as knowing what are the conditions of pure reflection? On his own premises, Sartre must regard his own self-consciousness as a case of impure reflection: but if so, then is he in a position to define for us the nature of pure reflection, and the content of a morality defined in terms of the pure reflector's will? Sartre must allow that one can somehow have a theoretical grasp of the requirements of pure reflection without oneself attaining that condition. But I shall not speculate how this is supposed to be possible, nor whether its possibility is indeed defensible.

Index of Names

Index of Subjects

Index of Subjects